Landscape Evolution in the Middle Thames Valley

Heathrow Terminal 5 Excavations Volume 1, Perry Oaks

by Framework Archaeology

John Lewis, Fraser Brown, Angela Batt, Nicholas Cooke, John Barrett, Rachel Every, Lorraine Mepham, Kayt Brown, Kate Cramp, Andrew J Lawson, Fiona Roe, Steve Allen, David Petts, Jacqueline I. McKinley, Wendy J. Carruthers, Dana Challinor, Pat Wiltshire, Mark Robinson, Helen A Lewis and Martin R Bates

Illustrations by Karen Nichols and Elizabeth James

Framework Archaeology Monograph No. 1

2006

The publication of this volume has been generously funded by BAA plc

Edited by Lisa Brown, John Lewis and Alex Smith

Typeset and designed by Karen Nichols

ISBN: 0-9554519-0-6
ISBN: 978-0-9554519-0-4

This book is the first of a series of monographs by Framework Archaeology, which can be bought from all good bookshops and internet bookshops.

Published by Framework Archaeology, a joint venture partnership between Oxford Archaeology and Wessex Archaeology

Oxford Archaeology, Janus House, Osney Mead, Oxford, OX2 0ES

Wessex Archaeology, Portway House, Old Sarum Park, Salisbury, SP4 6EB

Contents

CHAPTER 1: Introduction
by John Lewis

CHAPTER 2: Hunter-gatherers and first farmers: The Mesolithic wildwood to the end of the monumental landscape of the Neolithic (10,000 BC–1700 BC)
by John Lewis and Fraser Brown

List of Figures

List of Plates

List of Tables

The Freeviewer CD-Rom

The volume is accompanied by a CD-Rom containing the Framework Archaeology Freeviewer. This GIS viewing software has been developed to enable readers to have access to more data than would be possible in a traditional publication. The monograph and Freeviewer are designed to be used together so that if more data is required in order to view the evidence supporting a particular argument presented in the text, it will be possible to consult the particular dataset via the Freeviewer. Filters can be applied to show different distributions of finds material by date, and at the start of Chapters 1–4 in this volume there are there Freeviewer boxes referencing particular queries that are available within the Freeviewer (eg 'Bronze Age waterholes' or 'Roman buildings'). Please note that much of the data within the Freeviewer is essentially primary data, in that it represents material and ideas generated on-site, without additional post-excavation analysis. Because of this there may be the occasional discrepancy with the data as presented within this volume. In addition to the Freeviewer, the CD-Rom also contains the full set of finds and environmental reports in PDF form as listed below:

1 Prehistoric pottery *by Rachel Every and Lorraine Mepham*
2 Romano-British pottery *by Kayt Brown*
3 Flint *by Kate Cramp*
4 Bronze Age metalwork *by Andrew J Lawson*
5 Stone axe *by Fiona Roe*
6 Wooden finds *by Steve Allen*
7 Roman lead tank *by David Petts*
8 Human bone *by Jacqueline I. McKinley*
9 Waterlogged plant remains *by Wendy J. Carruthers*
10 Wood charcoal and charred plant remains *by Dana Challinor*
11 Palynological analysis *by Pat Wiltshire*
12 Insects *by Mark Robinson*
13 Soil micromorphology *by Helen A Lewis*
14 Sediments *by Martin R Bates*

Instructions for installing the Freeviewer are presented below:

1. Insert the CD-Rom in your CD Drive
2. If Autoplay is enabled then the Framework Archaeology Installer will start. Otherwise double-click on the CD-Rom Drive letter in My Computer or select Autoplay from the right click pop-up menu.
3. Once the Framework Archaeology Installer has started, you should install the Framework Archaeology Freeviewer (menu option 1). Click the button to start the installation.
4. This starts a standard install program for the Framework Freeviewer. Follow the instructions of this installer. At the end of this process, you will then need to install the data.
5. Use the menu option 2 to start the installation of the data for the Perry Oaks excavations and follow the instructions. You may need to be patient as this can take some time to complete. During the installation you will be prompted to either accept the default location on your computer for the data or you can specify a location of your choice.
6. Once you have installed the data you can then exit the Framework Archaeology Installer by clicking the exit button.
7. Now you can start to explore the data using the Framework Archaeology Freeviewer. You will find a short-cut on the desktop to start the program. The Programs section of the Start Menu will also contain a folder called Framework Archaeology which contains short cuts to start the program and a link to the Help File. Help can be accessed within the program by pressing the F1 key or by using the Help option on the pull-down menu.

System requirements

The program requires 12MB of disk space to install and once installed will take up 3.5MB of disk space. The data (varying by project) may require approximately 1.1GB of free disk space and will use approximately 500MB of disk space once installed for the largest Framework Archaeology project. You will require as a minimum a 500 Mhz processor or better. The program is a Windows®-based application designed to run on Windows 2000® and Windows XP® operating systems. It will also run on Windows 98® but with limitations. Running on Windows 2000® and Windows XP® you will typically require 256MB of memory. The program will run with less memory but with a performance impact. Since the program includes a Geographic Information System, you will find that using the program is more comfortable at higher screen resolutions. The program is designed to run on a minimum screen resolution of 800 by 600 pixels but a screen resolution of 1024 by 768 or higher will greatly improve your experience of the Framework Freeviewer.

Data formats

The data is presented using the following data formats:
Database attribute data is in Microsoft Access 2000® format (.mdb) and stored in the AttributeData folder under the project folder, Perry Oaks. The mapping data is stored in ESRI® shapefile format (.shp) and stored in the SpatialData folder under the project folder, Perry Oaks. Supporting images such as sections and digital photographs are in .jpg format and stored under Sections and Photos folders under the project folder, Perry Oaks. The data can be directly accessed using your preferred Geographic Information Software if required.

Foreword

Almost 9000 years ago humans who lived by hunting and gathering dug a series of small pits on land overlooking a small river valley in what is now West London; today that site is covered by part of the newly constructed Terminal 5 at Heathrow Airport. These two events form part of a continuous human history of this area linking the people of early prehistoric times to those of the present day. This volume seeks to illuminate that history in some detail. That we are able to do so is because of a substantial programme of archaeological excavations undertaken as part of the Terminal 5 development.

Archaeological excavation is now a normal and accepted part of many development projects. Terminal 5, however, has not been a normal development; it has been one of the biggest construction projects in the world and this has presented particular challenges. From the outset, BAA was determined to ensure that Terminal 5 set new standards and benchmarks for UK construction. Building on its pioneering approach to partnering and taking further inspiration from the 1998 Egan report, Rethinking Construction, BAA created a bespoke commercial partnering agreement with contractors and suppliers called the T5 Agreement. This was a contract based on relationships and behaviours, designed to expose and manage risk rather than transfer that risk to other parties. Open communication, collaboration and an ethos of continuous improvement in the interests of achieving excellence were expected as standard on the project. These principles were applied across the whole range of construction-related activities, be it the delivery of aircraft pavements, baggage handling systems or, indeed, archaeology.

The archaeological project required a particular blend of field skills, academic expertise and liaison with the client. Much of the success of the project has been due to the appointment of a strong archaeological team of contractor and consultants, and to the excellent working relationship which the team has established with BAA. It was considered that the size of the excavation would stretch the resources of any one archaeological contractor and BAA was instrumental in setting up Framework Archaeology, a joint venture of Oxford Archaeology and Wessex Archaeology, the first occasion such an arrangement had been employed in a development context. From the beginning it was seen that a commitment to excellence would involve academic guidance and Professor John Barrett of Sheffield University has acted as academic advisor and played an important part throughout.

The archaeological team's challenge was to put in place a programme which would result in the greatest possible contribution to knowledge in as cost-efficient a manner as possible. Development-led archaeology is sometimes criticised as being simply an exercise in recording the remains on a site, with insufficient thought being given to what the value of the results might be. The Terminal 5 research design lies at the heart of the archaeological programme and its focus has been the history of human lives, rather than the recording of material remains; it has been about people, not things. Our desire has been to make this history available to the widest possible audience. A key objective of the archaeological work was the production of a narrative of the human history of the site which would be both accessible and updated as work progressed. This strategy proved very successful during excavation and stimulated interest in and support for the archaeological programme across the entire construction project and also within the local community.

Managing research - a process of asking questions about the past and seeking answers from the archaeological evidence contained in the ground - on the scale demanded by the Terminal 5 programme was a major challenge. BAA provided development funding to enable the archaeological team to review established working practices and re-design the archaeological process. Above all, what was sought was the active engagement of every member of the archaeological team in writing the history of the site. By demanding that each excavator move beyond the simple requirements of recording to the challenge of understanding the historical conditions in which people had lived, the programme not only required more of the excavation team but reaped the benefits in high levels of motivation. The feedback from members of Framework Archaeology who worked on the site has been extremely positive.

The style of this volume has tried to capture something of the immediacy and freshness of the developing on-site narrative, an approach which has been made possible by the digital presentation of detailed data on disc. The archaeological project is still very much "work in progress"; in accordance with spirit of the Terminal 5 programme it is hoped that the approach will be developed in the future and will stimulate discussion and debate within the archaeological profession.

The successful implementation of the archaeological programme on a development the size and complexity of Terminal 5 has been a considerable achievement and the archaeological discoveries made have amply repaid the efforts expended by all concerned. The excavations described in this and the forthcoming volume have recovered remarkable detail about past lives and made a major contribution to our understanding of the past.

Gill Andrews
Archaeological Consultant to BAA plc

Summary

Between 1996 and 2000 Framework Archaeology undertook extensive excavations of an important prehistoric and Roman landscape at Perry Oaks sludge works, Heathrow, Middlesex. This volume presents the results of these excavations. Further archaeological work in advance of a fifth passenger terminal ('T5') at Heathrow Airport took place from 2002 onwards, and the results of those excavations will be integrated with the data contained in this volume, to be presented in Volume 2 of this series.

The earliest evidence of human habitation at Perry Oaks comprised a handful of pits which were dug in the 7th millennium BC at a location on the edge of the Colne floodplain. In the late 4th millennium BC, the landscape was transformed by the construction of the C1 Stanwell Cursus, one of the great monuments of Neolithic Britain. This event was followed by the construction of a second cursus (the C2 Cursus) and a small horseshoe shaped enclosure. In the space of a few centuries or less, people had transformed the landscape from one defined by memories of ancient locations to one defined by the architecture of earthen banks and ditches. However, by 1700 BC further changes led to the replacement of a system that apportioned land and resources through ceremony to one of physical demarcation: the first land tenure and field divisions. Settlements became archaeologically visible and landholdings developed into a landscape of small and large fields traversed by ditched trackways. This landscape supported a mixed arable / pastoral agricultural economy, supplemented by resources from the innumerable hedgerows which divided the fields. People maintained links with the past through ceremonies resulting in particular artefacts being deposited in the base of waterholes.

From the late 2nd millennium BC the pattern of small settlements scattered across the landscape changed to one of fewer and larger settlements. Little specific evidence was recovered for early Iron Age activity, but major elements of the Bronze Age agricultural landscape appear to have persisted well into this period. Waterholes appear to have retained their status as places of offering for generations of farmers during the late Bronze Age/early Iron Age whilst hedgerows were maintained and ancient trackways respected. Over this period, the Perry Oaks landscape came under the control of new cultural and economic influences and designs, culminating in a gradual transformation which saw the emergence in the middle Iron Age of a nucleated settlement of roundhouses. This in turn became a focal point for continuing occupation and ceremony through into the Roman period. However, the Perry Oaks landscape of the later Roman period largely overwrote the previous land divisions, focussing outwards and away from the ancient local community. Some fossilisation of this late Roman landscape can be traced in the medieval ridge and furrow and the alignment of a post-medieval trackway, although by this time the site appears to have reverted to localised rural inhabitation and agricultural regime.

Acknowledgements

The various phases of the Perry Oaks project have involved contributions from many people.

BAA

We are grateful to the Managing Director of the Terminal 5 Project, Eryl Smith, and Terminal 5 Construction Director, Norman Haste, for their interest and support.

The Framework Joint Venture was fostered on behalf of BAA by Andrew Gibson to whom we owe a great deal of thanks. The conduct of the excavations themselves was managed for BAA by Tony Power and David Harwood together with Ashley Hollington of EC Harris.

The staff of Laing O'Rourke provided essential advice and guidance, particularly Andy Anderson, Nick Harris and David Lloyd. Lorne Ireland and Jim Hodgekiss managed the plant, equipment and attendances with consummate professionalism.

BAA Consultancy and Advice

Many thanks are due to BAA's archaeological consultant, Gill Andrews, and academic advisor, John Barrett, who have provided constant support, advice and feedback through all stages of the project.

The principal contributions from Framework Archaeology staff

The Project was managed and directed by John Lewis and Ken Welsh. The planning of the project was aided by numerous contributors including Andy Crockett, Gill Hey, Sue Davies, George Lambrick, David Jennings and Jonathon Nowell. Linda Coleman undertook the topographic and truncation modelling. The difficult task of supervising the machine stripping and survey of the site under extremely bad weather conditions was undertaken by Nicholas Cooke. He and Jeff Muir were the principal Project Officers who oversaw the main excavations. The site supervisors were Angela Batt, Fraser Brown, Nicholas Mitchel (who also recorded the waterlogged wooden remains), Rob Johns, Jenny Morrison, Rod Brook, Richard Conolly, Jo Best and Simon Mortimer. Simon Mortimer also directed the excavations at Northern Taxiway (GAI99) and Grass Area 21 (GAA00), and was assisted at the latter by Phil Jefferson. Lorraine Mepham together with Leigh Allen managed the processing, recording and on-site analysis of the artefact assemblage which was undertaken by Rachel Every. Andy Bates recorded and reported on the animal bone assemblage. Dana Challinor was responsible for environmental sampling and processing. Kirsten Miller and Rosemary Wheeler scanned and digitised the plans and sections and oversaw the entry of data onto the database. Paul Miles provided computing support and advice. Anthony Beck developed the Framework database system and was responsible for surveying and all on-site computing. The scale of this achievement cannot be underestimated. Keith Westcott developed the stratigraphy-ranking algorithm. Niall Donald replaced Anthony Beck at the end of the fieldwork and has made a similarly important contribution. He has managed the data as well as stabilising and refining the database and GIS system. In particular, Niall has created the concept of entities as analytical tools and this has proved an important advance in the Framework Archaeology analytical process. The Framework Freeviewer software was also developed by Niall Donald.

Site archaeologists

The most important contribution to the project was from the site archaeologists in the form of the excavation, recording and on-site interpretation, without which there would be no report. However, the site staff not only shaped the nature of the excavation and the archive, but also the ethos of Framework Archaeology. The archaeologists involved were:

J Alcock, C Appleton, R Barrett, C Barton, A Bates, S Bates-Lacy, A Beaucock, C Bloor, K Blythe, P Breach, G Campbell, M Campbell, S Clelland, K Colls, R Court, S Craig, J Crisp, C Cropper, N Dagless, N Dale, M Davis, S Dennis, L Dicicilia, A Dicker, J Dilcock, P Durnford, J Eaton, F Edwards, S Exelby, T Fairclough, P Gajos, T Gent, F Gibson, J Gidlow, E Glass, R Golding, S Hamblett, D Harris, S Harris, J Helmsley, E Hemming, B Hennessy, R Hoyle, R Johns, C Jones, N Lambert, C Lawson-O'Brien, S Leech, B Lewis, C Lowe, G Mabbott, D Maricevic, L Martin, T Mellor, B Middleton, D Miller, S Morris, P McNulty, P Noble, E Noyce, M Orna-Ornstein, P Owen, A Page, A Paul, J Pearce, M Pearce, N Plunkett, P Poucher, A Prior, A Rackley, R Radford, N Redvers-Higgins, D Rodgers, J Rolfe, A Smallcross, J Stedman, D Stevens, M Stewart, D Sykes, E Taylor, S Thomas, M Thompson, S Thompson, R Villa, M Walter and R Woodgate.

The 1996 Museum of London Archaeology Service excavation at Perry Oaks (site code POK96) was managed by Simon Mason and directed in the field by Stuart Hoad.

Specialist support both on site and during post-excavation analysis

S Allen, M R Bates, K Brown, W J Carruthers, D Challinor, K Cramp, R Every, A J Lawson, H A Lewis, J I McKinley, L Mepham, D Petts, M Robinson, F Roe and P Wiltshire.

The post excavation analysis and publication programme also involved many staff in addition to many of those mentioned above. Fraser Brown, Angela Batt and Nicholas Cooke undertook the analysis and produced the first drafts of the main chapters. This was a particularly difficult task, since the format, style and content of the report was far from clear to anybody at the time. In addition, until Niall Donald developed the Framework Freeviewer software, the mechanism for distributing the digital data in a coherent form was absent. These chapters were subsequently reviewed and additional analysis and content provided by John Lewis with John Barrett, Alex Smith and Lisa Brown. Alex Smith edited the volume. The artefacts were drawn by Elizabeth James. The reconstruction work was done by Tom Goskar and Karen Nichols. Karen Nichols produced the final publication figures, typeset and designed the layout of the monograph.

Curatorial Advice

We would like to thank Greater London Archaeological Advisory Service (GLAAS) officers Robert Whytehead and Jez Reeve for advice throughout the project, and Jon Finney (Principal Architect/Planner, London Borough of Hillingdon) and Harvey Sheldon who monitored the fieldwork programme on behalf of the London Borough of Hillingdon. We are particularly grateful to Jonathan Cotton of the Museum of London who has provided much valuable advice, knowledge and encouragement over many years.

Framework Joint Venture Board and Management Team

The joint venture was agreed and overseen by the then chief executives of Wessex and Oxford Archaeology, Andrew Lawson and David Miles, together with Peter Dawes and Simon Palmer. This role has continued under the present Chief Executives, David Jennings and Sue Davies together with Clive Burrows who replaced Peter Dawes. The Framework Management team is composed of John Dillon and Bob Williams who provide guidance and advice.

CHAPTER 1
Introduction

by John Lewis

CD-Rom queries
1943 survey and cropmark survey drawings
Truncation model

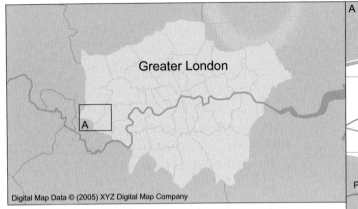

Figure 1.1: Site location

Introduction

This volume presents the findings of excavations at Perry Oaks sludge works, Heathrow, Middlesex between 1996 and 2000. The area investigated totalled *c* 26 hectares. Of this total, 21 hectares were exposed and excavated in a single phase in 1999, making it one of the largest open area excavations undertaken at the time.

The excavations at Perry Oaks were undertaken to mitigate the deleterious effects of the sludge works operation on the surviving archaeological deposits. However, they were also carried out with the expectation that the construction of the proposed fifth passenger terminal ('T5') at Heathrow Airport would be approved. In the event approval for Terminal 5 was granted and the Perry Oaks sludge works was relocated. Archaeological mitigation associated with the construction programme took place from 2002 onwards, and the results of those excavations will be integrated with the data contained in this volume, to be presented in Volume 2 of this series.

The main excavations outlined in this volume were carried out by Framework Archaeology, a joint venture agreement between Oxford Archaeology (OA) and Wessex Archaeology (WA) to provide archaeological services to BAA. The results of archaeological investigations by other organisations on the site have also been incorporated where appropriate (see below).

Figure 1.2: Aerial photograph of Heathrow Airport showing outlines of main excavation areas at Perry Oaks (© BAA)

Structure of Chapter 1

The results of the Perry Oaks excavations are presented in the form of a historical narrative, which is ordered chronologically but which seeks to explore a number of main historical themes and processes.

This introductory chapter seeks to guide the reader through the main body of the report by outlining the following key areas:

- Site location

- Geology and topography

- Modern land-use

- The archaeological background to the area

- The nature of the challenge and the solution

- Academic aim and approach

- Application: the recording system and data presentation

- Publication: scope, concept, presentation and archive

- Structure of the historical narrative and how the themes will be explored

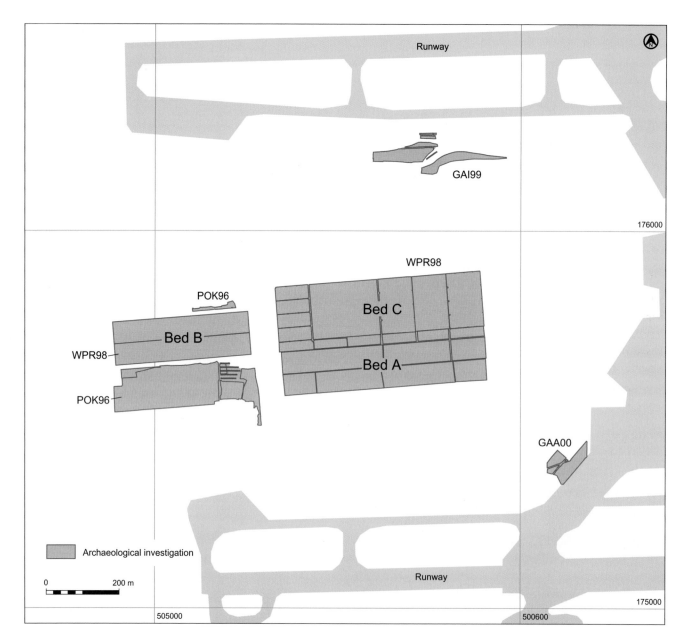

Figure 1.3: Archaeological investigations at Perry Oaks

4

Site location (Figs 1.1–1.3)

Perry Oaks sludge works was located on the eastern edge of the Colne Valley (TQ 055 756), bounded to the north, south and east by Heathrow Airport and to the west by the A3044 and the Western Perimeter Road (Figs 1.1 and 1.2). The sludge works covered an area of c 91 ha, of which the central drying bed area, comprising Beds A, B and C, occupied c 21 ha (Fig. 1.3). These drying beds were excavated by Framework Archaeology in 1999 (Greater London site code WPR98). Previous excavations in 1996 of sludge stockpile areas by the Museum of London Archaeological Service (MoLAS) comprised an additional c 5 ha (site code POK96). Two smaller excavations were undertaken by Framework Archaeology within Heathrow Airport at Northern Taxiway (GA199) and Grass Area 21 (GAA00) (Fig. 1.3; for more information see below).

Geology and topography (Fig. 1.4)

The Perry Oaks sludge works was situated on Taplow Gravel capped by the Langley Silt Complex ('brickearth'). The Taplow Gravel forms one of the sequence of gravel terraces created during the Pleistocene by the movement of the River Thames.

Throughout this report the area of Hounslow Heath now occupied by Heathrow Airport is referred to as the 'Heathrow Terrace'. We have used this term to describe the block of landscape

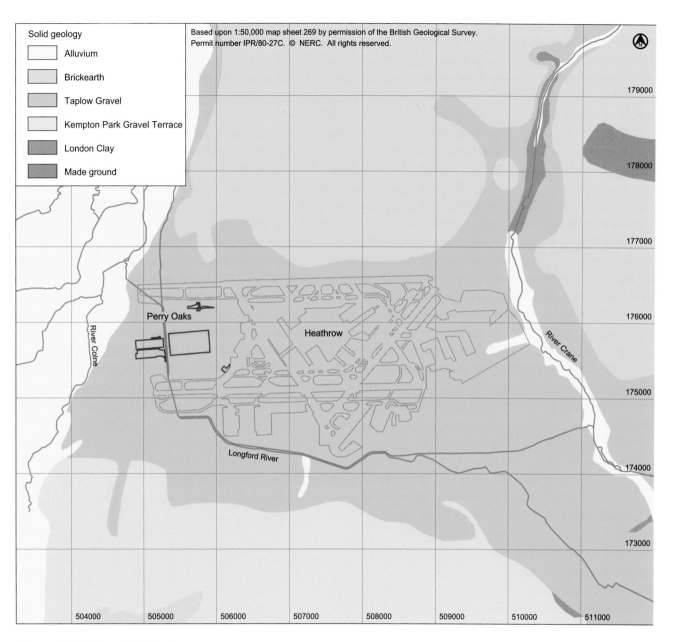

Figure 1.4: Geology of the Heathrow area

5

which is defined by the River Colne in the west and the River Crane in the east (Fig. 1.4). To the north, the Heathrow Terrace is defined by the junction of the Taplow and Lynch Hill Terraces, and to the south the junction of the Taplow with the Kempton Park Terrace. These geological boundaries appear on the ground as breaks in slope, sometimes almost imperceptible, sometimes quite marked. However, in the past their topographic effect would have been much more noticeable than today.

The Perry Oaks area lies immediately to the east of the River Colne floodplain at an altitude rising from c 21 m OD in the west to c 23.5 m OD in the east (Fig. 1.5). It is thus a broadly flat landscape with a very gentle upward slope from west to east. In addition, the 23 m contour can be seen to 'swing' away to the south-east, and we will show in Chapter 3, on the 2nd millennium BC agricultural landscape, how the field ditches and hedgerows also follow this change in topography.

Throughout the remainder of this volume we will make repeated reference to the flatness of the landscape. This flatness has shaped the 20th-century history of the area; it was one of the reasons for siting the sludge works at Perry Oaks, and of course for the subsequent construction of Heathrow Airport. Prior to any modern changes, however, the topography of the landscape was more varied, with slight rises and lower lying areas (such as palaeochannels), which would undoubtedly have held significant topographical importance (see below). Human modification of the landscape from the 4th millennium BC has

utilised these variations, usually to enhance them. Most importantly, almost any human endeavour that resulted in the raising of a mound, bank or other earthwork or timber structure would most likely have made a distinctive impression on this landscape.

Topography prior to the construction of the sludge works in the 1930s and the airport in the 1940s (Fig. 1.5)

In 1943 the Air Ministry undertook a levels survey of the Heathrow area prior to the construction of the airport (Fig. 1.5). The survey covered an area of 20 square kilometres of Hounslow Heath and survey readings were made every 20 feet producing a total of 23,763 points. Framework Archaeology digitised the original survey data and produced a computer-generated model, which also included survey data from the engineering drawings for the sludge works in the 1930s.

For the purposes of this report we have assumed that the 1943 ground surface would have equated with the prehistoric and Romano-British ground surface. Agriculture will, of course, have eroded some parts of the landscape, and colluviation and alluviation will have deposited material in others. Nonetheless, this model has provided the essential topographical framework within which we can consider the architectural modifications made by people since the 4th millennium BC. It also allowed the construction of the Truncation Model described below.

The Truncation Model (Fig. 1.6)

The Truncation Model consists of a contour and wire mesh drawing of the difference in heights between the pre-sludge works ground surface (derived from the 1943 Air Ministry Survey and the Perry Oaks sludge works engineering drawings described above) and the top of the gravel surface following archaeological stripping and survey. This was achieved by using the 'residuals' function in the Surfer computer program to subtract the OD heights in the 1933–43 grid file from those in the modern day grid file to produce a third grid file which could be contoured. The degree of truncation was then calibrated by examining the impact of truncation on archaeological survival in POK96. It was apparent during excavation, from archive aerial photographs and documentary research, that the eastern part of POK96 had undergone substantial terracing and truncation. The truncation model allowed the depth of disturbance to be quantified, and its effect on archaeological features to be assessed.

The truncation model proved to be a very valuable tool during excavation and post-excavation analysis since it could be used to assess the validity of artefact distributions, and to determine if the absence of features in a particular area can be attributed to the effects of the construction of the sludge works.

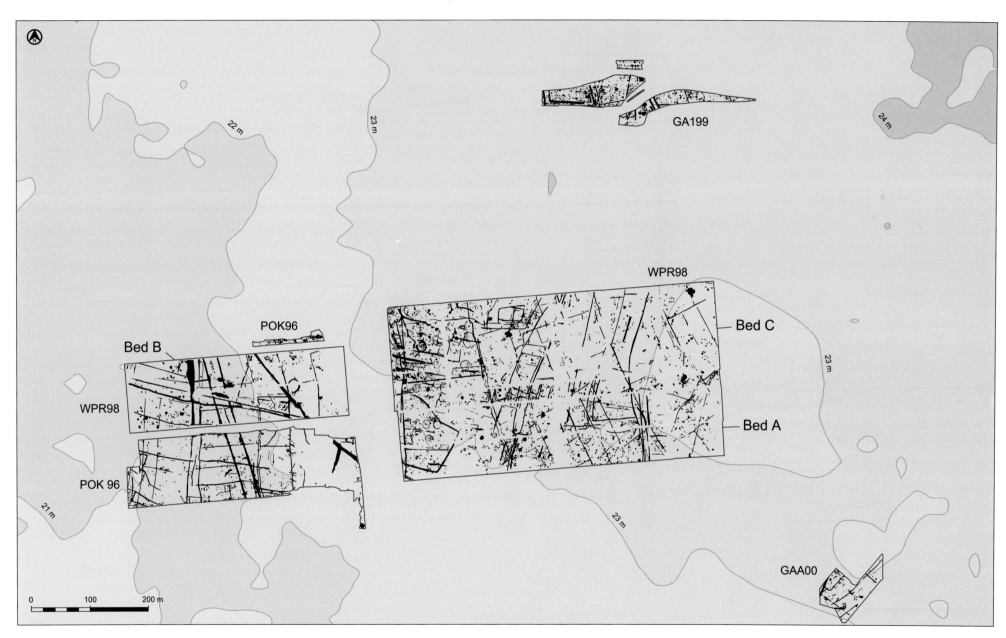

Figure 1.5: 1943 topography of Heathrow

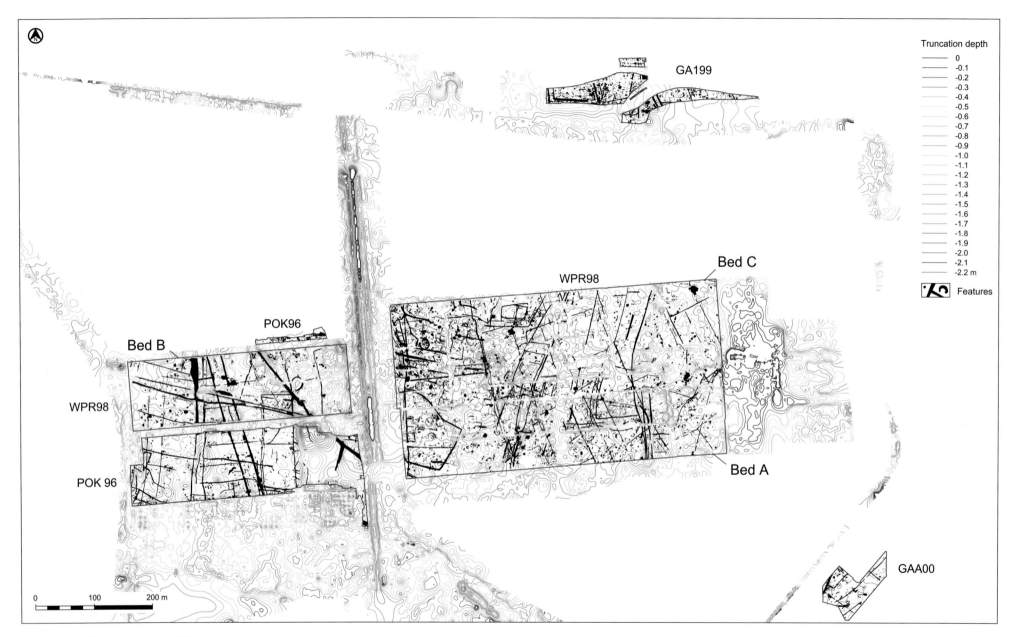

Figure 1.6: The truncation model

Plate 1.1: Aerial photo of Perry Oaks sludge works drying beds looking east with Heathrow airport in the background (© BAA)

Modern land-use

Perry Oaks sludge disposal works was built as one element of the West Middlesex Main Drainage Scheme. This scheme was conceived following the First World War, at a time when West Middlesex was developing rapidly in both industry and population. The Scheme was devised in 1928 by John D Watson, past President of the Institution of Civil Engineers, in order to replace 27 sewerage works operated by 22 local authorities.

John D Watson reported fully on the construction of the Perry Oaks works in 1937, and this was followed by a further report on the first 10 years of operation by Townend (1947). These reports— and the Thames Water Utilities Ltd engineering drawings—proved invaluable in both recording the history of the development of the works and also in assessing their impact on the surviving archaeological deposits.

The principal purification works was built at Mogden, near Isleworth. This contained all of the facilities for dealing with disintegrating and screening the sewerage as well as tanks for the primary digestion and sedimentation of the sludge. It was considered that there was inadequate space for sludge air-drying at the Mogden Works and that a more thinly populated area would be preferable for this process. Thus, primary treatment and digestion were located at Mogden and the resulting sludge was pumped the seven miles to Perry Oaks in a liquid state, where 10 secondary digestion tanks and 50 acres

Plate 1.2: Photograph looking south-east across Beds A and C at Perry Oaks

of drying beds (increased to 72 acres in 1939; Townend 1947, 384) were laid out. At Perry Oaks the liquid portion was separated off and pumped back for final treatment at Mogden. Initially, it was proposed to tip the resultant 'cake' at Perry Oaks, but in 1940 the decision was taken to sell the 'cake' to farmers as fertiliser (Townend 1947,

384), a practice which continues to this day. The following extract from Watson's 1937 paper is reproduced here as it illustrates the rural isolation of the Heathrow area prior to the Second World War, and the transformations that have occurred since that conflict.

Isolation from existing dwelling-houses and unlikelihood of building development taking place in the immediate vicinity recommended the Perry Oaks site for sludge-disposal, although the low cost of the land (about one-sixth the price per acre of the Mogden land) was an important factor. Although only 7 miles from Mogden, it is no less than 3 miles from the nearest railway station. The nearest habitable dwelling is an isolated farm 700 yards from the drying beds; the nearest building-development lies on the Bath road, more than ½ mile to the north of the site.

The whole complex of drying beds, sludge digestion tanks and sewers will not be described here; instead we will concentrate on the drying beds, for almost all of the Perry Oaks WPR98 excavations were undertaken in areas occupied by these structures (Plate 1.1). The POK96 excavations were carried out in an area which had been earmarked for conversion to drying beds, but which in the event was used for temporary storage of sludge 'cake' and earthmoving.

The main area of the WPR98 excavations consisted of drying beds A and C (see Fig. 1.3 above and Plate 1.2). These formed one of the original areas of the sludge works and were used for the air-drying and conversion of sludge to 'cake' to be resold as fertiliser. Watson described the construction of the beds thus:

.... the excavation was reduced to a minimum by grouping the beds at four different levels, the highest being 18 inches above the lowest. Turf and topsoil were stripped off 6 inches deep, even where filling was required. Excavation was computed at 68,000 cubic yards, and refilling at 3,500 cubic yards, exclusive of excavation for drainage-pipes and wall-footings. General excavation was carried out by scrapers drawn by tractors, and spoil was used to make embankments around the site.

The beds are underdrained with 3-inch porous concrete pipes, laid in herring-bone pattern at about 12-foot 6-inch centres, connecting to a main open-jointed stoneware pipe. This pipe runs parallel to a division-wall, and picks up the porous pipes from two beds.

(Watson 1937)

This construction method led to some areas being more deeply 'cut' than others, in order to provide a level fall across the site; this can be seen in the truncation model described later. The concrete walls dividing the drying beds and cells effectively destroyed any archaeological deposits and the underdraining concrete pipes also had a localised impact on archaeological features.

Under the initial scheme, dried sludge had been tipped on land lying between the Duke of Northumberland's River and the Longford River, which then flowed in a NW-SE direction (across WPR98 bed B and POK96). As part of the modifications of the late 1940s / early 1950s, the latter river was diverted to run parallel to the former, allowing more land to be annexed for further sludge tips and to allow the construction of additional sludge lagoons. The realigned rivers traversed the site contained within concrete troughs, probably to keep the river water separate as the rivers crossed the area enclosed by the puddle wall. This 'Twin Rivers' area only became available for excavation during the construction of Terminal 5, and is included in Volume 2. However, in 1999, this area represented a major break in the continuity of the archaeological investigations between POK96 and bed B in the west, and beds C and A in the east.

The archaeological background to the area

The Perry Oaks excavations were undertaken in a landscape that had been archaeologically investigated for over 50 years. Figure 1.7 shows the scale and extent of these investigations. Most excavations were undertaken by MoLAS (or its predecessors) from the late 1970s onwards, ahead of gravel extraction and other commercial development (MoLAS forthcoming).

Located a few kilometres to the south-west of Perry Oaks, the Yeoveny Lodge Neolithic Causewayed Enclosure was partially excavated prior to destruction through gravel extraction in the early 1960s (Robertson Mackay 1987). In the early 1980s the Surrey Archaeological Unit excavated a length of the Stanwell cursus, the 2nd millennium BC field system and Saxon features to the south of Perry Oaks (O'Connell 1990). In the 1990s Wessex Archaeology excavated large multi-period sites to the north of Heathrow at Prospect Park (Andrews 1996) and Imperial College Sports Ground (Crockett 2002; Wessex Archaeology 2004).

Within the airport itself, Canham undertook limited excavations in advance of the western extension of the northern runway in 1969 (Canham 1978), and Grimes excavated the famous Heathrow Romano-Celtic style 'temple' situated within an Iron Age enclosed settlement (Caesar's Camp), whilst the airport was being built in 1944 (Grimes and Close-Brooks 1993). This latter report also provided additional information on the archaeological and historical background of the area, demonstrating the destructive effects of arable agriculture in a relatively short space of time on standing earthworks (ibid., 306–307).

More general synthesis and discussion has also been published (eg Cotton, Mills and Clegg 1986), whilst the prehistoric archaeology of West London features in a recent assessment of the archaeology of Greater London (MoLAS 2000).

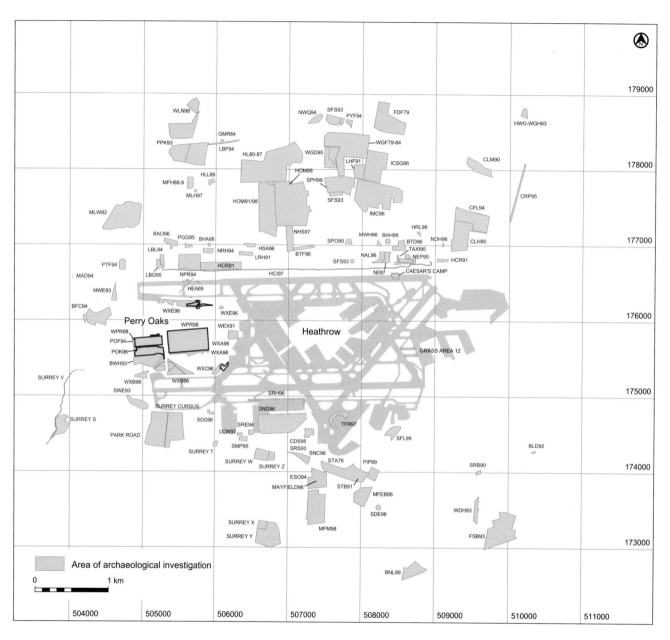

Figure 1.7: Extent of all known archaeological investigations at Heathrow

Summary of the Heathrow archaeological landscape prior to the Perry Oaks excavation

At the outset of the project, a chronological series of past landscapes was identified (based on Andrews and Barrett 1998). These comprised the following:

Hunter-gatherer communities and early agricultural practices (300,000–4000 BC)

Hand axes and other lithic tools of Lower Palaeolithic date were deposited amongst the Thames terrace gravels, but those located within the Taplow terrace, upon which Perry Oaks is located, have been acknowledged as being rolled and reworked from the higher Lynch Hill terrace (Gibbard 1985). The same has been suggested for artefacts within the Colney Street gravels of the River Colne (ibid., 131). Since this material is derived and redeposited, it did not feature as a research priority.

The surface of the Taplow gravels was occupied from the late Lower Palaeolithic (300,000 BC) onwards. Antiquarian observation and fieldwork over the last 100 years suggest that much of this material lies buried beneath the Langley Silt (Brickearth) deposit capping the Taplow gravels. At Perry Oaks, the sludge works had severely truncated this thin capping, and thus this early period did not feature as a research priority.

Late Glacial and Mesolithic occupation (from 9000–4000 BC) across the terrace would have taken the form of lithic and bone scatters, which were deposited on the contemporary land surface. Again, the severe truncation at Perry Oaks had removed all *in situ* traces of these remains. There was no opportunity for studying occupation of the landscape to the same level of detail as that of the Colne floodplain (Lacaille 1963). However, diagnostic lithics of this period did survive in tree throws and a handful of contemporary pits, as well as residing in later features.

Early agricultural and ritual practices (4000–2000 BC)

The construction of the first monuments in the Heathrow and West London landscape can be dated to the Neolithic period. These consist of linear cursus monuments (such as the Stanwell example described in this volume) as well as smaller circular or sub-circular enclosures. Notably absent are earthen long-barrows of the early 4th millennium BC. Along the Thames to the west of Heathrow lay a series of larger causewayed enclosures (eg at Yeoveny Lodge Staines and Dorney) of the 4th millennium BC, while the large double ditched enclosure to the east of Perry Oaks at Mayfield Farm may also date to this period.

The construction of small circular enclosures continued in the 3rd millennium BC, although the characteristic features of this period (middle and late Neolithic) in the area are pits containing either Peterborough Ware or Grooved Ware pottery. Overall, the emergence and chronological development of the monumental landscape at this time is far from clear.

Agricultural intensification and the rituals of reproduction (2000–100 BC)

During the 2nd millennium BC the monumental landscape of the preceding millennia was transformed into one of fields, settlements and trackways. Exactly when, why and how this took place remains uncertain, as is the extent of this agricultural landscape. Conspicuously absent from West London were many aspects of the late Neolithic / early Bronze Age material and monumental package: round barrows, burials and Beaker pottery. From c 1500 BC onwards, cemeteries with middle Bronze Age Deverel Rimbury pottery had been recorded (Barrett 1973), and together with the succeeding Post-Deverel Rimbury pottery of the late Bronze Age, were clearly associated with field and settlement systems. Relatively little is known about the early Iron Age in the region, although by the middle of the 1st millennium BC, middle Iron Age settlements comprising roundhouses, pits and four-post structures were spread across the landscape. The Heathrow 'temple' (Grimes and Close-Brooks 1993) was tentatively dated to the middle or late Iron Age, although the function of this structure remains far from certain (Black 1986, 203; Smith 2001, 64).

Rural landscapes and urban hinterlands (100 BC–AD 1700)

The transition from late Iron Age tribal society to post–conquest Roman province remains poorly understood in this region. The Romano-British landscape was characterised by small farmsteads consisting of enclosures, field boundaries and (probably) earth and timber buildings, which served the markets at roadside towns such as Staines and possibly Brentford, and of course the capital, Londinium. A growing number of such Roman rural farmsteads have been excavated along the Thames gravel terraces in recent years, and yet there is a notable lack of villas or other high status sites. There are indications that the landscape of the 3rd and 4th centuries AD underwent some form of reorganisation, which might reflect changes observed within the urban centres of Staines and Londinium.

The archaeology of the early and middle Saxon periods consisted of isolated or small concentrations of sunken-featured buildings. Sometimes these were located away from medieval and present-day villages and in other cases they were found close to villages such as Harmondsworth. These medieval villages presumably developed from their Saxon predecessors. A number of hamlets and villages were dotted across Hounslow Heath, which began to be enclosed in the 18th century. Finally, some of these settlements, such as Heathrow itself, were destroyed by the construction of the airport in 1944.

This briefly sketches the state of knowledge of the West London landscape prior to the MoLAS excavations at Perry Oaks in 1996. The Perry Oaks excavations thus had the potential to make a tremendous contribution to our knowledge of the history of human occupation within the Heathrow landscape, and of the middle Thames region in general. However, the scale of the project presented a number of challenges, that had to be addressed before undertaking any excavation, and these will be discussed in the following section.

The nature of the challenge and the solution

The excavations at Perry Oaks provided a number of important challenges. Evaluations undertaken by MoLAS on behalf of BAA during the early 1990s in support of the Terminal 5 planning application demonstrated that all elements of the Heathrow ancient landscapes described above survived to varying degrees within the confines of the sludge works (BAA Series reports). Subsequent excavations by MoLAS of the 5 hectares to the south of drying bed B (Site Code POK96; see Fig. 1.3) confirmed these results and served to refine the research philosophy and approach. It was clear from the POK96 excavations that archaeological deposits, though truncated, probably remained beneath the drying beds of the active sludge works and were thus threatened by the daily workings of the drying beds.

Framework Archaeology was appointed by BAA in 1998 to undertake all archaeological mitigation for the Terminal 5 project. Throughout the project Framework Archaeology worked in partnership with BAA's Archaeological Consultant, Gill Andrews, and BAA's Academic Advisor, Professor John Barrett. Gill Andrews and John Barrett prepared the initial T5 Research Design (Andrews and Barrett 1998) which was subsequently developed by John Barrett (see below).

One of the first tasks was to excavate and record the archaeological remains that were being destroyed by the daily workings of the sludge works. This would entail stripping and excavating a very large open area within an operating sludge works, which itself posed problems with regard to Health and Safety. However, were the proposal to build Terminal 5 to be approved, the archive and results of the Perry Oaks excavations (and those undertaken by MoLAS) would have to fit seamlessly into the rest of the landscape exposed during these subsequent excavations. The huge extent of the area that might ultimately be exposed demanded that all the archaeological features be surveyed digitally. Large quantities of written and graphical records, as well as artefactual and environmental material, were likely to be produced. The only practical way to manage this data was to adopt a database system, linked to digital plans via a Geographical Information system (GIS). By adopting a GIS approach, and by processing and assessing as much of the finds and environmental data as possible on site, the data could be used to inform the excavation strategy.

The process of historical inquiry that was demanded by the academic philosophy at the heart of the project (see below) could now be pursued through an iterative excavation and interpretative process. At the same time, the opportunity was taken to design a recording system focussed on those processes of excavation and interpretation. The GIS and database were then designed around the recording system.

Academic aim and approach *by John Barrett*

Various research designs have been prepared with the aim of providing guidance for British archaeological work. The most recent examples have operated within period-specific remits at either a regional or a national level and have tended to specify research issues in terms of particular categories of material, or with reference to particular period-specific research questions.

By contrast the T5 Research Design, was developed at a more 'generic' level of analysis. It established an approach towards the archaeology of all periods that was intended to be applied with reference to the resource model for the T5 development area and with reference to our current understanding of the archaeology of the Middle Thames Valley.

Principles

The aim of the T5 archaeological programme has been to move beyond the recovery and description of archaeological remains as they are distributed across the landscape and to arrive at an understanding of the history of human inhabitation. The archaeology of inhabitation demands more than the recording of the traces of human activity and the history of inhabitation involves more than tracing the changing organisation of activities in a landscape. Inhabitation concerns the practical ways in which people established their presence in the material, social and political conditions of their day.

To establish a presence involves having the power, common to all human agency, to move and act in the world according to available opportunities and constraints, where such actions express knowledge of various levels of technical proficiency, social adequacy and moral authority. The archaeology of inhabitation is therefore an investigation of the various ways the human presence was established in and contributed towards maintaining or transforming the material and social conditions of history. It is an investigation of the material, moral and political contexts of human diversity.

This understanding of history is therefore not a matter of simply tracing changes in material forms (be they cultural or 'environmental') as expressed by phased sequences of material, nor is it a matter of noting that people in the past 'did things differently'. Rather, it concerns the ways lives were shaped in terms of social and political realities. These realities created different identities by virtue of varying access to resources and to modes of authority. Historical change arose as these differences were negotiated or were otherwise transformed by human practices, and by virtue of the cumulative changes in material conditions.

Human practice necessarily occupies areas of time and space. Spaces are 'opened up' by the activities that people carry out within them, and attempts can be made to define them in material terms by such things as enclosures, pathways and focal markers. Spaces and times may be appropriated and allocated to people and resources.

Application

Current excavation procedures normally treat the recovered material as data that represent historical processes. This means that field technicians record evidence that is destined for future interpretation. Our approach treats the materials excavated as components of the material conditions of history. It therefore treats excavation as primarily the investigation of history, rather than a preliminary stage in facilitating future interpretation. This places a clear interpretative responsibility with the excavators, and it ensures that the production of a coherent and empirically validated site narrative remains the fundamental objective of the excavation programme.

Inhabitation may be regarded as the creation of human realities with reference to certain material conditions. Consequently the interpretative emphasis must be placed upon the ways people brought social conditions into existence through their performance of different practices.

Two concepts frame our inquiry. These are defined as *structural conditions*, which concern the ways in which the existing material conditions operated upon the lives of the landscape's inhabitants in any one period, and *structuring principles*, which describe the organisation and interrelationship of the practical performances by which the various schemes of political and cultural order were reproduced.

Structural Conditions

Structural Conditions identify the ways in which the occupation of time and space was partly circumscribed and partly guided by existing material conditions, including the various structures in their different stages of decay that had been built into the landscape by previous generations. It is possible to identify these major structural components at various levels of generality or detail as excavation and interpretation progresses. These components will be labelled as *entities*.

The definition of *entities* enables the isolation of major architectural components through and around which lives were performed, and significant deposits and residues associated with these activities accumulated. Talking about *entities* enables us to trace the ways the physical conditions of the world were modified. *Entities* will map out, for example, the ways in which different places were linked and thus different movements may have been choreographed, the way activities may be framed by various forms of architecture, and the dominant points of reference, both monumental and topographic, that were negotiated in the occupation of the landscape.

Each generation lives within its own archaeology of standing buildings, of ruins, and of a managed landscape of high antiquity. Understanding something of the structural modifications undertaken in any period should inform an understanding of the ways by which this archaeology of the past was accommodated in the contemporary landscape and thus the ways in which that archaeology was utilised, remembered or eradicated.

Structuring Principles

By emphasising the active ways in which social life is created we can identify four broad *spaces* which facilitated that activity. These spaces were inhabited with reference to those material conditions that are represented by the excavated evidence (the structural conditions). Analysis is directed at the ways these spaces were designed and the ways in which they interrelated. The four spaces are:

Routine. These were the spaces of every day activities. They were built by acting out commonly held, if conflicting, values for often mundane and routine purposes. These activities expressed the realities of life that were taken for granted.

Explicit order. These spaces brought into being explicit statements and claims to authority, political power and the demonstration of various kinds of supernatural, or indeed natural, orders that were presumed to govern the wider order of the world. Where routine knowledge is likely to have been taken for granted, these spaces evoked a more explicit form of knowledge.

Inscription and control. These were the spaces by which resources (material resources, forms of knowledge and people) were defined by others and could be acted upon. These spaces were made in the operation of power over the lives and material conditions of others.

Exclusion, marginality and resistance. These are the spaces that may have lain beyond dominant political authority. They may have been the routines that rarely expressed their own identities, or the spaces in which arose attempts to challenge or avoid the normality of routines and the control of dominant authority.

- Each of the different kinds of space outlined above are always related through performance.

- Routine practices must involve action on and control of resources, operate against the background of explicit forms of political and religious order, and contain alternatives within them.

- Explicit order always makes sense by reference to routine experience, supports power wielded over some portion of the world, and may ignore, seek to silence or capture those actions that question its validity.

The inscription and control of resources is achieved by an effective authority, imposes itself upon the routines of life, and its boundaries partly define the spaces of alternatives and resistance.

The hidden and marginal spaces of the world contain their own routines, may express alternative views of order and seek to avoid forms of dominant control. In other words none of the performances defined here occupied spaces that did not require mediation, negotiation or confrontation with other regions of social performance. The material entities that are identified in fieldwork formed part of the technology by which these social dramas operated, and history is driven by such processes.

The different ways in which these practices brought these spaces together is what defines the character of different historical periods, and can be summarised in Figure 1.8.

Application: the recording system and data presentation

The Framework Archaeology recording system and fieldwork methodology have been developed to apply the academic approach outlined above. The field procedures and database structure have been described previously (Framework Archaeology 1999a; 2002) and are documented in the *Framework Archaeology Field Manual*. This section will summarise the definitions of the key concepts employed in excavation and post-excavation analysis, demonstrate how those concepts are used in the analytical process, and briefly describe the final product in terms of published output.

Definitions

The following section defines the key concepts of *context, intervention, deposit, stratigraphic group, feature, entity* and *interpretative group* as used in the Framework Archaeology Database.

Context

The *context* is traditionally the primary unit of recording in British archaeology and the usual means by which artefacts and ecofacts are located to their site of recovery. Contexts are primarily sub-divided into cuts and deposits but also operate as a means of tracking all stratigraphic units on site. A context can be a stratigraphic unit or stratigraphic event, but the practice of excavation means that a context may represent a sub-division of a stratigraphic unit or event. For example, two excavators might excavate the same deposit in two different locations, assigning different context numbers to the deposit. This produces the need for the *stratigraphic group*. Within the Framework Archaeology recording system the value list for the context type therefore also includes SG (stratigraphic group), IG (interpretative group), and Void (context number not used).

Intervention

An *intervention* binds groups of contexts together. It is usually a cut or layer (taken here to include masonry and structural timbers) and it may contain other contexts, for example the fills of a cut. In the case of a cut, the intervention will normally consist of at least two contexts, one for

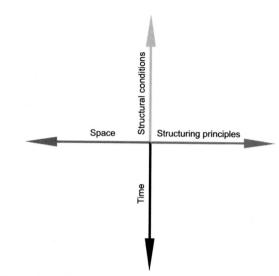

Figure 1.8: Diagram showing relationship between Structural Conditions and Structuring Principles

the cut and one discernible fill. The intervention must exist on the digital site plan and must represent an area of archaeological investigation. This is usually excavation but may on occasion be the result of a non-invasive recording method. The intervention is the primary method for producing artefact distribution plots within the Geographical Information System (GIS) and is the main method of displaying archaeological deposits three-dimensionally.

Deposit

The *deposit* is defined as a matrix that might contain finds or samples. Any context that might have produced a find or a sample, regardless of whether any were found or taken, is classified as a deposit. Each deposit is assigned to an intervention.

Stratigraphic Group

The *stratigraphic group* provides a means of describing the structure of the site. It is used to link equivalent contexts exposed in separate interventions within the same feature. For example, a stratigraphic group would be used to link together the separate context numbers given to the cut of a ditch in each of the interventions excavated, provided that it can be demonstrated to a reasonable level of confidence that they are stratigraphically equivalent. The same process would be applied to all fills within the ditch.

Figure 1.9: Modelling archaeological deposits

Feature

A *feature* is defined as one or more interventions that represent the remains of a past activity. It represents something that existed in the past, such as a ditch or a pit, which has been rediscovered through the process of archaeological investigation. The feature is defined through one or more interventions. It always consists of a stratigraphic group cut or a stratigraphic group layer and may contain other stratigraphic groups.

Entity

The *entity* is the basic tool of structural synthesis, a means of linking a group of related features together. For example, a number of postholes might form a structure or a number of ditches an

enclosure. This can be employed at an extremely detailed or a very broad level (eg an entity linking all the features making up a Bronze Age field system might contain hundreds of ditches). By definition, the entity includes all deposits within the assigned features. Not all features need belong to an entity, whereas some features may be assigned to more than one entity, depending on the analytical perspective.

Interpretative group

- To sub-divide entities into phases of time, which are defined as representing the construction of the entity, the use or disuse of the entity or the demolition of the entity. The distinction between disuse and demolition of the entity is defined by the visibility of the

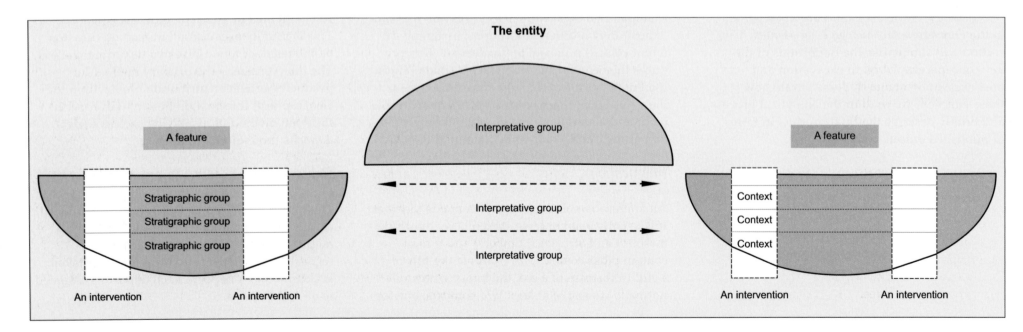

entity in the landscape. Disuse indicates that the entity was no longer used but still visible. Demolition indicates that the entity was no longer used and no longer visible in the landscape.

- To provide a method of linking deposits by a means unrelated to entities. An example would be the analysis of a landscape, which no longer exists as features, such as a Neolithic landscape where all features have been removed by later activity. Only Neolithic finds re-deposited within later features would indicate the existence of such a landscape.

The decision to define interpretative groups within an entity depends on the perceived degree of analysis required. Not all entities will be sub-divided into interpretative group time-slices. The diagram in Figure 1.9 shows how the Stanwell Cursus would be represented by *contexts, stratigraphic groups* and *interpretative groups* and as an *entity*. These elements can be used to model change through time and space, as demonstrated by the diagram (Fig. 1.8) showing *structuring principles* and *structural conditions*.

Information technology implementation

A computer system was installed on-site consisting of databases for matching up the records of features excavated, initial object identifications and the environmental samples with the plans of excavated and unexcavated archaeological features.

The purpose of the system was to allow cross-referencing of the recovered records and materials to produce initial phase plans and distribution plots of artefacts and samples which could be used to inform the excavation process.

Fieldwork procedures

The aim of the fieldwork programme was the creation of narratives of inhabitation, and those narratives were then further refined by off-site analysis. Interpretation at this level was the responsibility of the excavating team, rather than it being deferred to a post-excavation stage of analysis. Monuments, soils, organic and inorganic residues were therefore examined in the field in order to establish the changing form of the landscape, the processes operating across that landscape and the history of the landscape inhabitation. The development of *landscape generic* to *landscape specific* sampling, and the analytical shift between *structural conditions* and *structuring principles* were designed to facilitate the development of this line of analysis.

The issues raised as structuring principles are not derived from the material itself but from an inquiry into the way human life was ordered by occupying that material. For example, the inhabitants of an Iron Age settlement established and extended that settlement within the remnants of an ancient landscape, some worked the land, food was prepared, material needs were satisfied unequally, rubbish was deposited, the dead were given funerals, gods and spirits were

Plate 1.3: Site tour looking south-east with project team standing within middle Iron Age penannular gully 3 in WPR98 Bed C

acknowledged. Generally expressed they may be, but these issues impinge directly upon our understanding of the archaeological resource.

The above analytical sequence is one of increasing generalisation through which it will be possible to relate the archaeology of specific practices to more general historical themes and thus to a wider level of regional analysis for both the Middle Thames Valley and for southern Britain. In contrast, the excavation programme will, of necessity, have to move from the general to the particular, by initially assigning deposits to the chronological model proposed in the Research Design before interrogating those deposits to understand the operation of the structural principles through which the landscape was occupied.

Practical application

The excavation (Greater London Site Code WPR98) was undertaken in two phases. Phase 1 consisted of Thames Water Utilities Ltd (TWUL) removing any remaining dried sludge 'cake' from the drying beds and then any remaining overburden being removed by 360 degree tracked excavators under archaeological supervision. The archaeological features which were soon exposed were then digitally surveyed using electronic distance measurers (EDMs) to produce a digital map of the archaeological deposits. This was undertaken from October 1998 to February 1999, often under dreadful weather conditions. Heavy rainfall led to widespread flooding which required the use of pumps, and the archaeological team worked extremely hard under adverse conditions. This phase of the project clearly demonstrated that archaeological deposits had survived the construction and operation of the drying beds, but that survival was variable.

The excavation itself commenced in March 1999 and continued with a total team of *c* 60 individuals until the end of September 1999 (Plate 1.3). A small team was retained to finish data processing and limited excavation until Christmas 1999. To achieve the levels of analytical resolution demanded during the excavation, two main stages of investigation were identified, Landscape Generic and Landscape Specific. The main elements of these two stages were as follows:

Landscape Generic

- To characterise the overall nature of the archaeological resource and to understand the processes of its formation;

- To define in plan all archaeological features;

- To establish the character of those features in terms of cuts, soil matrices and interfaces;

- To recover across the site a sample of organic and inorganic material residues in order to understand site formation processes;

- To establish in outline a dated sequence of structures and thus to define changes in landscape organisation over time;

- To establish, within that dated sequence, the priorities for the investigation of a landscape specific archaeology of inhabitation.

The digital survey following the removal of overburden fully or partially met some of the above aims. Confidence in the interpretation of some features prior to excavation (eg the cursus monument and house circles) was more developed than for example, interpretation of linear ditches as field systems or enclosures. Our knowledge of these features was in turn more advanced than others such as pits and isolated postholes, about which little was known. The purpose of the Landscape Generic phase was both to build on our present interpretation and add to our knowledge of other landscape elements, and it thus addresses the need to understand the *Structural Conditions*.

In order to manage the excavation programme the Landscape Generic investigations were sub-divided into two stages: LG1 and LG2. The information recovered at each stage was used to inform subsequent interpretations and guided decisions on future excavation strategy. This staged approach facilitated a fluid and dynamic approach towards the management of the excavation and ensured that critical feedback and the construction of a narrative of human inhabitation was achieved within the constraints of the programme. Within these two stages therefore, excavation, analysis and interpretation was an on-going process in which objectives and the means of achieving them were the subject of constant critical review. This approach also had the advantage of allowing appropriate account to be taken of the varying levels of confidence in interpretation with which we started (see above).

LG1 was principally concerned with the following:

- dating and characterising a sample of the main types of features (eg linears, circular structures etc.);

- establishing a basic chronology and relative stratigraphy of the above features;

- assessing the quantities and analytical value of the artefactual and environmental material from these features.

The information gathered from LG1 sampling was analysed during excavation and the results determined the approach to the next stage (LG2).

LG2 was principally concerned with:

- determining the stratigraphic relationships between the excavated features to refine the chronological development of the landscape;

- increasing the sample size of excavated features in response to trends in spatial patterning of finds, environmental evidence and trends in constructional technique of linears etc.

In practice, LG1 interventions were located away from the junction of two features so that relatively uncontaminated finds and environmental samples could be obtained. LG2 interventions were located at the intersection of features to determine stratigraphic relationships. In addition, some LG2 interventions were located to clarify questions raised by LG1 interventions or to obtain more meaningful finds assemblages.

Constant re-assessment of data retrieved during LG1 and 2 allowed the appropriate sample size for investigation of unexcavated elements of LG1 to be determined. For instance, if LG1 determined that a meaningful sample excavation size for roundhouses was 50%, then the remaining unexcavated samples would be excavated to this size.

Following LG1 and LG2 the main elements of the stratigraphic groups were built (see Recording System above). Completion of the Landscape Generic phase provided the following:

- an understanding of the formation processes which led to the archaeological features and deposits which exist;

- a broad understanding of the structural conditions existing in successive landscapes;

- a baseline for future comparisons between human occupation of the different landscapes.

Landscape Specific

A series of period divisions in the history of landscape inhabitation was already defined in terms of the dominant traditions by which those landscapes were inhabited (see Previous work above). On-site analysis interrogated this model of chronological development, moving between the details of human inhabitation at a site-specific level of analysis and at the more general regional level.

In practice, the results of the Landscape Generic phase of work produced a number of research focussed tasks which were communicated in a Project Design Update Note in September 1999 (Framework Archaeology 1999b) whilst excavation was continuing.

It is important to note that none of the individual elements described below, or the processes that were used, are in themselves new. The basic level of recording remained the context, and these were grouped to form features and deposits, which in turn formed entities. Finds and environmental processing and assessment and analysis were undertaken in standard ways. The difference lay in where these tasks were positioned within the excavation and analytical sequence. For instance, Stratigraphic Groups (SGs) were produced at the end of the Landscape Generic (LG) phase of excavation: indeed, the construction of satisfactory SGs was a major test of whether enough data had been gathered during LG excavations. The creation of SGs allowed the excavators to interpret the construction, use and decay of features and deposits rather than disconnected contexts, and to consider how these operated in relation to contemporary and ancient landscapes. This was the beginning of the process that addressed the analysis of structuring principles and structural conditions (see above).

The requirement to address this level of interpretation during excavation, using finds and environmental data processed on site, facilitated the construction of the historical narrative in the field. The emerging narrative then acted as a source of inquiry for the Landscape Specific (LS) investigations, which may or may not have modified the initial interpretations. Excavation thus returned to the process that almost all archaeologists would agree it should be: a process of investigation of the past driven by questions and inquiry which demand observation, thought and interpretation, rather than attempting to achieve an arbitrary percentage sample across different features and deposits.

This system required site excavators and supervisors to engage with many elements such as grouping contexts and assessing dating evidence that has over the past 20 years tended to be deferred to the post-excavation phase of a project. It is our experience that one of the results of this deferral has been to narrow the skills base in British field archaeology, since field excavators usually have limited experience of post-excavation analysis. This project provided extensive training in this (and many other skills such as object identification and dating) in an attempt to raise excavators' interpretations from the context and intervention level to the feature, entity and landscape level. The results are contained in the interpretative text for the features and deposits and can be viewed through the Freeviewer software accompanying this volume (see below). The content is variable in clarity of thought and expression, but provides a much richer record than most archives: we feel it is still useful to be able to have the excavator tell us what a feature actually is, rather than trying to work this out from the convoluted 'context speak' we normally encounter.

By the end of the Perry Oaks excavations, a digital archive consisting of contexts grouped into features and deposits was available. The artefactual assemblages were quantified and dated and the environmental samples had mostly been processed and assessed for potential. In most respects the dataset was at a stage which most projects achieve after the post-excavation assessment phase, as defined by the Management of Archaeological Projects (English Heritage 1991). Nonetheless, a period following the excavation was required to enter a backlog of records into the database and to check through the digital archive for digitising, stratigraphic and dating errors. The archive was then used to refine the narrative and proposals for analysis and publication were presented in the Project Design Update Note 2 (Framework Archaeology 2000).

Post-excavation analytical procedures

The analytical phase of the project comprised specialist analysis of the artefactual assemblages and environmental samples, in conjunction with the stratigraphic evidence through the medium of the GIS, a process that took several years. Could this process be shortened? Is it possible to come off site with all this detailed analysis complete? In theory yes; however a number of practical factors prevent this.

Firstly, some forms of detailed analysis such as palynology simply take a long time, especially with a large project and numerous samples. Pottery fabric and form analysis is best undertaken once the whole excavated assemblage is available, not whilst more material is being recovered. Samples for radiocarbon dates (as with samples for environmental disciplines) need to be carefully selected and prioritised in the light of the full data set if cost-effectiveness is to be maintained.

Secondly, the structure of British archaeology is such that finds and environmental specialists with years of experience are simply not able to move and work on a single site for months or years at a time. They are based in offices or laboratories with extensive existing commitments. However, the publication of the narrative in this volume is dependent on this work, and until those skills can somehow be returned to the field then a lengthy post-excavation programme will remain.

Publication: scope, concept, presentation and archive

Scope of the work within this volume

This volume encompasses or draws upon the results of a number of different phases of archaeological investigation at Perry Oaks, as presented below.

- Several archaeological evaluations were undertaken by the Museum of London Archaeological Service (MoLAS) (BAA/902, /903, /905) in support of the Terminal 5 Public Inquiry in the early 1990s.

- Two aerial photographic surveys were commissioned by MoLAS and produced by English Heritage (RCHME 1995; 1997), showing the Stanwell Cursus, small circular Neolithic and/or Bronze Age monuments, and field systems dating from the 2nd millennium BC to the medieval period.

- In 1996, an excavation (Greater London site code POK96) was undertaken by MoLAS

Book	Freeviewer	Digital archive
Historical narrative with key supporting analysis and data. Discussion is based at the Entity and Feature/Deposit (Stratigraphic Group) level	Selected digital plans, sections and photographs. Landscape phasing and finds/environmental distributions and queries. Data is presented and described at the Entity, Feature/ Deposit (Stratigraphic Group) level. Contains context level data for each feature, but not descriptions	Full digital archive: all plans, sections, photographs, survey data. Data is presented at Entity, Feature/ Deposit (Stratigraphic Group) and Context level. Full Stratigraphic Group and context descriptions. All finds and environmental data. All specialist reports.

Increasing detail and complexity

→

Table 1.1: Levels of data in each stage of dissemination within the Perry Oaks Volume

(Andrews *et al.* 1998). This was located immediately to the south of Drying Bed B (Fig. 1.3) in order to mitigate the effects of the movement and stockpiling of processed sludge 'cake' by mechanical excavators, which was causing gradual truncation and loss of archaeological deposits (as demonstrated in the truncation model, see above).

- In 1998, Framework Archaeology was commissioned by Thames Water Utilities Ltd (TWUL) and BAA to mitigate the effects of the clearance of Drying Beds B, C and A, covering an area of *c* 21 hectares (Greater London site code WPR98). Excavations took place in 1999 and 2000.

- During 1999 Heathrow Airport Limited (HAL) commissioned Framework Archaeology to undertake further archaeological mitigation in advance of the construction of a new Northern Taxiway at Grass Area 6 (Greater London Site

Code GA199) and remote aircraft stands at Grass Area 21 (Greater London Site Code GAA00). Both areas, which lay within the perimeters of the airport, had been the subject of previous archaeological evaluations by MoLAS: WXE96 at Grass Area 6 and WXC96 at Grass Area 21 (BAA/905). Both evaluations had indicated the presence of archaeological remains, predominantly dating to the middle of the 2nd millennium BC. The Framework Archaeology excavations took place over a period from October 1999 until May 2000.

As far as possible, the field archives and finds data from all the MoLAS evaluations and excavations above (particularly POK96) have been digitised and incorporated within the Framework Archaeology GIS and database system.

With the approval of the application to construct Terminal 5, Framework Archaeology began further mitigation ahead of that project in March

2002. The data from those excavations (Greater London site codes PSH02, TEC05 and LONG-FORD) has been integrated with the datasets used here, and will be presented in Volume 2.

Publication concept, presentation and archive

This volume serves to develop the historical narrative and explore the major themes of landscape inhabitation. It has proved experimental in that it has explored the many issues of how to write a historical narrative, but at the same time present archaeological data. We cannot stress enough how difficult a process this has been. Writing an engaging historical narrative, which talks about the choices faced by people at different points in the past, what decisions they made and how that shaped their futures is a difficult enough task for historians. However, as archaeologists we need to build this narrative on a considered analysis of our excavated data. The presentation of the results of this analysis was problematic. Early drafts of this volume concentrated on historical processes and agency and high level theoretical synthesis of human occupation of the landscape. However, these early drafts proved unconvincing: enough data has to be presented within the narrative to provide examples to illustrate the historical points being discussed and to give the reader confidence in our conclusions, or at least provide a starting point for the reader to challenge those conclusions. Conversely, if too much data is presented, the narrative becomes disjointed and one returns to the format of more traditional publications, which tend above all to be descriptive catalogues of artefacts and stratigraphic sequences. Put simply, we have a tension between two main readerships. Firstly, those who wish to read about the history of human inhabitation of the landscape and are content with a historical narrative supported by detailed example. Secondly, there are those who want to 'know what pottery they found there' (Mercer 2002, 363); that is archaeologists who wish to use the data in their own researches, or are simply content with descriptions of how many monuments and trackways were excavated, their dating and finds assemblages. Our ideal, of course, would be to produce a publication that would satisfy both these groups and allow people to move from narrative to data and back again with ease.

Our solutions are not perfect, but we have been aided greatly by having all our data available in digital format. This has allowed us to distribute a distilled version of our data by creating the Freeviewer software. This is a GIS viewer, which allows the reader to view and interrogate a much larger dataset than would be possible with a normal publication. Should one want more detail than the Freeviewer can provide, then the full digital archive will be deposited with the Archaeology Data Service (ADS), and the physical archive with the Museum of London once the Terminal 5 excavation and publication programme is complete.

This approach seeks to provide a historical narrative backed by key analysis and data, but also provides a structured path into increasingly more complex data via the Freeviewer and the full digital archive. Table 1.1 shows the levels of data in each of these stages.

Structure of the historical narrative and how the themes will be explored

This section summarises how the results of the pursuit of the academic philosophy in the field has been presented in this volume.

The main part of this volume is divided into three sections (Chapters 2–4), which progress chronologically from the Mesolithic period in the 10th millennium BC to the end of the Romano-British period at the start of the 5th century AD.

Chapter 2, Hunter-gatherers and first farmers: the Mesolithic wildwood to the end of the monumental landscape of the Neolithic (10,000 BC–1700 BC)

This chapter outlines our chronological evidence before considering some of the historical processes through time. We will consider the significance of a handful of pits excavated by hunter-gatherers in the 7th millennium BC at a location on the edge of the Colne floodplain. In the 4th millennium BC a timber post–built structure was constructed a few metres south of these pits. In the late 4th millennium BC, the landscape was transformed by the construction of the C1 Stanwell Cursus, one of the great monuments of Neolithic Britain. This event, shortly after forest clearance associated with the 'elm decline', was followed by the construction of a second cursus (the C2 Cursus) and a small horseshoe-shaped enclosure. In the space of a few centuries or less, people had transformed the landscape from one defined by memories of ancient locations to one defined by the architecture of earthen banks and ditches. We will go on to suggest how people lived within this new world during the early part of the 3rd millennium BC. However, by the latter half of the millennium, new monuments and practices of artefact deposition signal a change in the way people lived in the landscape. By 1700 BC this change was to lead to the replacement of a system that apportioned land and resources through ceremony to one of physical demarcation: the first land tenure and field divisions.

Chapter 3, The emergence of the agricultural landscape from the early-middle Bronze Age to the end of the early Iron Age (c 1700 BC– 400 BC)

We will suggest a time and origin of the first land tenure boundaries that divided the Heathrow landscape in the first half of the 2nd millennium BC. We will show how settlements became archaeologically visible, how the landholdings developed into a landscape of small and large fields traversed by double-ditched trackways. This landscape supported a mixed arable/pastoral agricultural economy, supplemented by resources from the innumerable hedgerows which divided the fields. However, we will also show that during the middle of the 2nd millennium BC, people maintained links with the past and the overtly ceremonial world of monuments of the 3rd millennium BC through ceremonies resulting in particular artefacts being deposited in the base of waterholes. From the late 2nd millennium we will see how the pattern of small settlements scattered across the landscape changed to one of fewer and larger settlements. We can also see this change being reflected in different patterns of artefact deposition at the base of waterholes.

Little specific evidence was recovered for early Iron Age activity during the Perry Oaks excavations, but we shall see how major elements of the Bronze Age agricultural landscape appear to have persisted well into this period. Waterholes appear to have retained their status as places of offering for generations of farmers during the late Bronze Age/early Iron Age whilst hedgerows were maintained and ancient trackways respected.

Chapter 4, Development of the agricultural landscape from the middle Iron Age to the end of the Romano-British farmstead (c 400 BC–5th century AD)

This chapter deals with the period following the early Iron Age, after the abandonment of the small, dispersed settlements occupied by the Bronze Age inhabitants. We shall suggest that the Perry Oaks landscape came under the control of new cultural and economic influences and

designs, culminating in a gradual transformation which saw the emergence in the middle Iron Age of a nucleated settlement of roundhouses. This in turn became a focal point for continuing occupation and ceremony through into the early Roman period. However, we will show that the Perry Oaks landscape of the later Roman period largely overwrote the previous land divisions, focussing outwards and away from the ancient local community. This was perhaps produced by upheaval within the regional and imperial Roman administration during the 3rd century AD. We will demonstrate how some fossilisation of this late Roman landscape can be traced in the medieval ridge and furrow and the alignment of a post-medieval trackway that survive at Perry Oaks, although by this time the site appears to have reverted to localised rural inhabitation and agricultural regime.

Running through all three chapters are two main historical themes:

• The strategies used to decide access to land and resources and how these changed through time;

• How these strategies were intertwined with the tensions between individuals, families and communities, and how these dynamics changed through time.

The description of the archaeological remains will be considered in terms of these historical themes and used as examples of change or continuity in these processes. For example, we will examine how the construction of the Stanwell Cursus was undertaken by, and cemented the creation of, a community composed of kin-groups. For the next 1500 years the community apportioned access to land and resources to support the constituent kin-groups. We will show how this system weakened until just prior to 1700 BC, when the kin-groups came to the fore by physically apportioning land and resources through major landscape divisions. However by 1000 BC, the kin-groups had once more become unified into a community which lived in a single settlement and had pooled the resources of the individual landholdings into a larger landscape block.

CHAPTER 2
Hunter-gatherers and first farmers:
The Mesolithic wildwood to the end of the monumental landscape of the Neolithic
(10,000 BC–1700 BC)

by John Lewis and Fraser Brown

CD-Rom queries
Neolithic landscape
Mesolithic landscape
Burnt flint from cursus and Mesolithic pits
Neolithic Pre-C1 Stanwell Cursus postholes and pits
Postholes and pits
C1 Stanwell Cursus
Tree-throws
C2 Cursus
Neolithic HE1 enclosure
Early Bronze Age flint and pot distributions

Introduction

This chapter deals with the hunter-gatherer landscapes prior to *c* 4000 BC (the Palaeolithic and Mesolithic), and the appearance of the first agriculturists and transformation of the landscape through the construction of ceremonial monuments between 4000 and 1700 BC (the Neolithic and early Bronze Age). The chapter first lays out the framework of material evidence and assumptions regarding dating that will guide our analysis, relative to the research approach established in Chapter 1. This is then followed by a chronological narrative.

Summary of the evidence (Fig. 2.1)

Palaeolithic and Mesolithic

Five heavily rolled flint artefacts (including a small handaxe), none of which was in situ, are our only testimony to the Palaeolithic at Perry Oaks, whilst the Mesolithic is represented by *c* 80 flint artefacts, including 10 diagnostic types, mostly residing in features of much later date. Most notable were a cluster of pits excavated in the northern part of Bed B (WPR98; see Fig. 2.1) which contained burnt flint. This material provided thermoluminesence dates suggesting activity in the middle of the 7th millennium BC.

Figure 2.1: The Mesolithic and Neolithic dataset: excavated features

Neolithic

The Neolithic evidence from Perry Oaks consisted of three earthen monuments and one posthole complex, together with scatters of pits, tree-throws and occasional postholes. Neolithic flint artefacts and pottery fragments were also found residing in later features, as well as in the Neolithic features themselves.

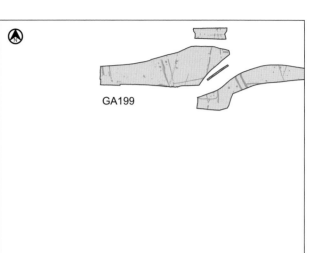

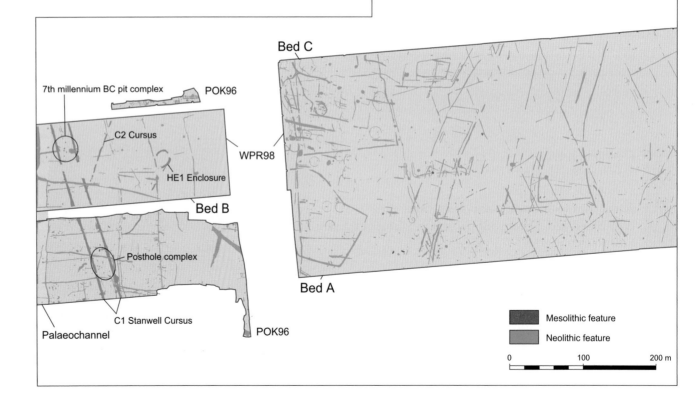

The specific Neolithic monuments excavated were as follows:

- A posthole complex within POK96. This was undated but was stratigraphically earlier than the construction of the C1 Stanwell Cursus.

- The C1 Stanwell Cursus. This monument consisted of two parallel ditches *c* 20 m apart, orientated NNW-SSE. It ran for at least 4 km and passed through Perry Oaks in Bed B and POK96. The cursus ran through the 7th millennium pit complex and earlier posthole complex, and was unusual in having a single central mound. More posts were erected in the area of the posthole complex when the cursus ditches began to silt up, suggesting a reaffirmation of this location. Roughly contemporary with this event, a second cursus (the C2 monument) was constructed.

- The C2 Cursus consisted of two parallel ditches, *c* 60 m apart and orientated NNE-SSW. This monument probably had the more usual arrangement of an internal bank adjacent to each of the two ditches. The C1 Stanwell Cursus served as the southern terminal of the C2 Cursus and the Terminal 5 excavations suggest this monument ran for at least 480 m.

- On the basis of pottery, stratigraphy and analogy with other monuments of this type, both the C1 and C2 Cursus were probably constructed sometime between 3600 and 3300 BC.

- The HE1 'horseshoe' shaped enclosure was located within the C2 Cursus. It is unclear whether this enclosure pre- or post-dated the C2 Cursus. No ceramic dating evidence was retrieved from the enclosure and the lithic material is inconclusive, but suggestive of a period of use in the 3rd millennium BC. The enclosure was *c* 17 m in diameter and probably consisted of ditches with internal banks. It was orientated on the mid winter sunset and the mid summer sunrise.

Ground water had completely leached out the collagen from all the skeletal material associated with these Neolithic features, making radiocarbon determinations impossible. Furthermore, the radiocarbon determinations of non-skeletal material conflicted with the stratigraphy and/or artefacts contained within the features, and so the chronology of the Neolithic landscape relies on a relative chronology of pottery styles which are present across much of southern Britain. In this respect, no Peterborough Ware pottery (3400 to 2500 BC) was recorded on site, although a small quantity of Grooved Ware pottery (3000 to 2000 BC) was recovered from a handful of pits scattered across the area.

Environmental evidence for the entire Neolithic period was very limited, with just a single pollen diagram presenting the results from a pit cutting one of the ditches of the C1 Stanwell Cursus. The pollen evidence suggests the location was either in a glade or on the woodland edge. The radiocarbon date for this feature is however contradictory. Another sample from a pit in Bed C was assessed and suggested a more open landscape, but it was not fully analysed due to poor preservation of pollen grains.

Early Bronze Age

Direct evidence of activity in the early Bronze Age is limited to a few diagnostic flint artefacts and pottery. A single sherd of Beaker pottery dating from some time between 2400 and 1700 BC was recovered, together with a few more sherds of less diagnostic pottery, which could either be Beaker or Collared Urn, and thus date from 2000 to 1500 BC. However, all these sherds appear to reside in features dated to later periods.

Outline of the narrative

Next we will outline the evidence for constructing a chronological framework for human activity during the huge time-span under consideration. The nature of the evidence for Palaeolithic and Mesolithic occupation is assessed, before turning to look at the Mesolithic in more detail. Several zones of Mesolithic activity are postulated, both from lithic material residing in later features and from the cluster of mid 7th-millennium pits. These locations are interpreted as meeting places for kin-groups, with the pit complex being especially important.

Moving forward to the Neolithic, the sequence of monument construction is explored. The construction of the C1 Stanwell Cursus is seen as revolutionary, both in terms of an architectural modification to the landscape, but also in being a physical manifestation of kin-groups coming together to form a community. This was achieved by communal effort to build a monument whose architecture linked locations of great importance (such as the Mesolithic pit complex and the pre-cursus timber complex) to kin-groups over several millennia. We suggest that this transformation occurred in a landscape which was becoming increasingly cleared following the 'elm decline', and may have occurred in response to the need for new mechanisms to apportion land and resources. These new mechanisms may have required architectural settings for ceremonies to negotiate these matters.

This transformation set in motion the construction of the C2 Cursus and probably the HE1 enclosure, as ceremony associated with access to land and resources rapidly became established as the way in which the community developed. Tree-throws and the occasional pit show that occupation was spreading across the landscape at this time, probably in the many woodland clearings that were being exploited for transient arable and pastoral agriculture.

This pattern of ceremony associated with monuments seems to have lasted through the currency of Peterborough Ware pottery, until perhaps the middle of the 3rd millennium BC. At this time, evidence from other West London sites suggests changes in the landscape, with a marked increase in the deposition of artefacts in isolated pits, starting with Peterborough Ware and continuing with Grooved Ware. These pit deposits can be interpreted as marking the end of a sequence of ceremonies, which started at the now ancient earthwork monuments. The pit deposits were the final act, which sealed the agreement over which kin-group had rights over a particular clearing or parcel of land. This represents the first physical act of marking a kin-group's rights over a piece of land, however small or however transient it may have been.

Other evidence from West London and the Terminal 5 excavations suggests that new small circular monuments were constructed in association with the use of Grooved Ware pottery from the latter half of the 3rd millennium BC onwards (see Vol. 2). There was thus a renewed requirement for architectural settings in which representatives of the kin-groups would meet and maintain the cohesion of the community.

The mechanisms by which the community had operated cohesively had been changing since the construction of the cursus monuments, up to 1500 years before, and so it is perhaps not surprising that we see changes at the turn of the 3rd and 2nd millennium BC. During this period, Beaker pottery and the associated burial rights seem to have been ignored in the Heathrow area. Instead, Collared Urn appears to have been utilised in similar ways to the Grooved Ware of earlier centuries, except that now it sometimes incorporated the remains of the dead in making claim to land. In many ways this marked the 'last gasp' use of monuments, ceremonies and discrete artefact deposits to negotiate access to land and resources in what was by now an increasingly open landscape.

In Chapter 3 we will show how, around 1700 BC, the whole process was replaced by the physical division of the land by boundary ditches, banks and hedgerows, a process as revolutionary in terms of the community and inhabitation of the landscape as the construction of the cursus monuments had been almost 2000 years earlier.

Chronological framework

In order to describe the human inhabitation of the Mesolithic, Neolithic and early Bronze Age landscapes, and to understand the transformation of one to the other, it is necessary to define the tools available to build a chronological framework for these periods. This framework is largely defined by ceramic and lithic artefacts, which can be dated with varying chronological precision.

The chronological framework adopted in this chapter is one that is generally accepted for southern Britain. Details are presented below.

The paucity of Mesolithic evidence, and in particular radiometric dates, from Perry Oaks frames our debate in terms of the early / late Mesolithic. With regard to the Neolithic, there persists in the literature a confusion of terms dividing the period. Two schemes have generally been adopted—earlier and later, and early, middle and late. This duality has arisen largely because researchers in different parts of the country have different components of the Neolithic 'package' in a variable mix and with varying and imprecise absolute chronologies.

However, recent developments in the dating of particular Neolithic ceramic traditions have allowed some refinement of chronology of the Neolithic monumental landscape at Perry Oaks.

Absolute dates

Absolute dates from the Mesolithic to early Bronze Age at Perry Oaks are extremely sparse. This is largely due to the poor state of preservation of many of the deposits. Most features lay above the permanent water table in conditions not conducive to organic preservation. The charcoal recovered was generally heavily comminuted, and bone collagen was depleted.

Mesolithic dates

Four thermoluminescence (TL) dates were obtained from burnt flint recovered from a series of pits sealed below the Stanwell Cursus (Table 2.1). The dates extended across the 7th millennium BC but it is probable, given the nature and spatial distribution of the pits, that they represent either contemporary activity or phases of activity confined to a few generations.

A radiocarbon date of 6240–5990 (cal BC 2 sigma) from the 2003 evaluations at Bedfont Court on the Colne floodplain attests to activity in this area at broadly the same time as the burnt flint pits of the terrace were filled (Framework Archaeology 2003).

Neolithic dates

The earliest Neolithic radiocarbon date came from sediment in a pit (150011) that cut the Stanwell Cursus ditch fills, although the date (4349–4047; NZA14902 cal BC 2 sigma) was very early, suggesting that the organic material tested was residual. A radiocarbon date of 3030–2870 BC (WK11473 cal BC 2 sigma) was obtained from a small bowl-shaped pit (137027) containing cremated human bone. In all pits of this type where ceramics were also present, the pottery was Grooved Ware, confirming the Neolithic date.

The more recent excavations associated with the construction of Terminal 5 (T5) have yielded more radiocarbon and Optically Stimulated Luminescence (OSL) dates (see Vol. 2). An OSL sequence was obtained from deposits in both ditches of the Stanwell Cursus, with the dates indicating that the monument's ditches were silting during the early Neolithic. Analyses of the T5 data is ongoing and the results are not included in this volume.

In view of the paucity of absolute dates, we will consider the relative dating of stratigraphy and the ceramic sequence.

Relative chronology

Lithic technology and typology

We will now look at the context and distribution of the Mesolithic and earlier Neolithic flint work within the Perry Oaks and wider Heathrow landscape, and try to construct a non-monumental geography of the period 9000 to 3000 BC.

Lithic artefacts and assemblages have an important part to play in defining a relative chronological sequence. However, in chronological terms, it is generally only possible to speak in terms of the following:

- Early and late Mesolithic

- Mesolithic or Neolithic,

- Earlier and later Neolithic.

This is partly due to the relatively undiagnostic nature of lithic waste and debitage. These terms cover much broader periods of time than the ceramic evidence and so the chronological resolution of the historical narrative is coarser when relying on lithic evidence alone, as Table 2.2

Pit context number	Lower date-range	Upper date-range	Mean date
165005	6840 BC	5580 BC	6210 BC
165005	7330 BC	6170 BC	6750 BC
165007	7160 BC	5760 BC	6460 BC
165009	7810 BC	6550 BC	7180 BC

Table 2.1: Thermoluminescence dates for Mesolithic pits in area of the Stanwell C1 Cursus at Perry Oaks WPR98

Lithic Period Division	Calibrated BC
Late Glacial	10,300-8800
Early Mesolithic	8800-7000
Late Mesolithic	7000-4000
Earlier Neolithic	4000-3200
Later Neolithic	3200-2400
Early Bronze Age	2400-1500

Table 2.2: Chronological divisions of lithic artefacts

indicates. Cramp, who analysed the lithic assemblage from Perry Oaks, makes the following observations on the chronologically diagnostic Mesolithic and Neolithic flint assemblages (full lithics report can be found on accompanying CD, Section 3).

While diagnostic tool types, such as microburins and microliths, provide a more reliable and quantifiable resource, it is possible that a significant quantity of undiagnostic Mesolithic flintwork is present but has been subsumed by the early Neolithic assemblage with which it shares many technological characteristics. This invisible element may, not entirely but to some extent, account for the apparent under-representation of the earlier period in terms of flintwork from the site. Examples include some of the blades, bladelets and rejuvenation flakes, along with the two blade cores from WPR98. These pieces were isolated according to general technological traits, such as the presence of platform edge abrasion and evidence for the use of soft-hammer percussion.

These potentially Mesolithic artefacts are quantified by feature and phase in Table 2.3, which provides an indication of the low numbers of flints involved.

(Cramp, CD Section 3)

Ceramic chronology

The ceramics cannot be used to achieve accurate absolute dating, but they can support the general sequence established using absolute methods. It is important to stress that the dates referred to in this section reflect the main period of use of the ceramics concerned.

Firstly, we will examine the Neolithic ceramics and assess their relative position in the chronology of the period.

Problems with ceramic fabrics

During initial analysis of the ceramics recovered from Perry Oaks a fabric type series was established. These fabrics, however, are not chronologically precise indicators of ceramic development. In the middle and lower reaches of the Thames in particular, a range of flint-tempered fabrics was used intermittently throughout the Neolithic and Bronze Ages. It follows that dating deposits on the basis of otherwise undiagnostic body sherds does not provide a precise chronology for these deposits. As a result, at Perry Oaks and other West London sites, it has been common practice to date features containing undiagnostic flint-tempered fabrics to the late Bronze Age. Therefore, during excavations at Perry Oaks in 1999 (WPR98) it was assumed, on the basis of the ceramics, that the ditches of Stanwell Cursus were open into the late Bronze Age.

During analysis, a reassessment of the flint-tempered pottery fabrics and their associations

with lithic artefacts, combined with detailed stratigraphic analysis, has shown that the pottery from the cursus and many other features (notably the horseshoe monuments and tree-throws) better accords with an early Neolithic date. For example, all of the pottery from the primary fills of the cursus was originally identified as flint-tempered fabric type FL1, assigned to the late Bronze Age. This would imply that no sediment had accumulated in these ditches although they had been open for many hundreds of years, contrary to the fill processes in other features in the vicinity. Alternately, it could suggest that the ditches had been entirely re-excavated in the late Bronze Age, although this is at variance with the observed stratigraphic relationships.

The associations between diagnostic lithic artefacts and pottery fabrics also played an important part in the reassessment of the dating of these fabrics. Tree-throws containing Neolithic flints and pottery fabric FL1 were classified as late Bronze Age, it being assumed that the flintwork was residual. However, we know that the landscape from the middle Bronze Age onwards was largely clear of trees, and therefore the lithic material could provide a more accurate date for the tree-throws. The pottery could then be earlier Neolithic rather than late Bronze Age in date.

This reassessment resulted in a reclassification of the pottery as early Neolithic fabric FL4, suggesting that the early Neolithic inhabitation of the Heathrow landscape was much more widespread and populous than was previously believed. Having discussed the problems of ceramic dating,

Feature	Interpretation	Feature cut date	Number of Mesolithic flints	Feature	Interpretation	Feature cut date	Number of Mesolithic flints
POK96				WRP98 continued			
961017	Gully	Early Neolithic	1	132199	Undefined	Unphased	1
961501	Ditch	Neolithic	2	133198	Waterhole	Romano-British	1
961508	Ditch	Late Bronze Age	1	134029	Ditch	Early Neolithic	2
961540	Natural feature	Mesolithic	1	135055	Pit	Late Bronze Age	1
962363	Ditch	Middle Bronze Age	1	136177	Pit	Neolithic	1
963163	Tree-throw	Unphased	1	137114	Pit	Middle Iron Age	1
963218	Ditch	Middle Bronze Age	1	141228	Pit	Neolithic	1
Undefined	Undefined	Unphased	14	147106	Ditch	Middle Bronze Age	1
WRP98				148029	Ditch	Early Iron Age	1
106013	Cremation	Late Bronze Age	1	148093	Ditch	Romano-British	1
107042	Ditch	Early Neolithic	2	148303	Pit	Middle Iron Age	1
107084	Ditch	Romano-British	1	149209	Posthole	Late Bronze Age	1
108022	Ditch	Middle Iron Age	1	151031	Pit	Unphased	1
113131	Ditch	Romano-British	1	156191	Tree-throw	Early Neolithic	11
119240	Ditch	Middle/late Iron Age	1	158143	Ring gully	Middle Iron Age	1
119259	Ditch	Middle/late Iron Age	1	160016	Ditch	Middle Bronze Age	1
120072	Tree-throw	Mesolithic	1	160104	Ditch	Late Bronze Age	2
121173	Ditch	Neolithic	1	163135	Tree-throw	Mesolithic	1
122036	Ditch	Late Bronze Age	1	166195	Ditch	Romano-British	1
122084	Pit	Mesolithic	1	167037	Ring ditch	Middle Iron Age	1
127022	Pit	Late Neolithic	1	172081	Tree-throw	Mesolithic	1
128028	Ditch	Neolithic (western cursus ditch)	5	180080	Well	Early Iron Age	1
129013	Posthole	Neolithic	1	GAI99			
129109	Pit	Neolithic	2	218038	Ditch	Middle Bronze Age	1
132190	Posthole	Middle Bronze Age	1	GAA00			
continued on right				401075	Ditch	Middle Bronze Age	1
				Total			**80**

Table 2.3: Distribution of possible Mesolithic flints, by feature

Date	Fabric Type	No. sherds	Weight (g)	ASW (g)
Early Neolithic	FL4	769	2216	
	FL8	1	15	
	QU13	17	119	
	Subtotal EN	787	2350	3
Late Neolithic	GR2	62	184	3
Early Bronze Age	GR1	32	75	2.3
Totals		881	2609	3

Table 2.4: Quantification of Neolithic and early Bronze Age pottery from Perry Oaks

we can return to the evidence from Perry Oaks and place this element of the pottery assemblage more precisely within the early Neolithic period. The majority of the pottery was of a single fabric type, FL4, with only a handful of sherds in other fabrics (see Table 2.4). This apparent homogeneity might suggest that the assemblage covers a relatively restricted time span, but evidence from across the region and beyond indicates that fabrics did not change significantly within this period, or indeed subsequently, during the currency of Peterborough Ware. The condition of the sherds from Perry Oaks is poor and diagnostic material is relatively scarce, but on the basis of the existing evidence a chronology for the ceramic assemblage can be proposed.

Carinated Bowls

The earliest ceramic form identified in Britain is the Carinated Bowl, generally dated to *c* 4000–3600 BC (Herne 1988; Gibson 2002, 70). However, Cleal has recently re-appraised the type, and concluded,

...that the majority were carinated in some way, but were not all of the Classic Carinated Bowl form, which should focus our attention and interest particularly on the minority which were not carinated at all

(Cleal 2004)

The evidence for this tradition at Perry Oaks is elusive, but could be represented by a single, possibly carinated, sherd from tree-throw 156191, although the remaining pottery from this feature appears to be later (see below).

Undecorated Bowls and Decorated Vessels

The bulk of the earliest ceramics from Perry Oaks probably dates to later within the early Neolithic sequence. This part of the assemblage consists of undecorated Plain Bowl Ware types, with a small proportion of decorated vessels. These types are thought to have emerged sometime before *c* 3600 BC, continuing in use to *c* 3300 BC (Gibson 2002, 70).

Early Neolithic pottery is scarce within the West London area, and parallels for the fabrics and forms found within the Perry Oaks assemblage are more common from a wider area of the Thames Valley, including Staines and Runnymede Bridge (Robertson-Mackay 1987; Kinnes *et al.* 1991). However, the lack of decoration within the Perry Oaks assemblage is in distinct contrast to these groups. In this respect the assemblage is closer to those from three sites in east Berkshire: Cippenham, Slough; Manor Farm, Horton and Charvil (Raymond 2003a; 2003b; Lovell and Mepham 2003). This may seem anomalous in an area that falls within Whittle's decorated style zone (1977), but the legitimacy of such stylistic classification has been questioned more recently (eg Cleal 1992). The relative lack of decoration within the Perry Oaks and Cippenham assemblages may be a chronological factor, suggesting that these assemblages fall earlier within the early Neolithic than those at Staines or Runnymede.

A large proportion (61.4 %; 541 sherds) of the Neolithic and early Bronze Age pottery assemblage derived from a single context, tree-throw 156191, with a smaller residual group of 80 sherds coming from Bronze Age field ditch 961508. In general, the condition of this material is poor but the fabrics, particularly the flint-tempered wares, tend to be extremely friable and a high degree of fragmentation does not necessarily reflect a commensurate level of post-depositional movement. The main group, from tree-throw 156191, seems to have been deposited as a single event, whilst the group from ditch 961508, while

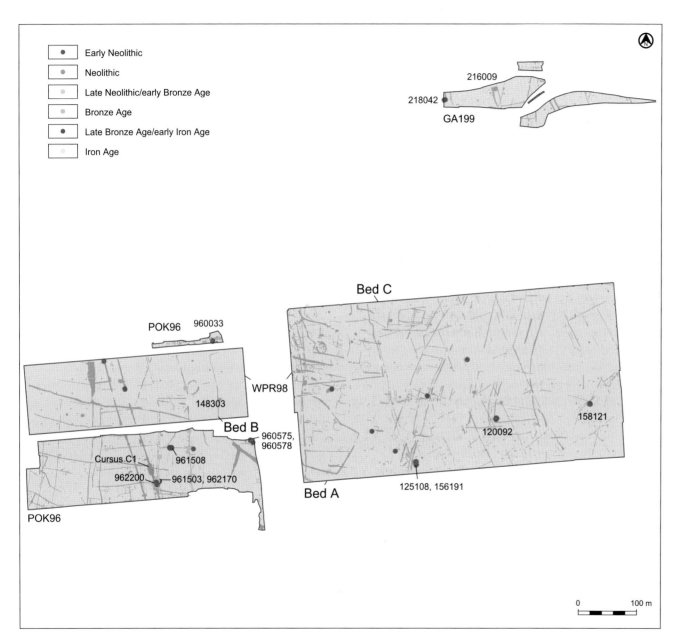

Figure 2.2: The distribution of early Neolithic pottery

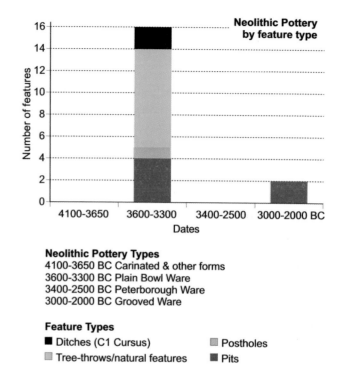

Neolithic Pottery Types
4100-3650 BC Carinated & other forms
3600-3300 BC Plain Bowl Ware
3400-2500 BC Peterborough Ware
3000-2000 BC Grooved Ware

Feature Types
■ Ditches (C1 Cursus)   ▨ Postholes
▨ Tree-throws/natural features ■ Pits

obviously residual, is likely to have derived from a disturbed deposit nearby. The original deposition of the two groups could have been separated by a wide chronological gap, but the homogeneity of the fabrics across the groups and the stylistic similarity of the rims suggests otherwise.

The distribution of early Neolithic pottery (Fig. 2.2) extends across most of the site. However, the complete absence of sherds to the west of the C1 Stanwell Cursus is notable. In fact, with the exception of two sherds from the western ditch, none were identified beyond the eastern cursus ditch. A rough clustering of findspots was apparent in part of the MoLAS excavations (POK96), where pottery was found in the fills of the eastern cursus ditch (most of the 31 sherds from the cursus were concentrated in this area) and within the fills of the Bronze Age field system, including the large group from ditch 961508. The identification of early Neolithic pottery within the cursus ditches has considerable implications for their dating. Most of the sherds came from secondary fills, but two were recovered from a primary fill within ditch 961501.

Other sherds came from a scatter of tree-throws, including the largest group from 156191 on the southern edge of Bed A, and from pits and other features. Tree throw 156191 was the only feature with a possible *in situ* deposit, perhaps the result of deliberate middening. Other occurrences were sporadic and more likely to be residual.

Peterborough Ware

A recent programme of radiocarbon dating has established a currency for Peterborough Ware ceramics *c* 3400–2500 BC (Gibson and Kinnes 1997). No Peterborough Ware was recovered from the Perry Oaks excavations but it is known elsewhere at Heathrow (Grimes 1961), including the recent T5 excavations (see Vol. 2). It has also been found at a number of other excavated sites in the West London area.

Grooved Ware

The ceramic sequence at Perry Oaks continues with the use of Grooved Ware. The overall currency of this ceramic tradition in southern Britain, based on radiocarbon dating, falls *c* 3000–2000 BC (Garwood 1999, 152). Some 62 sherds from Perry Oaks have been identified as Grooved Ware, primarily on the basis of decoration and fabric. The fabric is a homogeneous grog-tempered type, classified as GR2.

Forty-one sherds of Grooved Ware, the majority of the total, came from a single feature excavated at the Northern Taxiway (GAI99), pit 216009/216118 (respective secondary fills 216011 and 216120). A radiocarbon sample from pit 216009 produced a completely anomalous medieval date (sample WK9377). Additional small quantities of Grooved Ware came from six stratified contexts at the main central drying bed area (WPR98), one from Grass Area 21 (GAA00), and two from the MoLAS excavations (POK96).

This small group is significant, although a substantial assemblage of more than 500 sherds, representing approximately 12 vessels in Durrington Walls sub-style, had previously been recovered in Harmondsworth (Field and Cotton 1987). More recent fieldwork in Harmondsworth has added to this, with a further four vessels in the same sub-style from Prospect Park (Laidlaw and Mepham 1996) and a substantial assemblage of *c* 9.5 kg from Holloway Lane (unpublished data, MoLAS site code HL80; cf. Merriman 1990, 24–5). At the latter site, a few sherds of Peterborough

Ware were found in association with the Grooved Ware, but at Perry Oaks Peterborough Ware is notable by its absence (see above).

Beaker

The chronology of Beaker ceramics has been discussed in detail elsewhere (eg Kinnes *et al.* 1991; Case 1993), and here our main concern is the relationship between Grooved Ware and Beaker ceramics. A recent review by Garwood (1999) has concluded that there is little overlap between the two and argues that Beaker funerary deposits in southern Britain belong to the period after *c* 2500/2400 BC and persist until 1700 BC (also Needham 1996, 124).

Only one diagnostic sherd of Beaker pottery has been identified at Perry Oaks, although a small group of other undiagnostic grog-tempered sherds (fabric type GR1) may belong either to this or to the Collared Urn tradition. It is notable that lithic types contemporary with Beakers (such as barbed and tanged arrowheads and thumbnail scrapers) are present, the former only as unstratified finds. It seems therefore that the Beaker ceramic traditions were not adopted in this area, as was the case with Henge monuments and single burials, which also appear to be absent.

The absence of the Beaker complex seems, on current evidence, to be a genuine and widespread characteristic of the middle Thames gravel terrace. It is one of the factors that distinguishes this landscape from surrounding areas (eg Surrey, London and the Upper Thames Valley).

Collared Urn

Collared Urns are also scarce, both on this site and generally in the West London area. None have been identified at Perry Oaks although, as noted above, undiagnostic grog-tempered body sherds in fabric GR1 could belong to this tradition. Collared Urns emerged at around 2050 cal BC and lasted until *c* 1500 cal BC (Needham 1996, fig. 2). Reliable radiocarbon dates for Collared Urns are rare and there is insufficient evidence to demonstrate continuous development from Fengate Ware (Gibson and Kinnes 1997; Gibson 2002, 96).

Conclusion of ceramic technology

The relative ceramic chronology at Perry Oaks allows us to discuss historical change within the following time periods:

Ceramic type	Calibrated BC
Carinated bowl	4000–3600
Undecorated Plain Bowl	
& decorated vessels	3600–3300
Peterborough Ware	3400–2500
Grooved Ware	3000–2000
Beaker	2400–1700
Collared Urn	2000–1500

A number of caveats must be applied in using this relative chronology. Firstly, the currency of different ceramic types is apparently overlapping—they are not *chronologically* mutually exclusive. This overlap may be a product of the vagaries of radiocarbon dating, as discussed by several authors (eg Garwood 1999; Gibson and Kinnes 1997). Secondly, the ceramic types (particularly Peterborough Ware) cut across traditional chronological subdivisions of the Neolithic, 'earlier and later' or 'early, middle and late'. Thirdly, the chronology is based on national reviews of the ceramics and the regional and even local ceramic sequence could show significant variations.

Implications of a relative chronology for the Neolithic landscape at Perry Oaks

Having reviewed the chronological evidence from Perry Oaks, we now turn to what that evidence might mean in terms of landscape history in the 4th and 3rd millennia BC.

Cleal, in a recent paper, has described succinctly the current practice applied to chronological divisions of the early Neolithic and ceramics thus:

This focus on chronology raises a more general question of how pottery, if it could be better dated, would influence our understanding of the development of the Neolithic. At present there is not even a consensus on the terminology for describing the Neolithic period as a whole. There are two common usages, both of which are applied to the ceramics: some writers prefer a bipartite division into 'earlier' and 'later' Neolithic, the division occurring at around 3000 BC; others use a tripartite division into early (c 4000 BC to, variously, anything from c 3600–c 3300 BC), *middle (variously c 3600–3300 to 3000, or 2900/2800 BC) and late.*

(Cleal 2004)

After reviewing the ceramics in Wessex and the south-west of England for the 4th millennium BC, Cleal proposed a four part regional chronology for the period. Whilst geographically removed from the Heathrow area of the Thames Valley, this scheme is worth summarising as it does offer certain parallels.

Earliest or Contact Neolithic (c ?4100–3850 BC). This may have been virtually aceramic and is attested mainly by interventions in the environment which are often difficult to distinguish as Neolithic.

Early or Developing Neolithic (say c 3850–3650 cal BC). Ceramics of this phase are largely carinated, but…, other forms were used alongside these, principally inflected forms and cups and small bowls, nor were the carinated forms exclusively the Classic Carinated Bowl. By 3800 cal BC, as demonstrated by the Sweet Track, an early stage of woodland management, exploitation of the Levels, ceramics, polished exotic axes and flint axes were all current, in what could be termed the earliest phase of the Neolithic to have most of the features we recognise as typical of the period. Some of the earliest long mounds may belong here, although the dating is uncertain, and there are as yet no convincingly early mounds quite this early in the south-west.

(Cleal 2004)

As we have shown, the lithic and ceramic evidence for these early phases of the Neolithic at Perry Oaks is scarce. To all intents and purposes, the lithics are virtually indistinguishable from the latest Mesolithic and suggest a relative continuum in human inhabitation of the landscape in the late 5th and early 4th millennia BC.

'High' or Developed Neolithic (c 3650–3350 BC). This is the phase with features of the 'classic' earlier part of the Neolithic most fully developed: causewayed and 'tor' enclosures (and cursus) emerge here, joining long barrows, and ceramics; it also includes the origins of Peterborough Ware as part of a widespread developing pattern of impressed wares.

(Cleal 2004)

In the Heathrow area, this is the period which sees the main phase of construction of large communal monuments, such as causewayed enclosures at Yeoveny Lodge, Staines (Robertson-Mckay, 1987), Eton Wick (Ford 1986) and Runnymede (Needham and Trott 1987, 482 and fig. 2). At Perry Oaks, major elements of the C1 Stanwell Cursus and possibly the C2 Cursus were constructed.

Middle Neolithic (3350–3000/2950 cal BC). In ceramic terms this is the period in which the Peterborough tradition is fully developed and in which the bowl styles of the mid-late 4th millennium BC go out of use.

(Cleal 2004)

No Peterborough Ware was recovered during the Perry Oaks excavations although a small amount was found during recent Framework Archaeology excavations at Terminal 5 (see Vol. 2).

Although across southern Britain as a whole there appears to be some chronological overlap between Peterborough Ware and late Neolithic Grooved Ware, in West London the two are never found in the same contexts. In this region Grooved Ware is most frequently found deposited with lithics and often with charred plant remains such as hazelnuts and crabapple pips. This may be a continuation of the ritual autumnal deposition initiated during the Peterborough Ware phase. In addition, small circular or hengiform monuments were constructed during this period, but not large henge monuments. At Perry Oaks, Grooved Ware was recovered only from a small number of pits but was not present in the HE1 horseshoe enclosure.

Using the ceramic chronology described by Cleal and others—and noting the distribution of Neolithic ceramics by feature type at Perry Oaks—the chart in Figure 2.2 provides an indication of the modification of the landscape by people during the 5th and 4th millennia BC. Prior to 3600 BC there appears to have been little human activity in terms of monument construction. The decline through disease of the elm population in Greater London (the 'elm decline') has recently been dated to 3750 BC (Rackham and Sidell 2000, 22). The effects of the elm decline on human behaviour are outside the scope of this

volume, but it is surely no coincidence that following this event, during the currency of Plain Bowl Ware pottery, we see a sudden and extraordinary flowering of monument construction in the form of large causewayed and small circular enclosures and cursus monuments. The chart reflects the impact of the Stanwell Cursus, but also the level of tree clearance at this time. Whether this was deliberate felling or removal of dead trees (perhaps groups of dead elms) to produce glades and clearances in the forest is uncertain. These local clearances may have acted as foci for shifting settlement and agriculture, which left their mark in the form of pits excavated for domestic refuse and ritual deposits. However, it is clear that the construction of major linear monuments such as the Stanwell Cursus and the C2 Cursus would have required at least local clearance of the forest along their course. This is particularly true of the Stanwell Cursus, which deviates only slightly from a straight course over at least 3.6 km.

The chart in Figure 2.2 indicates that people made little physical impact on the landscape at Perry Oaks during the succeeding period from 3400 to 2500 BC. It is only in the late Neolithic that the adoption of Grooved Ware coincided with renewed deposition of material in pits, and the construction of new, small circular enclosures in the landscape.

Geographies of the Palaeolithic

The artefacts listed in Table 2.5 are our only evidence for the inhabitation of Perry Oaks prior to the last glaciation. This is not an impressive corpus and the artefacts do not conform to any specific technological type. Indeed some question must remain as to whether they do actually represent a Palaeolithic assemblage at all. We might also note the small assemblage of flakes and a crested core recovered from the Cargo Distribution Service Site, Heathrow (Lewis in prep.), dating to 28,000–24,000 BP. These suggest low intensity inhabitation of a periglacial steppe landscape, just prior to the onset of another epoch of glaciation proper.

We pick up the Heathrow narrative circa 10,000 BC, when steppe tundra conditions once more prevailed. No evidence was recovered from the Perry Oaks excavations but other sites in the Colne Valley system, notably Church Lammas (Jones 1995) and Three Ways Wharf, Uxbridge (Lewis 1991; Lewis et al. 1992; Lewis in prep.),

furnish us with analogues for the kind of inhabitation we might expect in the immediate area. These sites were characterised by distinctive late Upper-Palaeolithic long-blade lithic technology used by the first reindeer hunters to re-colonise major river courses from a North Sea Basin that was dry and habitable at that time. It is perhaps unsurprising that we have retrieved no long-blades from Heathrow, as these hunting bands were probably merely passing through the area, following the migrating herds that were most populous in the valley networks. As such, these people would have had little material need to venture up on to the terrace.

The second phase of the site at Three Ways Wharf is set against a very different material backdrop to the first. This is evident from the pollen data (Lewis et al. 1992), which places the site in a Holocene/Boreal environment: a sedge/reed swamp populated by pine, oak, hazel, birch and elm. The faunal remains recovered from this site included red and roe deer—sylvan species suited to such an ecology, as well as swan. The people

who hunted these animals had adapted their technologies and inhabitation strategies to suit their needs and to the local ecology. They probably restricted their movements to smaller territories than their reindeer-hunting predecessors and were, as such, the first post-glacial residents of the Heathrow landscape. It is now that we can start to talk about the Mesolithic, a period archaeologists identify from the microlithic toolkits people fashioned into the composite tools with which they carved out a world in wood, hide and horn.

Mesolithic / earlier Neolithic geographies

The Mesolithic period at Perry Oaks is characterised by geological and topographical features, a small number of cut features and a number of lithic scatters that occurred across a wide area as a residual component within later deposits (see Figs 2.3–4 and below).

Table 2.6 shows features dated to the Mesolithic period, between 8500 and 4000 BC. The majority

Site code	Bed	Context no.	Object no.	Object	Object description
WPR98		100000		Awl	Thermal fragment with possible retouch creating spur. Poor condition.
GAI99	1A	216040	4020	Tertiary flake 0%	Large, broad secondary flake in extremely poor condition. Very heavily rolled, iron-stained and damaged. May be Palaeolithic.
WPR98		100000	444	Secondary flake 1-74%	Secondary flake in very poor condition. With heavy cortication and deep surface iron-staining. Possibly an axe-trimming flake?
WPR98		100000	3531	Axe/adze	Small handaxe, bifacially worked. Very rolled and corticated. Found in a land drain.
GAI99	1B	214009	4019	Other scraper	Scraper made on a non-flake blank. Irregular, elongated thermal fragment with some abrupt scraper retouch to one end, c 30mm. Further small area of retouch to one of the longer edges, c 12mm, forming small notch, for hafting? Condition (rolled, iron-stained) suggests Palaeolithic.

Table 2.5: Palaeolithic finds from Heathrow

Feature interpretation	Feature
Natural feature	961540
Pit	120028
Pit	122084
Pit	137021
Pit	160021
Pit	162010
Pit	165005
Pit	165005
Pit	165007
Pit	165009
Pit	178054
Tree-throw	120072
Tree-throw	122086
Tree-throw	163135
Tree-throw	172081

Table 2.6: Mesolithic features from Perry Oaks

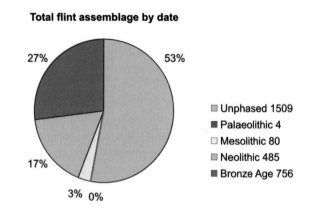

Total flint assemblage by date

- Unphased 1509
- Palaeolithic 4
- Mesolithic 80
- Neolithic 485
- Bronze Age 756

53%
27%
17%
3% 0%

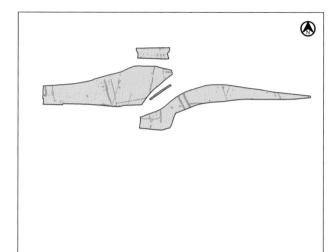

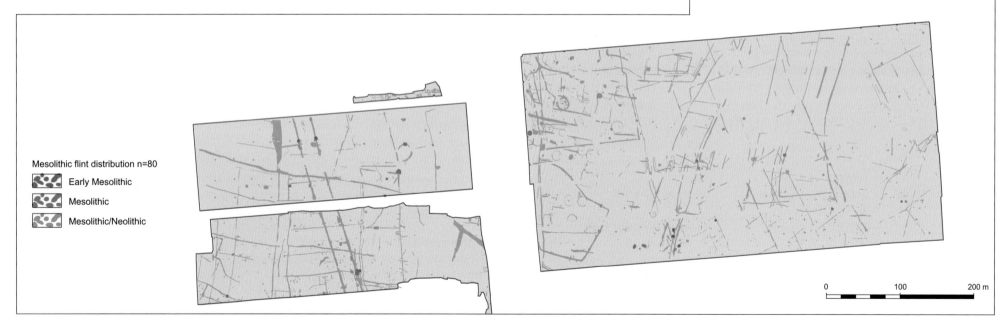

Mesolithic flint distribution n=80

Early Mesolithic

Mesolithic

Mesolithic/Neolithic

0   100   200 m

Figure 2.3: Quantity and distribution of Mesolithic and Mesolithic /earlier Neolithic flint

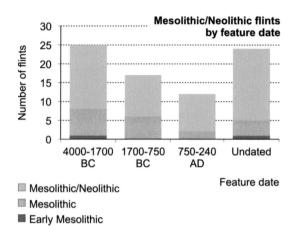
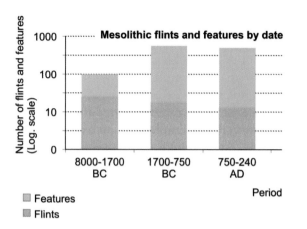
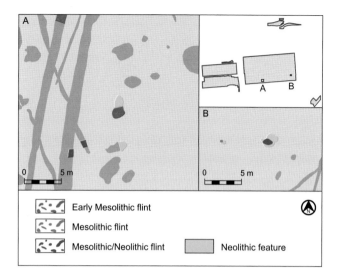

Figure 2.4: Mesolithic and Mesolithic/Neolithic flints by feature type and date

are pits containing burnt flint within the C1 Stanwell Cursus and dated by thermoluminescence. Some tree-throws have been assigned a Mesolithic date on the basis of stratigraphic relationships with Neolithic features, while some deposits contained only typologically dated Mesolithic flints. Only six diagnostic Mesolithic flints were recovered from deposits dated to the Mesolithic on the basis of stratigraphy or absolute dating. The vast majority of the remainder were recovered from deposits within later features, and it is those that we will deal with next.

The sludge works had removed all traces of the original ploughsoil, which in rural locations could be expected to contain lithic material derived from prehistoric flint scatters. Allen *et al.* have stated that without adequate preservation

or strategies (eg test-pitting or field walking) to recover this material from the ploughsoil, 'landscape studies in the Neolithic [and presumably the Mesolithic] are of limited value' (2004, 84). We would contend that it is the sort of questions and scale of analysis of the landscape that are the most important factors when considering lithic material. We would also contend that in some ways, lithic material which resides in later contexts can provide as precise a guide to activity locations as material collected from the ploughsoil by fieldwalking (see Fig. 2.4). Consider Neolithic flintwork residing in the middle 2nd millennium BC ditches of the field system. The excavation of those ditches took place perhaps 1500 years after the activity which left the lithic material, and locked those artefacts into the 2nd millennium features. In contrast, a Neolithic scatter in ploughsoil would have been subjected to a further 3500

years of post-depositional movement through agricultural and other processes. A single Mesolithic flint *could* be all that remains of an erstwhile scatter and several flints in close proximity increase the likelihood that a scatter was once located in the vicinity.

Chronology and distribution of Mesolithic activity

Distribution maps of the Colne Valley and Heathrow area (eg Lewis *et al.* 1992, 236; MoLAS 2000, map 2) display a series of Mesolithic findspots largely preserved below the alluvium of the River Colne. These sites, such as Three Ways Wharf, are often restricted to small areas (eg 100 sq m) and have little time depth, often encompassing only single episodes of inhabita-

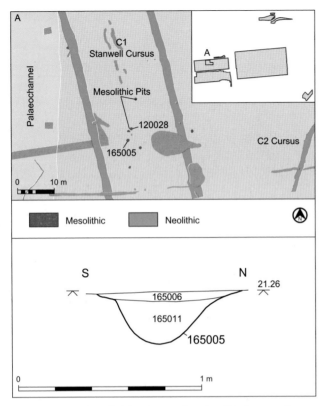

Figure 2.5: Mesolithic pits under the C1 Stanwell Cursus

tion. They provide us with a detailed record of short-lived inhabitation episodes and allow us to describe and distinguish types of activity in ecological and economic terms. However, they rarely afford us a history, in the sense that they do not provide us with the means to link these discrete places and temporalities into coherent narrative sequences.

In contrast, the Heathrow terrace, and indeed anywhere in Greater London outside the main valley, has an extremely sparse record of Mesolithic activity. But this does not mean that we cannot write the Mesolithic into a history of the landscape as a whole. The Mesolithic landscape as it has been defined at Heathrow (see above), consists of scatters of predominantly lithic material distributed over an extensive landscape. Archaeological analysis traditionally treats such material either at the scale of activity cluster or at the regional level (ie analysis of activity within a flint scatter of 100 square m, or as dots on the distribution map). The analysis in this volume will be at the local level of the Perry Oaks site and surrounding topography.

The problems of lithic chronology (the small number of datable lithics and the residual context of the majority in later features) have been discussed above. What can we say of this data that has historical meaning? Firstly, the lithic material attests to a human presence on the Heathrow plateau between 10,000 BC and 3000 BC. The assemblage is too small to allow particular activities to be defined and the blurred chronology leaves us with several different interpretations of the data. These may be summarised as follows:

- The lithic data may indicate repeated activity at (and therefore the continued importance of) certain locations in the landscape from the late Mesolithic through to the earlier Neolithic. We may be witnessing how the meanings and uses of these locations changed and were embellished architecturally from *c* 6500 BC to *c* 3300 BC.

- The data may represent chronologically short or closely grouped activity that is either entirely Mesolithic or entirely earlier Neolithic in date. If the former, then a case could still be made for continuity of place from the later Mesolithic into the 4th millennium BC. If the latter, then two further possibilities emerge. We could either be witnessing activity predating Neolithic monument construction dating to about 4000 BC to 3600 BC, or else activity associated with monument construction from 3600 to 3300 BC.

In actuality, the lithic data could have been generated by a combination of all these scenarios. The chronological problems of this data can be shown by looking at certain concentrations of flintwork in the landscape, as illustrated by the plan in Figure 2.4.

Two other concentrations of Mesolithic and/or Mesolithic/Neolithic flintwork were recovered adjacent to and within the C1 Stanwell Cursus and the small 'horseshoe' enclosure (HE1). The locations suggest most clearly the enduring importance of place from the middle of the 7th millennium BC to the construction of the Stanwell Cursus in the middle of the 4th millennium BC. This is discussed in more detail below.

Continuity of place: From late Mesolithic pits to the Stanwell Cursus

Prior to the construction of the C1 Stanwell Cursus, a small stream flowed north-south across the western part of the Perry Oaks excavations, now marked by the remains of a palaeochannel (see Figs 2.1 and 2.5). This area is known to have been wet in the later Neolithic, as spores of *Sphagnum* moss were detected in a core sample from pit 150011 that had been dug mid-way through the cursus ditch fill sequence. This is the only obvious source of surface water to have been detected in this part of the landscape, however, no finds were recovered from the fills of the palaeochannel, and no material suitable for radiocarbon dating was present. The watercourse flowed on the edge of the Colne floodplain, along which the Stanwell Cursus would later be constructed. At one point the alignment of the watercourse changed, following the topography westwards into the floodplain. This may have influenced the alignment of the C2 Cursus and established its general SW-NE trajectory. To the west of the C1 Cursus, the stream is well defined, having cut alluvial deposits of the Colne.

Adjacent to the stream, in the area that would later be sealed under the Stanwell Cursus bank, eight small pits were dug (Fig. 2.5; Plates 2.1–2). These were filled with burnt flint and stone and a few pieces of worked flint (Fig. 2.6), with extremely comminuted and mineralised charcoal. The pits were dated by thermoluminesence to the mid 7th millennium BC. The absence of burnt flint from the adjacent stream channel suggests

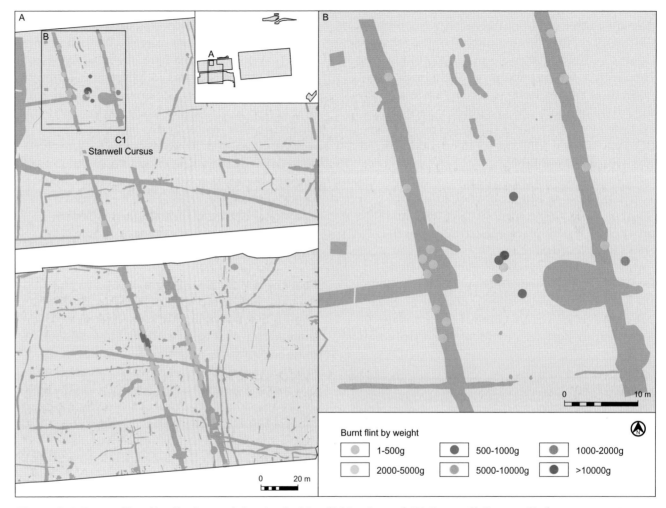

Figure 2.6: Burnt flint distribution and density in Mesolithic pits and C1 Stanwell Cursus ditches

that this had silted up by the middle of the 7th millennium BC.

The small assemblages of flint from the pits were undiagnostic and in an extremely poor condition. Almost without exception, the flakes appeared to be heavily rolled and glossed, often exhibiting a considerable degree of post-depositional edge-damage. Given the condition of the material and the lack of diagnostic traits, it is probable that they represent residual material incorporated into the fill of later features.

43

A small cluster of Mesolithic/earlier Neolithic flint work occurred in the ditches of the Stanwell Cursus in the area adjacent to the Mesolithic pits. However, it was impossible to distinguish if the majority of this material was contemporary with the 7th millennium pits or with the construction and use of the C1 Cursus in the 4th millennium BC. Only a burin from the western cursus ditch was typically Mesolithic.

It is impossible to establish whether the pit digging was a single event of the Mesolithic or whether it took place episodically, but the consistency in form of the pits suggests the former. The location was probably somehow marked, whether by distinctive vegetation in the form of a clearing, topographically by their proximity to the stream channel or by a man-made feature such as a midden. The distribution

Plate 2.1: View from C1 Cursus ditch looking towards the Mesolithic pits

of burnt flint in the Stanwell Cursus ditches adjacent to the pits (Fig. 2.6) suggests that whatever activity was undertaken here, the residues were originally more widespread, perhaps covering an area 30 m in diameter. The low density of burnt flint in the cursus ditches to the north and south of this location demonstrates that this activity was very localised. No comparable features have been detected anywhere else at Perry Oaks, and perhaps the break in slope between the Colne floodplain and the Taplow terrace formed a traditional routeway through the landscape, presenting a cleared or convenient route through flanking forest.

Both the specific distribution of the pits and the close focus on one place in the landscape, implies that a certain awareness had dictated some highly structured activity. Slight though these remains are, their significance lies in the fact that in the 7th millennium BC, a community had marked a significant place in the landscape by digging into the surface of the earth, piling up the residue and filling the void with culturally derived material. These activities had now become incorporated in the permanence of the place.

The practice of breaking the ground and processing the earth in a way that explicitly realised human intent, operating within a structure defined by the natural topography and a geography of cleared pathways and places, was to give rise to the inscription of a monumental landscape that pre-figures the Neolithic.

Plate 2.2: Mesolithic pits 120028, 160021 and possible Mesolithic pit 159025

We have seen how, during the 7th millennium BC, one location was marked by a distinctive pattern of activities. We have previously seen that other parts of the landscape contained lithic residues that also indicate activity sites during the Mesolithic/earlier Neolithic. When we consider the construction of the C1 Stanwell Cursus in the 4th millennium BC, we will show how it came to incorporate the location of the Mesolithic burnt flints, and how the residual meaning attached to that location was transformed into something new.

Monumentality and the architectural transformation of the landscape in the 4th and 3rd millennia BC

In previous sections we have described how human activity took place at various locations around the Heathrow landscape from the early Holocene to the early centuries of the 4th millennium BC. We have shown that the dating of the lithic assemblages means that our understanding of historical change is limited. With one or two exceptions, our crude datasets do not allow a fine resolution of human activity at particular places and times. However, we have been able to demonstrate that the first visible architectural modification of a specific location in the landscape occurred in the middle of the 7th millennium BC with a series of pits containing burnt flint. We have argued that as a result of the activities undertaken at this point, the location gained an importance which may have lasted for centuries if not longer. We have also suggested that this also occurred at certain other locations in the landscape which saw the deposition of Mesolithic and/ or Mesolithic / Neolithic flintwork.

In this section, we will look at how these places were marked, embellished and finally transformed in the 4th and 3rd millennia BC, through the use of architecture in the form of ditches, banks and standing-post structures. This architectural transformation, which we know as monumentality, is one of the key elements along with the adoption of ceramic and novel lithic technologies and the use of domesticated animal and plant species, of a period which we understand as the Neolithic.

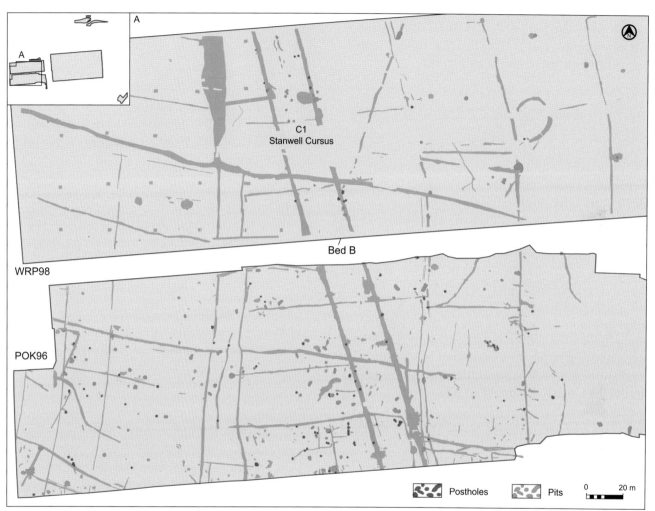

Figure 2.7: All pits and postholes around the C1 Stanwell Cursus

Firstly, we will examine a series of postholes and pits which predate the C1 Stanwell Cursus and show how particular locations of social importance became marked by architectural and physical means. Secondly, we will study the two

cursus monuments excavated at Perry Oaks, and compare their construction, development, and possible use. We will then move on to the small sub-circular monument, the horseshoe enclosure, and show how this served to demarcate locations which were used at particular times of the year for ceremonies, and how the cursus monuments served to link these locations together.

Activity predating the C1 Stanwell Cursus

We have already discussed the 7th millennium BC pit complex and shown how this location became overwritten by the C1 Stanwell Cursus 3000 years later. Figure 2.7 shows that the western area of the site, POK96 in particular, contained many small pits and postholes, the majority undated and some post-dating the middle of the 2nd millennium BC. A few features, however, contained burnt or struck flint, although problems of residuality make it impossible to say whether any of these features were associated with late Mesolithic or Neolithic pre-cursus activity. One exception is a handful of postholes which were stratigraphically related to the C1 Cursus ditches (Fig. 2.8).

A pit (178054) and five postholes (962132 962063, 962054, 962067 and 962081) can with some confidence be shown to predate the cursus, although none had any dating (Fig. 2.8). Pit 178054 lies at the extreme north of the site and may be associated with the adjacent mid 7th millennium BC burnt flint pit complex. The remainder of the features were clustered south of the junction of the C1 and C2 Cursus, and only one (962132) was located in the eastern C1 ditch. Only two of the section drawings demonstrate the stratigraphic relationship with the cursus (Fig. 2.8). These features vary in size, and some

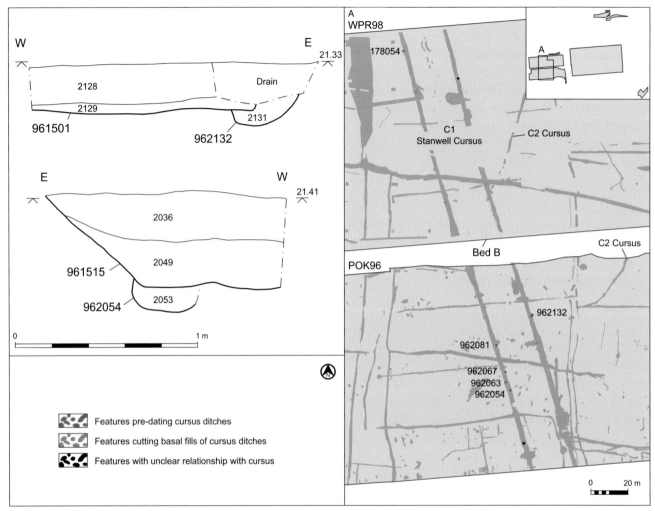

Figure 2.8: Postholes and pits with stratigraphic associations with the C1 Stanwell Cursus

could have supported substantial timbers when the effects of ground level truncation are considered. Posthole 962054, for example, was 0.5 m in diameter.

The function and date of these postholes is unknown. They may date to the later Mesolithic and be associated with the burnt flint pit complex to the north. They may thus have been similar to the early Mesolithic "totem pole" like structures at Stonehenge (Allen 1995, 471). Alternatively, they may have formed part of a pre-cursus Neolithic timber monument, possibly a post 'screen' or façade. They may even have been associated with the construction of the C1 Cursus. The important point is that they represent the construction of some sort of structure at a location along the interface between the Colne floodplain and the Heathrow Terrace. Together with the burnt flint complex, it demonstrates how these sites formed a string of locations along this axial border and how subsequently people felt compelled to physically link those sites together with the construction of the C1 Cursus, turning it into a monumental pathway.

C1 Stanwell Cursus

The history of investigation

The Stanwell Cursus was first recognised from cropmarks on aerial photographs (see Chapter 1, Fig. 1.1). Excavation of a length of the cursus to the south of Perry Oaks conclusively proved that the twin parallel ditches were stratigraphically earlier than a Bronze Age field system, and that the few finds contained within their fills dated to the Neolithic (O'Connell 1990). Although the monument was now recognised as being a Neolithic cursus, its exact architectural form was unclear. O'Connell (ibid., 33) favoured a central mound between the two ditches rather than the more common twin banks adjacent to the ditches (Plate 2.3).

Plate 2.3: Excavation of the C1 Stanwell Cursus looking north

Location and orientation

The location and orientation have been discussed in some detail elsewhere (O'Connell 1990) and will only be summarised here.

Cropmarks indicate that the monument ran for at least 3.6 km from the Colne Valley in the north-west to Stanwell in the south-east. The northern terminal was apparently rounded in plan before destruction through gravel extraction and lay close to the Bigley Ditch, an arm of the Colne Valley which originally formed part of the Middlesex county boundary. The southern terminal was destroyed beneath the housing of Stanwell, but it is likely that it lay close to the marked topographic break in slope caused by the boundary of the Taplow and Kempton Park Gravel terraces. The cursus runs along and almost defines the 22 m contour that separates the Colne Valley floodplain from the Heathrow Terrace.

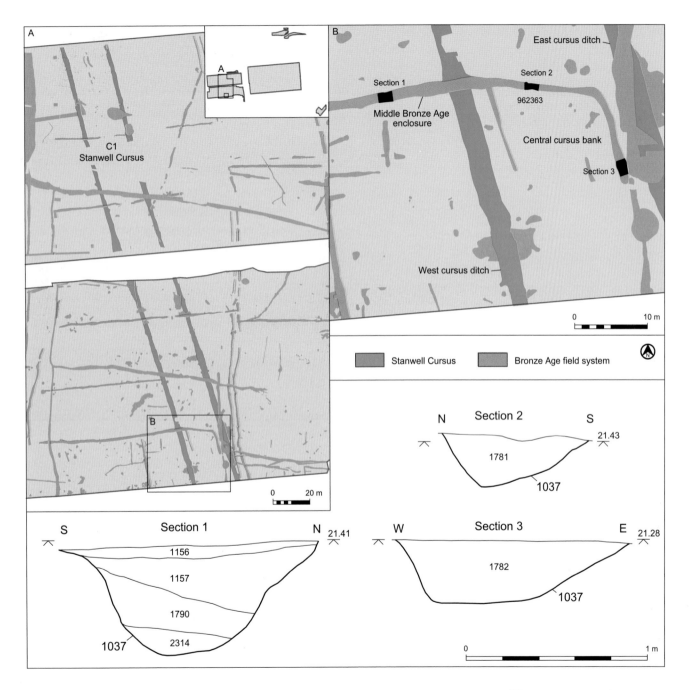

Form

Excavations at Perry Oaks in 1996 (POK96) and 1999 (WPR98) confirmed that the Stanwell Cursus consisted of two parallel ditches between 20.5 and 22 m apart, the spoil from which was used to construct a single central bank. The width and depth of the ditches will be explored in more detail below, but they averaged *c* 2.6 m wide and between 0.20 m and 0.5 m deep. The evidence for a central bank takes two forms.

Firstly, it is clear from Figure 2.9 that the middle Bronze Age field system ditches which cross the cursus become shallower and narrower as they cross the central part of the monument. In some places they actually stop just inside the cursus ditches. Perhaps the best example is middle Bronze Age ditch 962363, which has a distinctive hourglass plan as it crosses the central cursus area. Sections across these 2nd millennium BC ditches confirmed that they became much shallower between the two cursus ditches (Fig. 2.9), as they were dug across an already decayed central bank. The sections excavated across these ditches suggest that by the middle of the 2nd millennium BC the cursus bank was *c* 13 m wide and at least *c* 0.23 m high.

Figure 2.9: The Stanwell C1 Cursus in relation to the Bronze Age field system

The second piece of evidence for a central cursus bank comes from the Air Ministry survey of Heathrow undertaken in 1943. Whilst the surveyors did not notice a remnant bank at the time, the digitisation and processing of the survey data for this project revealed the presence of just such a feature coincident with the cursus cropmarks, running from Stanwell and terminating just to the south of Burrows Hill, immediately south of Perry Oaks. At the time of the 1943 survey, the broad remnant bank was *c* 0.20 m high and *c* 30 m wide, and it was this that led originally to the identification of the cursus as a Roman road.

Classification

Throughout this report, we have continued to refer to the Stanwell monument as a cursus, whilst others have started to refer to it as a bank-barrow. We continue to refer to it as a cursus for two main reasons. Firstly, the English Heritage Monument Protection Programme monument class description definition of bank-barrows states, *'Specifically excluded from the class of bank barrows are cursus that have a central bank'*. The term 'barrow' has funerary connotations which none of the excavations of the Stanwell Cursus have yet suggested. However, the Stanwell-type cursus with its long central bank is clearly architecturally different from most cursus monuments, which generally have two banks and external ditches. The central-bank cursus is widely distributed, with other examples being found as far apart as Scorton in Yorkshire (Harding 1999) and Cleaven Dyke in Perthshire (Barclay and Maxwell 1998).

The exact terminology and classification of these monuments is outside our scope, and to us, it does not matter. This is our second reason for continuing to call it a cursus: we are clear that the architecture of the C1 Stanwell and C2 Cursus at Perry Oaks was radically different. We are also clear that this difference reflected the variable responses to the structural principles that existed at different times in the late 4th millennium BC. Thus to us, whether these monuments are called cursus, bank-barrows or long mounds is irrelevant; they are simply labels.

When was the C1 Stanwell Cursus built?

Cursus monuments have traditionally proved very difficult to date accurately, due to the general paucity of artefactual material in their ditches. Recent work on dating cursus monuments has concluded that they were built between 3640–3380 cal BC and 3260–2920 cal BC

(Barclay and Bayliss 1999, 24). However, we have already made the point that the Stanwell Cursus belongs to a class of monuments with radically different architecture to traditional cursus, and therefore chronological parallels with these monuments must be viewed with caution. None of the samples of organic material from the C1 Stanwell Cursus submitted for radiocarbon determination produced a result (see above), and thus we are reliant on the relative chronology provided by pottery and flintwork from the ditch fills. Based on radiocarbon dates on comparable pottery from other sites, it would appear that the Stanwell Cursus was built sometime between 3600 and 3300 BC. However, before examining in detail the implications of this material, it is worth exploring an alternative hypothesis. That is, that the Stanwell monument could have been constructed in the 5th millennium BC, and the timber postholes which predate the cursus ditches (see above) may also be of this date or earlier.

Intervention	SG number	Stratigraphic order	East or west ditch	Fabric type	Ceramic tradition	No. of objects	Weight (g)
230326	230336	Top	E	FL4	Plain Bowl Ware	1	1
230329	230336	Top	E	FL4	Plain Bowl Ware	2	5
230328	230336	Top	E	FL4	Plain Bowl Ware	2	2
133016	134033	Top	E	GR1	early Bronze Age Grog tempered	2	2
133016	134033	Top	E	FL4	Plain Bowl Ware	1	2
230327	230335	Middle	E	FL4	Plain Bowl Ware	4	2
230329	230335	Middle	E	FL4	Plain Bowl Ware	4	8
133016	134032	Middle	E	FL4	Plain Bowl Ware	1	5
230333	230334	Basal	E	FL4	Plain Bowl Ware	2	7
229242	230334	Basal	E	FL4	Plain Bowl Ware	2	4
157188	128029	Basal	W	FL4	Plain Bowl Ware	2	25
Totals						**23**	**63**

Table 2.7: Neolithic ceramic assemblage from the C1 Stanwell Cursus

For instance, there is now good evidence for early Mesolithic 'totem pole' like structures at Stonehenge (Allen 1995, 471). Unfortunately, in the absence of radiocarbon dates from the lowest fills of the Stanwell Cursus, we are reliant on ceramic material for dating, which suggests a mid to late 4th millennium BC date.

Before turning to ceramics and relative chronology, it is worth remembering that the wide berm (ledge/path) prevented any bank material entering the ditches, the fill sequence of which suggests a natural process of silting with no deliberate back filling, at least within the segment excavated in WPR98 (the T5 segments to the south were somewhat different; see Vol. 2). The natural silting of cursus ditches in general has been contrasted with the deliberate backfilling of many other contemporary monuments (Harding 1999, 34), and they can therefore be taken to provide a reliable stratigraphic succession against which the ceramic assemblage can be viewed.

It is worth acknowledging, however, that the cursus ditches contain intrusive pottery from later periods (see above). Most of this later pottery was recovered from locations adjacent to the points where 2nd millennium BC or medieval features cut the cursus and so intrusion can be easily explained. Even the two small sherds of grog tempered early Bronze Age pottery were recovered from a section of the cursus cut by a small gully and could therefore be intrusive. The Neolithic ceramic assemblage, discounting these later contaminants and arranged by west or east ditch and stratigraphic order, is presented in

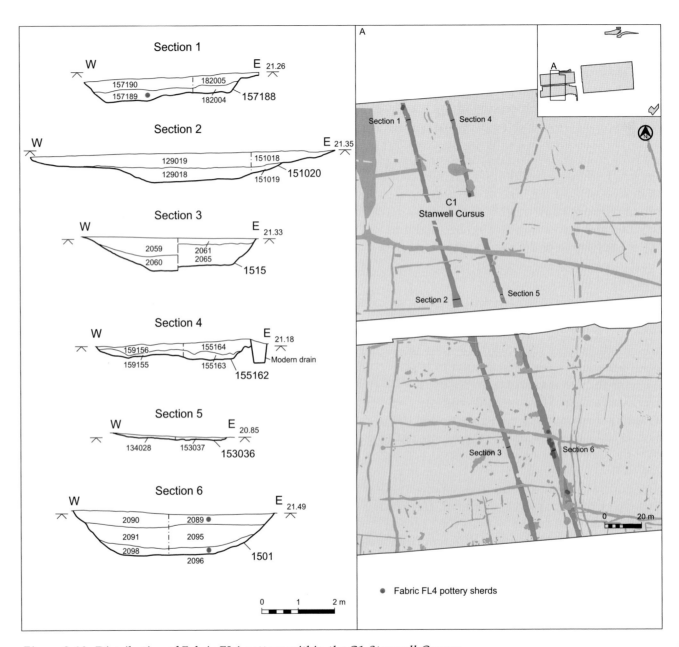

Figure 2.10: Distribution of Fabric FL4 pottery within the C1 Stanwell Cursus

50

Category	Sub-category	East ditch Basal	Middle	Top	East ditch total	West ditch Basal	Middle	Top	West ditch total	Other	Total
Flake/broken flake	Primary flake		3	1	**4**	4	4	2	**10**		**14**
	Secondary flake	1	6	10	**17**	2	11	13	**26**		**43**
	Tertiary flake	1	15	6	**22**	4	3	4	**11**		**33**
	Bladelike flake		2	1	**4**	1			**1**		**5**
	Unclassifiable waste			2	**2**		2		**2**		**4**
	Flake from a polished implement					1			**1**		**1**
Blade/broken blade	Blade						2		**2**		**2**
Thinning/sharpening flake	Axe/adze thinning flake		1		**1**						**1**
Spall	Spall	2	6	1	**9**	6		9	**15**		**24**
Core/core fragment	Single platform flake core						1		**1**		**1**
	Multi-platform flake core		1	1	**2**	2	1	1	**4**		**6**
	Single platform blade core					1			**1**		**1**
	Core on a flake					1			**1**		**1**
Nodule	Partially worked nodule	1			**1**	1			**1**		**2**
Retouched flake/blade	Retouched flake		2	1	**3**	2	2	1	**5**	1	**9**
	Retouched blade(let)						1	1	**2**		**2**
Scraper	End scraper			1	**1**						**1**
	Thumbnail scraper							1	**1**		**1**
	Unclassifiable scraper			1	**1**						**1**
Serrated/denticulate	Serrated piece		1		**1**						**1**
	Denticulate			1	**1**						**1**
Knife	Notched piece	1		1	**2**			1	**1**		**3**
	Backed knife		1		**1**						**1**
Total		**7**	**38**	**27**	**72**	**25**	**27**	**33**	**85**	**1**	**158**

Table 2.8: C1 Stanwell Cursus lithic assemblage

Table 2.7. It shows that the Plain Bowl Ware fabric FL4 occurs throughout the fills, with a slight concentration in one area of the eastern ditch (Fig. 2.10).

The later excavations at Heathrow Terminal 5 (T5) have produced larger sherds of plain undecorated Neolithic pottery of this date from the cursus, 874 m to the north of Perry Oaks. Conversely, the T5 excavations also produced Peterborough Ware pottery from the higher fills of the C1 Cursus, 860 m further south along the

course of the monument. Peterborough Ware sherds were also retrieved from the upper fills of the cursus during excavations by O'Connell immediately to the south of the T5 site (Cotton 1990, 28–9).

As outlined earlier, if we rely on ceramics to provide a relative chronology, this would mean that the cursus was constructed sometime between 3650 and 3350 BC. The presence of abraded Peterborough Ware in the upper fills would suggest that these were accumulating, or

perhaps parts of the cursus were re-worked, sometime between 3400 and 2500 BC. The lithic evidence broadly agrees with this, but is less precise than the ceramic evidence. Analysis of the flint from the C1 Cursus is summarised in Table 2.8 and as follows:

A total of 158 struck flints and 883 pieces (4352 g) of burnt unworked flint were recovered from various interventions along the length of the two ditches that compose the C1 Stanwell Cursus. The material is in fresh condition and is mostly uncorticated. The flintwork probably dates mainly to the later Neolithic or Bronze Age, although a small residual component was also isolated. This element probably dates to the Mesolithic or early Neolithic period, and includes a burin, an axe-thinning flake and a number of blades/bladelike flakes.

In terms of their vertical distribution, the majority of struck flints occurred in the upper ditch deposits. The basal fills contained just over 20% of the material, compared to 42% and 38% in the middle and upper fills respectively. The distribution is consistent with the assertion that the uppermost fills of the ditch were laid down in the later Neolithic and early Bronze Age. An analysis of the condition of the flintwork, however, showed no distributional patterning. Pieces in poor condition were scattered throughout the deposits and, as such, do not contribute to the discussion of the chronological development of the ditch fills.

(Cramp, CD Section 3)

With regards the sedimentary processes that led to the filling of the C1 Stanwell Cursus ditches, Bates (CD Section 14) makes the following observations:

- The magnetic susceptibility determinations from the western ditch fills….. perhaps indicates gradual, slow and continual accumulation of sediment.

- Infilling of the eastern ditch suggests that progressive infilling of the feature resulted from a winnowing out of the finer elements of the bedrock, and their subsequent deposition as ditch fills, and a decrease in gravel content

up-profile (Bates, Figures 4 and 6). Infilling of the central section of the eastern ditch (155165) suggests differing patterns of infilling dominated here.

The peaks of values for both magnetic susceptibility and organic content within the eastern ditch (Bates Figures 7 and 8) suggest variation in the nature of patterns of sedimentation and the possibility that a phase of stability exists within the middle part of the profile (thus implying a period of ditch fill stability and cessation of infilling – this may be reflected in the age distribution of finds from the uppermost fills being considerably later than the assumed age for the early fills).

The construction of the C1 Cursus between 3600 and 3300 BC took place at the same time as the construction of other ceremonial monuments in the Middle Thames Valley and nationally. In the West London area the C1 (and, as we will suggest, the C2) Cursus was contemporary with the Thameside causewayed enclosure complexes such as Yeoveney Lodge, Staines (Robertson-Mckay 1987), Eton Wick (Ford 1986) and Dorney (Needham and Trott 1987).

What drove people to build these monuments at this time? If we accept that the architecture of the cursus monument reflects its various uses, then a detailed study of its original form, how it was built and how many people might have built it may allow us to partially understand some of the historical processes that led to the monumentalisation of the landscape.

The function of the C1 Stanwell Cursus

In the recent publication arising from a session of The Neolithic Studies Group that specifically set out to explore the cursus phenomenon (Barclay and Harding 1999), a number of interpretations concerning cursus monuments were offered. Negotiating a line between the various theoretical positions, outlined in the introductory chapter of this volume, the position taken here concerning the cursus monuments at Heathrow can be summed up as follows:

- They were arenas for the production of explicit knowledge.

- They were constructed in the early Neolithic but their existence was acknowledged into the later Neolithic and their use in some form continued.

- They reinterpreted a Mesolithic geography, thereby reinterpreting subtleties of the local topography and hydrology.

- They represented an axial and connective focus within the wider monumental landscape.

- They had long histories of development.

- The construction of the monuments was probably at least as important as their continued use.

- They were associated with the rivers and may have metaphorically embodied or acknowledged them.

- In conjunction with the other monuments of the terrace, they may have been used as foci of mediation with the ancestors and a parallel metaphysical world.

- They may have embodied a cultural core that expressed group identity but was not overtly concerned with demarcating territory.

- They united communities, landscapes and histories.

- They were socially and politically significant locations, serving as arenas of social contestation within which social equilibrium could be negotiated and groups or individuals could acquire increased power and status.

- They were not obviously exclusive in the same sense as the monuments of Wessex. They had an open form, accessible as theatres for the performances of the living or conduits of the dead.

The linking of locations by the C1 Stanwell Cursus

In plan the Stanwell Cursus is remarkably straight, although some minor deviation has been noticed (O'Connell 1990, 9). We propose that the cursus was constructed along a pre-existing pathway of great antiquity to physically link and tie together numerous important places along the route such as the timber post alignment and the remnants of the 7th millennium midden and pits (see above). The Dorset Cursus

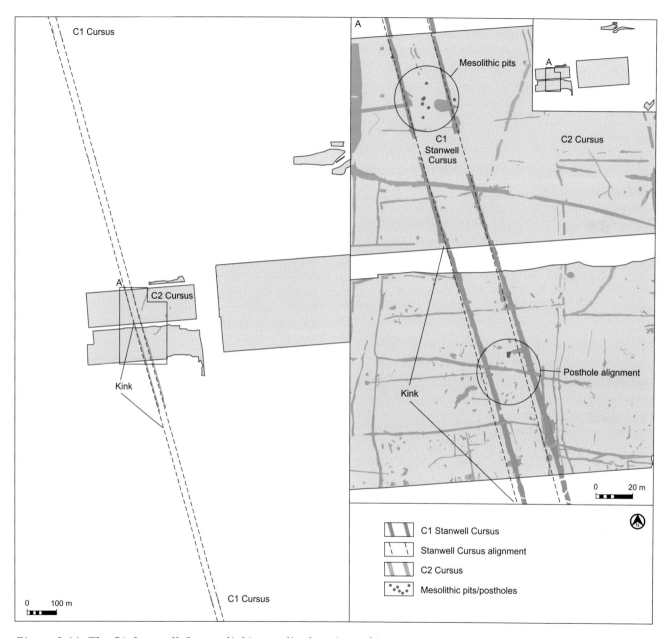

Figure 2.11: The C1 Stanwell Cursus linking earlier locations of importance

performed a similar function by linking together the separate long barrows along its course (Barrett *et al.* 1991, 58). Within the Perry Oaks excavations, the Stanwell Cursus makes an almost imperceptible deviation (the 'kink' in Fig 2.11) to accommodate these two locations, but almost as importantly, to accommodate the area between these two places. This location was subsequently further enhanced by becoming the terminus of the C2 Cursus. The ditches in the kinked section, *c* 150 m long, are also slightly shallower than those to the north and south, suggesting that this section may have been constructed separately, perhaps by a different construction team. We suggest, therefore, that the C1 Cursus was excavated in relatively short lengths by different teams, but within an overall rigid plan.

The uniformity of the cursus over at least 3.6 km suggests that it was laid out in a landscape that was at least locally cleared, and was very carefully aligned to incorporate special locations. It may even have been that the course of each ditch was marked on the ground with string or rope for the construction teams to follow. The Dorset Cursus contained clear examples of deviation from the main course once the sighting point the construction team was aiming at (eg a long barrow) temporarily disappeared from view (Barrett *et al.* 1991, 47). With the Stanwell Cursus, even necessary deviations, such as the kink described above, were accommodated almost imperceptibly. Achievement of such uniformity would suggest that the initial construction period, the length of time that the whole length of the cursus was set out and remained an active project, would have spanned

decades at most. The T5 excavations have revealed a complex history of back- filling and re-cutting over parts of the cursus, and these re-workings may have spanned centuries (see Vol. 2). However, they are re-workings within the template of the original layout, not extensions or additions.

What did the C1 Stanwell Cursus originally look like?

By the time the Stanwell Cursus was excavated at Perry Oaks in 1999, nothing survived of the remnant central bank. In order to understand the constructional history of the cursus and its architectural development, we must therefore rely on the stratigraphic sequences contained in the western and eastern flanking ditches to reconstruct the central bank.

The depth of the ditches was not consistent, but varied by 0.25–0.30 m. The western ditch, furthermore, tended to be deeper than the eastern ditch over much of the exposed length. The varying amounts of spoil generated from ditches of fairly uniform width but differing depth would have led to corresponding variations in the width and or height of the central bank. The long section in Fig. 2.12 shows longitudinal sections through both cursus ditches, from north to south. The vertical scale has been exaggerated by a factor of 10 to make the differences in depth of the ditches clearer.

Between 0.40 m and 0.66 m has been lost between the 1943 ground surface and the uppermost fills of the cursus ditches as excavated. So at any given length along the cursus, the ditches were

on average 0.40 m to 0.60 m deeper when dug in the 4th millennium BC than when excavated in 1999. When the depth is measured from the 1943 ground surface, the eastern ditch varied in depth between 0.65 m and 0.95 m, with the majority of the length varying between 0.70 m and 0.82 m. The western ditch varied between 1.3 m and 0.62 m deep, but was more variable in depth within this range than the eastern ditch. Excavations at Terminal 5 have subsequently shown that the cursus ditches become deeper to the north and south of the Perry Oaks excavations (see Vol. 2). Further south, O'Connell (1990) recorded several sections through the cursus ditches as up to *c* 1.80 m deep from the 1980s ground surface, which had not changed greatly since 1943.

In order to attempt to recreate the architecture of the cursus as originally constructed, the volume of spoil excavated from various lengths of each of the ditches was calculated. This was done by comparing cross sections along the monument, both from the WPR98 and O'Connell excavations (O'Connell 1990, figs 7, 16 & 17), and working out their cross-sectional area. It soon became apparent that the profiles of the ditches were generally very uniform, so uniform in fact that a chart could be plotted and an equation calculated to produce the cross sectional area of a cursus ditch for any given depth from the 1943 ground surface (Fig. 2.12).

The regularity in spacing of the Stanwell Cursus ditches and the straightness of their alignment over 3.6 km has been remarked upon many times. The ability to produce such a chart relating to

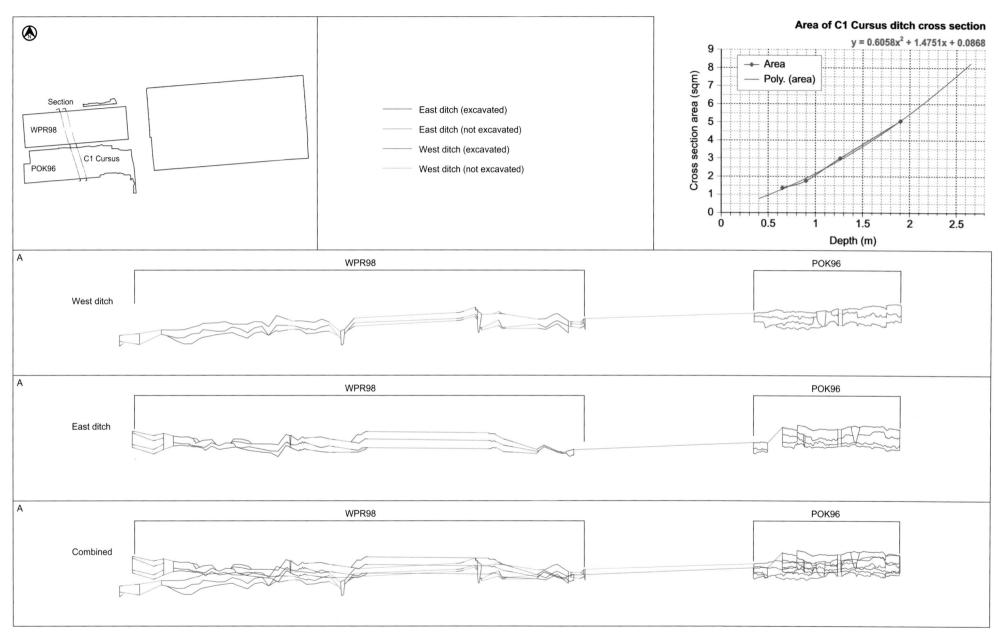

Figure 2.12: Longitudinal sections through both cursus ditches, from north to south, and area of C1 Stanwell Cursus ditch cross section

	Sections of cursus from N-S (m)	Average depth from 1943 surface (m)		Volume (cubic m)			Height of bank of various widths	
		West ditch	East ditch	West ditch	East ditch	Total volume after expansion factor of 1.1	Middle Bronze Age 13 m	Neolithic possibly 5 m
North	50	1	0.75	108.39	76.69	203.59	0.23	1.23
	20	1	0.88	43.35	37.08	88.48	0.28	1.37
Kink	27	0.75	0.8	41.41	44.67	94.70	0.14	1
	40	0.9	0.8	76.20	66.18	156.63	0.20	1.17
	36	0.85	0.75	64.02	55.22	131.16	0.16	1.06
	46	0.85	0.8	81.80	76.11	173.71	0.18	1.11
South	24	1	0.9	52.02	45.72	107.52	0.29	1.39
Totals (or average depth of ditch/height of bank)	**243**	**0.91**	**0.81**	**467.40**	**408.87**	**963.90**	**0.21**	**1.19**

Table 2.9: Volume of spoil excavated from Stanwell Cursus at Perry Oaks (WPR98)

depth and cross-sectional area suggests that the ditches were also dug to a well defined template.

Table 2.9 shows the volume of spoil excavated from various lengths of the Stanwell Cursus ditches at WPR98, arranged from north to south. The geology at Perry Oaks is fine grained 'brick-earth' and gravel, and the expansion factor for spoil volume would therefore be similar to that employed by Startin (Startin 1998) of about 1.1. Unfortunately, we do not know the actual dimensions or shape of the cross section of the bank when it was constructed. A turf revetment, for example, could have radically altered the shape and height of the bank. However, in this attempt to reconstruct the central bank, we have adopted the following assumptions:

- Without turf or any other revetment the angle of the slope of the bank would have been unlikely to exceed *c* 40 degrees.

- If our assumption that that one of the functions of the bank was to provide an elevated ceremonial processional route, then we can assume that the top of the bank was flattened, and for ease of use would have been up to 2 m wide.

- The base of the bank would have been comparatively narrow, leaving a large berm (ledge/path) between bank and ditch. This is clear from the distinct lack of evidence from the C1 Cursus ditch sections for an adjacent bank.

If we apply these assumptions to the first 50 m length of the cursus, they produce a bank 5 m wide at the base, *c* 1.2 m high and 2 m wide at the top. Table 2.9 shows that these dimensions, particularly height, would have varied along the length of the cursus depending on the depth of the flanking ditches. For instance, the bank along the 'kink' section of the cursus could have been *c* 0.20 m lower than the lengths immediately adjacent to the north and south. This may seem, and indeed may have been insignificant, but in a relatively flat landscape, small variations in vertical height would stand out.

Plate 2.4: Reconstructed cursus looking south

At the end of the Perry Oaks excavations, a short length of the C1 Cursus was reconstructed using a mechanical excavator (Plates 2.4–6). The resultant bank was not quite as wide at the base and top as our calculations, but it does give some indication of the original form of the monument at this location.

How much effort was required to build the C1 Stanwell Cursus?

We have made a case above for the cursus to have been constructed as relatively short, connected lengths, possibly each having been excavated by a different team. If we take the length of the cursus we have described as the 'kink', then we can estimate how this was constructed and by how many people and how long it took.

The method used by Startin (1982; 1998) for the Abingdon causewayed enclosure and Cleaven Dyke cursus has been followed. Startin assumed a rate of excavation of 0.35 cubic m per person per hour. From personal experience of excavating the compacted gravel and brickearth deposits of the Perry Oaks area, a more likely rate would be c 0.25 cubic m per person per hour. We can assume that for each ditch, the team consisted of

Plate 2.5: Reconstructed cursus central bank looking east

one digger with antler picks and one shoveller using scapulae and baskets, who would also carry the spoil to the central bank. If all the trees and vegetation were cleared from the course of the cursus and the course had already been set out, then two teams of two people working 10 hour days, six days a week, could complete the 150 m long 'kinked' section of the cursus in 16 to 18 weeks.

If we suppose that the C1 Cursus was built in similar 150 m long segments, then the whole 3.6 km could be built by 24 teams of two people per ditch (a total workforce of 96 using c 97,000 man hours) in 16–18 weeks. Of course, we have already noted how the ditches were deeper in some sections of the cursus and the bank would have been higher, but this calculation gives some idea of the effort required. It is apparent that the cursus could have been constructed by relatively few people, within a relatively short time scale. It is probable that the labour was spread over more than one year to accommodate other domestic activities, but as we have suggested, the regularity of the scheme would suggest that it would have taken a few years at most.

What was the architectural impact of the C1 Stanwell Cursus?

The resulting monument would have been a long, low mound or 'causeway', bisecting and radically altering the landscape. Its impact cannot be understated. Until this moment, the only human architectural modifications or construction within the landscape consisted of pits and postholes.

Plate 2.6: Standing on reconstructed cursus bank looking east

The major landscape impact up to this point would have been forest clearance, but its extent and the involvement of human agency are still unclear. The C1 Cursus was therefore without precedent, and it reflects the desires and motivation of the people who built it.

In order to explore those motivations further, we will consider firstly the way the cursus was used and experienced by people who would have processed along its course, and secondly how the cursus affected people outside the monument, both in terms of what they could see of ceremonies and the general impact of the monument on the landscape.

It is impossible, due to profound changes to the landscape, to attempt to construct the sort of perceptual narrative for the Stanwell Cursus that Tilley (1994, 173–200) produced for the Dorset

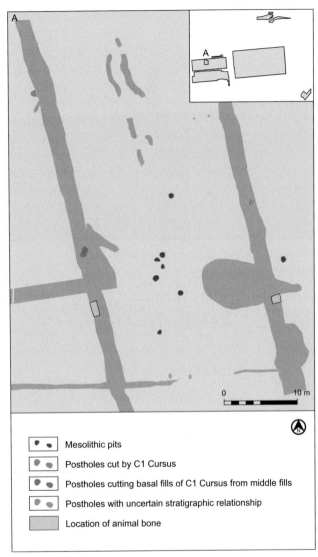

Figure 2.13: Relationship between animal bone, Mesolithic pits and postholes in C1 Stanwell Cursus

Legend:
- Mesolithic pits
- Postholes cut by C1 Cursus
- Postholes cutting basal fills of C1 Cursus from middle fills
- Postholes with uncertain stratigraphic relationship
- Location of animal bone

0   10 m

Cursus. Nonetheless, prior to the construction of the C1 Cursus, people moving from place to place along the floodplain margins did so along a path that was only formalised and maintained by human memory and agreement. Each place visited may have been consecrated with a ceremony that may or may not have included the deposition of artefacts, but the important element of the ceremony would have been the ritual, the display and the words exchanged between the participants and onlookers.

What was the importance of these locations and why were they revisited? We of course cannot answer this, but it is our view that one of the important subtexts of the ceremonies and processions was the concern with access to the resources of the landscape. Throughout the Mesolithic this concern may have been settled in many different ways, and had to take into account mobile and seasonal resources of animals as they moved through the landscape. Indeed it is possible that the burnt flint pit cluster and possible midden described above may have acted as a meeting place and context for settling these concerns in the 7th millennium BC. It is now generally agreed that the adoption of agriculture and domestic animals from 4000 BC in this county did not at first cause a radical shift in the late Mesolithic subsistence economy. As we have shown previously, with the exception of 'type fossils' such as microliths and leaf-shaped arrowheads, it is hard to distinguish chronologically the lithic assemblage for this period, and this must reflect a minor change in the subsistence economy.

However, as the first 500 years or so of the Neolithic unfolded, the cumulative impact of agriculture and pastoralism, coupled with new technologies and new expressions of old practices in the form of the first monuments, meant the world was being transformed. Individual kin-groups now had to resolve questions and conflicts regarding access to land and resources. How was it decided where a group would plant this year's crops? Who grazed their animals on a certain stretch of the floodplain? Who placed this year's settlement in the old woodland clearing, or burnt some fallen trees to create a new field? We suggest that the ceremonies undertaken at certain locations in the landscape helped to facilitate these decisions. Perhaps each location was of importance to separate kin-groups. As the generations passed, the ceremonies changed and developed. Some locations were forgotten, others increased in importance, new ones emerged and others were embellished architecturally, for example, the timber post alignment. If so, then the string of locations which grew up along the boundary of the Colne floodplain and the Heathrow Terrace to the east show that this zone was of crucial importance, since it marked the boundary between the water resources of the floodplain and the dryer, higher terrace to the west. It is perhaps not surprising then that the places and ceremonies began to be linked together by ceremonial processions.

We do not know how many people took part in these processions and ceremonies or how they were arranged or led. Without formal demarcation, the processions and ceremonies could have been viewed by all. The important point is that the kin-groups or communities associated with individual locations were now linked together by processional pathway and ceremony. Through this process the separate groups started to form into a larger, more cohesive community. Whereas before disputes and negotiations over land and resources occurred *between* separate kin-groups and were resolved through ceremony at distinct locations, now negotiations were contained *within* a wider community, whose important ceremonies and locations were linked by procession.

The creation of a *community* at this time is pivotal. It could be said that, without a community, the opportunities for forest clearance and agricultural expansion represented by the 'elm decline' could not have been exploited, and causewayed enclosures and cursus could not have been built. We view the construction of the C1 Cursus in particular as a physical manifestation, formalisation and celebration of the emergence of a community. We have shown how the cursus was built in sections, each by a small team of people, and we can see how each section was built by a team drawn from the individual kin-groups, and each group probably built a length of cursus associated with their own ceremonial location. The result was a monument that physically tied together all the groups through shared labour in a common enterprise to build a communal monument, which bound together the histories of the individual groups as invested in special locations.

Although the architecture of the mound served to restrict the numbers of people who could process

along its length, most of the community would probably have been engaged more in observing the ceremonies than in taking part. The architecture of the Stanwell Cursus now served to emphasise the processional ceremonies along the top of the bank in a way that was impossible with an informal pathway at ground level. Although the leaders of the processions might have been differentiated from the rest of the community, the community remained an essentially open one. The participants were now on very obvious display against the horizon and visible for all to see (see Plate 2.6 and Fig. 2.25 below). Thus the architecture of the C1 Cursus did not mask the activities that went on inside to the exclusion of those outside, unlike those with a pair of flanking ditches such as the Dorset Cursus. The C1 Cursus was the product and celebration of an essentially open community.

The cursus acted as a unifying device for the community, and there is some evidence that the special places now cut or buried by the monument retained their importance, and may even have been involved in the ceremonies associated with the processions. Two examples serve to demonstrate this. The first is the occurrence of fragments of cow skull in the middle fills of both cursus ditches adjacent to the Mesolithic burnt flint pit complex (Fig. 2.13). Burnt flint clusters also occur in these locations. We consider the flint to be of Mesolithic date, and this may also be true of the skull fragments. However it is conceivable that they represent the residues of ceremonies enacted at the location following the construction of the cursus. In the absence of

radiocarbon dates this is impossible to determine. If the animal bone is contemporary with the middle fills of the cursus, then this would explain the presence of a posthole cutting the basal fills of the western ditch from this level, and another posthole in the eastern ditch, which had unclear stratigraphic relationships. Put simply, the posts may have been driven into the basal fills of the ditch to serve as markers signifying the location of the pit complex and midden once the cursus had buried these sites. The burnt flint and animal bone may then be seen as the remnants of ceremonies undertaken once the procession had stopped at this location.

This association of burnt flint and postholes sealed by the middle fills of the cursus is repeated further south at the location of the earlier timber post alignment (Fig. 2.14). Again, one or possibly more postholes were driven through the basal fills of the cursus from the middle fills. These fills also contained relatively large amounts of struck and burnt flint. A glance at Figure 2.10 shows that the distribution of FL4 fabric pottery sherds in the C1 Cursus shows a similar association. This material may be the residues of ceremonies carried out as the processional group halted at the now ancient ancestral location. The graph in Figure 2.14 shows the vertical distribution of these artefact types through the fills of the cursus, and shows that the C1 Cursus remained a focus of activity throughout the remaining depositional sequence.

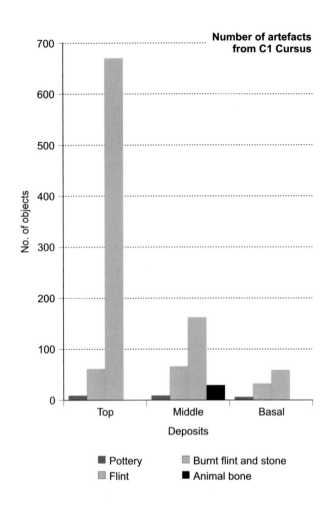

Number of artefacts
from C1 Cursus

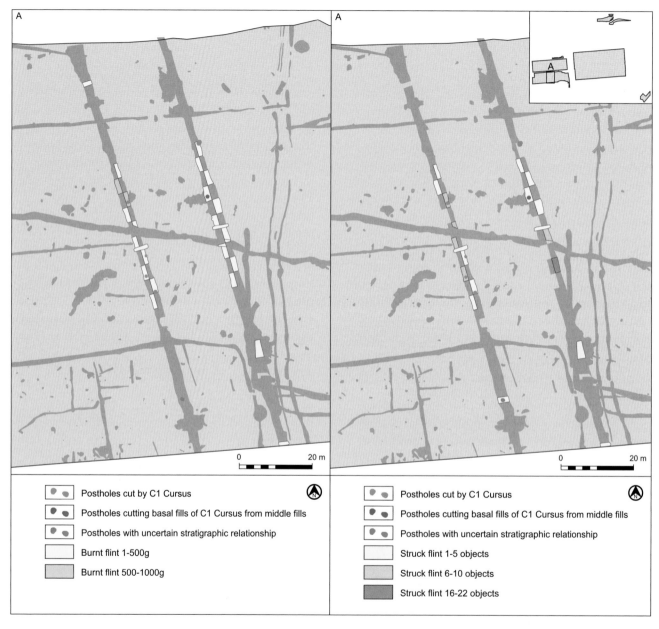

Figure 2.14: Relationship of postholes, burnt/struck flint and other artefacts with the C1 Stanwell Cursus

What did the landscape look like at this time?

The following is derived from Pat Wiltshire's analysis of the pollen sequences and the full report can be found on the accompanying CD-Rom (Section 11).

Unlike their descendants in the middle Bronze Age, Neolithic people did not dig deep pits and waterholes across the Heathrow Terrace. This means that, for the period prior to about 1600 BC, there is a dearth of suitable waterlogged deposits yielding well-resolved environmental evidence. Thus, our conception of the impact of these people on the local landscape is fragmentary and blurred.

The lack of convincing environmental evidence from Perry Oaks during this period means that we need to rely again upon information gleaned from other sites in the region. Data from Meadlake Place, Egham, Surrey (Branch and Green 2004, 12) suggest that between 8000 and 5860 uncal BP (approximately 6800 to 4800 cal BC), dry ground supported mixed, deciduous woodland while *Alnus* (alder) and *Salix* (willow) dominated the riverine environment.

The nature of the early to middle Neolithic landscape in Surrey and the middle/lower Thames has recently been reviewed by Branch and Green (2004). The Lower Thames Valley around Southwark is seen as consisting of, 'an ever changing mosaic of closed and open woodland, temporarily cultivated land, grazing land, and meadows interrupted by tributary rivers

and streams, small ponds, and lakes' (Branch and Green 2004, 13). It might be reasonable to imagine the Lower Colne Valley and the Heathrow Terrace in a similar way.

Unlike in Southwark, the sequence at Runnymede produced no evidence for the elm decline (Scaife 2000). However, evidence for this event has been outlined by Sidell and Rackham (2000) for the London area, and for Surrey by Branch and Green (2004) who date the horizon to about 5000 uncal BP (3700 cal BC). The elm decline coincides with the period of use of Plain Bowl Ware early Neolithic pottery. In later sections of this volume, we will discuss further the chronology of this ceramic, and demonstrate that the major monuments of the Heathrow area were constructed during the currency of this pottery type. The link between monument construction and the elm decline has been discussed previously, but it is pertinent in this context since the major monuments of the early Neolithic, such as the Stanwell C1 Cursus and the C2 Cursus, would have required a terrain that had been at least partially cleared of woodland. Certainly, the landscape picture presented by Scaife (2000, 184–5) for the Neolithic at Runnymede appears to have been similar to that described by Branch and Green (2004).

Pollen evidence

The pollen evidence from pit 150011, which cuts the basal fills of the cursus adjacent to the burnt flint pits, suggests that the cursus was located either at the edge of woodland or in a woodland glade (Fig. 2.15). The pollen suggests that the pit

was cut some time after the elm decline of 3700 BC, but a radiocarbon date of 4349–4047 BC (NZA14902 cal BC 2 sigma) from sediment from the upper silts of this feature appears to be far too early, and was probably obtained from residual organic matter redeposited in the pit.

The results of the pollen analysis are shown in Figure 2.15 (full report by Wiltshire on CD-Rom Section 11). The three pollen zones were designated 150011/1–3 respectively. Changes in the pollen spectra in this sequence are rather subtle and indicate that only moderate changes were happening in the landscape around the feature. It must be stressed, however, that pits can become infilled very quickly and the sediments might represent a single generation of trees. Many forest trees are potentially long-lived; a healthy specimen of *Quercus* (oak) can live for at least 600 years (Mitchell 1974), and managed trees (pollarded and coppiced) can live even longer (Rackham 1986).

Zone 150011/1: The deposits represent a period some time after the elm decline of approximately 5000 years ago. The soils around the waterhole were wet enough to support occasional Cyperaceae (sedges) and some *Sphagnum* moss but there is no evidence of the feature having had an aquatic and emergent community in or around it. People were certainly active in the environs of the site since microscopic charcoal levels were relatively high throughout the zone. Furthermore, occasional cereal-type pollen grains were found. Considering the nature of the palynological assemblage, these grains are unlikely to be those of *Glyceria* species. These aquatic grasses produce pollen grains within the size range of some cereals and their presence at riverine sites can cause confusion. It is more likely that the cereal-type grains recorded here are of cereals. There is little doubt that there were many trees near the waterhole when these deposits were accumulating, and arboreal pollen accounts for up to 80% of total land pollen and spores (TLPS) throughout the zone. This area appears to be more heavily wooded than at Runnymede. Whether this is due to natural spatial heterogeneity in tree distribution or whether it actually reflects the density of the woodland canopy is difficult to assess.

But *Hedera* (ivy) was abundant, especially towards the end of the zone where total arboreal pollen falls and that of Poaceae (grasses) actually rises. This suggests that the canopy was becoming open enough to support flowering ivy and, indeed, the high tree/shrub pollen values might be the result of some degree of tree clearance creating the edge effect outlined above. The woodland community included ferns such as *Polypodium* (polypody fern), monolete *Pteropsida* (possible *Dryopteris* spp. - buckler ferns), and Pteridium (bracken) but all these respond favourably to openings in the woodland canopy.

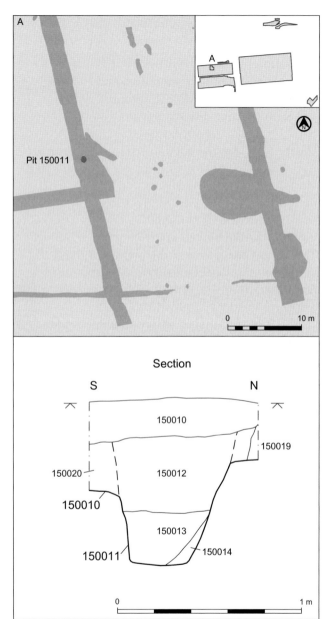

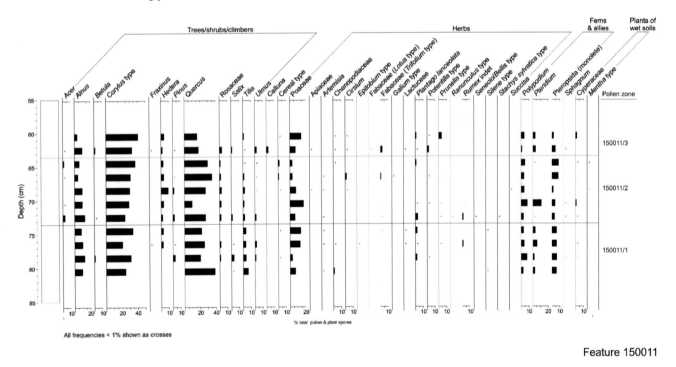

Feature 150011

Figure 2.15: Pollen monolith sample from pit 150011

The suggestion that the feature was close to a woodland edge or in a glade is supported by the presence of Poaceae (grasses), Rosaceae (hawthorn, bramble, rose), *Salix* (willow) and a range of weeds and ruderals such as *Artemisia* (mugwort), Chenopodiaceae (goosefoot), *Rumex* (docks), Lactuceae (dandelion-like plants), and *Plantago lanceolata* (ribwort plantain). There were also herbs such as *Lotus* type (bird's foot trefoil), *Prunella* type (eg self heal), *Silene* type (eg red campion), and *Epilobium* type (eg greater willowherb). All these could have been growing in grassy areas and places where the soil was disturbed.

Oak and hazel dominated the local woodland although *Alnus* (alder) was well represented and probably growing on the wetter soils near the river. *Betula* (birch), *Pinus* (pine), and *Fraxinus* (ash) were growing in the catchment area but were either some distance away or present in small numbers. *Tilia* (lime) and *Ulmus* (elm) were both growing in the vicinity but their relatively low abundance suggests that they might have been already been subjected to management. Both plants produce highly nutritious foliage and they could have been exploited for cattle fodder. Lime is also the source of many other useful commodities (Bates and Wiltshire 2000) and was probably targeted by early settlers.

Zone 150011/2: This zone is characterised by small but discernible changes in the local vegetation. The relatively high levels of microscopic charcoal attest to a continued human presence. Both *Tilia* and *Alnus* declined slightly and there

was a drop in *Quercus* in the middle of the zone. This may have been the result of pollarding trees close to the feature. The fall in *Quercus* was reciprocated by a rise in Poaceae and ferns, and *Acer* (maple) was recorded. Rosaceae were also consistently represented at fairly high level and *Hedera* increased at the end of the zone. There was very little change in the herbaceous plants other than the rise in grasses as described above. It would seem that the local oaks were being exploited and that this allowed more light to reach shrubs and herbs. Cereal-type pollen was found which shows continued (though very small-scale) arable activity nearby.

Zone 150011/3: The amount of microscopic charcoal accumulating into the feature declined in this zone and the centre of activity might have moved away slightly. *Corylus* (hazel) continued to be a dominant member of the woodland, while *Alnus* and *Tilia* both declined. *Quercus* also declined towards the top of the zone but the more light-demanding shrubs (*Salix, Acer, Hedera* and Rosaceae) were all well represented. Some light-demanding herbs flowered more prolifically than before, and ferns certainly increased. This suggests that there was more light available to the area so that marginal shrubs and herbs were able to flower more profusely. It is tempting to suggest that animal grazing played some role in these changes at the site and the drop in Poaceae might be a function of grazing of flowering heads. Certainly, arable agriculture seems to have increased, and the canopy was open enough to allow *Calluna* (heather) to grow in the area.

Summary

Pit 150011 shows that the Neolithic landscape supported mixed, deciduous woodland, dominated by oak and hazel in the vicinity of the site. However, some impact was being made on the wildwood. Because of the relatively short life of the feature, the picture presented here may represent a brief period, certainly within a single generation of oak, lime, and alder trees. There appear to have been relatively small areas of grasses and herbs, and the environs of the pit had moist soils. There seems to have been some arable agriculture being carried out locally and it is possible that cereals were being grown in the woodland glades, the so-called practice of 'forest farming' (Coles 1976; Göransson 1986; Edwards 1993). Unfortunately, we cannot be sure whether pit 150011 and therefore the C1 Stanwell Cursus were located within a local clearing, or at the edge of the transition from a wooded environment (perhaps on the floodplain) to a more open landscape on the terrace.

The taphonomy associated with pollen fallout in woodlands is highly complex, and high arboreal values need not reflect very densely wooded conditions. There can be higher tree/shrub values for pollen in open-canopied woodland, or at the woodland edge, than in the dense interior (see Tauber 1965). Certainly in some mixed woodlands, the canopy component does *not* seem to fall through to the woodland floor when trees are growing densely, but it *does* reach the ground beneath the parent trees where they are more spaced, or the branching is relatively open (personal observation). Modern pollen studies have

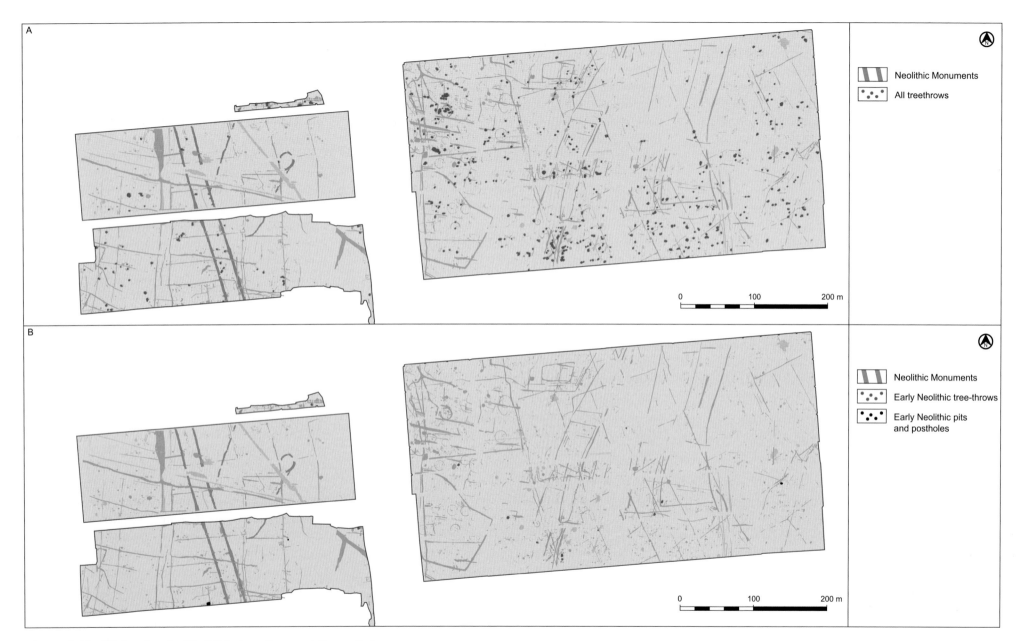

Figure 2.16: All dated early Neolithic tree-throws at Perry Oaks

revealed many inconsistencies in palynological profiles obtained from a variety of woodland types and, indeed, open ground. As much as 50% arboreal pollen can be recorded on very open sites (such as the middle of a golf courses) while over 80% can be obtained from woodlands where the canopy is relatively open. Herbaceous pollen is often recorded in some closed woodlands, and these can even include significant levels of pollen from cereals and hay meadow. Invariably in this instance the pollen has been derived from the dung of grazing animals (horses in the modern context). In ancient woodland, dung from browsing and grazing animals (including stock animals) could create the same effect. Furthermore, it must be noted that considerable amounts of herbaceous pollen can find their way into deposits well within the heart of woodland if there is adjacent open ground (Wiltshire 2003).

There is little doubt then, that interpretation of data relating to woodland cover in the Neolithic period is fraught with difficulty. The patchiness of the landscape and the essentially low sampling frequency mean that complexities of taphonomy cannot be easily resolved. But, in spite of the difficulties listed here, wherever arboreal pollen levels are very low indeed, the catchment must be very open (see Chapter 3 for discussion on the middle Bronze Age landscape). To get low arboreal pollen values, the woodland edge would have had to have been some (unknown) distance away from a feature, or the local trees would have had to have been very heavily exploited so that flowering was suppressed. In spite of the high arboreal pollen values, the Neolithic

landscape around pit 150011 might have been more open than the pollen diagram might suggest.

The problems associated with identifying the extent of woodland clearance from palynological data alone ensure that the local environment at Perry Oaks during construction and the life of the cursus remains unclear. The monument itself is testimony to the creation of open ground, and yet pit 150011, which cut the cursus ditch, seems to indicate densely wooded conditions. However, as outlined above, this may be because higher pollen levels are often associated with freer dispersal facilitated by an open canopy.

Settlements and clearance?

We have one other strand of evidence for clearance and activity on the Heathrow Terrace in the 4th millennium BC, in the form of tree-throws, the bowls left by falling trees as their roots are torn out of the ground. A handful of pits and postholes are also tentatively ascribed to this period. The dating evidence from all these features consists mostly of small fragments of Plain Bowl Ware pottery and/ or lithic material datable broadly to the 4th millennium BC. Some of the lithic and ceramic material is contradictory and far from clear. What is clear is that the 11 dated tree-throws in Figure 2.16 seem to be distributed through the centre of the site and perhaps all that can be made of such a small sample is that they show that clearance (either humanly or naturally induced) was occurring during the 4th millennium BC.

Tree-throw 156191 produced the largest pottery and lithic assemblages, and Figure 2.17 shows that it lay in an area with a relatively large number of other Mesolithic and early Neolithic residual finds. The assemblages from this feature are revealing and will be discussed more fully:

Tree throw 156191 produced 541 sherds of Plain Bowl Ware fabric of total weight 1444g. In general the condition of this material is poor; sherds are small and moderately to heavily abraded. However the fabrics (in particularly the flint-tempered fabrics) tend to be extremely friable, and a high degree of fragmentation does not necessarily reflect a commensurate level of post-deposition movement. Tree-throw 156191 seems to have been deposited as a single event. 156191 is the only tree-throw, pit or other feature where an in situ deposit can be postulated, perhaps resulting from deliberate middening. Other sherd occurrences are sporadic and are more likely to be residual.

(Every and Mepham, CD Section 1)

The lithic assemblage from tree-throw 156191 consisted of 230 flints (Table 2.10), all recovered from the upper fill, sub-group 223003. Within this, the flint was recovered almost exclusively from context 148109, although one piece, a broken tertiary flake, was retrieved from context 156190. A further 137 pieces of burnt unworked flint were also recovered from the tree-throw, weighing a total of 514g. Again, the majority of the burnt flint derived solely from context 148109. Further details of this deposit, as derived from the archive flint report (in CD-Rom Section 3), are as follows:

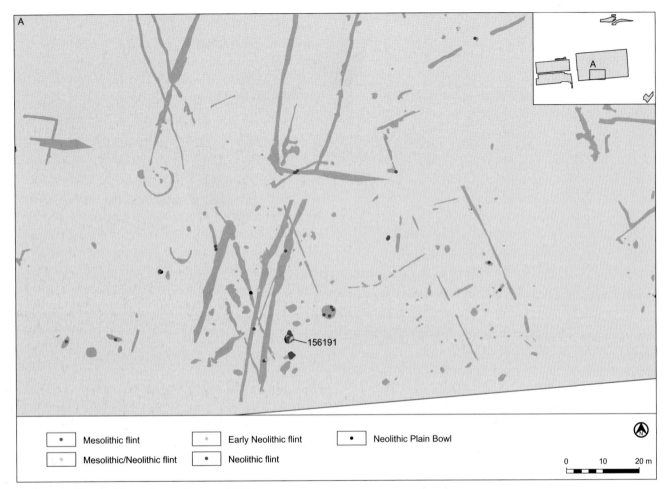

The assemblage is dominated by flakes (101 pieces) and chips (86 pieces), which together provide around 80% of the struck assemblage. One of the flakes has been struck from a polished implement, probably an axe, and can be dated to the Neolithic period. Blades, bladelets and bladelike flakes are represented by a combined total of 25 pieces that provide around 20% of the debitage component. While less common than flakes, blades are nonetheless sufficiently numerous to suggest a date in the earlier Neolithic (e.g. Ford 1987). The majority of flakes have been struck using a soft percussor, such as an antler hammer, and many display abraded platform edges and dorsal blade scars.

A total of 86 chips were recovered from the deposit, almost certainly reflecting in situ knapping activity. Along with several of the flakes, these chips seem to be the product of a single core and probably result from a discrete knapping event. Only one core (42 g), manufactured on a flake, was recovered from the feature; this suggests that the larger elements of knapping waste were removed and deposited elsewhere. Some of the flake material may refit, although brief attempts were unsuccessful.

The assemblage contains twelve retouched tools (8.3%, excluding chips), ranging from retouched flakes and scrapers to piercing tools and serrated flakes. Numerous unretouched flints also display utilised edges. These retouched and utilised pieces are combined with the knapping waste described above, suggesting that the assemblage results from a series of activities performed on several occasions.

(Cramp, CD Section 3)

Figure 2.17: Location of tree-throw 156191

The flintwork is in fresh, uncorticated condition and can be dated to the early Neolithic on technological and typological grounds. While the majority of the struck flints represent the use of locally available river gravel, bullhead flint and chalk flint are also present in small quantities. One of the serrated flakes, for example, has been manufactured on a bladelike blank of bullhead flint. Local nodules, on the other hand, seem to have been preferred for burning.

At this location at least, we can picture a domestic settlement dating sometime between 3600 and 3300 BC and located within a clearing. The settlement would therefore be roughly contemporary with the construction of the C1 and C2 Cursus monuments. The size of both clearing and settlement is unknown, but both could have been extensive.

Summary of C1 Stanwell Cursus

We have suggested how the construction of the C1 Stanwell Cursus, sometime between 3600 and 3300 BC, was an act of celebration by physically manifesting the emergence of a cohesive, essentially open community composed of individual kin-groups. These groups had histories and associations with places dotted along the edge of the Colne floodplain, which in some cases stretched back several millennia. At these locations the individual groups would have met other groups for the necessary social interactions: births, passage, marriages, funerals and negotiation of access to landscape resources. We have suggested that with the introduction and increasing importance of agriculture throughout the early 4th millennium BC, these individual groups had to become more closely associated and this led to the linking of their important locations and histories by ceremonial procession. With this, the community was born, and it was to lead to the construction of the C1 Cursus.

We have also shown that the previously important locations remained significant foci for ceremonies as groups processed on top of

Category	Sub-category	Total
Flake/broken flake	Primary flake	10
	Secondary flake	54
	Tertiary flake	37
	Flake from a polished implement	1
	Unclassified	1
Blade/broken blade	Blade	11
	Bladelet	6
	Bladelike flake	8
Core preparation flake	Core face/edge rejuvenation flake	1
	Rejuvenation flake tablet	1
Axe/adze sharpening flake	Axe/adze thinning flake	1
Chip/sieved chip	Chip	86
Core/core fragment	Core on a flake	1
Retouched blade/flake	Retouched flake	3
	Retouched blade(let)	1
Scraper	End scraper	2
	Side scraper	1
	Unclassified scraper	1
Serrated/denticulate	Serrated piece	2
Piercer	Awl/piercer	1
	Spurred piece	1
Total		**230**
No. of burnt struck flints		**14**
No. of broken struck flints		**64**
No. of burnt unworked flints		**137**
Weight (g) burnt unworked flints		**514**

Table 2.10: Lithic assemblage from tree-throw 156191

the Stanwell Cursus bank. The landscape and social trajectory of the community had been transformed by the construction of this monument, and the community now turned to the construction of a second cursus, which we have called C2. The C2 differed in architectural form to the Stanwell monument, and more closely resembled traditional cursus monuments. In the next section we will explore the form and function of this monument and what it might tell us of the evolution of the community that built it.

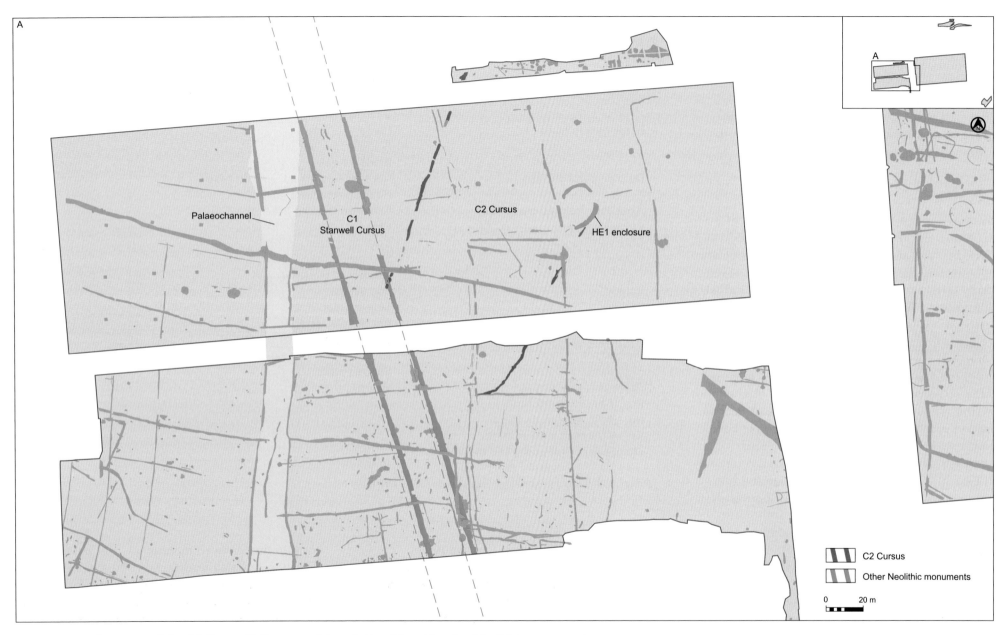

Figure 2.18: The extent of the C2 Stanwell Cursus and its relationship with other Neolithic monuments

C2 Cursus

The two parallel, widely spaced discontinuous ditches that represent the C2 Cursus were considered during excavation to date to the early Bronze Age, possibly representing the earliest attempts at land enclosure. Subsequent analysis of the field system of the 2nd millennium BC, together with analysis of the C2 Entity itself, has led to its reclassification as a cursus monument. The extent of the C2 Cursus and its relationship with other Neolithic monuments is shown in Figure 2.18.

Original architecture of the C2 Cursus

The distance between the ditches of the C2 Cursus is 80 m to *c* 90 m. These dimensions are similar to other more traditional cursus monuments rather than the C1 monument, with for example the Dorset Cursus ditches being *c* 90 m apart (Barrett *et al.* 1991). Although no conclusive evidence for the above ground architecture of the C2 Cursus is available it is unlikely to have had a central bank and probably had a bank running parallel to each of the flanking ditches. The parallel ditches are typically 1.4 m wide and relatively shallow at 0.15–0.30 m deep. Truncation since 1943 has removed between 0.4 m and 0.8 m from the original ground surface. The lack of clear evidence for asymmetric silting or sudden collapse of material into the ditches suggests that the associated banks were relatively wide, stable and low. If we apply the same sort of calculations to the C2 Cursus as we used for the C1 monument (see above), the flanking banks could have been between *c* 2.6 m and 3 m wide and *c* 0.75 m to 1.0 m high.

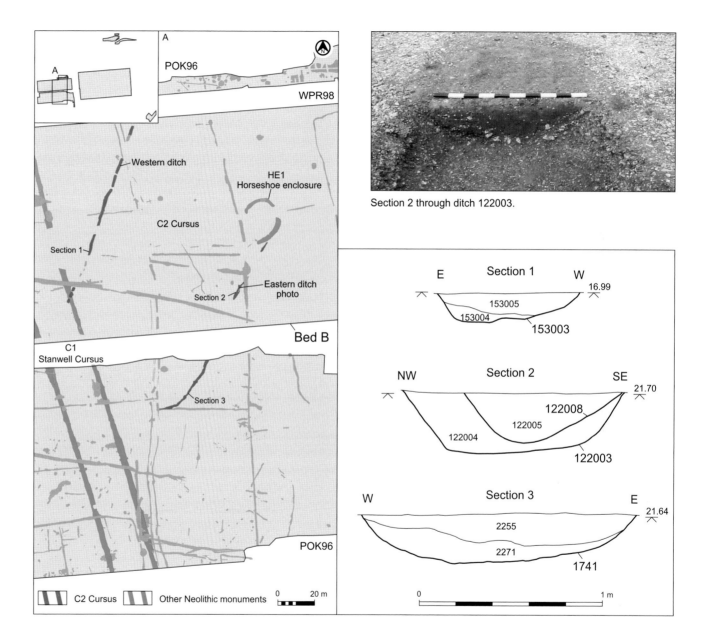

Section 2 through ditch 122003.

Figure 2.19: The C2 Stanwell Cursus

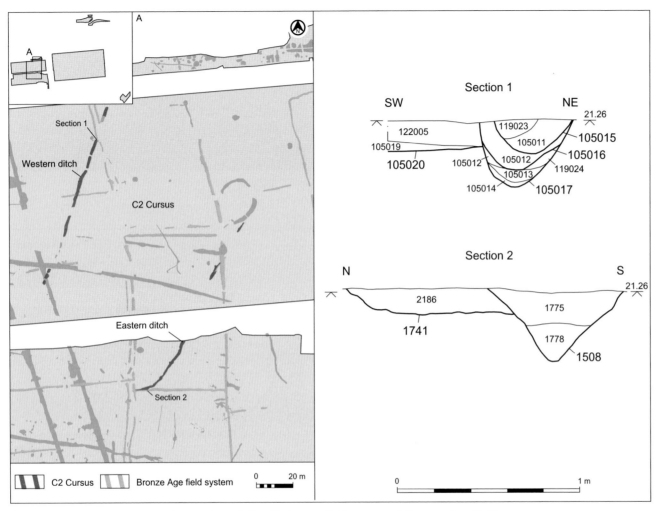

Figure 2.20: Stratigraphic relationship of the C2 Stanwell Cursus and Bronze Age field system

The southern terminal of the C2 Cursus is formed by the Stanwell C1 Cursus bank and ditches. The northernmost C2 ditch cuts the eastern Stanwell Cursus ditch and probably terminated just short of the C1 central bank. (see Fig. 2.19). The southern C2 ditch makes a distinct curve and terminates some 26 m from the eastern C1 Cursus ditch, and this gap would have formed a wide entrance into the C1 Cursus from the south-east, between the C1 and C2 Cursus ditches.

From this southern terminus, the C2 monument had been traced as cropmarks and was revealed during the Terminal 5 (T5) excavations running at least 430 m further north-east, before a lagoon associated with the former sludge processing works completely destroyed the land surface. The C2 Cursus was not identified in excavations north of the lagoon, and it is possible that a Neolithic rectangular enclosure partially recorded during the T5 excavations in Area 61 (N-S central Perry Oaks Road) formed the northern terminus. This enclosure will be mentioned later, but its analysis and full consideration will appear in Volume 2 of this series.

For the purposes of this volume, the southern part of the C2 Cursus will be considered, in particular its relationship with the Stanwell C1 Cursus and the small 'horseshoe' enclosure, HE1.

In absolute chronological terms, the C2 Cursus remains undated. The only finds recovered were a handful of undiagnostic flint flakes and a small core fragment, together with c 60g of burnt flint. No material suitable for radiocarbon dating

The ditches were constructed as a series of intercutting, elongated discontinuous segments, leaving several causeways. These causeways would have afforded access/egress to the monument and potentially clear lines of sight

if internal banks were also absent at these points. The C2 Cursus does not follow the same rigid template as the C1 Stanwell Cursus, and appears more 'informal' in its layout.

survived and no ceramic material of any description was recovered from the numerous interventions excavated through this entity. However, during the later T5 excavations, eight sherds (12g) of early Neolithic Plain Bowl Ware were recovered from the basal and middle fills of the southern C2 Cursus ditch in a narrow previously unexcavated strip between POK96 and WPR98. These sherds are not presented in the dataset distributed with this volume, but will appear in more detail in Volume 2 following further analysis. Nonetheless, although the few small sherds were abraded and may be residual, they do at least suggest that the silting of the C2 and C1 Cursus ditches were broadly contemporary events.

Stratigraphic relationships of the C2 Cursus

In several places, the C2 Cursus was cut by the ditches of the early-middle 2nd millennium BC field system, convincingly demonstrating that the monument predated this period (Fig. 2.20).

The stratigraphic relationship between the C1 and C2 Cursus monuments is ambiguous, but there is some limited evidence to further refine their relative chronologies. The excavated section of the intersection of the eastern C1 and northern C2 ditches was cleaned and examined repeatedly in order to determine a stratigraphic relationship. That relationship is, nonetheless, far from certain. The conclusion of the excavator was that the C2 ditch cut the fills of the C1 Cursus and the section drawing (Fig. 2.21) does indicates the lower fills of the C1 ditch were cut, but uncertainty remains since the illustrated C2 cut was projected

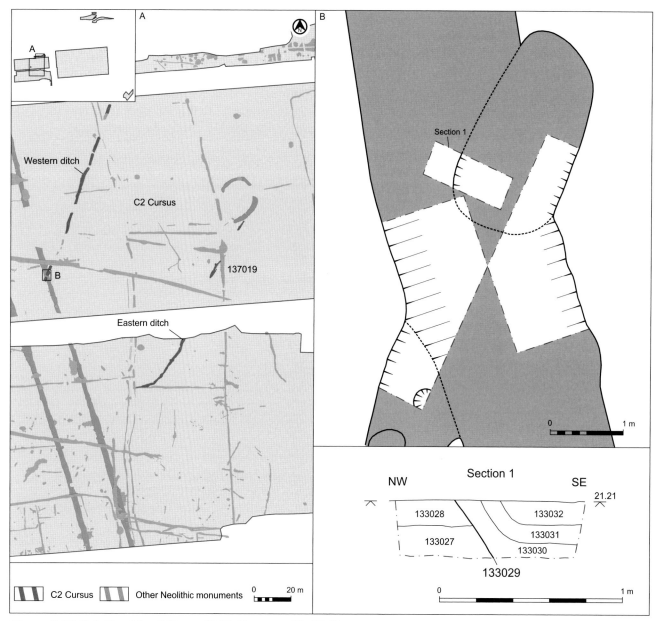

Figure 2.21 Relationship of Stanwell C1 Cursus with C2 Cursus

by a dotted line into the upper fills. As has been argued elsewhere, it is likely that the C1 Cursus ditches were completely silted by the early Bronze Age. If so, then it is more likely that the C2 Cursus ditch was excavated through the lower fills of the C1 Cursus, after which time both ditches continued to silt-up simultaneously.

The ditch silts of the C2 Cursus were very similar to those of the C1—predominantly dark greyish brown. In places an upper and lower fill could be distinguished, but neither fill produced finds in any significant quantity. The HE1 horseshoe enclosure had no direct stratigraphic relationship with the C2 Cursus. In one area south of the enclosure the southern C2 ditch, 11001, had been re-cut as feature 137019 (Fig. 2.21). There was no dating evidence from the recut, so it is unclear whether this was a roughly contemporary modification of the monument, or if it was excavated during the 2nd millennium agricultural transformation of the landscape (see Chapter 3).

Despite the radical architectural difference between the C1 and C2 Cursus, both defined significant pathways through the monumental landscape. For instance, the southern terminus of the C2 Cursus coincided with—and reaffirmed the importance of—the section of the Stanwell C1 Cursus south of the Mesolithic pit cluster and just north of the postholes cut by the western C1 Cursus ditch. The C2 monument then extended to include the location of the HE1 horseshoe enclosure and probably terminated at the location of the rectangular enclosure excavated in Area 61 of the T5 excavations (see Vol. 2).

We have described how the C1 Stanwell Cursus was a celebration and manifestation of the newly emerged community, but if we are to understand the part the C2 Cursus played in the lives of the community, then we must look at the locations and monuments that it incorporated, and in particular, the HE1 horseshoe enclosure.

We will now explore in detail the other monuments on the terrace, examine their development and demonstrate how they integrated the cursus with its immediate landscape setting, or depending on one's perspective, linked places to it.

Horseshoe Enclosure 1

The western area of the Perry Oaks site appears to have been a place of strategic importance within the monumental scheme at large. We have seen how the C1 and C2 Cursus monuments intersected in an area that had been repeatedly modified by the construction of postholes and pits. If the cursus monuments are accepted as denoting formal and traditional paths through the landscape, then this area was an interchange, controlling and concentrating people, information and knowledge. We have discussed above the focal nature of this location—the local topography and its long and acknowledged history demonstrated by the presence of the Mesolithic pits. The siting of the HE1 horseshoe enclosure lends further weight to this assertion (Fig. 2.22). This enclosure was initially recognised as a cropmark, and significantly, two similar cropmarks lie adjacent to the C1 Cursus, upon a promontory of land on

the opposite side of the watercourse, just to the north-west of Perry Oaks.

The HE1 enclosure was located within the C2 Cursus. The 1943 contour survey indicated that the HE1 was located on a slight gravel ridge, up-slope from the Stanwell Cursus and just under 0.5 m higher than it. This slight topographic elevation together with cultural determinations must have led to this choice of location for its construction. In such a flat landscape any upstanding architectural features would have been visible at quite a distance, especially if the eye were drawn to them by cleared 'rides' through scrub or woodland. Generally however, unless wooden structures were used to augment the monuments, they would not have been visually impressive in the same way as the comparable monuments of Wessex, for example. The HE 1 enclosure may never have been intended to make an impressive visual statement, rather it would have been inferred from afar and only fully revealed through close encounter. It was, therefore, primarily concerned with the circumscription of the area it enclosed and segregation from the world of the everyday.

Form and architecture of the HE1 enclosure

HE1 was just in excess of 20 m in diameter and comprised two continuous but segmental ditches arranged as opposing horns, with unexcavated causeways between them to the north-east and south-west (Fig. 2.22). The internal diameter of this sub-circular monument was approximately 17 m and the monumental ditches enclosed an

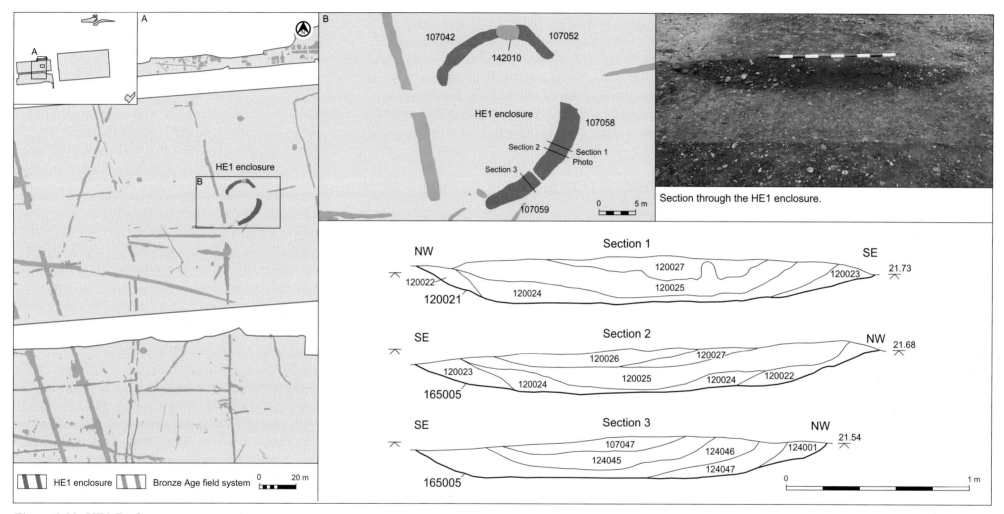

Figure 2.22: HE1 Enclosure

area of 225 m². The northern ditch (107042 and 107052) was on average 1.3 m wide and 0.2 to 0.3 m deep. The southern ditch (107058 and 107059) was wider at 2.3 to 2.4 m but of a similar depth to the northern ditch. Both ditches had a shallow 'U' profile. The south-west causeway or entrance faced the C1 Cursus and was 16 m wide; the north-east causeway was much narrower at 6 m wide. The north-east causeway was directed towards the segmented ring ditch (Site A) excavated in 1969 (Canham 1978, 6) that is possibly of a similar date.

73

The exact architecture of the HE1 monument cannot be confidently reconstructed, as only the footprint survives and superstructures in wood may have enhanced upstanding earthen features. The evidence of asymmetric silting of the southern ditches suggests that an internal bank or mound of some type existed (see Fig. 2.23), and the splayed and open arrangement of the monumental ditches suggest internal banks rather than an internal mound. The incorporation of this monument into the Bronze Age field system as a means of channel movement supports this interpretation of its construction (see Chapter 3).

During excavation the HE1 enclosure did not appear to have been a particularly imposing monument. However, the Truncation Model (see Chapter 1) shows that approximately 1 m of deposits and topsoil have been lost since the construction of the sludge works in the 1930s. This may, however, be an overestimate, since the remnant bank material would have made the local ground surface artificially higher. It is more likely that *c* 0.8 m has been lost from the original pre-monumental ground surface, and if this is

accepted, then the ditches would originally have been much deeper and slightly wider. More importantly, the resulting internal banks would have been significant structures, especially considering the monument was located on a slight natural rise. Tables 2.11 and 2.12 provide some estimates for the dimensions of the ditches and banks as originally constructed.

Figure 2.23 shows a possible layout of the internal banks, based on the simulated data in the tables. The north-eastern entrance is very narrow or even non-existent, whilst the south-western entrance was substantial. The southern bank is slightly longer, wider and higher than its northern counterpart. Whatever the original architecture, it is clear that the HE1 monument would have been a substantial feature in the relatively flat Heathrow landscape. In Figure 2.23, the circles represent the area occupied by a standing adult with an outstretched arm (Fairweather and Sliwa 1970, 44). These suggest that approximately a dozen people could have stood within the embanked enclosure and still have left clear the central space and sight lines out of the monument.

	Estimated Northern bank	Estimated Southern bank
Length (m)	15.2	17.7
Width at base (m)	3.2	3.3
Height (m)	1.6	1.9
Volume (cu m)	38.9	55.5

Table 2.12: Estimated dimensions and volume of HE1 banks

Chronology of the HE1 enclosure

As with many of the 3rd and 4th millennium features in the Perry Oaks landscape, dating the construction of the HE1 enclosure is difficult. The extensive contamination from the activities of the sludge works has ensured that no attempt was made to obtain radiocarbon dates from the cominnuted fragments of charcoal recovered from the monument. The small fragments of associated pottery were found to be the result of contamination by later features. For instance, a shallow pit, 142010, was excavated into the fills of the northern circuit of the enclosure ditch (Fig. 2.22). This was not recognised during excavation, but the dense concentration of late Bronze Age pottery in this intervention, together with some evidence from the section drawings, confirms this interpretation.

	Northern ditch SG 107042 & 107052	Southern ditch SC 107058 & 107059
Length of ditch (m)	19.3	19
Depth on excavation (m)	0.3	0.3
Estimated original depth (m)	1.1	1.1
Width on excavation (m)	1.4	2.4
Estimated original width (m)	2.2	3.2
Estimated original cross-sectional area (sq m)	1.8	2.6
Estimated original volume after expansion factor 1.1 (cu m)	38.5	55.2

Table 2.11: Estimated original dimensions and volumes of HE1 ditches

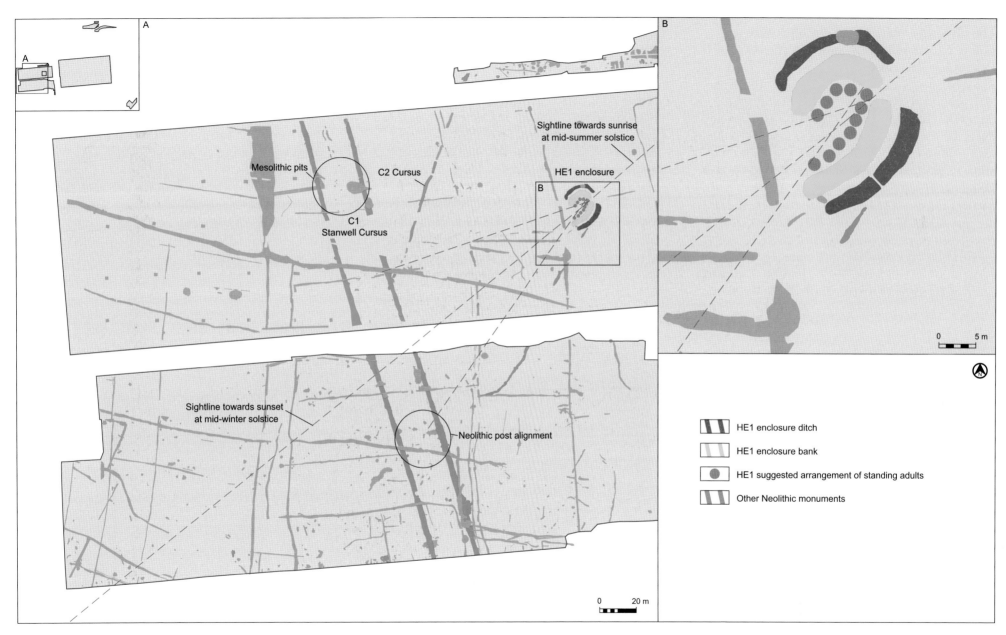

Figure 2.23: Plan of the estimated dimensions of the internal banks of HE1 enclosure and suggested arrangement of standing adults with site lines

The lithic assemblage from the enclosure (Table 2.13) is relatively undiagnostic, as Cramp has described:

As a group, the assemblage consists mainly of nretouched debitage. Excluding spalls (51 pieces), flakes are the most common removal type. These pieces tend to be small and squat in shape. The reduction strategy involved a mixed hammermode and the occasional use of platform edge abrasion. Although one bladelet and one bladelike flake were recovered, blades are conspicuously absent from the collection. The flake-based character of the assemblage might indicate a date in the later Neolithic or Bronze Age for the majority (Pitts and Jacobi 1979; Ford 1987), although much of the material is chronologically undiagnostic.

The flintwork from the ditch deposits is in very variable condition, but some significant differences were noted in the relative severity of the damage observed on the flints from the lower and upper fills [Table 2.14]. The flints recovered from the primary fills (SG 107051, 107053, 107064 and 107065) have suffered more extensively from post-depositional damage and rolling, suggesting that the assemblage is composed mainly of residual material. By contrast, the material from the upper deposits is in much fresher condition and forms a more technologically coherent assemblage. It seems likely that the material contained within the primary deposits derives from a pre-existing scatter of lithic material, perhaps formed over several millennia, that was incorporated unintentionally

into the later ditch cut. A microburin was recovered from the late Bronze Age intrusive context 107037.

The flintwork from the upper fills is probably associated with the use of the monument and may have been deposited over a much shorter period of time...and...probably relates to the use of the monument...which..., morphologically and technologically, is most consistent with a later Neolithic or Bronze Age industry, although the paucity of chronologically distinctive types does not allow much confidence in dating.

(Cramp, CD Section 3)

Category	Sub-category	Lower 107015	Lower 107053	Lower 107064	Lower 107065	Upper 107041	Upper 107042	Upper 107043	Upper 107056	Upper 107057	Upper 107061	Upper 107063	Total
Flake/broken flake	Primary flake >75%		2	3				3		1		1	10
	Secondary flake 1-74%		7	6	4	1		2	1		1	6	28
	Tertiary flake 0%	2	1	3	1			1			1	2	11
	Bladelike flake											1	1
	Unclassified debitage		2					3					5
Blade/broken blade	Bladelet	1			1								2
Spall/spall bag	Spall	3	6	14	4	7	2	6	2			7	51
Core/core fragment	Core on a flake										1		1
	Unclassifiable/fragmentary core											1	1
Nodule	Partially worked nodule					2		1					3
Retouched blade/flake	Retouched flake	1				1							2
	Miscellaneous retouch					1							1
Serrated/denticulate	Serrated piece											1	1
Total		**7**	**18**	**26**	**12**	**10**	**2**	**16**	**3**	**1**	**3**	**19**	**117**
No. of burnt unworked flints			199	6	43	14		6181	386	65	97	62	7053
Weight (g) burnt unworked flints			73	6	5	6		1605	24	2	10	23	1754

Table 2.13: Lithic assemblage from the HE1 enclosure

This confirms our view that the location of the HE1 enclosure had already had a long history of human activity. We have suggested previously that the residual lithic material in later features in this area was produced as a result of activity in the late Mesolithic or earlier Neolithic, perhaps within a small forest clearing. The HE1 enclosure therefore served to architecturally enhance a place which was already of some importance. Unfortunately, the lithics do not closely date the construction of the HE1 monument. When considering the lithic material, it is worth remembering that the terms upper and lower fills are strictly relative when bearing in mind that up to 1 m depth of deposits had been removed prior to the excavation of this monument.

In summary, the lithic material suggests that the monument was constructed at a location which had a history of activity dating to the late Mesolithic/ early Neolithic, and the construction of HE1 probably post-dated that activity. The lithics from the upper fills of the monument ditches suggest that it was in use anywhere between 3300 and 2000 BC. In addition, the major north-south field boundary, 138018, and much of the rest of the 2nd millennium field system changed orientation at this point, with respect to the HE1 enclosure.

Turning to the relationship with the C2 Cursus, the lack of a direct stratigraphic relationship between the two monuments means that it is impossible to be sure if the cursus was built to incorporate the existing enclosure, or whether the enclosure was built within the extant cursus.

Condition category	Lower fill		Upper fill	
	No. of flints	% of total	No. of flints	% of total
Fresh	7	11.11%	12	22.22%
Slight post-depositional edge damage	9	14.29%	15	27.78%
Moderate post-depositional edge damage	22	34.92%	19	35.19%
Heavy post-depositional edge damage	25	39.68%	8	14.81%
Total	63	100%	54	100%

Table 2.14: Comparison of flint condition from the upper and lower fills of the ring ditch (HE1)

In some respects, it makes little difference which came first. The important point is that the C2 Cursus and the HE1 enclosure (and probably the rectangular enclosure excavated in T5) worked together as a ceremonial complex.

Function of the HE1 enclosure

We will now turn to our final question: what purpose did the HE1 monument serve, and what does it and other similar enclosures tell us about human inhabitation and social change?

In order to answer this, we must look at the architecture of the monument, its location and relationship with the existing monuments of the 4th millennium BC, and the finds assemblage from the ditches.

We have already shown that the architecture of the monument would suggest that a small group of people could undertake ceremonies around a central space. We have shown that the banks would have been substantial and would have prevented views into and out of the monument apart from through the two entrances. The north-eastern entrance would have been very narrow; the south-western entrance would have allowed open views towards the Stanwell C1 Cursus, but only that section where the C1 and C2 Cursus meet. It is also notable that the area of post alignments in the western and eastern C1 Cursus ditches would not be visible from inside the HE1 monument and neither would the location of the late Mesolithic pits to the north. The focus was emphatically on the junction of the two cursus monuments.

Figure 2.23 shows that sunset at the mid winter solstice fell centrally to the field of vision from the HE1 monument. At sunset on the shortest day of the year, a group of people inside the HE1 monument would have observed the sun disappear behind the mound of the Stanwell Cursus (see Fig. 2.25 below). Conversely, the narrow north-eastern entrance would allow the observation of sunrise at the mid summer solstice. This would have been aided by the large gap in the southern bank and ditch of the C2 Cursus, affording views across the landscape. However, these sight lines do not take into account topography and vegetation. For instance, the sun is more likely to have disappeared at mid winter behind the higher ground now occupied by Windsor Great Park than the Stanwell Cursus mound. Nevertheless, we feel the coincidence is strong enough to associate the HE1 monument and possibly the C2 Cursus with the general Neolithic monumental association with astronomical events (eg Parker Pearson 1993, 62–65).

We have already mentioned the small rectangular enclosure, which possibly formed the north-eastern terminus of the C2 Cursus, and which was excavated in T5. More detailed analysis of this enclosure will be presented in Volume 2, but before discussing how these enclosures and observations were tied together by the C2 Cursus, we will consider what people may have done at the HE1 enclosure.

Use of the HE1 enclosure

The finds assemblage from the HE1 enclosure was relatively large in comparison to others thus far explored at Heathrow (eg Canham 1978), which might suggest more intensive use and the relative strategic importance of this area in general (Fig. 2.24). The finds included worked flint, burnt flint and animal bone (a rare find from deposits at Heathrow from this period). The upper fills were charcoal rich and contained high frequencies of burnt flint, all of which appear to have tipped in from the centre of the monument. The upper fills also contained 'tested' flint nodules and cores.

Cramp compares the lithics from the lower fills with the upper fills (Table 2.13) and makes this point:

In terms of function, this later assemblage [from the upper fill] is hard to characterise. The presence of small quantities of knapping waste in combination with burnt, broken, retouched and utilised pieces implies a range of tasks. Given the presence of animal bone, it is possible that some of the flintwork results from feasting activity.

(Cramp, CD Section 3)

The animal bone was poorly preserved and very fragmentary (apart from a cow maxilla from basal deposit 107063), and consisted of cattle and sheep/goat as well as indeterminate fragments of large mammal. These remains were present throughout the sequence, as was burnt flint. This latter material was significantly more frequent in the upper than the basal fills.

Spatially, the animal bone and other finds are largely coincident, with a particular concentration in the southern ditch (see Fig. 2.24). Whether these deposits were produced by activity inside the enclosure or in the immediate vicinity of the monument is unclear. We believe that the primary use of the monument was to facilitate the meetings of groups of people (Figure 2.23 suggests *c* 12 individuals) at particular times of the year. These people negotiated, through various media, access to land, water and other resources. These negotiations may have taken place via ceremonial occasions such as marriages, births and rites of passage and may have been facilitated through rituals which involved slaughter and / or consumption of animals. Although fragmentary, the finds signature

from the remnants of the ditches could be interpreted in this way.

If the HE1 enclosure was built for a small group of people to meet, perform ceremonies and observe solar events in relative seclusion, then the architecture of the C2 Cursus would seem to cater for a large group of people, especially when compared to the C1 Stanwell Cursus. The widely spaced ditches and banks would allow a relatively large gathering of people, perhaps most of the community, to congregate inside the C2 Cursus, with perhaps only selected individuals or leaders entering the HE1 enclosure to take part in the most sacred rituals.

We may thus picture the events that may have taken place in this landscape.

The community that built and used the C1 Stanwell Cursus may have used the monument in ceremonial processions by a small number of people along the top of the bank, while the rest of the community observed. It is possible, even probable, that the location of the HE1 enclosure and the T5 enclosure were already important and used for solar observations. Due to increasing concerns over land and agricultural resources, the community may have needed to architecturally formalise these locations, which would also more clearly differentiate the leaders of those ceremonies as representatives of the constituent kin-groups. It would be this smaller group that would now lead and take part in the most sacred ceremonies, but the rest of the community ensured that they were involved in these as well

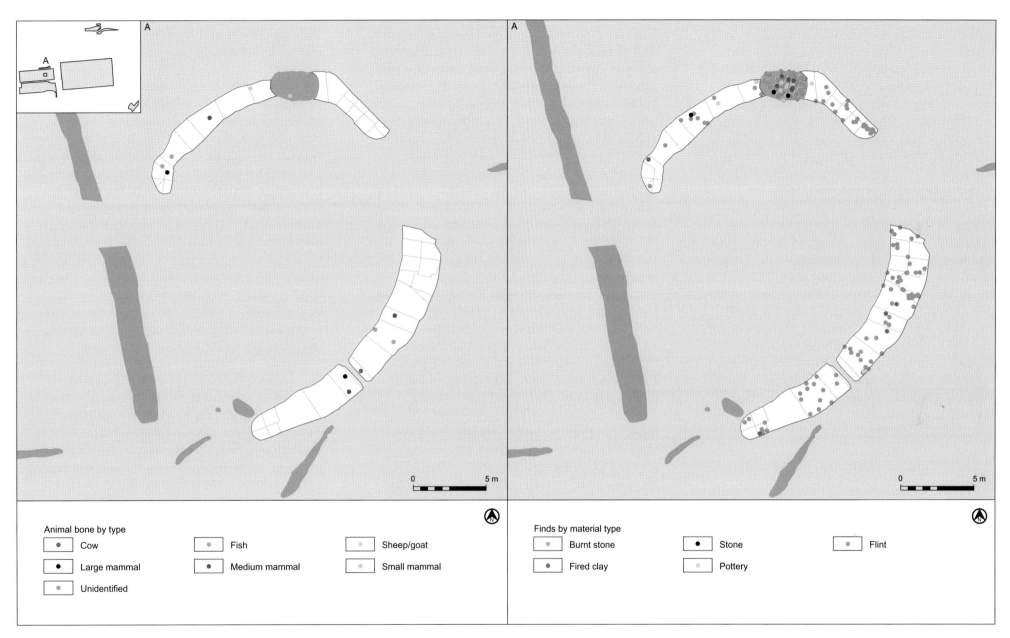

Figure 2.24: Finds distribution within the HE1 Enclosure

in the construction of the C2 Cursus. This linked together the C1 Stanwell Cursus and the two small enclosures, and allowed the community to take part in the processions between these locations. For instance, at sunset at the mid winter solstice, the community would gather outside the HE1 enclosure, possibly having previously observed their leaders processing along the C1 Cursus to this point. The leaders would take part in ceremonies inside the enclosure which included observing the sun setting in the south-west. The community and their leaders may have continued ceremonies and feasting through the night until before dawn, when they all processed along the C2 Cursus to the rectangular enclosure at its northern terminus. Here, the leaders would enter the small enclosure whilst the community waited outside, and the sunrise in the south-east would be greeted with further ceremony. This sequence would be reversed at the mid summer solstice. Figure 2.25 shows an artist's reconstruction of this solstice ceremony.

Architecture, monuments and society: a summary

Through the preceding pages we have demonstrated and suggested how the architecture of the C1 and C2 Cursus and HE1 enclosure reflected the major changes which came about in the latter half of the 4th millennium BC. We have suggested how a loose association of small kin-groups chose to become a cohesive community in response to growing concerns of access to land and resources following the adoption of agriculture and the opening of the forest canopy. They did this at first by ceremony and procession between ancient ancestral locations, but soon formalised this process by constructing the C1 Stanwell Cursus. This monument's precision in layout and adherence to a specific template also allowed for the incorporation of earlier locations, and the continuation of ceremonies at these locations. Its construction was a product of the community and tied together the disparate histories of the constituent kin-groups. However the C1 Cursus also reflected the transformation in society and the landscape. A smaller group of people would now actively take part in the processions along the top of the bank. Ceremonies, the sub-texts of which were concerned with land and resources, would be led and mediated by that smaller leadership group. Nonetheless, the wider community was not isolated: the C1 Cursus facilitated their involvement and allowed all to see the ceremonies and processions.

Very soon the community encompassed other landscape locations with banks and ditches forming small enclosures, which reflected the increasing importance and detachment of the leaders and negotiators. However even now the community still played an active part in this process, through the construction of the C2 Cursus. The architecture of this monument was radically different from that of the Stanwell monument, for it served a different purpose. The C2 Cursus tied together important locations, but it allowed the community to take part in the procession between these locations, even if they were physically excluded from the ceremonies that took place within the small enclosures.

We can view the monumental complex of the latter half of the 4th millennium BC as being revolutionary and transformational in that a community was born and within that community was the emergence of a small leadership group. The tensions between community and leadership reached an equilibrium through the inclusion of the wider community in observation and participation in ceremonies conducted on their behalf at crucial times of the year. Nonetheless, the construction of small circular enclosures such as the HE1 example illustrate that spaces of 'explicit order' were becoming more closely defined and possibly more exclusive in terms of the select group that occupied those spaces during the later 4th and 3rd millennia BC.

Our ceramic-based relative chronology has allowed us to place these observations within the currency of Plain Bowl Ware Neolithic pottery between 3600 and 3300 BC. The WPR98 excavations revealed relatively little in the way of monuments or artefacts from the succeeding 3rd millennium BC. No Peterborough Ware, current from 3400 to 2500 BC, was encountered, and only four pits containing Grooved Ware dating from 3000 to 2000 BC were excavated. More substantial evidence for human activity in the 3rd millennium BC was recorded during the T5 excavations and will be presented in Volume 2. However, for our purposes here, we will conclude our chapter with some general observations on inhabitation of the landscape in the 3rd millennium BC.

Figure 2.25: Artist's reconstruction of the monumental landscape at the end of the 3rd millennium BC

3300 to 2000 BC: Peterborough and Grooved Ware

The period following the construction of the major monuments from 3300 BC to the emergence of the first field boundaries between 2000 BC and 1700 BC is not well represented in the WPR98 dataset at Perry Oaks. For instance, no Peterborough Ware was recovered during the WPR98 excavations and Grooved Ware was only recovered from a handful of pits. In addition, as we have seen, our lithic chronology is not sufficiently refined to allow us to use those artefacts to examine this period in detail. It is worth discussing the meagre data from WPR98 at the outset, before moving on to outline some of the trends that may have taken place in the community of the 3rd millennium BC. We will do this by analogy with the material in West London and nationally.

The evidence from Perry Oaks

We have already described the HE1 horseshoe enclosure, which on the basis of the meagre lithic assemblage from the ditch fills, could date to the 3rd millennium BC. However, our evidence for the 3rd millennium BC at Perry Oaks in general consists largely of Grooved Ware and lithics residing in later contexts. Only two pits containing Grooved Ware could confidently be dated to this period (216121 and 127022; Figure 2.26), and even these were far from normal Grooved Ware pits. Pit 127022 for instance was contaminated by slag deposits from the construction of the sludge works, and contained only 5 g of Grooved Ware

GR2 fabric. It also contained 22 g of an indeterminate grog-tempered fabric, GR1, which could date to the early Bronze Age.

On the basis of technology, the lithic assemblage from pit 127022 appears to date to the late Neolithic or early Bronze Age and contains evidence of both knapping and tool use (Table 2.15).

Pit 127022 contained a total of 52 struck flints and 289 pieces (1203 g) of burnt unworked flint within SG deposit 127017. Technologically, the assemblage is in fresh condition and probably dates to the late Neolithic or early Bronze Age, although several residual pieces are present, including one microburin and one, probably later Neolithic, Levallois core. Retouched tools include five retouched flakes and two piercers.

(Cramp, CD Section 3)

Given the problems of distinguishing with certainty changes in lithic technology between 2400 and 1700 BC, we must conclude that this pit (127022) could date to anytime between 3000 and 1700 BC. It is even conceivable that the pit dates to the period between 2400 and 2000 when both Beaker and Grooved Ware pottery appears to have been in use (but see Garwood 1999, 161). Nonetheless, the lithics do represent the traces of some sort of specialised domestic (?) activity.

Pit 216121 contained 132 g of Grooved Ware and 12 flint flakes of broadly late Neolithic date (Fig. 2.26). However, a radiocarbon date on seeds from context 216011 of this feature produced a medieval date of AD 1180 to 1400 (WK9377 cal AD 2 sigma).

Table 2.15: Late Neolithic/early Bronze Age lithic assemblage from pit 127022

Category	Sub-category	Total
Flake/broken flake	Primary flake	4
	Secondary flake	13
	Tertiary flake	11
Blade/broken blade	Bladelike flake	1
Microburin	Microburin	1
Chip/sieved chip	Chip	13
Core/core fragment	Multi-platform flake core	1
	Levallois/other discoidal flake core	1
Retouched blade/flake	Retouched flake	5
Piercer	Awl/piercer	2
Total		**52**
No. of burnt struck flints		**1**
No. of broken struck flints		**18**
No. of burnt unworked flints		**289**
Weight (g) burnt unworked flints		**1203**

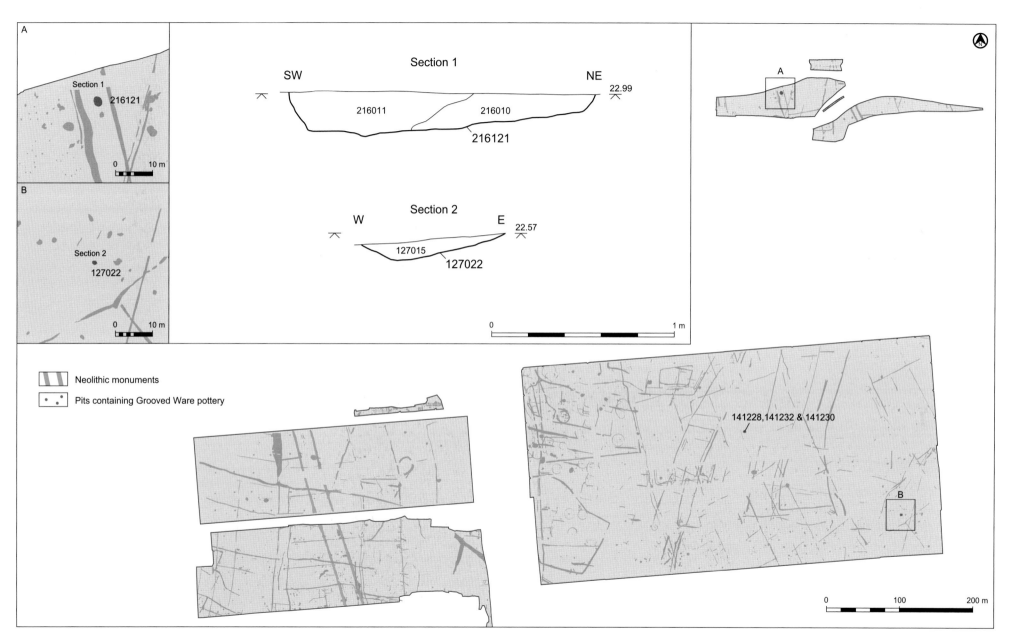

A

Section 1

216121

0   10 m

B

Section 2

127022

0   10 m

Section 1

SW   NE   22.99

216011   216010

216121

Section 2

W   E 22.57

127015

127022

0   1 m

A

141228,141232 & 141230

B

▨ Neolithic monuments

⬚ Pits containing Grooved Ware pottery

0   100   200 m

Figure 2.26: Pits containing Grooved Ware

A radiocarbon date of 3030–2870 BC (WK11473 cal BC 2 sigma) was obtained on *Arrhenatherum elatius* (onion couch) tubers from pit 137027, which also contained cremated human bone. No Grooved Ware pottery was recovered from this pit, but the radiocarbon date places the cremation during the use of Peterborough Ware and the emergence of Grooved Ware. Unfortunately, the pit was again contaminated by the construction of a nearby concrete wall. In addition, the human bone report noted the presence of pyre goods in the shape of copper alloy and animal bone. The presence of copper alloy and the association of *Arrhenatherum elatius* (onion couch) tubers with cremations is more indicative of the Bronze Age, and certainly unlikely for the beginning of the 3rd millennium BC.

Three intercutting features (141228, 141232 and 141230) contained fragments of Grooved Ware (Fig. 2.26), but they also contained various sherds of early Bronze Age, early Iron Age and late Iron Age fabrics.

Pit 129109 in the north-eastern part of WPR98 contained a sizeable lithic assemblage (Fig. 2.27), broadly dated to the 3rd millennium BC. Nearby were two further pits (148324, 148328), which contained no finds, and a tree-throw (148326) containing one struck flint and some burnt flint. Although undated, these further features could well be contemporary with pit 129109. The lithic assemblage from pit 129109 provides a good example of the sort of features which resulted from inhabitation of the 3rd millennium BC landscape.

A total of 57 struck flints were recovered from two deposits in pit 129109, which was excavated in quadrants. The flintwork can be dated to the Neolithic on the presence of one fragment and three flakes from three polished implements; the general technological appearance of the flintwork might support a date in the later half of the period.

The majority of flints are in a fresh, uncorticated condition. While most is local gravel flint, a few flakes of bullhead flint along with several pieces of a distinctive derived flint are also present. Local nodules seem to have been preferred for burning.

Most of the material (53 pieces) came from the upper fill; only four pieces were recovered from the lower fill. A further 710 pieces (4130 g) of burnt unworked flint came from the pit, again mainly from the upper fill

Category	Sub-category	SG deposit 129110	SG deposit 129111	Total
Flake/broken flake	Primary flake		1	**1**
	Secondary flake		12	**12**
	Tertiary flake	3	22	**25**
	Flake from a polished implement		3	3
Blade/broken blade	Blade		1	1
	Bladelet		1	1
	Bladelike flake		5	5
Core preparation flake	Rejuvenation flake tablet	1		1
Axe/adze sharpening flake	Axe/adze thinning flake		2	2
Chip/sieved chip	Chip		1	1
Core/core fragment	Single platform flake core		1	1
	Core on a flake		1	1
Retouched blade/flake	Retouched blade(let)		1	1
Serrated/denticulate	Notched piece		1	1
Axe/core tool	Polished axe fragment		1	1
Total		**4**	**53**	**57**

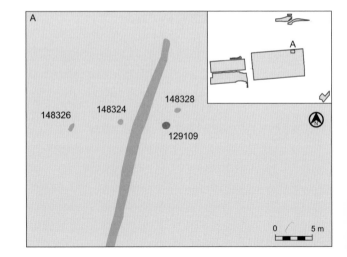

Figure 2.27: Lithic assemblage from pit 129109

(707 pieces, 4113 g). There was little horizontal variation in the distribution of either struck flint or burnt unworked flint.

The assemblage is mostly composed of flakes (38 pieces). Blades, bladelets and bladelike pieces are less numerous (seven pieces), suggesting a flake-based later Neolithic technology. The majority of flakes are broad and thin with fine dorsal flake scars. Many have been carefully struck from an abraded platform edge using a soft-hammer percussor. The presence of a platform rejuvenation tablet reflects attempts to maintain the flaking angle during knapping. Two possible axe-thinning flakes were also recovered.

The paucity of preparatory flakes, pieces of unclassifiable waste, chips and cores suggests that the assemblage contains little knapping waste. No refits were found, despite the presence of several related groups of flint, which again suggests that the assemblage does not result directly from knapping activity. An important exception is the polished axe fragment from the northeastern quadrant and the indirectly refitting flake from the southeastern quadrant. It is possible that other pieces that might have refitted have been lost to truncation, although it is not uncommon to find that only elements of a polished implement have been selected for deposition; examples of both 'cores' and flakes are known from the nearby Neolithic causewayed enclosure at Staines, Surrey (Robertson-Mackay 1987, 104 and 107).

Two additional polished flakes, originating from two different axes, were recovered from the northwestern and northeastern quadrants. As seen at Ascott-under-Wychwood in Oxfordshire (Cramp forthcoming), it is

not unusual for several axes to be represented by single flakes. It seems that, once knapped, the flakes from polished implements had a fairly wide and perhaps prolonged circulation, with the effect that material from the same implement was only rarely - and perhaps unintentionally - recombined for deposition.

Beyond the group of polished flakes, there were very few formal tools in the pit. A retouched bladelet was recovered from context 129104 (NW quadrant) and a notched flake was recovered from context 129095 (SW quadrant). Numerous unretouched edges show evidence of use.

(Cramp, CD Section 3)

Environmental samples taken from pit 129109 (1124 and 1125) yielded no arboreal pollen and only Poaceae (grasses) and ruderal weeds were found. The occasional cereal-type pollen grain supports the possibility of nearby cultivation, but some reworking of sediments is a possibility. Microscopic charcoal was present in moderate amounts but palynomorph preservation was poor and it is difficult to characterise the landscape from such impoverished data. The absence of tree and shrub pollen might reflect a genuinely open Neolithic landscape, but the paucity of palynomorphs makes interpretation tenuous. Furthermore, the pit can only be dated on the lithic assemblage, and could thus have been excavated anytime between 3000 and 2000 BC. This Neolithic pit might, indeed, be reflecting a cleared landscape, although other areas of the site may yield evidence of wooded conditions. For instance, an example from a long barrow at Redlands Farm in Northamptonshire (Wiltshire,

forthcoming) illustrates the difficulty in extrapolating data obtained from features separated by only a short distance. Analysis of the ditch deposits in this feature showed that the local landscape was extensively open in the early Neolithic but this failed to be recorded in contemporaneous palaeochannel sediments of the nearby River Nene (Brown and Keough 1992), which indicated an extensively wooded catchment throughout the period. It is not surprising that trees fringing a river bank would dominate the local pollen record and filter out regional pollen, and the wider landscape may have consisted of woodland with a mixed mosaic of newly created and neglected clearings, similar to Perry Oaks.

Another factor of importance is the tendency to ascribe 'periods' to features that may, in fact, be temporally separated. For example, two waterholes separated by a short distance might both be regarded as being late Neolithic, but this period may span 800 years. There might be clearance and abandonment at the site several times within that period and the features might just be reflecting one set of environmental conditions. This could prove problematical for landscape interpretation for the late Neolithic.

Data relating to the 3rd millennium BC have been recovered in greater quantity and with more reliable provenance during the T5 excavations, and these will be discussed in Volume 2. In the meantime, we will briefly turn to some of the broader trends of the 3rd millennium BC within the wider West London landscape.

Evidence for the wider landscape in the 3rd millennium BC

In the West London area, Peterborough Ware was deposited in three main contexts. Firstly, isolated or small clusters of pits, often with lithic material and charcoal. Secondly, from the upper fills of causewayed enclosures (eg Yeoveny Lodge Staines) and the Stanwell Cursus (O'Connell 1990). Thirdly, Peterborough Ware is often associated with the modification of earlier Neolithic small circular monuments. Examples include Manor Farm Horton (Preston 2003) and Staines Road, Shepperton (Bird *et al.* 1990).

Taken together, the three main contextual occurrences of Peterborough Ware give the impression of a time when people inhabited a landscape defined by ancient places and relatively new monuments and practices. However, this landscape did not see a continuation of the major architectural constructions undertaken in the period 3600 to 3300 BC. Rather, existing large monuments continued in use in some way, even if they were in advanced decay, whilst small monuments were modified and / or enlarged. Groups of pits, possibly to accept the ceramic, lithic and ecofactual residues of autumnal rituals, were dug in woodland clearings that had been or were to be used for cultivation or pasture.

We have termed the Peterborough Ware Phase of the Neolithic the 'Period of Contentment' in West London, as it appears to have been a time when the community that built the major monuments of the latter part of the 4th millennium were content to live their lives within the physical and social framework they provided. Hence new monuments were not constructed, but old ones were modified or re-used.

If we can detect a subtle change in this period, then it is in the practice of pit digging and the assemblages they contain when compared to the earlier 4th millennium BC.

If the overtly ritual aspects of life as expressed through monuments showed continuity or gradual evolution, then how people behaved in the wider landscape showed a more pronounced change during the period 3400 to 2500 BC, and one which would accelerate during the currency of Grooved Ware pottery. This change concerned a shift from deposition of pottery and flintwork in tree-throws and pits to almost exclusive pit deposition.

Evans *et al.* (1999) have drawn attention to the patterns of artefact deposition in tree-throws across southern Britain in the 4th millennium BC, and suggested that many were the deliberate receptacles for midden material. Allen *et al.* (2004) have drawn similar conclusions from their excavations at Dorney, near the Thames, eight miles (13 km) away from Terminal 5. They support the findings of Evans *et al.* that middening occurred after the trees had fallen, and possibly after significant clearance in the early Neolithic (Allen *et al.* 2004, 91). Furthermore, they go on to suggest that the deposition of early Neolithic material within tree-throws can be seen as a continuation of a Mesolithic tradition (ibid., 92).

We have already discussed the lithic and ceramic assemblage from tree-throw 159191 and suggested that it represented just such a midden deposit from a settlement of the 4th millennium BC, probably dating to between 3600 and 3300 BC.

Allen *et al.* (2004) have contrasted this pattern with that of pits dated by radiocarbon to the period 3350–2900 BC containing Peterborough Ware. They have suggested that these pits saw the deliberate deposition of selected pottery and flint assemblages rather than the general midden deposits of the early Neolithic, which were placed in tree-throws. Pits 127022 and 129109 at Perry Oaks both contained lithic assemblages which show some specialisation and selection of pieces for deposition, and of course the former also contained Grooved Ware.

This pattern is repeated across the West London area, where excavations by the Museum of London and others, for example at Imperial College Sports Ground (Crockett 2001), in the latter quarter of the 20th century recorded isolated or small clusters of pits containing Peterborough Ware, often with lithic material and charcoal.

If we are to try to understand this trend beyond ascribing it to ritual practices, we should consider how people moved around a landscape divided by monuments and tradition—how they decided where people would live, graze animals, gain access to water and plant crops. By whatever process, these issues had to be resolved and settled, perhaps every year or season. We have already suggested that the cursus and small circular monuments constructed between 3600 and 3300 BC played a vital role in this process of negotiation. These meetings may have become cloaked by rituals involving worship and even disposal of the dead, but the subtext remained the fundamentals of ordering life. In the 3rd millennium BC, new monuments were constructed and were associated with Grooved Ware. These take the form of small 'hengiform' enclosures, but are essentially very similar in plan and dimension to the small circular enclosures of the 4th millennium BC. One such small Grooved Ware enclosure was revealed in Area 77 (Pond 17) of the T5 excavations, and will be discussed in more detail in Volume 2. For the time being, we can say that with the adoption of Grooved Ware, there was a re-emphasis on the monumentalising of meeting places for small groups of people to undertake ceremonies.

We cannot know the details of these negotiations, rituals and ceremonies, and in this context negotiation is taken to cover a wide range of possibilities. It may have taken place in the context of peaceful discussions with ritual feasting or negotiation by force through trials of strength or combat. The deliberate digging of pits and the deposition of pottery and flint may be part of the process of negotiation itself, or it may be an outcome of that process. In other words, once agreement had been reached over access to a particular resource or part of the landscape under the guise of a ceremony undertaken at one of the monuments, a small ritual may have been undertaken at the part of the landscape under contention. This may have ended with a ceremo-ny laying claim to the land at issue, involving burying some of the ceramic and lithic material used in the ceremony, or derived from the respective settlements of the people involved. Allen *et al.* (2004, 92) have noted that the material deposited in Grooved Ware pits was carefully selected, not merely a sample of occupation debris. It is not surprising, therefore, that some pits containing Grooved Ware in the West London area also contained wild autumnal fruits such as sloes, crab apple and hazelnuts. These suggest that representatives of the produce of the wild, non-domesticated landscape also formed part of the ceremonies, and were deposited in acts of affirmation. These deposits were the final link in a chain of events which commenced with ceremonies undertaken at the monuments.

As we will see in our final section of this chapter, these practices were to change during the period 2000–1700 BC, as people, kin-groups and the community came to terms with new conditions in society, and adapted the mechanisms of the 3rd millennium BC to a point where the manner in which land was apportioned was completely transformed.

The social origins of the landscape transformation of the 2nd millennium BC

The period between the late Neolithic (*c* 2000 BC) and middle Bronze Age (*c* 1600 BC) saw a major transformation of the Heathrow landscape that was so conspicuous that it clearly represented a correspondingly significant transformation of human engagement with the landscape. This was principally concerned with agricultural production enclosed by boundaries marked by ditches, banks and hedges. Within the enclosed areas lay fields, waterholes and permanent settlements accessed by trackways that gradually developed along the lines of the boundaries. This was a marked shift from the character of the Neolithic landscape, which was defined by highly visible major monuments set within open tracts of land that preserve more subtle traces of human activity. The society that was marked by the coming together of peoples using Grooved Ware pottery appears to have been transformed from *c* 2000 BC. A comparison between the Neolithic and Bronze Age landscapes as shown in Figure 2.28 clearly demonstrates this radical transformation, from an ancient, monumental landscape at *c* 2000 BC to the rural agricultural landscape of *c* 1700–750 BC, which would be more familiar to us today.

The change to a pattern of enclosed field systems and settlements implies an ethos of claiming ownership of land by individuals or communities, although this may not have been either sudden or dramatic, either in landscape or in ideological terms. In addition, the pattern of enclosure was not chronologically or morphologically consistent across the Heathrow area. It may have been either a relatively swift or a gradual and cumulative process, reflecting emerging and shifting relationships between individuals, communities and settlements, negotiated with reference to a consciousness and memory of the landscape they inhabited.

Chronology

Our first concern in trying to understand this revolution in landscape use is to consider chronology. The excavations at WPR98 produced over a dozen radiocarbon dates from 1600 BC to 900 cal. BC from a range of waterlogged contexts, but we have nothing from the early Bronze Age. Therefore, ceramic evidence continues to play a large part in understanding the chronology of the 2nd millennium BC (see Table 2.16).

Firstly, we must consider the chronological overlap between Grooved Ware pottery of the 3rd millennium BC and Beaker pottery which spans the late 3rd and early 2nd millennium BC. Both Grooved Ware and Beaker utilised grog-tempered fabrics, and we have already discussed the pattern of Grooved Ware deposition. The Perry Oaks excavations produced even smaller quantities of Beaker pottery, and in fact there is very little in the way of Beaker pottery at Heathrow generally, although south of the Thames it is more common. Furthermore, if

Pottery type	Date range BC
Grooved Ware	3000-2000
Beaker	2400-1700
Collared Urn	2000-1500
Deverel Rimbury	1700-1150
Post-Deverel Rimbury	1150-750

Table 2.16: Ceramics of the 2nd millennium BC

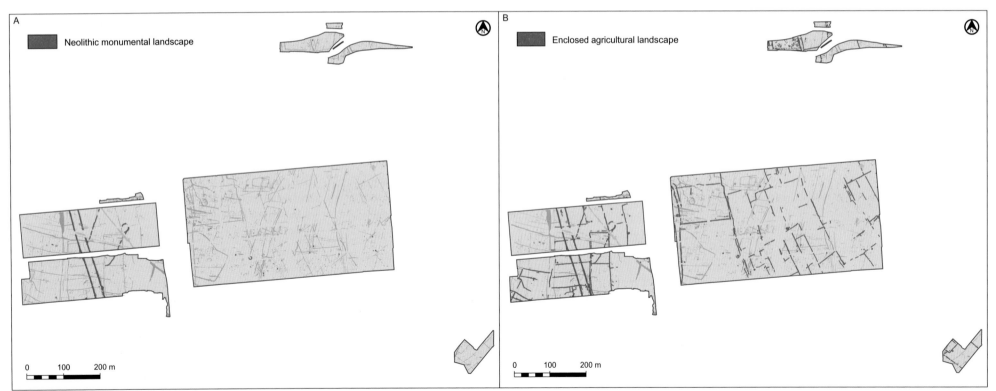

Figure 2.28: Transformation from monumental to enclosed landscape

Garwood (1999, 161) is correct, then there may have been relatively little chronological overlap in the use of Grooved Ware and Beaker pottery. In ceramic terms Heathrow has a greater representation of Collared Urns, which, although still not common, are a clear element of activity of this date. Subsequently, during the middle Bronze Age and into the late Bronze Age there was a return to an almost universal flint-tempered tradition, and body sherds can sometimes be only broadly dated as middle/late Bronze Age. The Deverel Rimbury ceramic tradition embraced a relatively conservative repertoire of forms—essentially thick-walled bucket and barrel shaped urns in coarse fabrics and smaller globular urns—generally containing better sorted and finer temper.

Lithic material can be broadly dated to the late Neolithic/early Bronze Age, a somewhat crude chronological range, apart from individual diagnostic artefact types. Lithics in the latter part of the 2nd millennium BC become increasingly crude and flake-based, and so serve as only broad chronological indicators.

There is no direct evidence from the site for environmental conditions or prevalent vegetation cover prior to 1600 BC.

Social changes

We have argued in the previous section that by the end of the 3rd millennium BC small groups of people negotiated, through ceremonies at monuments, access to and use of areas of landscape for settlement and agriculture. Tenure of land, probably on a seasonal basis, was then confirmed by the enactment of ceremonies, which included the deposition of Grooved Ware ceramics and associated lithics. Wild fruits and nuts also accompanied the process of deposition, suggesting that the ceremony occurred in autumn. We have argued that the monumental architecture and absence of large henge monuments suggests that society remained organised around smaller groups, possibly at the kin or clan level.

Our next firm chronological horizon is defined by a raft of radiocarbon dates associated with Deverel Rimbury pottery. The dates span the period 1600 to 1100 cal. BC and were obtained on material derived from pits and waterholes associated with fields and settlements contemporary with the full floruit of the middle Bronze Age 'complex' (see Chapter 3).

The period of transformation thus coincides with the early Bronze Age and corresponds, in terms of Needham's chronology (1996), with his Periods 3 (2050–1700 BC) and 4 (1700–1500 BC). These periods in West London, however, are better defined by the rarity or absence of diagnostic artefacts and monuments rather than their presence. There are no individual burials, barrows or large henge monuments unequivocally associated with Beaker pottery. Collared Urns, by comparison, are more abundant but still scarce. As Needham (ibid., 131) has pointed out, nationally there is a large degree of overlap in the chronology of late Beaker and the early and middle Bronze Age Collared Urns (Burgess 1986).

For West London and the Middle Thames in general, we are therefore unable to resolve the relationship between Collared Urns and Beaker pottery, in contrast to Burgess' treatment of the link between Collared Urns and food vessels in northern Britain (ibid., 348–9).

Early Bronze Age metalwork occurred as isolated finds across the site, but was very uncommon. The chronology of the early Bronze Age lithic repertoire, represented particularly by barbed-and-tanged arrowheads, is, as already mentioned, insufficiently precise to allow us to understand changes within the period 2000 to 1600 BC. It is also difficult to determine the association of the lithics generally with Beaker and Collared Urn ceramics.

The plan in Figure 2.29 shows the distribution of pottery and lithics that can be dated to the late Neolithic or early Bronze Age with any degree of certainty. Early Bronze Age pottery is relatively uncommon at Perry Oaks—only 32 sherds (75 g) have been tentatively assigned to this period, in almost every case on the grounds of fabric alone. All late Neolithic sherds are grog-tempered and all have been assigned to a single fabric type (GR1). While the fabric itself is visually very similar to Grooved Ware fabric GR2, sherds in GR1 are invariably oxidised, at least externally, a trait more characteristic of early Bronze Age ceramics. Only one diagnostic sherd was identified amongst this group—a comb-impressed body sherd, probably from a Beaker vessel. The remainder are all plain body sherds, and could belong either to Beakers or Collared Urns.

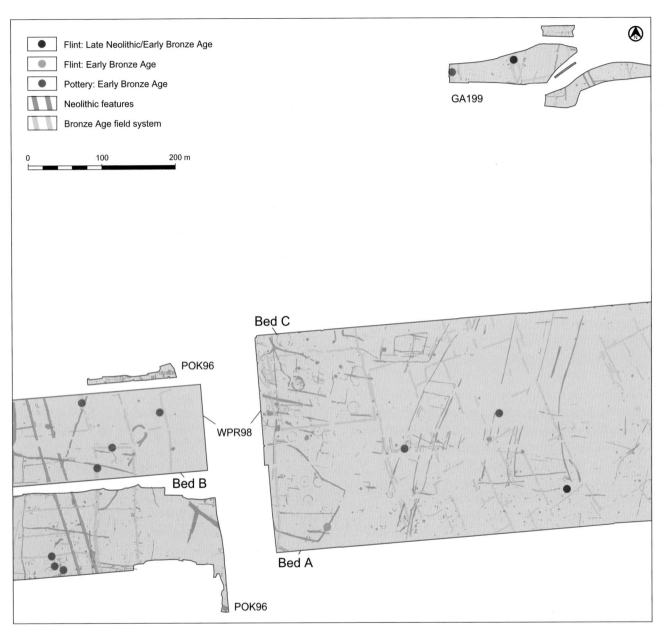

Figure 2.29: Distribution of pottery and lithics dated to the late Neolithic or early Bronze Age

Sherds were recovered from 15 contexts. Condition overall was poor, sherds are very small and abraded (mean sherd weight 2.3 g) and no context produced more than 22 g of pottery. The diagnostic Beaker sherd came from a primary ditch fill (ditch recut 105009). The overall distribution is quite dispersed across the excavated areas (Fig. 2.29), although some loose clustering can be observed on the southern edge of POK96 (ditches 961009 and 962366; pit 961024), and to the north in WPR98 Bed B (secondary fill of the eastern cursus ditch; ditch recut 105009; ditch 107029, 129006). Sherds from all of these contexts can be regarded as residual.

Lithic material is similarly sparse. Small assemblage size, residuality and chronologically imprecise technological evolution all combine to restrict the range and usefulness of lithics of definite early Bronze Age date.

The distribution pattern of artefacts residing in later features is generally similar to patterns from the 4th and 3rd millennia BC, and from this we may infer that settlement and activity patterns in the early Bronze Age landscape were broadly similar to the latter part of the 3rd millennium BC. In contrast, ceremonial monuments unequivocally dated to the early Bronze Age are rare. In West London as a whole, many small circular cropmarks attributed to the early Bronze Age, have, on excavation, proved either undatable (eg Heathrow Site A, Canham 1978) or to date to the 4th and 3rd millennia BC (eg the Perry Oaks HE1 enclosure). Excavations by Wessex Archaeology at Imperial College Sports Ground, however, recorded a round barrow that had been inserted into an existing small Neolithic circular enclosure, although unfortunately the associated primary cremation was undated (Crockett 2001). However, a barrow with a Collared Urn cremation was excavated adjacent to the Thames on the Surrey bank at Hurst Park (Andrews 1996).

Early Bronze Age round barrows are usually associated with individualised burial rites and personalised artefacts, despite the occurrence of successions of later inserted burials. Barrows and Beakers tend to denote individuality and high status. The paucity of evidence of this type from across the large area excavated at T5 suggests that this tradition was virtually absent in the vicinity of Heathrow.

Clearly people were still present in the landscape, and living in a broadly similar fashion to the late 3rd millennium BC. The reasons for the extreme scarcity of Beaker ceramics, burial traditions and monuments are unclear, although it is possible that Beaker ritual and funerary activity were re-located to a focus on the floodplains of the Thames and its tributaries, as suggested by wider distributional patterns (Brown and Cotton 2000, 85). It is also possible that in this part of the Middle Thames at least, there was a closer chronological relationship between Neolithic Grooved Ware (or even late Peterborough Ware) and Collared Urns. The Beaker 'package' was adopted only in part, for example lithics, and did not find a hold in society. We have argued previously that late Neolithic society in West London was not geared towards the sort of

powerful individuals and leaders who emerged from the ceremonies associated with the large monuments of the day. Instead society was centred on small kin or extended kin-groups, whose mechanism of land access and usage we have previously described. However it is clear that between 2000 and 1600 BC that centuries-old mechanism was breaking down or transforming. Society sought new ways of dealing with the problems of land access and tenure, although why this occurred we do not know. It could have been due to population growth or any number of other interrelated or unrelated factors. Nonetheless, we can see from the depositional contexts of Collared Urns an attempt to accommodate new monumental and burial traditions with old traditions of ceremonies resulting in deposition of material in pits.

For example, the six Conygar Hill type barbed-and-tanged arrowheads used to kill an aurochs, which was butchered and buried in a large pit at Holloway Lane to the north of T5 (Brown and Cotton 2000), are nationally associated with food vessels and Collared Urns (Green 1980 130). No ceramics were recovered from this pit, but the act of deposition clearly has echoes of the Grooved Ware pits of the late 3rd millennium BC. In fact, the pit containing the aurochs was excavated through a small pit containing Grooved Ware (Brown and Cotton 2000, 86) and other Grooved Ware pits were close by. Cotton has speculated (Lewis 2000, 74) that the aurochs burial may be the culmination of the Neolithic 'structured deposition' tradition, although if it is the culmination, then it also heralds changes. The aurochs was a

wild animal of some rarity by the early 2nd millennium BC, and its deposition is in contrast to the wild fruits and nuts predominantly associated with Grooved Ware depositional practices.

Excavations in Area 91 of T5 revealed a pit containing Grooved Ware, which was cut by another pit containing relatively large quantities of Collared Urn (see Vol. 2). There were no traces of cremated bone, and this too appears to be an attempt to continue the tradition of ceremonies culminating in the deposition of material employed in the ritual. It may well be, however, that these attempts at continuing the tradition of negotiated land access eventually proved insufficient and that social agreements following ceremonies of deposition gave way to more formal agreements manifested in more blatantly physical demonstrations of the negotiation process.

We have already mentioned the first occurrence of barrows and cremation burials, perhaps the first indication of a concern with treating certain individuals differently and erecting monuments around them. It would be logical to suggest that this provided the more formal mechanism for asserting land tenure which people adopted in the early 2nd millennium BC. However, even in these cases there is a clear link with the past. For example, the Imperial College barrow was constructed within an existing small Neolithic enclosure, and although undated, it must be presumed to date to the early Bronze Age. Elsewhere on the Imperial College site, two Collared Urns were associated with cremated remains buried in a pit, located close to a deep shaft or well containing Peterborough Ware. At Hurst Park, the barrow enclosing a Collared Urn cremation burial enclosed a shallow oval 'scoop' or tree-throw containing Grooved Ware. Located 30 m to the west of the barrow was a large rectangular feature containing six sherds of Peterborough Ware.

In all of these cases we see a clear link with the practices of the 3rd millennium BC, which we have argued were concerned with ceremonies relating to affirmation of land access and resources. The practice of cremation and the construction of barrows at these locations could represent a change in the methods of laying claim to land and resources. Instead of the deposition of ceramics, lithics and wild produce following ceremonies, human bodies were cremated, buried with Collared Urns and the places marked with monuments. The monuments were clear physical markers of territory and the association of individuals of defined ancestries with that land.

Once again we have no refined chronological outline for this process, and do not know how long these practices continued. Put crudely however, the Imperial College and Hurst Park Collared Urns fit in the Late Series of Burgess' classification, which in turn accords with Needham's Period 4, 1700–1500 BC (Needham 1996, 132). These would appear to be crucial

centuries, since evidence from Perry Oaks indicates that the first division of the landscape by formal field boundaries took place during this period or even earlier. Most importantly, Needham (1996, 132) has suggested that Deverel Rimbury pottery probably originated in his Period 4, which accords with the appearance of land division and the first proper settlements (see Chapter 3).

If we accept that the adoption of cremation burial, sometimes accompanied by barrows and Collared Urns, was an attempt at formalising claims to land and resources, then it would appear that after an unknown period even this approach was not sufficient to achieve a long lasting agreement over access to resources. The strategy of excavating a series of banked and ditched boundaries across the landscape was thus a logical progression in a series of progressively more overt attempts at claiming land tenure.

It would thus appear that the unified community which built the Neolithic monumental landscape of 3600 to 3300 BC had itself undergone transformation during the 3rd millennium BC. After many years of the community living contentedly within the monumental and social architecture they had constructed in the latter half of the 4th millennium BC, we have suggested the second half of the 3rd and early 2nd millennia BC saw an increasing trend towards more overt

ceremonial and physical affirmation of claims to land and resources. It would thus appear that the unity of the community was breaking down, and these mechanisms may have developed as an increasingly desperate attempt to maintain orderly access to resources, and therefore to retain community cohesiveness. Indeed, if we accept the physical division of the landscape by the first field boundaries as being a logical progression of this process, then it would appear that the community of kin-groups had finally broken down.

It could be argued that the act of landscape division was itself an expression of the importance of the individual and the small group, an imperative which elsewhere in the country was expressed by the adoption of high status monuments and artefacts such as barrow burials, rich grave goods, metalwork, Beaker and other forms of ceramics. However, in the Heathrow area there may have been a more egalitarian backdrop to the apparently personalised activity of splitting off plots of land from a previously communal landscape. In the following chapter we will examine how the landscape was divided and how it developed through the latter half of the 2nd millennium BC. We will show how the individual landholdings reflected the individual kin-groups, and how these locked together to form a field system which was the product of the overarching community.

CHAPTER 3

The emergence of the agricultural landscape from the early-middle Bronze Age to the end of the early Iron Age (*c* 1700 BC–400 BC)

by John Lewis and Angela Batt

CD-Rom queries
Trackways and landholdings
Insect analysis from Bronze Age waterholes
Pollen analysis from Bronze Age waterholes
Plant analysis from Bronze Age waterholes
Radiocarbon dates from Bronze Age waterholes
Bronze Age metal objects
Bronze Age trackways 1-7
Bronze Age landholdings 1-7
Settlement 1
Settlement 2
Settlement 3
Settlement 4
Settlement 5
Settlement 6
Waterholes and pits
Burnt flint from fields and trackways
Bronze Age burnt mound complex

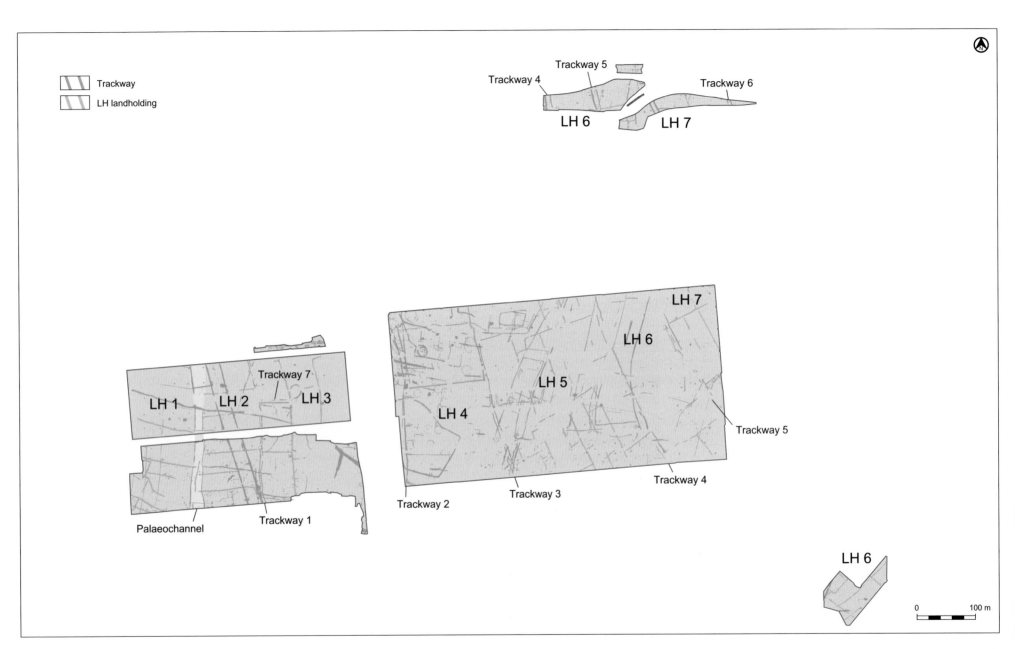

Figure 3.1: Bronze Age trackways and landholdings

Introduction

This chapter is concerned with the history of the 2nd and early 1st millennium BC, roughly from *c* 1700 to 400 BC. During these 1300 years the landscape was transformed from one dominated by the monuments and practices of the preceding two millennia to a landscape of fields, hedgerows, settlements and trackways: the kind of landscape we would recognise today. Figure 3.1 shows the landscape as it had developed by *c* 750 BC. We have divided the landscape into a series of landholdings (LH) divided by north-south trackways (and one east-west trackway), and the development of this system will be examined in some detail. We will explore the reasons for and mechanisms of this transformation, and how the development of the landscape through the 2nd millennium BC drove changes in society.

Throughout this chapter we will continue the theme developed in the preceding chapter: the dynamics of the relationship between the individual, the kin-group and the wider community. We will discuss how sometimes during the 2nd millennium BC the community may have been weakened at the expense of the kin-groups, but how through various social mechanisms and the success of the mixed agricultural farming regime,

Pottery type	Date range BC
Beaker	2400 - 1700
Collared Urn	2000 - 1500
Deverel Rimbury	1700 - 1150
Post-Deverel Rimbury	1150 - 750

Table 3.1: Date range of Bronze Age pottery

the kin-groups became subsumed into the community once more during the period 1150–750 BC.

Chronological framework

We will attempt to follow the chronology outlined by Needham (1996) wherever possible, and Figure 3.2 is a simplified amalgamation of the tables presented in that paper. The main chronological indicators will be discussed throughout this chapter, but can be summarised as: radiocarbon dates, pottery assemblages and metalwork.

A total of 25 radiocarbon dates were obtained, ranging from 1610–1390 cal BC to 840–480 cal BC at two standard deviations, with majority clustering in the period 1600–1100 cal BC. Unfortunately the two standard deviation range of most of these dates is not very precise, only allowing us to assign activity to the general periods 4, 5 or 6 in Needham's scheme, and usual only to the latter two.

The ceramic assemblages from Perry Oaks contain residual scraps of Beaker and Collared Urn, but are dominated by Deverel Rimbury and Post-Deverel Rimbury ceramics (Table 3.1). These allow us to differentiate between the periods 1700 to 1150 BC and 1150 to 750 BC. However, Figure 3.2 implies a chronological overlap between these two ceramic assemblages, and many features, such as field ditches and waterholes, contained both types of pottery. Common sense might dictate that the two types coexisted at some time, but we are unable to be precise about this at Perry Oaks.

Only two pieces of Bronze Age metalwork were recovered from Perry Oaks: a spiral finger- or thumb-ring and a side looped spearhead. Both date to the Taunton metalwork phase, between 1500 and 1200 BC, and are discussed more fully in the next section.

The inception of the 2nd millennium BC field system

This section explores the chronology of the enclosed landscape of the 2nd millennium BC and considers how it emerged from the Neolithic landscape of the 3rd millennium BC. Such a transformation from the open, monumental Neolithic landscape to the Bronze Age pattern of enclosed fields and trackways is a crucial development in the history of the British landscape, and four sources of information have been used in establishing a chronology for this period (see Fig. 3.2):

- radiocarbon dates

- stratigraphy

- metalwork

- palaeoenvironmental evidence

This evidence has indicated that the enclosure system originated sometime between 2000 and 1700 BC and reached its maturity around 1600–1500 BC, although in Landholding 4 the development of enclosure may have begun later in the Bronze Age, after 1500 BC.

Calendrical dates BC	2300	2200	2100	2000	1900	1800	1700	1600	1500	1400	1300	1200	1100	1000	900	800	700
Traditional periods	Metal using Neolithic			Early Bronze Age						Middle Bronze Age			Late Bronze Age				Iron Age
Needham's periods	Period 2		Period 3					Period 4		Period 5			Period 6		Period 7		
Metalwork assemblages						MA VI: Arreton											
							Acton Park 1 & 2										
								Taunton									
									Pennard/Wallington								
										Wilburton							
											Blackmore						
												Ewart Park					
Pottery assemblages	Beaker																
		Collard Urn															
					Deverel-Rimbury												
								Post-Deveral-Rimbury									

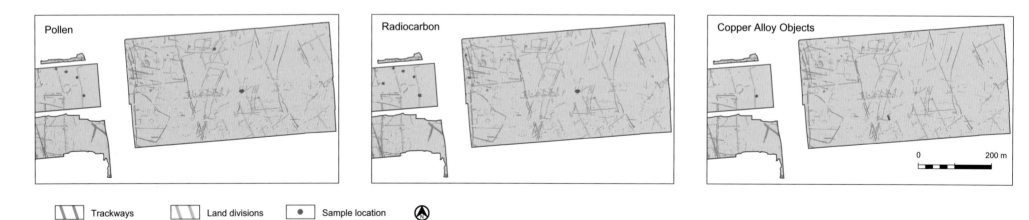

Pollen   Radiocarbon   Copper Alloy Objects

0   200 m

◫ Trackways   ◫ Land divisions   • Sample location

Figure 3.2: Late Neolithic/Bronze Age chronology (simplified version of Needham's 1996 figures 1, 2 and 3) and location of chronological evidence at Perry Oaks

Radiocarbon dates

The radiocarbon sampling strategy sought to establish a chronological framework for the emerging landscape of the 2nd millennium BC, and was designed to address several key questions:

- to date the formation and filling of features;

- to date deposits containing coherent groups of pottery in order to provide absolute dating for the ceramic type series;

- to date the manufacture and use of organic artefacts;

- to secure dates from the palynological sequences.

This section is concerned with radiocarbon dates obtained from the fills of large waterholes and associated organic objects (Fig. 3.3). Many of the best-preserved waterlogged sediments and wooden objects were located within c 100 m of each other in Landholding 3 (see Fig. 3.4), the earliest part of the developed landscape. The dated materials comprised two wooden socketed axe/tool hafts, two wooden 'beaters', stakes from pit revetments, cereal glume bases and organic sediments. The dates obtained range from 1610 BC to 1210 BC.

Results

Although the dates are spread, it is clear that the waterholes were excavated and began filling at a time when Deverel Rimbury pottery was in use. The major land divisions occurred c 1600–1300 BC, with the boundary ditches subsequently silting up. Waterholes 110107 and 156031 in Landholding 3 cut two of these silted major north-south land divisions, indicating that they were later insertions into the landscape.

A date was obtained from a wooden haft preserved in the socket of a copper alloy spearhead, recovered from the re-cut of a silted field ditch in Landholding 5. The significance of the 1308–940 BC date is discussed below. The date is somewhat late compared to those from Landholding 3, but provides a benchmark for comparison of metalwork typology with an absolute date.

Radiocarbon dates were obtained from waterhole 124100 in Landholding 5 (WK 10023, WK10033 and WK10034). The date range of 1520–1100 BC (cal BC 2 sigma) is contemporary with those from Landholding 3 to the west.

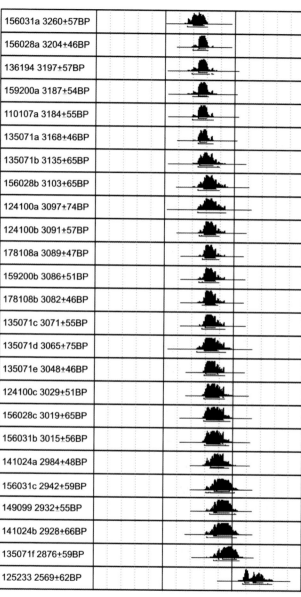

3000Cal BC   2000Cal BC   1000Cal BC

Figure 3.3: Bronze Age radiocarbon dates

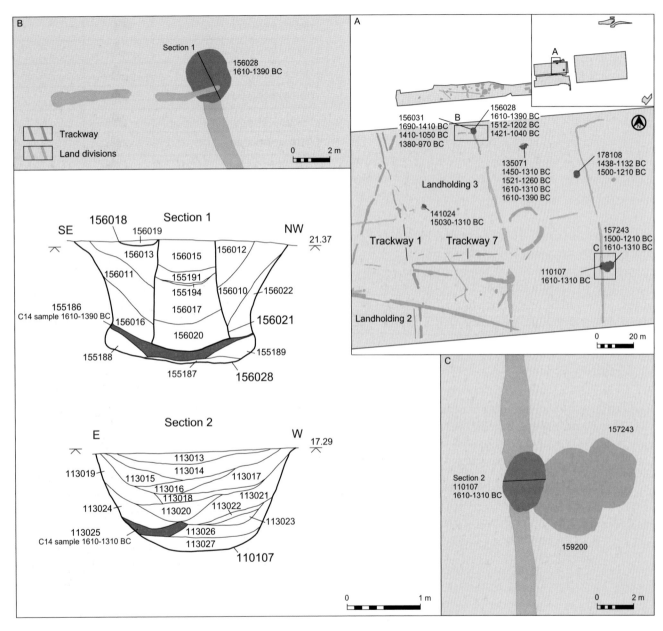

Figure 3.4: Radiocarbon dates from Landholding 3

Stratigraphy: Bronze Age land enclosures with the Neolithic monuments of the 3rd and 4th millennium BC

At some point between *c* 2000 BC and 1600 BC a major transformation of the landscape took place. Previously open areas were enclosed and the construction of boundaries would have restricted movement. This process began with the integration of the monuments of the 4th and 3rd millennia BC into the enclosed landscape of the 2nd millennium BC. The stratigraphic relationships that attest to this transformation within Landholdings 2 and 3 are examined in detail here (Fig. 3.5).

Two important stratigraphic relationships are apparent.

- None of the major 2nd millennium BC north-south aligned enclosure ditches cut across Neolithic monuments.

- The east-west enclosure ditches clearly did cut across Neolithic monuments.

The first observation is illustrated by the C1 Stanwell Cursus and the adjacent 2nd millennium north-south aligned boundaries, which all respect the cursus. Other north-south boundaries also avoid the early monuments or navigate through existing gaps in ditches and banks. For instance, ditch 110009, a recut of 110014, curves around the western side of the horseshoe enclosure and through a gap in the southern bank and ditch of the second cursus. Similarly, field boundary

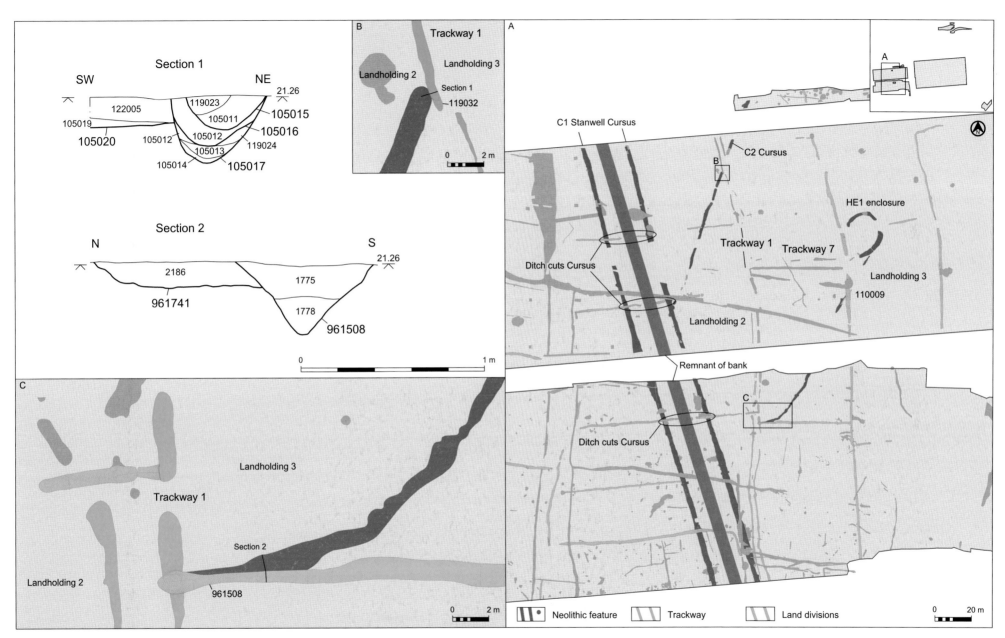

Figure 3.5: Stratigraphic relationships in Landholdings 2 and 3

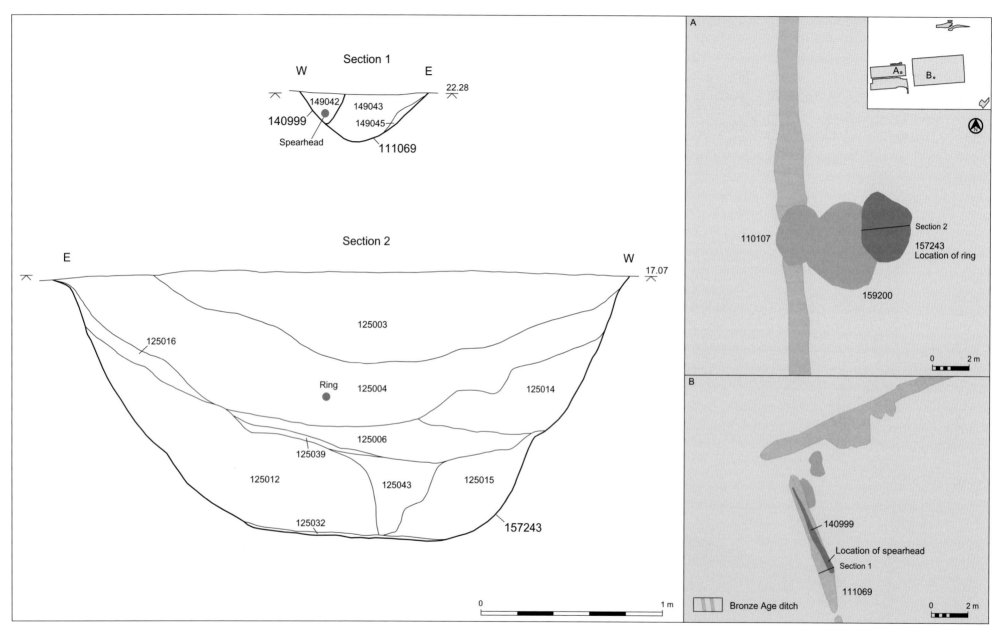

Figure 3.6: Plan of site with copper alloy objects located

119032 carefully negotiates the existing gaps in the northern ditch and bank of the second cursus.

In contrast, a series of east-west aligned ditches cut across the Stanwell Cursus, demonstrating that these boundaries do not respect the monument. The gaps in the east-west ditches at the centre of the cursus indicate the points at which the ditches cut into the decayed and eroded remnant of the central cursus bank (see Fig. 3.5). Furthermore, the east-west field boundary ditch 961508 cuts the southern terminal of the southern ditch of the C2 Cursus.

These stratigraphic relationships are important, since elsewhere in this chapter we will show that, in general, the first elements of the 2nd millennium BC land enclosures were the north-south ditches, followed by east-west subdivisions. Clearly then, the earliest elements of this enclosure system respected the Neolithic monuments, although by the time the later sub-divisions were constructed, the Neolithic landscape was being overwritten by the imperatives of living in a changed world.

Bronze Age Metalwork

Two copper alloy objects dating to the 2nd millennium BC were recovered, a spiral finger ring and a spearhead (Fig. 3.6). Both provide some evidence that contributes to our understanding of the chronology of land enclosure during this period. The objects are typologically assigned to the Taunton phase of the middle Bronze Age and are paralleled elsewhere.

The Ring (Fig. 3.7)

The ring is formed from a stout, coiled rod of oval section with smoothly rounded ends. Objects of this type are normally regarded as personal ornaments on the basis of continental parallels, but they may have served other functions. The diameter of the ring is more consistent with an interpretation as a thumb rather than a finger ring, although a toe ring is also a possibility. The ring was recovered from the central part of an upper fill (125004) within a well (157243) (see Fig. 3.6). The significance of this location is twofold:

- The well was situated close to a north-south aligned ditch, which was possibly associated with an old hedgerow.

- The well cut waterhole 159200, which was also cut by waterhole 110107. This suggests that this particular location was a focus of regular use.

Two interpretations for the deposition of the ring can be suggested. It may have been redeposited from the earlier waterhole, or else it could have been deposited as a curated, significant votive object. The presence of possible Post-Deverel Rimbury pottery in the waterhole suggests that the former explanation is most likely.

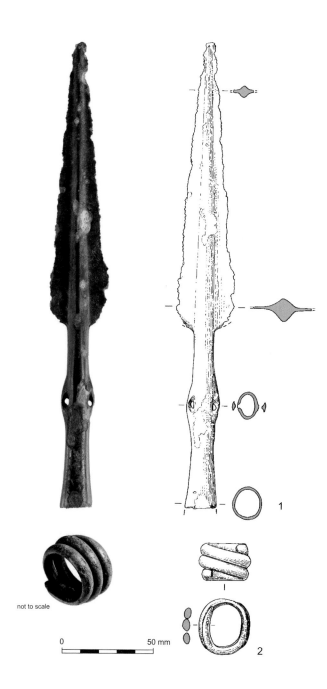

not to scale

0   50 mm

Figure 3.7: Copper alloy ring and spear head

The Spearhead (Fig. 3.7)

The spearhead is a Taunton phase middle Bronze Age type, cast with a hollow socket and side loops. It was recovered from recut ditch 149099 (Fig. 3.6), the western boundary of a Bronze Age field system in Landholding 5.

The chronology of this type has been discussed at length (eg Ehrenburg 1977, 7–9; Rowlands 1976, Ch. II 3), while associated radiocarbon dates have been assessed by Needham *et al.* (1997). Although Needham *et al.* (ibid., 85) admit to some imprecision in the dating of metalwork of the Taunton phase, as a result of the re-use and long functional life of spearheads, a date between 1450 and 1250 cal BC would seem appropriate.

A radiocarbon date from wood (ash) preserved in the haft of the spearhead confirmed the middle Bronze Age date (NZA14907; 2932±55 BP) of 1308–940 cal BC (2 sigma), which could appear slightly later than the suggested typological date. Repeated re-hafting of the spearhead over several hundred years may explain this anomaly. Re-hafting would also emphasise the potential for reuse of functional bronze and acts of deliberate deposition of curated or 'heirloom' objects, where the antiquity of the object is recognised and valued.

The context of the spearhead is even more significant than that of the ring. It was located within a shallow recut (feature 149099) of a Bronze Age ditch (111069) in Landholding 5. If the spearhead had been deposited in the recut sometime between *c* 1308 and 940 BC, the construction of the original ditch and associated field bank could have preceded this event by several centuries.

Palaeoenvironmental evidence for hedgerow origins prior to 1600 BC

Figure 3.8 shows the position of waterholes which provided palaeoenvironmental evidence from the period *c* 1600 to 750 BC. The detailed reports on this data (pollen, Wiltshire; insects, Robinson; waterlogged plant remains, Carruthers) are contained on the accompanying CD-Rom. In this section we will summarise the pollen evidence from the middle Bronze Age waterholes 124100, 135071, 178108 and 156031 (discussed in more detail below), and show how this information has contributed to our belief that the initial construction of the land boundaries pre-dated *c* 1600 BC. All of these waterholes were located adjacent to ditches and banks which would have supported hedgerows, with the exception of 135071 which was equidistant between two hedgerows.

Wiltshire has summarised the pollen evidence to address two main questions:

How did the hedges form?

There are several possibilities for hedgerow formation. They can be formed from (a) selective clearance of primaeval woodland (assarting), (b) by default (natural colonisation after erection of semi-temporary artificial boundaries), and (c) by active planting of appropriate and available shrub species. The existence of obvious banks and ditches at Perry Oaks precludes the development by assarting so this leaves natural colonisation or planting. Either was possible.

When did the hedges form?

The hedges themselves were very diverse. There is little doubt that trees such as alder, birch, pine, and elm were growing away from the immediate settlement but some trees (such as lime and possibly ash) and a wide range of shrubs were growing very locally and could have been components of the managed hedgerow systems. Shrubs included field maple, hazel, dogwood, purging buckthorn, alder buckthorn, hawthorn, sloe, elder, and guelder rose. It is also possible that the hedgerow supported standard oaks, which could have provided important resources, while honeysuckle, ivy, and bramble were also significant components of the hedge community. The presence of ivy and honeysuckle gives additional credibility to the contention that the shrubs had been allowed to grow fairly tall. Herbaceous plants are always important components of any hedgerow and bank. They provide soft and palatable food for many animals, and the hedge itself provides a protective haven for this complex community. Many of the herbs and ferns recorded in both the palynological and macrofossil record for the site could have been well established in the hedgebank.

Based on the species composition deduced from the palynological and other environmental evidence, and relying on suggestions made by

Figure 3.8: Waterholes dating from 1600 to 750 BC containing palaeoenvironmental evidence

Rackham (1986), it is likely that the hedges were at least 500 years old by the time that the waterholes were dug. It has been suggested that both hazel and field maple take a long time to colonise natural hedgerows and, further, that any hedgerow containing field maple is likely to be at least 400 to 500 years old (ibid.). This confirms that the hedgerows at Perry Oaks were well established and, indeed, very old before the waterholes were dug. Even some herbaceous plants are indicators of old hedges. *Mercurialis* (dog's mercury) was found in waterhole 124100 and it was probably growing at the base of the hedge adjacent to this feature. Even today, this plant is an indicator of ancient woodland, and is a frequent member of herbaceous communities associated with ancient hedges.

Given the reliability of radiocarbon estimates (at 2 sigma) from the four waterholes (see above), this would mean that the hedges originated some time between 2020 and 1610 BC (cal). This implies that the landscape was extensively cleared by the early Bronze Age to allow the setting out of the major land boundaries.

Building the system—Development of the trackways and landholdings

In the previous section we discussed the chronology of the inception of the enclosed landscape of the 2nd millennium BC. In this section we will explore how the enclosure of the landscape developed through the 2nd and into the early 1st millennia BC. But let us start by continuing

the palaeoenvironmental summary of the palynological, entomological and other botanical evidence to paint a picture of what the landscape would have looked like during the formation of the waterholes and development of the trackways and landholdings between *c* 1600 and 1100 BC. The following section is derived from Pat Wiltshire's pollen report, which can be found in full on the CD-Rom, Section 11.

What did the landscape look like during the latter half of the 2nd millennium BC?

The landscape of the latter half of the 2nd millennium BC had already been established for many centuries, with the terrain largely cleared of woodland. However, there were certainly some trees in the landscape, with alder probably growing further towards the river and small stands or isolated trees, including birch, pine, lime and elm, dotted around Landholding 3 and beyond. The pattern of land use and management had long been in existence and had resulted in a patchwork of fields, lanes, and hedgerows that provided for the needs of the local communities.

There is little doubt that people were engaged in mixed farming, and the environmental evidence tells the story of everyday domestic and small-scale agricultural activity and management. The ditches (and associated banks) of the field boundaries, as well as functioning as land divisions, could also provide drainage for the brickearth-derived soils overlying the Thames gravels. Gradually, through natural succession,

these banks became colonised by vegetation and eventually by shrubs and even trees. Thus, productive hedgerows could have developed by default and, once established, were probably nurtured and maintained through careful management. Essentially, hedgerows represent 'woodland edge', the most productive part of any woodland in terms of food and other resources.

The palynological evidence suggests that the shrubs in the hedgerows were allowed to grow tall enough to produce flowers. They were not maintained by regular severe cutting as is characteristic of the modern British landscape. The base of the hedgebank would have provided a haven for many herbs—grasses and flowering plants—and been home to small mammals, birds, invertebrates, and even reptiles. In short, the hedgerow provides a rich, diverse habitat for plants and animals and these can be exploited by people. The palynological evidence also suggests that by the second half of the 2nd millennium BC, these hedgerows were already established and certainly very old.

The hedges and banks separated the fields, which were seemingly used for stock animals and crop growing (see below). Successful pastoral farming implies good pasture and there is evidence for established grassland. The only evidence for crop plants was of barley, wheat (emmer and spelt), and flax but it is possible that other foods and utility plants were also being grown. Animal husbandry was important and there is tentative evidence that sheep were kept as well as cattle and pigs. It is probable that the farming community also exploited the wider landscape for food, wood, and other resources such as fibre, fodder, medicines, and dye plants. The hedges and woodland edges were certainly rich in berries and nuts and there is ample evidence for bramble, hazel, purging buckthorn, sloe, and elder.

Settlements were built within each of the landholdings (see below), and around these areas was evidence for broken trampled soils and waste ground. There was certainly some degree of soil impoverishment during the life of the settlement; bracken and heather were recorded at low level and these imply poor, acidic soils. These plants may have been infesting poor pasture outside the settlement.

There is little doubt that the picture presented by the environmental evidence from the waterholes at Perry Oaks is of the modern concept of a rural idyll. It must have been exceedingly colourful with hedges full of spring flowering shrubs, full of honeysuckle in summer, and providing rich autumn colour from berries and foliage. Verdant fields offered herb-rich grassland— buttercups, daisies, flowering grasses, and milkwort. Even the trampled areas under herds and flocks, and around the settlements, supported diverse herb-rich ground and pretty grassy edges. Some of the waterholes themselves must have been very attractive with meadowsweet, loosestrife, watermint, crowfoot, pondweed and iris.

Social context of landscape division

If, as discussed above, social pressures led to creation of the first land boundaries in the first half of the 2nd millennium BC, we may pose the following question: does the division of the landscape mark the fragmentation of the community into smaller constituent groups, or did the community evolve to accommodate the increased importance of group identity?

We have chosen to explore this question by studying the way the landscape developed and became increasingly sub-divided during the 2nd millennium BC. By seeking to understand these physical developments, we can attempt to interpret the social dynamics that drove them. A relatively coarse level of analysis has been adopted at this stage, since a much greater area of landscape will be available for study once excavation at T5 is complete, and will be presented in Volume 2.

Figure 3.1 at the beginning of this chapter shows that the field system is divided into seven landholdings and seven double-ditched trackways. The trackways have been numbered from 1 to 7 (all but Trackway 7 north-south), and the blocks of field systems defined by these trackways have been referred to as Landholdings (LH) 1 to 7.

The trackways and landholdings have undergone varying degrees of recent truncation. In general, the eastern landholdings (6 and 7) and trackways (4 to 6) have been subject to most destruction but others (eg Landholding 3) have also undergone severe truncation. This variability in survival has affected analysis, with, for example, very few of the field or trackway ditches retaining their stratigraphic relationships. This has proved a major obstacle in understanding the developmental history of the field system. Even from an incomplete plan, however, it is clear that the fields within each landholding maintained a general coherence in size, shape and orientation, although these properties differ markedly between each landholding. With the exception of short east-west Trackway 7, the trackways are all on a north-south or NW-SE orientation.

We can see from Figure 3.1 that the double-ditched trackways defined distinct blocks of land that were laid out and developed in different ways. To understand that development, we must look first at the history of the trackways.

Development of the trackways

As already discussed above, circumstantial and indirect evidence may lead us to believe that the first major land boundaries were laid out sometime between 2000 and 1600 BC, and that these boundaries were aligned north-south. We believe that those boundaries which developed into double-ditched trackways were the first to be dug, and served as the major boundaries for individual landholdings. A number of strands of evidence lead us to this conclusion.

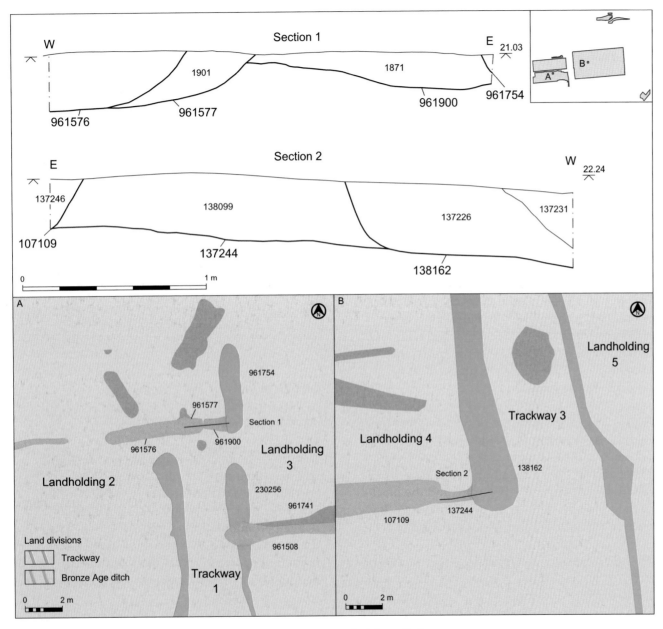

W
Section 1
E 21.03

1901

1871

961577
961900 961754

961576

E
Section 2
W 22.24

137246

138099
137226 137231

107109
137244

138162

0   1 m

A

961754

961577

Section 1

961576 961900

Landholding 3

Landholding 2

230256

961741

Land divisions

Trackway

Bronze Age ditch

0   2 m

Trackway 1

961508

B

Landholding 5

Trackway 3

Landholding 4

Section 2

138162

107109 137244

0   2 m

Figure 3.9: Relationships between trackway ditches and landholding ditches

Stratigraphy

Only three unambiguous stratigraphic relationships between trackway ditches and landholding ditches were recorded (Figs 3.9–10). The first lay within the area of Trackway 1, where ditches from Landholdings 2 and 3 converge with the southern ditch of the Neolithic C2 Cursus (Fig. 3.9). Here, C2 Cursus ditch 961741 is cut by north-south ditch segment 230256, which is part of Trackway 1. This is in turn, cut by east-west ditch 961508, which is part of Landholding 3. However, immediately to the north the primacy of the north-south trackway ditch is less clear. Here, the first feature appears to be an elongated pit, 961900. This is cut by both trackway segment 961754 and ditch segment 961577 in Landholding 2.

Small pits of this type are present in other areas of the landscape, such as where Trackway 3 ditch 138162 and Landholding 4 ditch 107109 meet (Fig. 3.9). In plan it looks as though a short length of ditch 137244 was dug to link the two, but the reverse is true. Ditch/pit 137244 is stratigraphically the earliest feature, and is cut by the trackway and landholding ditches. These small pits and their associated spoil may represent a temporary marking out of the main landholding boundaries, but their small size and subsequent digging of the field and trackway ditches have obscured their original function.

The second example concerns the relationship between Trackway 2 and Landholding 4 (Fig. 3.10). Eastern trackway ditch 119303 cuts

Landholding 4 ditch 108043. However ditch 119303 is shallower (0.6 m deep) than western trackway ditch 160233 (1.0 m deep), suggesting that the western ditch was the original boundary. The recent T5 excavations have confirmed that 119303 is a later addition which forms the double ditched trackway. In this case there is no stratigraphic relationship between Landholding 4 ditch and the primary element of the land boundary (ditch 160233) that became Trackway 2.

The relationship between Trackway 5 and Landholding 7 is the final example (Fig. 3.10). Here, trackway ditch 121104 is cut by landholding ditch 121106. However, on the opposite side of the trackway, it appears as though ditch 149131 is superseded by ditch 149141, presumably in order to reduce the width of Trackway 5.

To summarise, there are two examples of east-west field boundaries cutting trackway ditches, and one example of the reverse. Additional stratigraphic relationships have been recorded between field boundaries within the landholdings. In six of eight examples, east-west ditches are cut by north-south ditches and in one case the reverse is true. The final example resembles that shown in Fig. 3.9, with a small gully cut by two later ditches.

The stratigraphic evidence indicates that the original ditches and banks which were modified as trackways were the earliest division of the open landscape. Had they been inserted into a pre-existing field system, many more stratigraphic relationships would have been apparent. It seems

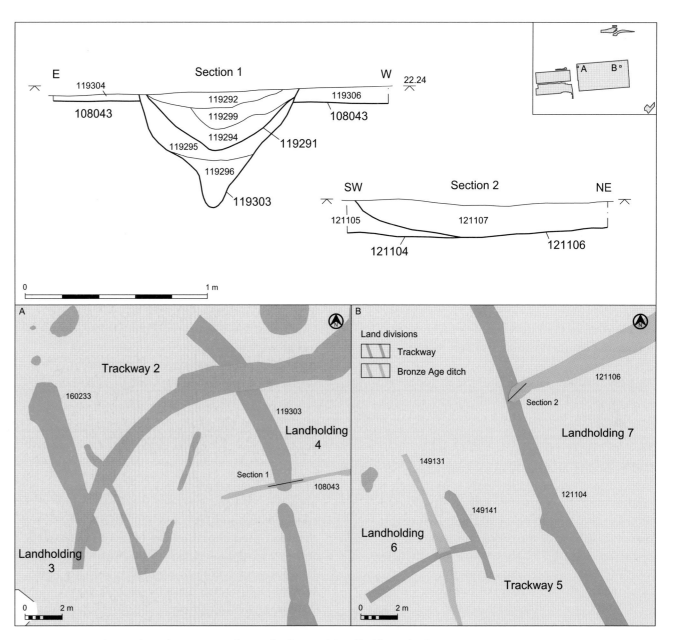

Figure 3.10: Relationships between trackway ditches and landholding ditches

also that the first land boundaries superseded pits and associated spoil heaps that acted as markers for early landholdings.

This apportionment of land may have reflected the break-up of the community of the 3rd millennium BC into constituent kin-groups, each with their own landholding. This division of the landscape was apparently undertaken in an orderly way, as blocks of land may have differed in width, but they lay on the same orientation. This apportionment of land was probably not imposed by a single authority, since, as we have noted previously, high status artefactual and burial paraphernalia of the early Bronze Age are conspicuously lacking in West London. Instead, the constituent groups within the community appear to have agreed on a system of land division that resolved the increasing conflict over access and resources.

As previously discussed, the first major boundaries respected the monuments of the 4th and 3rd millennia, but also took clear account of small variations in the relatively flat topography of the area (Fig. 3.11). Once the major land boundaries had been dug and the banks constructed, the field system evolved differently within each landholding. Each possible kin-group divided their landholding to best suit their own requirements and those of the topography and local resources. Figure 3.11 shows how the ditches of Landholdings 1 and 2 cut across the contours and ran towards the floodplain of the River Colne. In contrast, the landholding ditches and trackways to the east of Trackway 2 ran roughly parallel with the 23 m contour.

There appears to have been a general trend for the long rectangular north-south aligned landholdings to have been initially divided into smaller fields by east-west ditches and banks, before further sub-division by additional north-south ditches. This is, however, a generalisation, and the long north-south orientated fields of Landholding 3, for example, seem to be an exception. Of course, in order to lay out major linear land boundaries and finer field divisions the landscape must, to some degree, have been cleared of trees, and we will consider the palaeoenvironmental evidence for this later in this chapter.

It appears that the development of the landholdings and trackways reflected the ascendancy of individual kin-groups over the larger community, but as we shall see when we examine the chronological development of the system, this may have been a short lived phenomenon.

Chronology of the development of the trackways and landholdings

The first major land boundaries were dug between 2000 and 1600 BC, probably in the centuries around 1800 and 1700 BC. We have demonstrated above, on the basis of relatively few stratigraphic relationships, how these major landholdings were sub-divided into fields and how the land boundaries developed into double-ditched trackways. The chronology of these developments is, however, far from clear for several reasons. Firstly, there are no radiocarbon

dates from the field boundaries and trackways, as organic materials were preserved only at the base of large pits and waterholes. Secondly, the relative ceramic sequence is based on Deverel Rimbury and Post-Deverel Rimbury wares. On the basis of Needham's (1996) chronological framework, Deverel Rimbury pottery could have been in use through Periods 4 and 5 (1700 BC to 1150 BC) and Post-Deverel Rimbury pottery through Periods 6 and 7 (1150 BC to 750 BC). The context of these ceramics within the trackways and field systems should, therefore, provide a relative chronology of Period 4/5 or 6/7, although recutting of the upper fills of ditches has resulted in the mixing of Deverel Rimbury and Post-Deverel Rimbury ceramics. Furthermore, the truncation of much of the field system by the construction and operation of the sludge works has removed the upper part of many of the ditches, thus depriving us of the full silting sequence. However, if we chart the amount of Deverel Rimbury and Post-Deverel Rimbury pottery from each trackway and landholding, we can at least gain an idea of the relative development of these entities in the periods 1700–1150 BC and 1150–750 BC.

The chart (a) in Figure 3.12 is presented by trackway and landholding from west to east across the landscape. The chart reflects the relative area of landholding available for excavation and the varying degrees of truncation.

There is a trace residue across the landscape of pottery from Needham's (1996) Periods 3 and 4 (The early Bronze Age, 2050–1700 and 1700–1500 BC) in the small sherds of Beaker and Collared

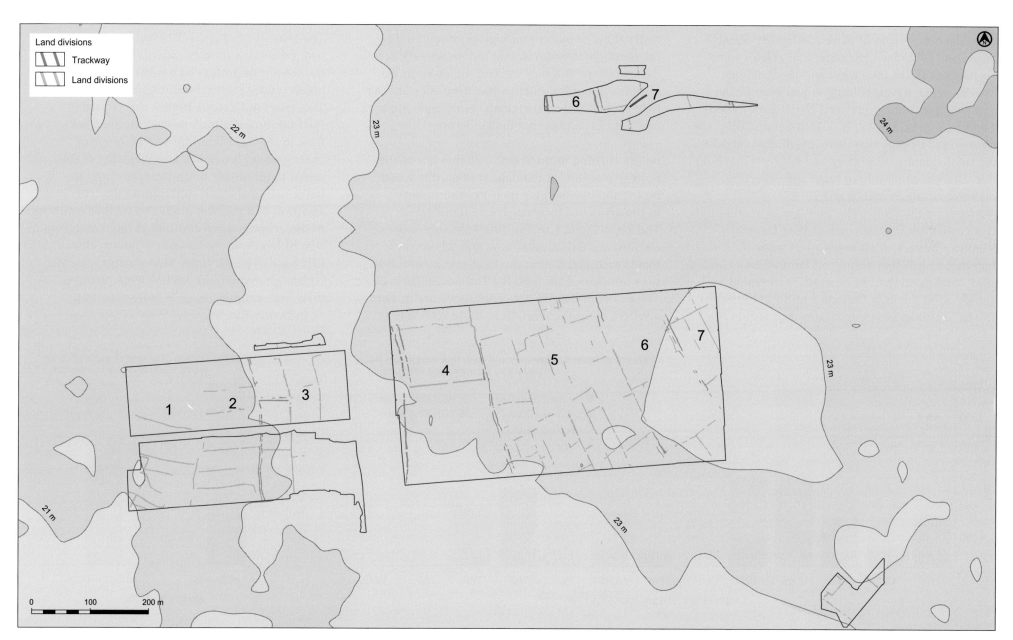

Figure 3.11: Landholdings, trackways and topography

Urn. The occurrences of Deverel Rimbury Bucket/ Barrel and Globular Urns show that at least some elements of all the trackways and landholdings (except perhaps Landholding 4) had been laid out and were functioning between Needham's Periods 4 and 5 (1700 BC to 1150 BC). That Landholding 4 is represented by only two east-west ditches explains the small quantity of pottery and suggests that both ditches were either dug or recut and collecting material during Periods 6 and 7.

It is clear from the presence of Post-Deverel Rimbury pottery in all areas apart from Landholding 1, that almost all landholdings and trackways continued to be used, maintained and sub-divided through Periods 6 and 7 (1150 BC to 750 BC). This evidence indicates that within the restrictions of our chronological understanding, the landholdings developed independently across the landscape through the 2nd millennium BC, once the major boundaries had been set out. The field system did not originate in any specific area and then expand across the landscape.

Before turning to more detailed analysis of the pottery residues of the field system, it is worth noting the peaks in the quantities of pottery in the areas of Trackway 1, Landholding 3, Trackway 2 and Landholding 6. In subsequent sections we will discuss how and where settlements emerged within the field system and how they developed through the 2nd millennium BC. The peaks in the pottery chart above are in part a reflection of the location of those settlements.

The chart (b) in Figure 3.12 has been produced using the same data as chart (a), but displays the weight of pottery as a percentage of the combined trackway and landholding assemblages. This chart indicates a higher percentage of Post-Deverel Rimbury pottery in the trackways than in the field boundaries, the result of continued maintenance and recutting of the initial landholding boundaries through the latter half of the 2nd millennium BC. The addition of a parallel ditch and further recutting of the original ditch completed the transformation of landholding boundary into trackway. This process can be demonstrated stratigraphically. Although many field ditches were recut, there was proportionately more recutting of trackway ditches.

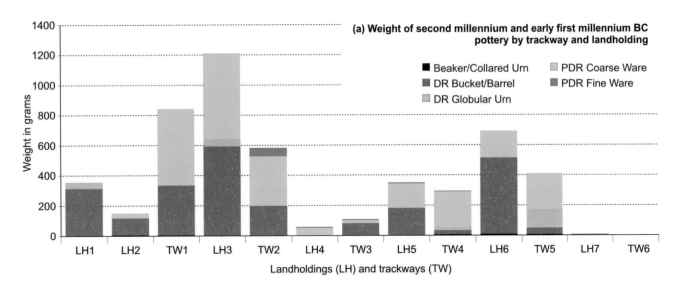

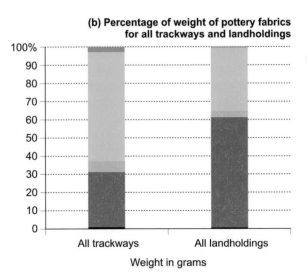

Figure 3.12: Graphs showing (a) weight of 2nd millennium and early 1st millennium BC pottery by landholding and trackway and (b) percentage of weight of pottery fabrics for all trackways and landholdings

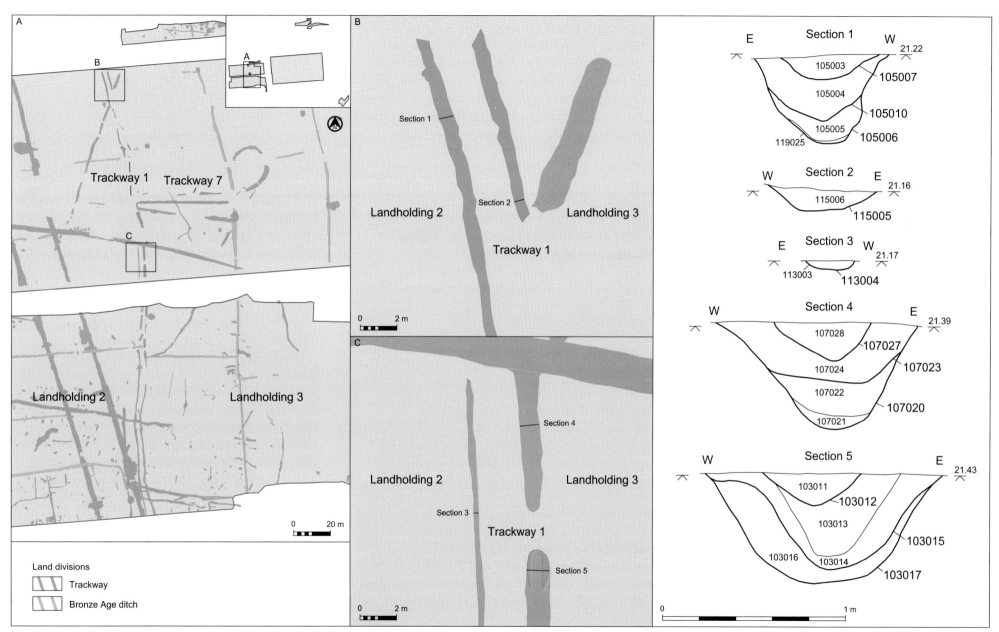

Figure 3.13: Sections across Trackway 1 (north)

Trackway 1 provides a good example of the process (Figures 3.13 and 3.14 present sections across this trackway). At the northern end of the site (Fig. 3.13), the western ditch (section 1) was maintained by recutting, whilst the eastern ditch (section 2) had a single phase of digging and silting. However, south of the east-west aligned double-ditched trackway (Trackway 7) that led towards the Neolithic HE1 enclosure, the pattern was reversed, the eastern ditch (Fig. 3.13 sections 4–5; Fig. 3.14 sections 2 and 4) being repeatedly recut and maintained. In some areas the western ditch became very shallow (Fig. 3.13 section 3; Fig. 3.14 section 1) with the same dimensions as the final recut of the eastern ditch. At one point the eastern ditch bifurcated, indicating that this boundary was recut on a slightly different alignment.

The small pottery assemblage from Trackway 1 was dominated by Deverel Rimbury Bucket Urn (Table 3.2). Only one sherd (2 g) of Post-Deverel Rimbury ware fabric was recovered, from deposit 107014. Although this was the fill of a secondary recut of the eastern boundary ditch, a single sherd remains a reliable indicator of the date of the silting.

At present the stratigraphic and artefactual evidence is insufficient to indicate at what point in the 2nd millennium BC the landholding boundaries became double-ditched trackways. However, we may suggest a reason as to why these boundaries underwent this change.

We have suggested that the entities that became fully developed trackways started as the first major land divisions—the initial boundaries of blocks of land that were held by individual kin-based groups. Once the process of division and land apportionment was set in motion, the only way to move around the landscape without crossing neighbouring landholdings was to travel along the boundaries of these landholdings. These boundaries became practical and acknowledged routes for people and animals to move through the landscape without causing disputes. Over time, routes became formalised into trackways and additional parallel ditches were dug as control of movement of livestock became ever more important.

In the next section we will turn to examine the development of settlements within the individual landholdings.

Settlement

Settlement genesis

In the previous chapter, we demonstrated the presence of Neolithic occupation localities from the occurrences of flintwork residing in later features. Here we will show how middle Bronze Age settlements also developed at such locations. First we will explore the nature of human occupation of the landscape prior to the division of the landscape in Periods 2 and 3 (2300–1700 BC), traditionally referred to as the early Bronze Age.

Evidence for occupation during the late 3rd/early 2nd millennium BC is sparse, restricted to a

Pottery ware	Fabric	No. sherds	Wt g.
Beaker/Collared Urn	GR1	2	5
DR Bucket/Barrel	FL2	33	330
DR Globular Urn	FL3	0	0
PDR Coarse Ware	FL1	1	2
PDR Fine Ware	FL5, FL12	0	0

Table 3.2: Pottery assemblage from Trackway 1

handful of grog-tempered sherds and a few diagnostic flint artefacts, including barbed-and-tanged arrowheads. This may represent a very low level of landscape occupation, or may reflect a lack of archaeological visibility of the type seen elsewhere at the time (mainly burial evidence).

It is reasonable to assume that early Bronze Age settlement dynamics resembled those of the late Neolithic in that settlements were relatively transient, with perhaps the major focus of occupation lying on the Thames floodplain rather than on the higher terraces (eg Brown and Cotton 2000, 90). However, diffuse lithic scatters of late Neolithic / early Bronze Age date do appear to have been associated with the Perry Oaks Neolithic monuments, and probably represent semi-permanent settlements dating to the early 2nd millennium BC. Their location adjacent to such monuments is perhaps to be expected, as these structures had served as arenas for the negotiation of land utilisation and access to resources during the 3rd millennium BC (see Chapter 2).

The construction of the first major land boundaries between 2000 and 1600 BC led to the emergence of the middle Bronze Age settlements,

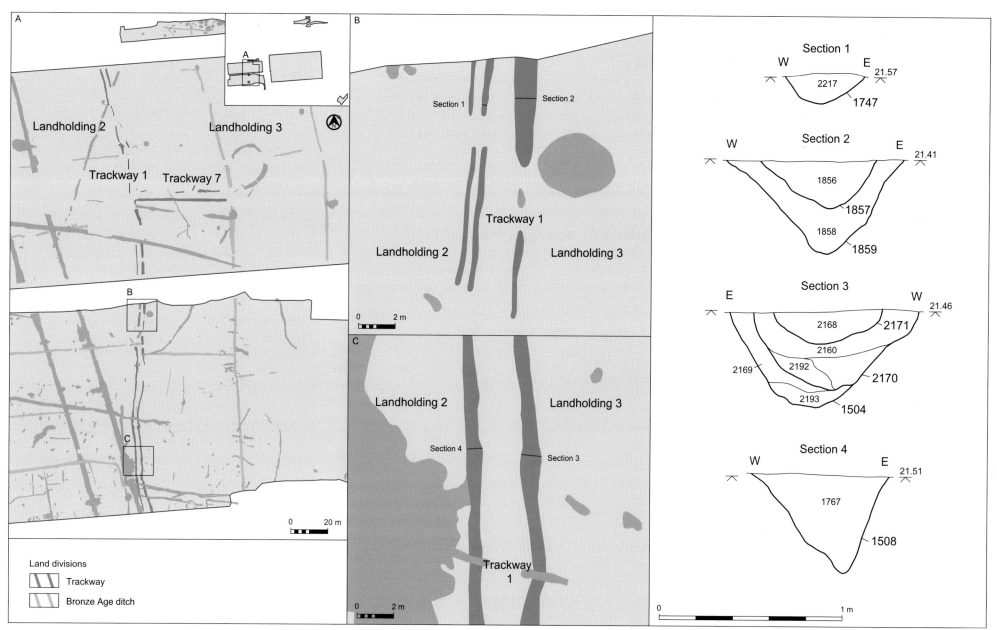

Figure 3.14: Sections across Trackway 1 (south)

albeit still in similar locations linked to the earlier Neolithic monuments. With the breakdown of traditional practices and the first division of the land, the primary resource for a residential group would be the produce of their land block. The 2nd millennium BC thus saw the emergence of a new concept of land tenure, the holdings defined by physical boundaries and reinforced by the physical linkage of settlement with ancient locations.

Settlement and landholding

Division of the landscape into landholdings had a number of consequences. We have shown how large landholdings were subdivided into smaller fields of varying patterns and orientation, and how the boundaries evolved into double-ditched trackways. With the sub-division of the landscape came the need for the supply of water to fields, animals and settlements and so large waterholes and wells were excavated in the fields and adjacent to settlements. These features will be examined below. This section explores another major consequence of landscape division—the development of archaeologically visible domestic structures and settlements in Periods 4 and 5 (1700 to 1150 BC). It also presents the possibility of a change in settlement nature and location during Periods 6 and 7 (1150–750 BC).

The structure of individual settlements is not discussed in detail here, nor is there detailed discussion of the palaeobotanical evidence for the economy of the settlements. The settlements exposed during this excavation were either very

heavily truncated, partially exposed, or lacking good organic preservation. These problems have been redressed during the recent excavations at T5, where complete plans of the settlements mentioned in this volume have been revealed, providing a better sample of palaeobotanical remains upon which to base a study of landscape/settlement interrelationships and economics. A fuller discussion of settlements will therefore be presented in Volume 2.

Middle Bronze Age settlement location

Six possible middle Bronze Age settlements have been identified (Fig. 3.15). In order of decreasing certainty they are:

Settlement 1: This consisted of four or five subrectangular structures, enclosed to the west and east by north-south aligned field boundaries which developed into double-ditched trackways. Although the northern part of the site remained inaccessible beneath the airport operational area, the southern boundary was defined by postholes representing a fence line. Immediately to the south of this line, the edge of a large pit or quarry contemporary with the settlement was exposed.

Settlement 2: This settlement consisted of a number of palisade trenches and gullies sub-dividing a large square enclosure adjacent to the Stanwell Cursus. First identified from the higher density of burnt flint and pottery in the area, subsequent excavations produced the full settlement plan.

Despite the presence of large pits containing domestic refuse and loom weight fragments within one of the palisade trenches, no accompanying post-built structures survived. Since most of this settlement was excavated as part of the T5 programme, it will be described fully in Volume 2.

Settlement 3: This small post-built structure could be part of a settlement, but it is small and apparently isolated.

Settlement 4: No structures were identified in this area but the presence of Coleoptera in samples from pit 178108 and recut 178122 suggests that timber buildings may have been located in the vicinity of this feature.

Settlement 5: Only circumstantial evidence suggests the presence of a settlement here as no structural evidence was identified.

Settlement 6: Only field system patterning and finds distributions suggest the presence of a middle Bronze Age settlement in this location.

Some general observations can be made with reference to middle Bronze Age settlement. Settlements, fields, and waterholes had developed in the landscape between 1600 and 1300 BC. The settlements post-date the initial major north-south land boundaries, and some (eg Settlement 2) appear to post-date the sub-division of the large blocks. Most settlements are located adjacent to major land boundaries that evolved into double-ditched trackways. This is not surprising, since trackways developed in order

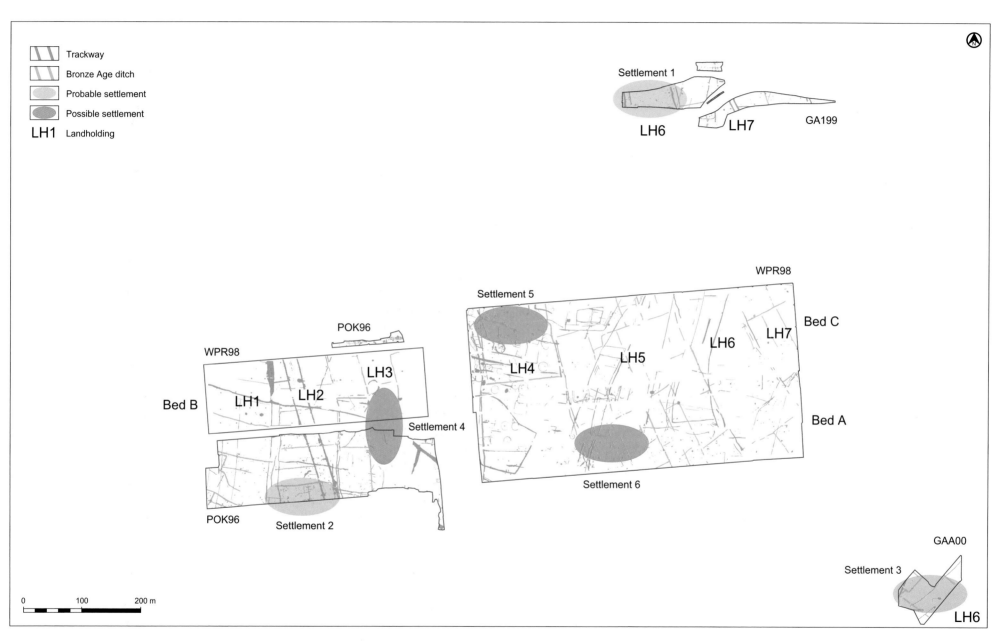

Figure 3.15: Location of middle Bronze Age settlement

to facilitate movement between settlements and fields. Figure 3.15 shows the location of the settlements and highlights the double-ditched trackways. Even if some of the more improbable 'settlements' (eg Settlement 5) are discounted, a clear pattern of settlements located within landholdings remains.

The description above presents all the middle Bronze Age settlements as contemporary, although there is little direct evidence to corroborate this and current theories suggest that middle Bronze Age settlements may have been relatively short lived and have 'migrated' across the landscape (eg Pryor 1996, 323). Unfortunately, we have no radiocarbon dates directly associated with structural features and the pottery chronology allows us to distinguish only between Deverel Rimbury and Post-Deverel Rimbury ware (see above).

The six possible settlements are discussed in more detail below.

Settlement 1 (Fig. 3.16)

The settlement was located in Landholding 6, within the excavated area known as Northern Taxiway (GA199), 300 m north of the main excavations.

Pre- and early settlement activity (Fig. 3.16)

The history of this part of the landscape has been discussed in Chapter 2, specifically concerning the way the distribution of Grooved Ware in shallow pits relates to the Neolithic landscape as a whole. The 2nd millennium BC settlement at Northern Taxiway was located c 50 m south of an undated, interrupted ring ditch partially excavated in 1969 (Canham 1978). The ditches of Trackway 5 appeared to lead directly towards this monument, which probably dates to the 4th or 3rd millennium BC (see Fig. 3.17). Pit 216009, which contained 3rd millennium BC Grooved Ware pottery, lay between the ditches of Trackway 5, suggesting that the 2nd millennium BC settlement had close spatial ties with the past landscape that were not fortuitous.

In the previous chapter we proposed that the small circular monuments of the late 3rd millennium BC were the original sites of ceremonies held to negotiate control of land and resources. The ceremonies apparently culminated in rituals performed within the area of land under negotiation and involved the deposition of artefacts including Grooved Ware pottery. We can argue that the kin-group that constructed the 2nd millennium BC settlement at Northern Taxiway and held Landholding 6 merely formalised the tenure established during the late 3rd millennium BC and previously maintained through ceremony and ritual.

There is some evidence of the activity that preceded the construction of north-south Trackway 4 ditch 218035 on the western boundary of the settlement (Fig. 3.16). Two short east-west gullies (218042 to the north and 217061 further south) were cut by this ditch, and 218042 contained 3 sherds (13 g) of grog-tempered pottery. The sherds were in fabric GR1, and possibly belonged to a Beaker or Collared Urn. Another small sherd was recovered from the upper fills of ditch 218035, and presumably derived from gully 218042. Gully 218042 was the western extension of another gully, 218038. Another short length of ditch (218058) probably functioned in association with this gully complex, until it was superseded by the construction of the Trackway 4 ditches.

The gullies and their intersection with Trackway 4 ditch 218035 were excavated as part of a programme of field evaluation by trenching in 1996 (site code WXE96, trench 5B5: BAA /905, 1996). The finds remain at the Museum of London and were unavailable for examination during this analysis, although the fieldwork report (BAA /905) described a small green glass or faience bead and part of a Deverel Rimbury Globular Urn, recovered from gully 218038. The presence of the grog-tempered Beaker / Collared Urn sherds would imply activity on the site prior to 1700 BC.

Another feature which probably pre-dated the main settlement was shallow ditch 212055, which lay just to the west of the large Trackway 5 ditch 212086. Although undated, ditch 212055 could be an early trackway ditch which was replaced by 212086, as we have previously shown that Trackway 5 may have been narrowed further to the south in the WPR98 area (see above).

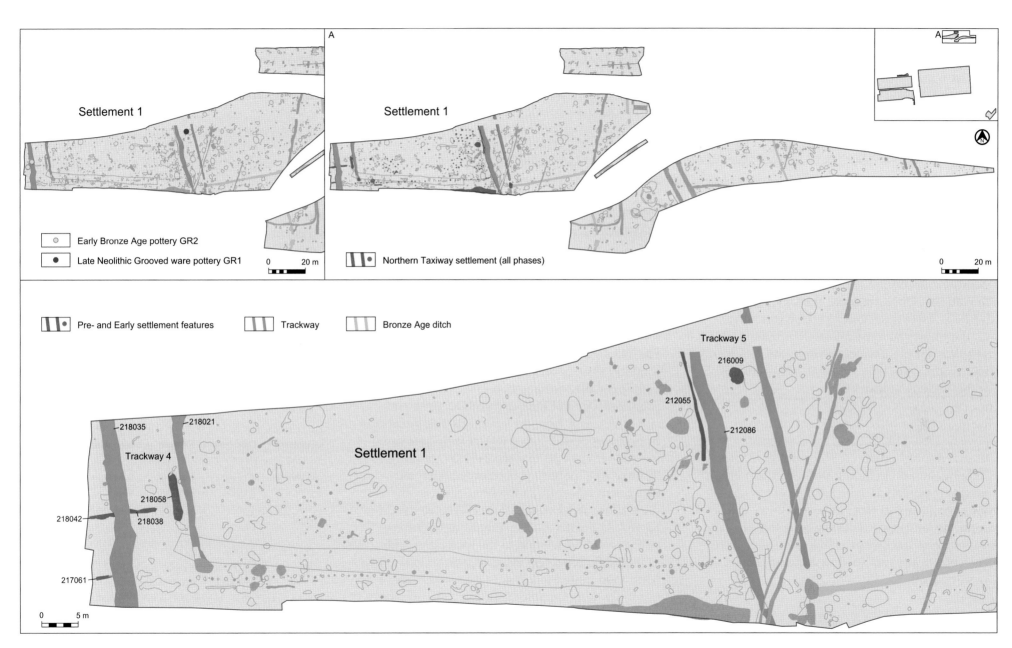

Figure 3.16: Settlement 1: Northern Taxiway

The 2nd millennium BC settlement (Fig. 3.17)

An east-west transect was excavated through the Northern taxiway settlement, which was defined to the west and east by the double ditches of Trackways 4 and 5. The southern extent of the settlement appears to have been defined by a post-built fenceline, while the northern part of the site remained unexcavated, preserved below the airport operational area. Within this area a number of post-built buildings were recognised.

The plan of the settlement is at best partial and interpretation is further hampered by the scarcity of stratigraphic relationships between the features. The contexts of the Deverel Rimbury and Post-Deverel Rimbury pottery recovered are, therefore, the most reliable chronological indicators for the development of the settlement, and this provides only a very broad sequence for the settlement history.

The main phase of activity seems to date to between 1700–1150 BC and to be associated with Deverel Rimbury pottery. The parallel ditches of the trackways bounding the settlement are unusual in being spaced *c* 7.4 m apart, wider than the spacing of most other trackway ditches across the landscape. This suggests that the land boundaries / trackways at this point may have been specifically modified to accommodate the settlement.

The dimensions of the trackway ditches adjacent to the settlement indicate that ditch 212086 in Trackway 5 and 218035 in Trackway 4 were sub-stantially wider and deeper than other trackway ditches. They were also more substantial than their respective parallel ditches, but 212086 very rapidly became shallower and narrower at its southern point, past the fenceline demarcating the southern settlement boundary. If we look at the above ground architecture, the excavators have suggested that both ditches of Trackway 5 were banked to the west, and the Trackway 4 ditches were banked to the east. It is normally expected that double-ditched trackways had banks external to the ditches in order to confine animal movement along their length. It is, therefore, likely that the larger, deeper trackway ditches were later enlargements or embellishments of the settlement boundary, although the evidence for this is circumstantial.

The Trackway 5 ditches contained Deverel Rimbury pottery and burnt flint in the middle and upper fills, whilst ditch 218021 of Trackway 4 produced Deverel Rimbury pottery, fired clay and struck flint from the basal fills and burnt flint from the upper fill. No artefacts were recovered from the lower fills of ditch 218035, although 'Bronze Age' pottery was recorded from an equivalent lower fill of the same ditch in an evaluation trench to the north (BAA/905, figure E3 and Appendix 1). The quantities of pottery (159 g) were, in relation to the total landscape assemblage, relatively insignificant. Globular Urn fabrics amounted to 125 g, as opposed to the generally more numerous Bucket / Barrel fabrics. It is likely, therefore, that the middle and upper fills of the ditches at least were contemporary with the settlement activity.

Turning to the area enclosed by the trackway ditches, direct evidence for the presence of a settlement comprised a number of postholes, some of which formed reasonably convincing building plans.

For example, Posthole Group 1 (Fig. 3.17) covered an area *c* 10 m long and 5–6 m wide. The postholes appear to have made up a substantial structure (although the exact form remains uncertain), with two intercutting postholes indicating a phase of repair. Perhaps the most interesting aspect of this structure was the extraordinary number of Deverel Rimbury Bucket Urn sherds deliberately placed in two postholes or pits, 210026 and 221005. Table 3.3 shows the quantity of pottery from these two features, which is particularly striking in contrast to the total of 2612 g of Deverel Rimbury pottery from all of the seven landholding field ditches. Table 3.3 also shows that both FL2 and FL10 fabrics were present in both postholes, suggesting the presence of at least two vessel elements in each.

Feature	Deposit	Fabric	No. sherds	Wt g.
210026	21005	FL2	92	124
	21003	FL10	113	5167
total			**205**	**5291**
221005	21004	FL10	4	3
	221003	FL10	21	1305
	221003	FL2	44	1442
total			**69**	**2750**

Table 3.3: Quantity of pottery from postholes or pits 210026 and 221005

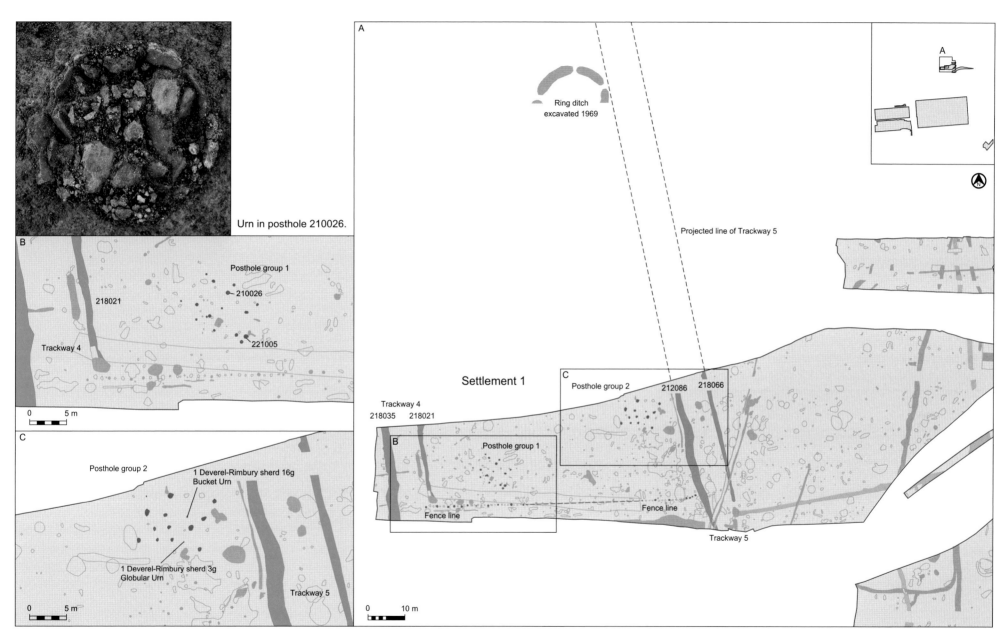

Urn in posthole 210026.

Posthole group 1

218021

210026

221005

Trackway 4

0   5 m

Posthole group 2

1 Deverel-Rimbury sherd 16g
Bucket Urn

1 Deverel-Rimbury sherd 3g
Globular Urn

Trackway 5

0   5 m

A

Ring ditch
excavated 1969

Projected line of Trackway 5

Settlement 1

Posthole group 2   212086   218066

Trackway 4
218035   218021

Posthole group 1

Fence line   Fence line

Trackway 5

0   10 m

Figure 3.17: Settlement 1: The 2nd millennium BC settlement showing posthole groups 1-2

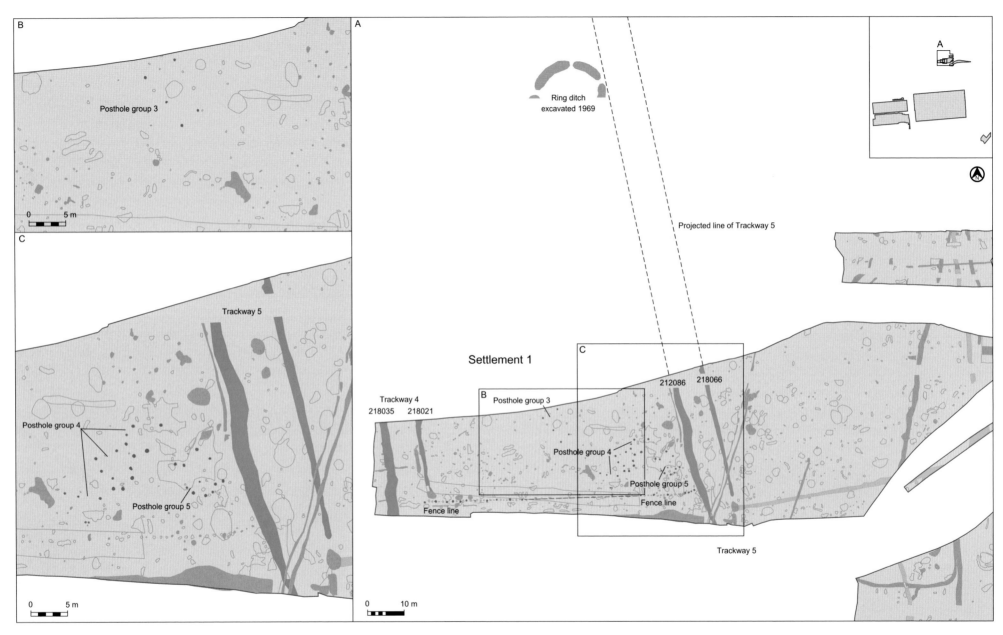

Figure 3.18: Settlement 1: The 2nd millennium BC settlement showing posthole groups 3-5

The photograph in Figure 3.17 shows a complete pot placed on the base of 210026 and a similar deposit was found in 221005. The absence of burnt bone indicates these were not cremation burials. If they were indeed postholes, the complete or near complete vessels may have been 'foundation' deposits.

A group of postholes designated Group 2 (Fig. 3.17) in the north-eastern part of the enclosed area probably also represented a series of buildings, but the plan is even less clear. Group 2 contained two small postholes / stakeholes, each of which produced a sherd of Deverel Rimbury pottery.

Three other posthole groups (Groups 3–5) were recognised within the enclosed area, all of which probably made up at least one building (Fig. 3.18). Posthole Group 5 must have either pre-dated the bank associated with Trackway 5 ditch 212086, or have been partially constructed on the decaying mound, but there is insufficient evidence to clarify this. None of the features produced any datable finds.

Post-Deverel Rimbury activity 1150–750 BC

Whilst there are no structures that can be definitely ascribed to the period 1150–750 BC, there are sufficient Post-Deverel Rimbury ceramics and features to suggest that some level of activity continued at the settlement during this period (Fig. 3.19).

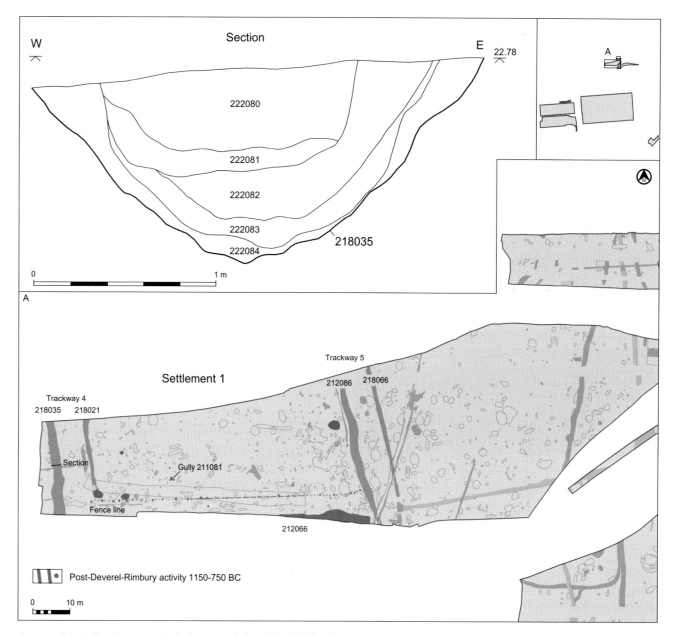

Figure 3.19: Post-Deverel Rimbury activity 1150-750 BC

121

Plate 3.1: Trackway 4: recut boundary ditch 218035 looking north

The major features include the recutting of the westernmost boundary ditch of Trackway 4 (218035; Plate 3.1) and the excavation of a very large feature, 212066, immediately to the south of the fenceline. The fills of the recut ditch were stained dark with comminuted charcoal and contained pottery, burnt and struck flint, fired clay and burnt stone, the sort of material that would be produced by domestic activity. Very little Post-Deverel Rimbury pottery was recovered from the silts of the other trackway ditches defining the settlement, suggesting that they had silted up by this time.

Feature 212066 was only partly exposed within the excavated area. It may have been either a large ditch or a series of pits or quarries. The fills produced 94 g of Deverel Rimbury pottery and 168 g of Post-Deverel Rimbury pottery, along with struck flint and a small quantity of fired clay and burnt flint.

Within the settlement area, a few postholes produced small sherds of possible Post-Deverel Rimbury pottery, as did a small 'T' shaped gully (211081) near Posthole Group 1. These features are sufficient to suggest the presence of structures of some sort during the period 1150–750 BC, although alternatively gully 211081 at least may be related to Posthole Group 1. Additionally, there are a number of shallow pits on the periphery of the enclosure that can be dated to this period. Pits are conspicuous by their absence from the Deverel Rimbury phase of the settlement, and their appearance in this later phase suggests a change in the nature of activity within the enclosure. Finally, we have dated the southern fence line boundary to this later phase of activity on the basis of a few sherds of Post-Deverel Rimbury pottery in two of the postholes, and on the relationship of the fenceline with the western and eastern trackway ditches. At the western end of the fence, the posts ran slightly beyond the line of ditch 218021, whilst at the eastern end, the fenceline clearly curves northwards to meet ditch 212086. The last three eastern postholes of the fence line were 50 mm to 80 mm shallower than the average depth of those to the west, suggesting that they perhaps cut remnant bank material adjacent to the ditch.

Conclusion

The phasing of the Northern Taxiway settlement is somewhat tenuous but a number of important points have emerged.

- The location of the settlement close to a 4th or 3rd millennium BC ring ditch and the 3rd millennium BC Grooved Ware pit, together with residual pottery of the early Bronze Age, demonstrates a link with previous mechanisms of securing access to land and resources.

- The settlement seems to have developed after 1700 BC within an area initially defined by major landholding boundaries which became trackways. The trackways were subsequently modified and emphasised to provide more impressive boundaries to the settlement.

- There is evidence to suggest continued activity at the settlement after 1150 BC, with the recutting of one of the boundary ditches and the addition of a fenceline along the southern boundary.

Settlement 2 (Fig. 3.20)

The settlement at Burrows Hill Close was located adjacent to the major monument of the Neolithic, the C1 Stanwell Cursus. The main part of this site was excavated as part of the T5 programme, and will be described in detail in Volume 2. However, it is worth summarising the major features of this settlement here.

Origins

There is some evidence for the presence of late Neolithic settlement activity in the area where the Burrows Hill Close middle Bronze Age settlement developed, comprising a few small fragments of Beaker or Collared Urn (2400 to 1700 BC) from the northern enclosure ditch and some of the internal settlement features. This was a similar pattern to that at the Northern Taxiway site.

Structure

The settlement was enclosed to the north and south by east-west field boundary ditches, both of which were modified following the construction of the settlement. The northern boundary ditch was extended eastwards over the western ditch and central bank of the C1 Stanwell Cursus, and the latter feature formed the eastern boundary of the settlement. Double-ditched Trackway 1 ran immediately to the east of the Stanwell Cursus.

Figure 3.20: Settlement 2: Burrows Hill Close

A recut of the southern boundary ditch contained significantly more middle Bronze Age pottery than the original fills, suggesting that the recut was contemporary with the settlement. To the west, the boundary of the settlement was formed by a series of shallow north-south aligned ditches and the palaeochannel, which would have been a low-lying boggy area.

No internal building plans survived but a relatively substantial double palisade trench probably represented the demarcation of an area that divided a domestic zone from the larger enclosed area (not all shown on plan). This domestic zone was sub-divided by a series of gullies.

Development

This settlement emerged as a highly visible entity from a more transient late Neolithic/early Bronze Age settlement. The middle Bronze Age settlement was constructed in the corner of an existing field, the boundaries of which were modified accordingly. The presence of large proportions of Deverel Rimbury pottery within the assemblages from the settlement features indicates that these developments took place between 1700 and 1150 BC. Table 3.4 shows the proportion of Deverel Rimbury to Post-Deverel Rimbury pottery from this settlement. As with the Northern Taxiway settlement, Post-Deverel Rimbury pottery is present in features at Burrows Hill Close, but with a much lower frequency and concentrated at the periphery of the settlement. This may be the result either of deposition of material through agricultural practices such as ploughing and manuring or of more specialised intermittent activity. This pattern may be modified as a result of analysis of the T5 excavations, but the current evidence indicates that settlement activity had declined at Burrows Hill Close during the late Bronze Age.

Settlement 3 (Fig. 3.21)

A relatively small area of the Heathrow landscape was investigated at Grass Area 21 (GAA00) to the south-east of the main excavation area, and despite the identification of a post-built structure, evidence for settlement here is tenuous.

Origins

A single Mesolithic and a handful of Neolithic flint artefacts were recovered from a middle Bronze Age field boundary. Unlike other settlement locations, however, no Neolithic monuments lay within the excavated area.

Structure and development

Five or six postholes belonging to a rectangular structure measuring 2.73 m x 2.27 m were the only settlement features identified. The only dating evidence was a single small sherd of Deverel Rimbury Bucket Urn from posthole 404032. The building was situated immediately adjacent to the ditches that formed part of Bronze Age Landholding 6. The ditches had been recut several times and contained both Deverel Rimbury and Post-Deverel Rimbury pottery.

Pottery type	Weight (g)
Beaker/Collared Urn	9
DR Bucket/Barrel	1188
DR Globular Urn	108
PDR Coarse Ware	104
PDR Fine Ware	0
Total	**1409**

Table 3.4: Proportion of Deverel Rimbury to Post-Deverel Rimbury pottery in the Burrows Hill settlement (Settlement 2)

They also contained large quantities of burnt flint, which had apparently derived from the rectangular building. Analysis of the charcoal from the postholes suggested that it was came from the remains of domestic fires associated with the building (Challinor, CD Section 10).

Precise interpretation of the function of the Grass Area 21 structure is difficult. It somewhat resembles the four or five structures identified at Settlement 1, but is distinct in that it is solitary.

Post-Deverel Rimbury pottery was found in the fills of the field ditches around the building, but it is unclear whether this was derived from activity associated with the building or with agricultural activity in the adjacent fields.

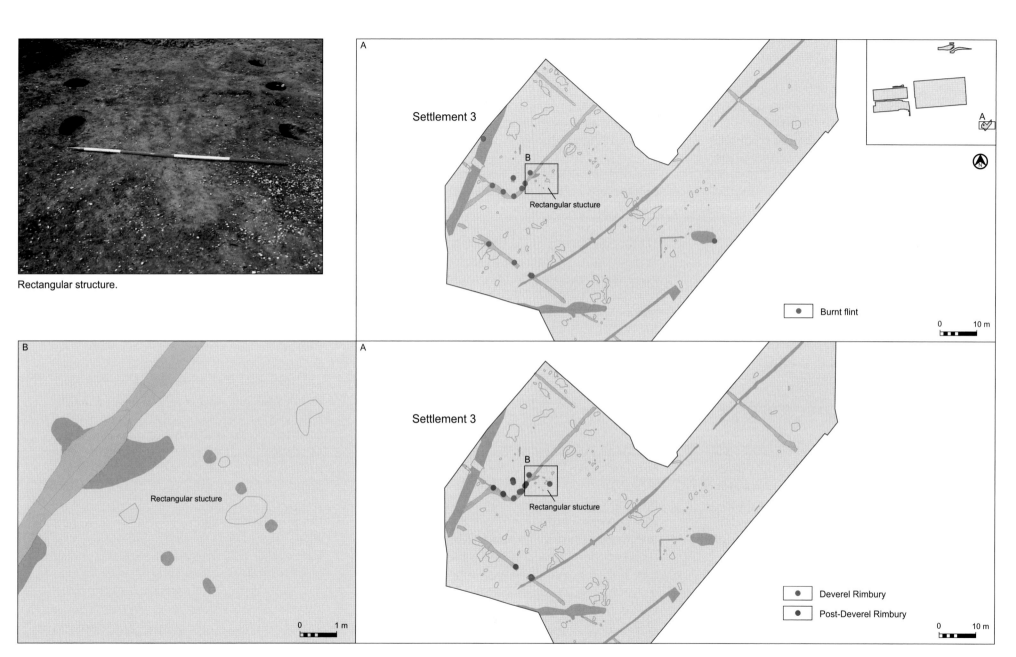

Rectangular structure.

Settlement 3

B

Rectangular stucture

Burnt flint

0   10 m

Settlement 3

B

Rectangular stucture

Deverel Rimbury

Post-Deverel Rimbury

0   10 m

Rectangular stucture

0   1 m

Figure 3.21: Settlement 3: Grass Area 21

125

Settlement 4 (Fig. 3.22)

Settlement 4 lay to the east of Settlement 2 within Landholding 3. No structural evidence was identified, and the only evidence for settlement activity is provided by insect assemblages from pit 178108 and its recut, 178122. The layout of the trackways in this area, the presence of Neolithic horseshoe enclosure HE1, and a scatter of pits and waterholes provide additional circumstantial evidence to support this evidence.

Origins

As we have seen at settlements 1 and 2, middle Bronze Age settlements tend to be located adjacent to Neolithic monuments. The proposed Landholding 3 settlement lay close to two monuments, the HE1 Horseshoe Enclosure and the C2 Cursus.

Structure and Development 1700–1150 BC

Despite the absence of structural elements, the layout of the middle Bronze Age field system and trackway in this area hint at the presence of a settlement. The site contained the only east-west aligned trackway in the entire excavated area (Trackway 7), which led from north-south Trackway 1 and terminated at the Neolithic horseshoe enclosure HE1. Elsewhere on the site, trackways generally connected settlements, with Trackway 1 for example probably originating at Settlement 2, and it would be reasonable to assume that the east-west trackway led to a settlement in Landholding 3.

Middle Bronze Age pits in Landholding 3 were distributed in a rough elipse with a radius of 52 m to 72 m from a central point at the eastern end of the east-west trackway. This could represent an arrangement of pits and waterholes surrounding a settlement.

The best settlement evidence comes from one of these pits, 178108, its recut, 178122, and well 156031. Sample 857 from 178121, one of the lowest fills of pit 178108, and sample 856 from 178120, the lowest fill of 178122, both produced evidence of Coleopterae, which suggests the presence of buildings in the vicinity. A radiocarbon date of 1450–1210 BC (WK10029 cal BC 2 sigma) was obtained from 178123, which sealed fill 178121 and was sealed by fill 178120. On the basis of this result, the following data can be firmly assigned to the middle Bronze Age.

Woodworm beetles of Species Group 10, mostly Anobium punctatum but also Lyctus linearis, ranged from 2.2 to 3.6% of the terrestrial Coleoptera in these samples. They are rare members of the British woodland insect fauna under natural conditions because their habitat of dry dead wood is uncommon, but they thrive in timber structures. The cerambycid beetle Phymatodes testaceus, which was present in both samples 856 and 857, could have attacked old oak timbers on the outside of a building or have emerged from firewood, rather than being from naturally occurring dead wood. The general synanthropic beetles of Species Group 9a, represented by Ptinus fur, ranged from 1.2 to 3.0% of the terrestrial Coleoptera. Ptinus fur naturally feeds on debris in bird and rodent nests but flourishes in much larger numbers

inside buildings amongst stable debris, in old hay, in thatch and amongst relatively dry waste in neglected corners from food preparation. The values for these two groups of beetles from the two samples strongly suggests that there was a building adjacent to the pits or that debris from a building was dumped into them. Feature 178122 cut Feature 178108 after it had silted up, so the results imply that there was some continuity to the presence of a building or buildings on this part of the site. Members of the Lathridiidae (Species Group 8) comprised around 5% of the terrestrial Coleoptera in the two samples. They tend to occur in old hay, thatch, sweet compost etc. The two most numerous, Lathridius minutus gp. and Corticaria punctulata, tend to flourish in settlements.

The insects from samples 856 and 857 gave no other evidence for high concentrations of organic refuse associated with any settlement. They did, however, give some indication of nettle-covered disturbed ground as occurs around settlements. The beetles Brachypterus urticae, Apion urticarium, Cidnorhinus quadrimaculatus and Ceutorhynchus pollinarius, all of which feed on Urtica dioica (stinging nettle), comprised 3.1% of the terrestrial Coleoptera in these samples. They only made up 0.5% of the terrestrial Coleoptera in Samples 229 and 277, from the other two waterholes. Samples 856 and 857 were the only Bronze Age samples to contain the nettle-feeding bug Heterogaster urticae. Many of the beetles that occur in arable fields (see above) also occur on disturbed and weedy ground. For example, the ground beetle Agonum dorsale and the Polygonaceae-feeding leaf beetle Chaetocnema concinna already mentioned could as readily have been occurring on waste ground in a settlement as in cultivated fields. However, several of

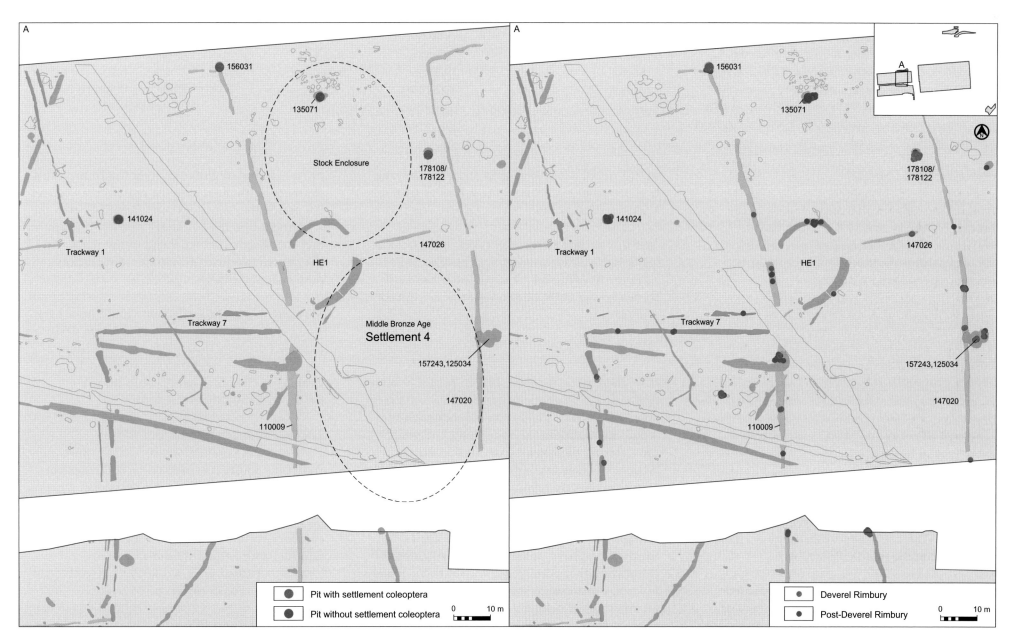

Figure 3.22: Settlement 4 in Landholding 3

the samples contained beetles which feed on members of the Malvaceae, particularly Malva sylvestris (common mallow), such as Podagrica fuscicornis and Apion aeneum. The Malvaceae are very vulnerable to grazing and are most likely to have grown in areas from which stock were excluded, such as waste ground in settlements

(Robinson, CD Section 12).

Sample 227 came from deposit 156034 at the bottom of well shaft 156031, which re-cut waterhole 156078. This sample also produced some synanthropic beetles, providing further evidence of settlement nearby.

Three individuals of Anobium punctatum (wood-worm) and an example of the synanthropic beetle Ptinus fur, which tends to occur inside buildings, raised the possibility that there was a settlement, or at least a timber building, close to Feature 156031. However, members of the Lathridiidae (Species Group 8) and insects of foul organic refuse were not particularly high. There was no strong evidence of any waste-ground type habitat.

(Robinson, CD Section 12)

Deposit 156034 yielded three consistent radiocarbon dates (Table 3.5), again placing any settlement firmly within the middle Bronze Age.

In contrast, pits 135071 and 141024 provided no indication of the presence of settlement or buildings. It may be that the settlement was fairly small and probably contained within ditches

SG Deposit	Context	Lab No.	Material	Results BP	Cal Date - 2 sigma
156034	156020	WK9376	Seeds	3015 +/- 56 BP	1410-1050 BC
156034	156020	WK10031	Wooden chips	3260 +/- 57 BP	1690-1410 BC
156034	156020	WK10028	Wooden chips	2942 +/- 59 BP	1380-970 BC

Table 3.5: Radiocarbon dates from 156034 within well 156031

147020 and 110009. Robinson observed that the high levels of scarabaeoid dung beetles from pit 178108 indicated that,

'domestic animals were concentrated in the vicinity of the middle Bronze Age pit. It is possible that the enclosure in which this pit was situated was used for management of stock which grazed over a much wider area.'

(Robinson, CD Section 12).

If so, then east-west ditch 147026 probably served to divide the stock enclosure from the settlement area to the south. The northern stock enclosure would then contain the waterholes and wells for watering the animals, whilst the southern settlement enclosure contained none. The nearest water sources are separated from the settlement by boundary ditches and banks.

The plan on the right in Figure 3.22 shows the distribution of pottery within Settlement 4. It indicates that pottery is confined to the waterholes in the northern stock enclosure, which may be the result of deliberate dumping of settlement rubbish from the southern settlement enclosure, hence the presence of building timbers, and crop

processing waste in the waterholes. In the southern settlement area the pattern may reflect the accidental incorporation of rubbish from the settlement into the boundary ditches. It follows that the absence of settlement in the northern enclosures produces a corresponding lack of pottery in the ditches.

Movement into the settlement would have been along east-west Trackway 7, which was designed to funnel animals through the old Neolithic horseshoe monument into the stock enclosure. People, on the other hand, could turn southwards into the settlement.

The late Bronze Age, 1150–750BC

With only indirect evidence of a settlement in Landholding 3, it is difficult to establish whether such a settlement would have continued to be occupied into the late Bronze Age. The only evidence for this is that the upper levels of the middle Bronze Age waterholes described above were either filled or re-worked/recut in the late Bronze Age. For example:

- The uppermost fills of 141024 contained Post-Deverel Rimbury pottery.

- The upper levels of the central shaft and surrounding fills of 156031 were cleaned and re-lined between 1150 and 750 BC.

- The top of waterhole 135071 was recut as 135055 and infilled with a range of material, including Post-Deverel Rimbury pottery.

- Two pits, 157243 and 125034, to the east of the possible settlement cut through two earlier middle Bronze Age pits. Both of the later pits contained Post-Deverel Rimbury pottery as well as abraded Deverel Rimbury sherds.

It is unclear whether the later re-working of existing middle Bronze Age pits signifies continuing settlement activity, or a continuing concern with supplying water to animals. However, the shallow depth of the later pits suggests they were associated with settlement rather than an attempt to reach the water table, as was the case with the earlier pits.

Settlement 5 (Fig. 3.23)

No definite structures dating to between 1150 and 750 BC were identified during the Perry Oaks excavations, but there was a concentration of Post-Deverel Rimbury pottery in the area of Landholding 4, leading to an assumption that a Bronze Age settlement may have occupied the site. Truncation of the excavated area would have removed the majority of postholes, leaving only the deeper pits and waterholes identified during excavation. The hypothesis was augmented by the recovery of loom weights from ditch 103046 and pit 125233 that dated from the middle of the 2nd millennium to the first quarter of the 1st millennium BC. Figure 3.23 shows the distribution of Deverel Rimbury and Post-Deverel Rimbury pottery in the area, and demonstrates that the majority of this material resides in Iron Age and Romano-British features.

The evidence from Settlement 2 shows that double-ditched trackways served to channel movement to and from settlements. Trackways 2 and 3 terminated at the northern enclosure in Landholding 4, the possible location of a 2nd millennium /early 1st millennium BC settlement. At settlements 1, 2 and 4, large waterholes were separated from the domestic areas of the settlement. In settlement 5, the large waterholes and pits lay to the west of Trackway 2 (see above).

However, unlike the other possible settlements described so far, little in the way of artefactual or monumental evidence from the period pre-1700 BC was recovered in the vicinity, and, even taking into account the effects of truncation, the absence of structures in this area is clear. The recent excavation of the Twin Rivers area (described in Volume 2) to the west of Landholding 4 has emphasised the extensive spread of Post-Deverel Rimbury pottery in this area, again mostly residual in Iron Age and Romano-British features or in situ in large early first millennium BC waterholes.

Table 3.6 shows the quantity of Deverel Rimbury and Post-Deverel Rimbury pottery from later features in and around Landholding 4. The small total of 2.66 kg is significant in view of the fact that the total weight of Deverel Rimbury and Post-Deverel Rimbury pottery from all the 2nd and early 1st millennium BC Trackways and Landholding ditches amounted to only 5.06 kg.

Although analysis of the recent T5 excavation is not sufficiently advanced to allow final identification of structures, there appears to be no significant concentration of structural features that would account for the comparatively large concentration of Post-Deverel Rimbury pottery in the area of Landholding 4, although a range of possible explanations could account for this phenomenon. A number of other sites dating to the late 2nd/early 1st millennium BC, including East Chisenbury (McOmish 1996) and Potterne (Lawson 2000), are characterised by the accumulation of large concentrations of pottery, flint and animal bones. During analysis of the Potterne site, Lawson (2000, 264–272) conducted a wide-ranging review of formation processes and the structure of similar sites in southern Britain. This discussion will not be repeated here, but the northern parts of Landholding 4 and the Twin Rivers area resembled these sites in some respects, particularly in terms of the presence of large accumulations of domestic rubbish at a single location. Occupation of Settlement 1 and possibly 2, appeared to continue into the period 1150–750 BC. If this were the case, then the contrast in the sparse concentration of Post-Deverel Rimbury pottery and other settlement debris in and around these sites, along with the relatively high concentration in Landholding 4,

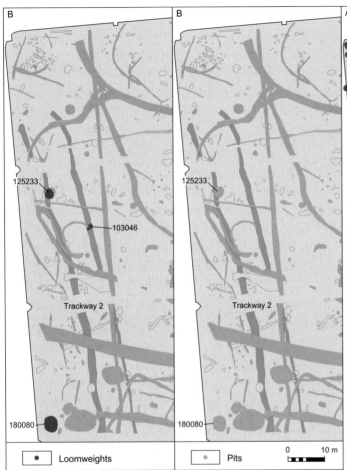

Figure 3.23: Settlement 5: Landholding 3 and 4

Pottery type	No. sherds	Weight (g)
Deverel Rimbury	47	342
Post-Deverel Rimbury	246	2322
Total	**293**	**2664**

Table 3.6: Quantity of pottery from later features in and around Landholding 4

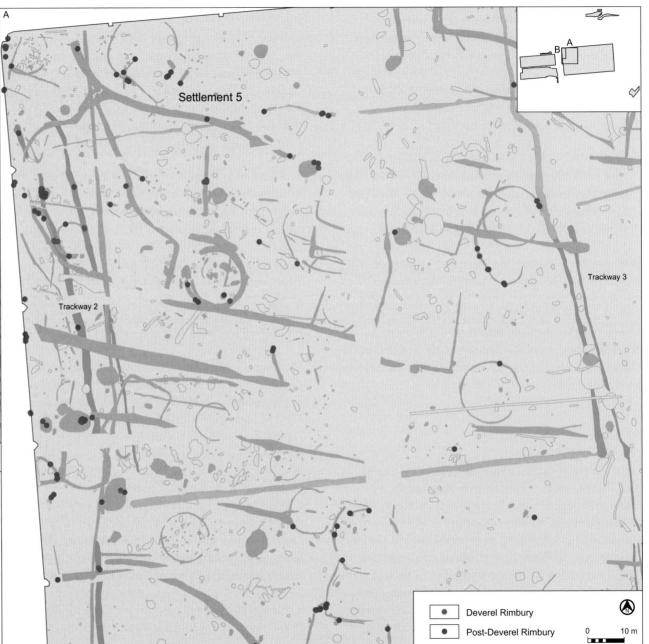

could indicate the presence of a 'midden' in this area. But the terminology must be qualified. Needham and Spence (1997) have argued that the term 'midden' should only be used for deposits generated by deliberate dumping of material in a particular place. Lawson favours the interpretation that the Potterne deposit accumulated *in situ* within the settlement in a wider context of periodic meetings of groups of people to engage in feasting, sacrifices and slaughter of animals (Lawson 2000, 271).

The effects of construction and working of the 20th century sludge works would have removed most evidence of deposits of the type preserved at East Chisenbury and Potterne. Nonetheless, the possibility of the existence of a late Bronze Age settlement or midden (or both) in Landholding 4 and the Twin Rivers area will be explored in Volume 2.

Settlement 6 (Fig. 3.24)

There is relatively little evidence for a middle Bronze Age settlement in this location (Landholding 5) but its existence was suggested by a number of factors.

A small, heavily truncated ring gully, 128119, which contained undateable struck and burnt flint, lay within this area (Plate 3.2). This feature has been interpreted either as a 4th / 3rd millennium BC ring gully or an eaves-drip gully for a 2nd or 1st millennium BC house. As a house, it would be smaller than most of the middle Iron Age

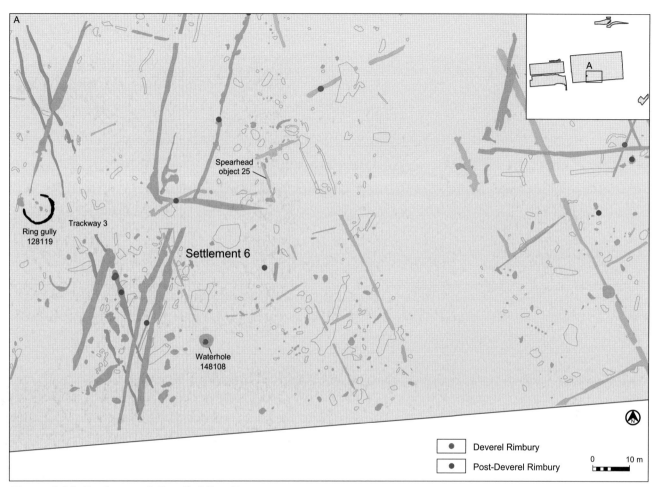

Figure 3.24: Settlement 6: Landholding 5

structures exposed to the north-west, and clearly isolated from the core of the Iron Age settlement. It was located close to Trackway 3 and the balance of evidence indicates that it is more likely to be a small late 2nd-early 1st millennium BC house than an earlier monument. The lack of dating evidence, however, allows for either possibility.

Another factor that suggests the presence of a settlement in this area is that the field system pattern in Landholding 5 to the east of Trackway 3 is more closely sub-divided than other parts of Landholdings 4 and 5. The sub-divisions could represent a series of small paddocks around a settlement. Finally, the side-looped Taunton

131

Plate 3.2: Ring gully 128119 within Settlement 6, looking north-west

phase spearhead (object no. 25) was recovered from a recut in the upper fill of ditch 149099 (see above), possibly close to the boundary of a settlement. The general patterning of other finds such as pottery, however, is not dissimilar to that of the surrounding field system. The lack of clear evidence for settlement in this area precludes further profitable discussion.

Structural elements of settlements

The structural evidence for Bronze Age settlement is relatively limited, but the possible settlement sites described above share a number of traits:

- The original major land boundaries and field sub-divisions were sometimes further modified to accommodate a settlement and provide

more substantial boundaries, particularly to the east and west (eg Settlements 1 and 2).

- Some settlements were sub-divided to form an outer animal compound and an inner or separate domestic area (Settlements 2 and 4).

- The southern boundaries of settlements or internal domestic areas were demarcated with fence lines or palisade trenches (Settlements 1 and 2).

- Waterholes, wells and pits were separated from the domestic area and tended to be located outside the settlement or within the animal compound area. Where buildings survived, they were rectangular or subrectangular in plan and exclusively post-built with no eaves drip gullies. At Settlement 1 complete pots were deposited as foundation offerings in the postholes of some of the buildings.

- The economic basis of the settlements can only be inferred from the general environmental evidence (see below).

- At a general level, we have a good understanding of how permanent settlements originated, why and where they were located, how they were structured and how they became central to the tenure of large land blocks. We are less clear about the contemporaneity and duration of occupation of the settlements. Were they all occupied from 1700 to 1150 BC, and if so, what happened to the settlements following 1150 BC in the late Bronze Age?

Settlement post-1150 BC

Almost all the middle Bronze Age settlements showed evidence of some survival into the late Bronze Age. This took the form of late Bronze Age pottery incorporated in ditch fills of the field system bordering the settlements, recutting of the middle Bronze Age pits and waterholes fringing the settlements and occasionally the digging of new features of this type. However, there is no good chronological control over the ceramic assemblage assigned to the Post-Deverel Rimbury tradition and the material does not include distinctive late Bronze Age forms. The settlements may therefore not have survived long into the late Bronze Age.

Analysis of pottery distributions suggests that whatever the nature of settlement activity, there was a substantial concentration of late Bronze Age pottery in the area of Settlement 5. This could represent the transition from a pattern of dispersed smaller settlements to nucleated settlement. Alternatively, this material may represent the creation of a large rubbish 'midden' similar to the one at East Chisenbury (McOmish 1996). Alternatively, as at Potterne (Lawson 2000), this material may have been the product of a range of ritual, ceremonial and domestic activities which gave rise to a 'tell-like' deposit. It is unlikely that the Perry Oaks deposit would have been on a scale equivalent to those at Potterne and East Chisenbury, but until analysis of the more recently excavated Terminal 5 sites is complete, all possibilities must be considered.

It is clear that, in terms of settlement, the next archaeologically visible settlement developed sometime during the early Iron Age and continued through the middle Iron Age in Landholding 4. We will discuss the changes that occurred in the landholdings, settlements and trackways between 1150 and 400 BC later in this chapter. Here we will describe additional components of the agricultural landscape of the 2nd millennium BC—pits, wells and waterholes. These features produced a wealth of artefactual and environmental material, and we will seek to understand their role in the enclosed landscape of this period.

Waterholes and water management in the 2nd and early 1st millennium BC

As discussed above, at around 1700 BC the landscape was divided into landholdings which were subsequently subdivided into fields or paddocks within which settlements developed. In this section we will look at another consequence of this modification of the landscape—the excavation of large pits originally constructed to supply water (Table 3.7, Fig. 3.25). The waterholes were generally wider and/or deeper than the pits, certainly deep enough to have reached the present day water table, although there is a continuum gradiation in size between pits and waterholes, so the division between the two is somewhat arbitrary. Various attempts have been made elsewhere to differentiate 'wells' from 'waterholes' (eg Brossler 2001, 133), but for ease of analysis, 'waterhole' has been used here to describe all large features we believe were originally intended to provide water.

Waterhole shape	Feature	Feature date (widest range)
Ramped access	108101	Pre-1700 BC?
Steep sided	963267	1700-1150 BC
Steep sided	963114	1700-1150 BC
Steep sided	960514	1700-1150 BC
Steep sided	178122	1700-1150 BC
Steep sided	178108	1450-1210 BC
Steep sided	159200	1610-1210 BC
Steep sided	156031	1690-1050 BC
Steep sided	156028	1610-1040 BC
Ramped access	148108	1700-1150 BC
Steep sided	141024	1380-940 BC
Steep sided	135071	1500-1100 BC
Ramped access	124100	c. 1500-1100 BC
Steep sided	110107	c. 1600-1300 BC
Ramped access	103040	1700-1150 BC
Steep sided	961744	1150-750 BC
Steep sided	960529	1150-750 BC
Ramped access	180080	1150-750 BC
Steep sided	157243	1150-750 BC
Steep sided	157065	1700-750 BC
Originally steep sided became ramped	155144	1150-750 BC
Ramped access	148042	1150-750 BC
Steep sided	146048	1150-750 BC
Steep sided	146043	1150-750 BC
Steep sided	146039	1150-750 BC
Steep sided	136194	1150-750 BC
Ramped access	135055	1150-750 BC
Ramped access	126025	1150-750 BC
Steep sided	125244	1150-750 BC
Steep sided	125233	1150-750 BC
Steep sided may have been ramped	103038	1150-750 BC

Table 3.7: Bronze Age waterholes at Perry Oaks

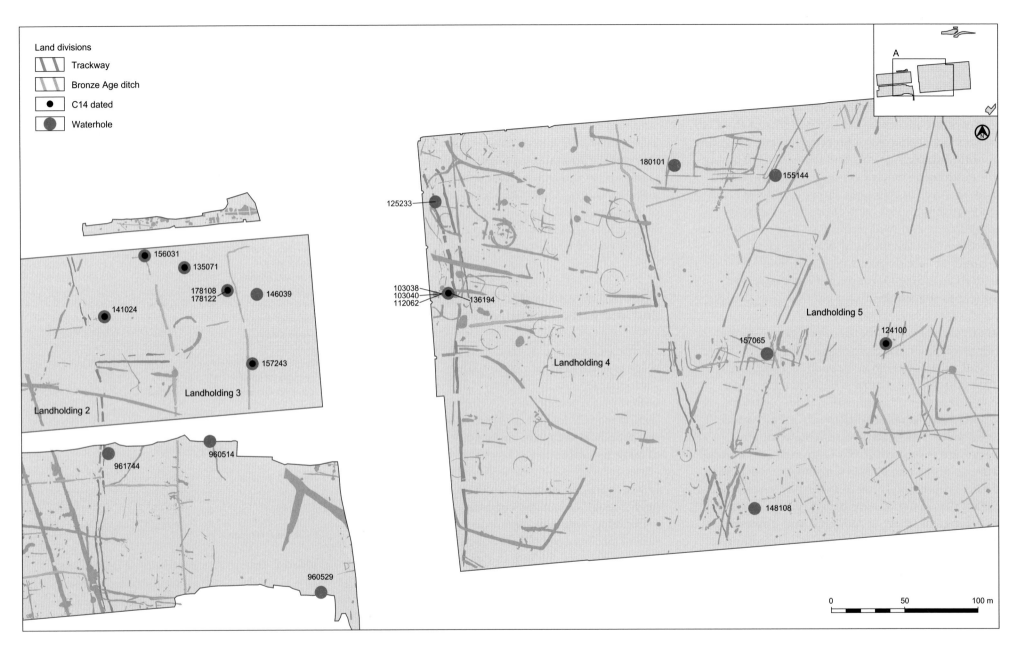

Figure 3.25: Location of Bronze Age waterholes

134

The waterholes at Perry Oaks have produced several important types of evidence:

- Waterlogging of basal deposits preserved a range of rare wooden objects.

- The wooden objects produced a series of radiocarbon dates ranging from 1600 to 940 BC. These helped define the chronological sequence of landscape development.

- The waterlogged deposits also preserved microscopic and macroscopic palaeobotanical remains which provided a clear picture of the landscape, its flora and some indication of farming practices.

When were the waterholes excavated, what did they look like and what were they used for?

Thirty waterholes of two basic forms were identified and are listed in Table 3.7 by feature number. One type was steep or vertical sided, the second had a shallow ramped access on one side. The steep-sided waterholes would have required people to draw water either by buckets or by climbing into them on log ladders, some of which were partially preserved (see reconstruction, Fig. 3.32 below). In several of the steep sided waterholes wicker or wooden revetments were also preserved, which would have stabilised the sides of the holes and acted as a filter to maintain a clear pool of water at the base. These water-holes would have been suitable for supplying

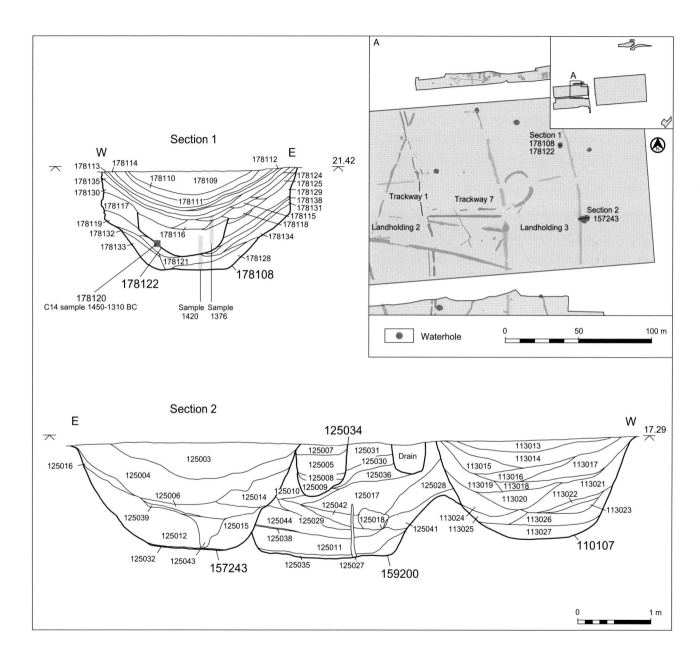

Figure 3.26: Waterholes 178108, 157234, 159200 and 110107

135

settlements with water, and contrast with the ramped waterholes that may have been designed principally to allow access to water for animals without the assistance of people. The artefacts contained in some of the waterholes, however, suggest that they may also have served other, less clear cut functions. Before looking at the distribution of the waterholes, we will consider when they were constructed.

A number of large waterholes cut some of the silted north-south field ditches. Wooden artefacts or palaeobotanical material in the lower waterlogged fills of some waterholes produced radiocarbon dates of the 2nd and the first quarter of the 1st millennium BC (see Table 3.7).

Several waterholes dug and used during the period 1700–1150 BC subsequently became receptacles for domestic settlement rubbish and crop processing waste before being recut between 1150 and 750 BC (eg 178108; Fig. 3.26). In some cases there is evidence of multiple phases of recutting and reuse within the general footprint of the original waterhole (eg 112062, 103038, 136194) or in the form of intercutting waterholes

(eg 157243, 159200, 110107; Fig. 3.26 and Plate 3.3). In other cases (eg 156031) the waterholes silted up with rubbish dumped in them before 750 BC. The repeated re-use and recutting has led to deposition of residual material. For example, the radiocarbon date of 1620–1320 BC (WK9375 cal BC 2 sigma) on seeds from the central shaft of 136194 does not correspond with the 8th century BC dates for complete pottery vessels recovered from the base of the feature. Similarly, many waterholes demonstrate some mixing of Deverel Rimbury and Post-Deverel Rimbury ceramics.

Figure 3.27: Distribution of waterholes in the two main phases of use

Plate 3.3: Wattle structure excavated in waterhole 159200

The evidence demonstrates that the practice of constructing large steep-sided and ramped waterholes occurred once the landscape had been divided into landholdings, presumably in response to the restriction of access to natural sources of water in rivers, streams and pools. Once constructed, it would appear that after a period of use a waterhole would typically fill by a combination of natural silting / slumping and deliberate backfilling with domestic or agricultural waste. Frequently, the partially or wholly filled waterhole would be recut to a shallower depth and reused, and in most cases this final phase occurred between 1150 and 750 BC. Figure 3.27 shows the distribution of waterholes across the two phases.

Distribution: where were waterholes dug and why?

The earliest excavated waterhole was probably 180101 in Landholding 5 (Fig. 3.28). It was a large ramped-access waterhole which produced no datable artefacts. The lower fill, however, contained bones of an aurochs and red deer, as well as cattle and other undifferentiated large mammals. The presence of the wild animal element is interesting, particularly the aurochs, which appears to have become extinct in the early 2nd millennium BC (eg Tinsley 1981, 219). The latest British aurochsen date is that from Charterhouse Warren Farm in Mendip (dated to 3245+/-37BP (1620–1430cal BC) BM-731; Burleigh and Clutton-Brock 1977; Yalden 1999, 109). Cotton *et al.* (in press) have recently reviewed the British evidence for aurochs in the archaeological record and have observed that many dates cluster either side of 2000 BC. A large, fierce, wild beast such as the aurochs would have had an uncomfortable existence in the divided landscape of the second half of the 2nd millennium BC.

In considering the distribution of waterholes in the landscape between 1700 and 750 BC (see Fig. 3.27), it must be remembered that the area excavated at Perry Oaks was a comparatively narrow transect across the seven landholdings, subsequent excavation has shown such landholdings to extend much further in all directions. Despite this partial view, Table 3.8 shows that different types of waterholes were dug in different parts of the landholdings.

During the period 1700–1150 BC two ramped access waterholes were dug in Landholding 5, and another adjacent to Trackway 2 in Landholding 3. Although we do not know how extensively Landholding 5 was divided at this time, it appears that the network of paddocks in this area was principally concerned with stock management, for which ramped access water-holes would be appropriate. It is notable that ramped access waterholes were comparatively rare, and were not dug in landholdings (or parts of landholdings) that incorporated larger, less finely sub-divided fields. In contrast, ten of the twelve steep-sided waterholes were dug in Landholding 3. These waterholes may have been sited to provide water for a settlement in Landholding 3 and to water stock that had been moved close to the settlement. Some of the waterholes may also have served nearby Settlement 2 in Landholding 2.

Whether fortuitously or by design, the waterholes in Landholding 3 appear to have encircled the Neolithic HE1 enclosure (see Fig. 3.29). This arrangement, together with the nature of the artefacts recovered from two of the waterholes in Landholding 3, suggests these features served functions beyond the purely practical need to sup-ply water. The two waterholes (135071 and 156028) around the HE1 enclosure containing the artefacts will now be described in some detail, before other waterholes across the site are considered.

Date	Waterhole type	Landholding							Total
		1	2	3	4	5	6	7	
1700-1150 BC	Steep sided	2		10					12
	Ramped			1		2			3
1150-750 BC	Steep sided			6	2	1	1		10
	Ramped			2		1	2		5
	Total	2	0	19	2	4	3	0	30

Table 3.8: Waterholes: Type, location and date

Context no.	Object No.	Species	Object count	Weight	Description
180100		Cow	3	146	
180100		Large mammal	1	2	
180100	214	Aurochs	23	537	Distal humerus fused. Htc= 561.2mm.Bd (minimum as worn around this area=98.2)
180100	215	Red deer	26	27	

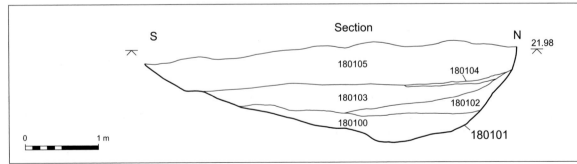

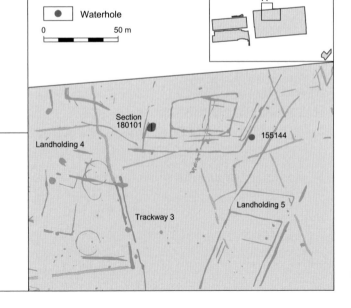

Figure 3.28: Waterhole 180101

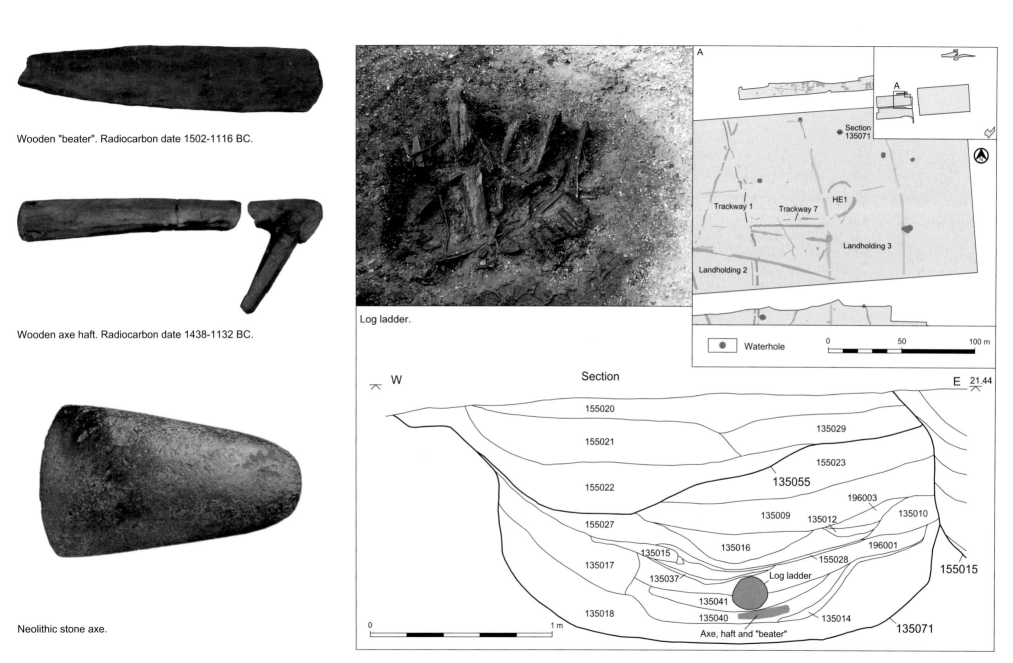

Wooden "beater". Radiocarbon date 1502-1116 BC.

Wooden axe haft. Radiocarbon date 1438-1132 BC.

Neolithic stone axe.

Log ladder.

Figure 3.29: 'Ring' of waterholes around Neolithic HE1 enclosure with detail of waterhole 135071 and ramped re-cut 135055

139

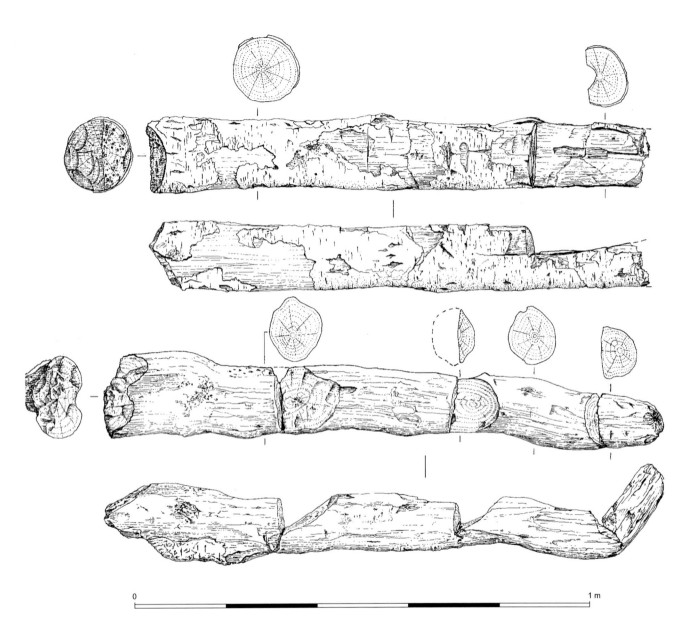

Figure 3.30: Wood ladder 135042

Waterhole 135071 (Fig. 3.29)

The sequence of deposition is as follows:

Episode 1

The lowest fills (eg 135018) were deliberate deposits to provide a more solid platform for drawing water. There was no conclusive evidence of wattle revetment but the lack of primary erosion from the sides of the waterhole suggests some level of maintenance during the initial use of the feature.

Episode 2

The next phase appears to represent a time when the waterhole was going out of use. Waterlogged organic-rich deposits 135040 and 135041 produced wooden artefacts, including:

A deposit of bark (135045- Alnus sp.), a log ladder (135042; Fig. 3.30) and artefacts (basketry SF 543–544, axe haft SF 88 (Fig. 3.29) and a 'beater' SF 323; Fig. 3.29). 106 other loose pieces of wood were recovered from the same feature including wood chippings (1 of Prunus, 2 not identified, 3 each of Populus and Fraxinus, 6 Quercus, 11 Salix and 14 Alnus spp.), bark chippings (1 Salix, 1 Fraxinus and 11 unidentified), sections of round-wood (1 each of Frangula, and Fraxinus, 2 unidentified, 5 Alnus, 6 Quercus, 11 Prunus and 22 Salix spp.) and stake points (1 Salix and 4 Quercus spp.). It is possible that among this assemblage are the remains of a disarticulated wattle lining. However the diverse composition and the fact that much of the roundwood consists of twig-type material suggests rather that this is a more casually derived assemblage. (Allen, CD Section 6)

The log ladder (Fig. 3.30) had probably been partially sunk into the basal deposits to provide a firmer seating. During excavation it was suggested that a deposit of bark was the remains of a bark container but specialist examination cast doubt on this interpretation. What seems likely is that a wooden haft (object 88) for a socketed tool and a Neolithic polished stone axe (object 500) were deliberately placed on the surface of deposit 135067. This was then covered by a deposit of wooden material (135091) which contained a wooden 'beater' (object 323).

Episode 3

The depositing of these artefacts seemed to signal a change in the history of the waterhole, which was allowed to silt slowly with material derived mainly from the erosion of the surrounding ground surface. Deposit 135062 (not on section), an organic fill, formed between these episodes of natural silting, perhaps at a hiatus in the erosion sequence, before reverting to natural silting again.

Episode 4

The waterhole was finally deliberately backfilled, possibly to level the ground.

Sometime between 1150 and 750 BC, the waterhole became a focus of activity again when a ramped-access waterhole, 135055, was dug into the top of the original feature (Fig. 3.29). A small pottery vessel was placed in the uppermost fill of the new waterhole, echoing the deposits of artefacts in the base of the original feature.

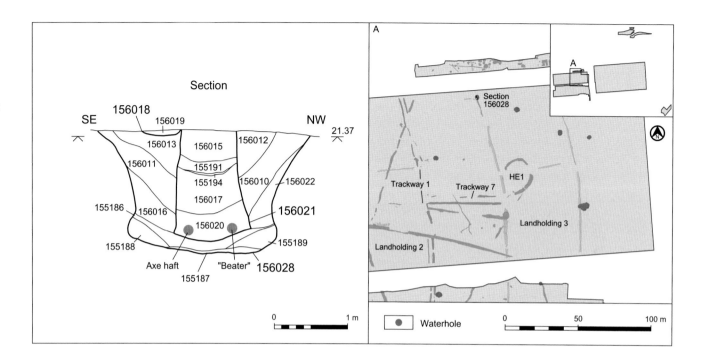

Wooden "beater", radiocarbon date 1421-1040 BC and wooden axe haft, radiocarbon date 1512-1202 BC.

Figure 3.31: Waterhole 156028

141

Waterhole 156028 (Fig. 3.31)

The deposition history of waterhole 156028 varied somewhat from that of 135071. The primary fills were caused by rapid slumping of the sides of the feature. Above this material was placed a wooden haft (object 207) for a socketed tool and a wooden 'beater' (object 208) (see below). This was followed by an episode of more gradual silting. It appears that the waterhole was then radically redesigned, with a wattle panel inserted to form a cylindrical revetment (156021; Fig. 3.31). This produced a vertical shaft into which spoil was deposited. Nine chippings (1 Pomoidiae, 8 *Quercus* spp.) and 12 sections of roundwood, 6 to 20 mm diameter (1 each of *Acer*, *Alnus*, Pomoidiae, *Salix*, *Ulmus* and 7 *Quercus* spp.) were recovered from a panel (156020) of the wattle revetment. A second assemblage, which produced 15 sections of roundwood 5–12 mm diameter (7 unidentified, 6 *Quercus* and 2 *Salix* spp.), may be derived from brushwood trimmings or sweepings.

Radiocarbon dates of 1410–1110 (WK9376 cal BC 2 sigma), 1410–1390 (WK10031 cal BC 2 sigma) and 1380–1340 (WK10028 cal BC 2 sigma), obtained from wooden chips and seeds from the first organic silting of the shaft (deposit 156034; not shown in section), placed this event firmly in the middle Bronze Age. Post-Deverel Rimbury pottery from the upper fills of the shaft indicated that it continued to fill during the period 1150–750 BC.

The occurrence of similar pairs of wooden artefacts in two waterholes *c* 26 m apart is unlikely to be coincidental or to be considered as casual losses, especially taking into consideration the presence of the Neolithic polished stone axe. How are we to interpret this evidence, and what were the historical processes that led to these deposits?

Deposits within waterholes 135071 and 156028

In Chapter 2, we suggested that deposition of material in pits in the 3rd millennium BC formed the final act in a sequence of actions that served to establish control and access to land and resources. We discussed how this system finally ended and was transformed in the centuries prior to 1700 BC, culminating in the division of the landscape into landholdings that physically defined land tenure. This led to the emergence of archaeologically visible settlements and waterholes. However, in addition to providing the essential requirements for water, the spatial distribution of the waterholes and the artefacts in the two examples described above suggest an historical and probably spiritual link with the past and its ceremonies and rituals. The waterholes served the settlements, but they were arranged around an ancient horseshoe enclosure where, generations before, representatives of the wider community met at certain times of the year. It is even possible versions of such gatherings still took place at this monument during the latter part of the 2nd millennium BC, and the waterholes were in some way linked to this. It

has been widely argued (eg Bradley 1984, 100; 1998; Bradley and Gordon 1988) that during the 2nd and 1st millennia BC, and probably during the earlier prehistoric periods as well, water and 'watery contexts' fulfilled a special and mystical place in people's lives (see artist's reconstruction of a middle Bronze Age 'waterhole ceremony' in Fig. 3.32). The artefacts in the two waterholes may have been part of a symbolic repertoire, and it is worth considering them in some detail.

Axe/adze handles (Fig. 3.33)

The two axe/adze handles were clearly intended for, and used with, socketed axes. Both were worked from long shafts, forming the handles, with one principal side branch worked to create a tine to fit into the socket. The angle of the tine to the handle (62.5 and 66 degrees) was deliberate; the tines were worked slightly off the centre of the side branch and there was sufficient wood available for the angle to have been made somewhat closer to a right angle had this been required. There is no evidence to suggest whether the blade on SF207 (Fig. 3.33, no. 1) was an axe or an adze but the cross section of the tine on SF88 (Fig. 3.33, no. 2) is more likely to have been associated with an axe. A shaving tool appears to have been utilised to trim the handle shaft but a sharp axe blade appears to have been all that was necessary to shape the butt and the head.

A number of socketed axe/adze handles of Bronze Age date are known. The remains of an oak tine were found in a socketed axe from Horsford, Norfolk (McK. Clough 1970–73, 491).

Figure 3.32: Artist's reconstruction of a middle Bronze Age 'waterhole ceremony'

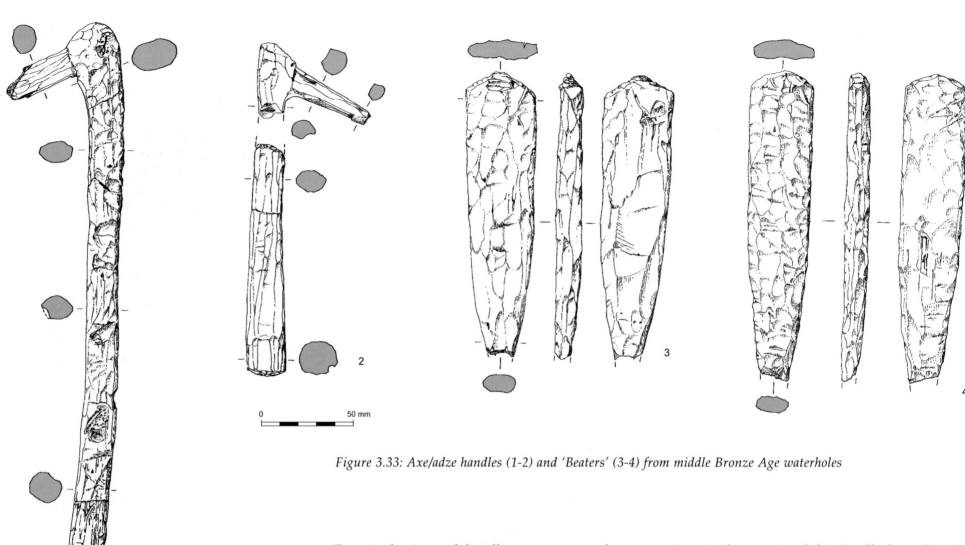

Figure 3.33: Axe/adze handles (1-2) and 'Beaters' (3-4) from middle Bronze Age waterholes

0   50 mm

Two single-piece oak handles were excavated at Flag Fen (Taylor 1992, 494), though in the complete example the tine was carved from the main fork and the handle from the side branch, reversing the practice at Perry Oaks. An alder handle is known from Inishmuck Lough, Co. Cavan (Green 1978, 139).

Axes, in their various lithic (eg Clarke *et al*. 1985, 47) and metal (eg Barrett 1985, 103) forms, are believed to have embodied value and meaning beyond the purely practical. We could interpret the deposition of the axe hafts and the Neolithic axe as clear references to the traditions of the past. Indeed, in the case of the stone axe, its excellent condition suggests that it was an heirloom passed down by generations before final removal from the world of the living and deposition in a waterhole.

'Beaters' (Fig. 3.33)

The enigmatic 'beaters' may be somehow linked to the axes.

The two 'beaters', SF 323 (Fig. 3.33, no. 3) and SF 208 (Fig. 3.33, no. 4), found in association with the axe/adze handles are of uncertain function. The wood they are cut from might be any of a number of fruit woods, such as apple, pear or hawthorn. They are fine grained and hard wearing. It would not be out of place to expect these artefacts to have been intended for some form of pounding or crushing activity, such as food preparation or, if hafted, as mattocks.

The wear on these objects though is quite uniform and as such probably occurred during burial rather than through use. It is questionable whether these are in fact finished artefacts. The axe marks are not smoothed off, the damage appears to have taken place during burial and there is no trace of any hafting or mounting for these tools. In appearance, these 'beaters' are very similar to unpolished stone axe/adzes. If ritual explanations for the depositions in these waterholes are invoked, then it may be worth considering whether these 'beaters' are wooden substitutes for the bronze axe/adze heads removed from the handles with which they are associated.

(Allen, CD Section 6)

The 'beaters' may, therefore, be mid-2nd millennium BC representations of 3rd millennium BC stone axes. The axe hafts, stone axe and wooden axe representations all directly refer to the past and the traditions of the past and these references were made at a time when the old world had been transformed into landholdings and when the community of the 3rd millennium BC had become less cohesive at the expense of the kin-group. Perhaps the excavation and use of the ring of waterholes around the Neolithic HE1 monument and the deposition of the artefacts described above was an attempt by the community to maintain a level of cohesion by drawing on the artefacts and traditions of the past but reworking them in the milieu of new depositional contexts, features and landscapes.

Waterhole 124100 (Fig. 3.34)

Waterhole 124100 was teardrop shape in plan with a sloping ramp on the western side (124105) leading to a shallow pool, created by the construction of a timber and wattle revetment (13048; Plates 3.4–5). It was excavated to a depth of 1.30 m. The revetment produced three radiocarbon dates (WK10023, WK10033 and WK10034) of between *c* 1500 and 1100 (cal BC 2 sigma; see Fig. 3.3). Following an uncertain period of time, the pool was deliberately filled with dumped material (124101) that was rich in burnt flint. Subsequent fills of the waterholes contained varying quantities of burnt flint until mid-way down the sequence, where an episode of stabilisation with a sterile deposit (123047 and 124109) was evident.

Plate 3.4: Wooden revetment within waterhole 124100

More burnt flint was deposited above this level, peaking in the upper fill (124092). A shallow rectangular feature (124085) lying 1.6 m to the north-west of waterhole 124100 also contained a very large quantity of burnt flint, particularly in the upper fills, and may have been a water trough (Fig. 3.35; see below).

Burnt flint was also recovered from interventions through the 2nd millennium BC field ditches adjacent to the waterhole and shallow pit. These deposits indicate that the function of the waterhole may have changed quite suddenly from watering animals to providing water for boiling by adding heated flint. The burnt flint debris was probably strewn over a wide area following successive episodes of heating and boiling, and a 'burnt mound' probably formed adjacent to the waterhole. A steep sided waterhole, 157065, 80 m to the west also produced relatively large quantities of burnt flint and small quantities of Post-Deverel Rimbury pottery (Fig. 3.35). This waterhole may have replaced 124100 as a water source associated with the burnt mound during the period 1150–750 BC.

Burnt mounds have been the subject of much research (eg Buckley 1990), which has tended to polarise interpretation. On the one hand, the mounds, together with water sources and boiling troughs (124085), are interpreted as sites of communal cooking of meat, possibly associated with feasting (Hedges 1975; James, 1986). The alternative view is that they represent sites

of saunas, sweat lodges for ritual cleansing (Barfield and Hodder 1987). However, Ray (1990) has developed yet another line of interpretation whereby the mounds became '...one locus of mediation of interests and strategies among several others' (Ray 1990, 10).

The Perry Oaks burnt mound complex was located amidst the sub-divided fields of Landholding 5, some distance away from any of the postulated settlements discussed above. The exact function of the burnt mound complex will probably remain uncertain but the depositional sequences in waterhole 124100 and possible trough 124085

Plate 3.5: Part of wood and wattle revetment on the base of waterhole 124100

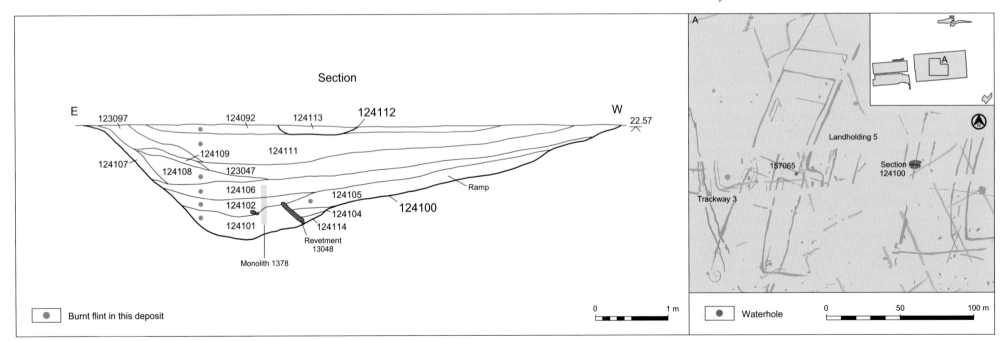

Figure 3.34: Ramped waterhole 124100

suggest that people periodically gathered at this location to take part in activities that produced the residues recovered during excavation. It has already been suggested that the ring of waterholes and unusual artefacts around the HE1 horse-shoe enclosure served to reinforce the ties that bound together the kin-groups in order to retain a form of community. The burnt flint complex may testify to a need to satisfy a similar requirement, acted out in a different physical and social setting, but retaining the element of water. In other words, members of the kin-groups might have come together in a relatively isolated part of the landscape in order to reaffirm community ties, undertaking unknown ceremonies and rituals that may have included cooking, feasting or bathing.

The developing role of the waterholes into the late Bronze Age

The waterholes and artefacts in Landholding 3 and the burnt flint complex in Landholding 5 seem to have fulfilled similar functions to the monuments of the 4th and 3rd millennia BC, but within a different structure, architecture and pattern in the landscape. All served to display, accommodate and negotiate the tensions between individuals, kin-groups and the wider community.

These examples demonstrate the role played by waterholes in the routine of social connections during the period 1700–1150 BC. Between 1150 and 750 BC many waterholes were re-cut and reinstated and new ones were excavated. Figure 3.27 and Table 3.8 above have shown that, whilst steep-sided waterholes continued to concentrate in Landholding 3 around the HE1 enclosure, they had a more even distribution across the landscape in the later period. Perhaps importantly, one steep-sided waterhole (125233) was excavated through ditch 113124, which formed part of Trackway 2. This suggests the abandonment of this trackway as an active routeway.

The numbers and distribution of ramped waterholes also increased slightly between 1150 and 750 BC. The current sample is too small to suggest a change in stock management and the stock/ arable balance before and after 1150, although this theme will be explored further in Volume 2.

Turning to the role of waterholes in maintaining late Bronze Age communities, one or two examples of unusual artefact deposits in the bases of these features appear to continue the pre- 1150 BC traditions.

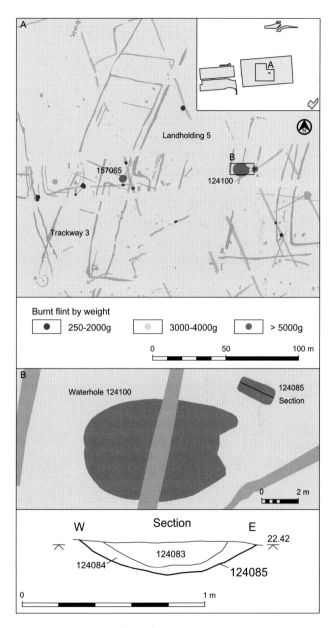

Figure 3.35: Burnt flint features around waterhole 124100

Waterhole complex 103040, 103038, 136194

Waterhole 103038 was a steep-sided recut of ramped waterhole, 103040 (Fig. 3.36). The excavator believed that 103038 was cut by shaft 136194 to form a well, but, due to extremely difficult excavation conditions, precise interpretation of this complex sequence is not possible. Nevertheless, the original interpretation is described here, with the shaft shown on the section in Figure 3.36 as cut 136194. The base of waterhole 103038 was revetted to retain the soft, unconsolidated fills of the earlier ramped waterhole, 103040. A significant artefact assemblage was recovered from the basal fills of shaft 136194 and waterhole 103038, comprising an almost complete Post-Deverel Rimbury bipartite jar (from 112062), and a carinated bowl with two carinated drinking vessels (from 136193) (Figs 3.36-7).

A radiocarbon determination on waterlogged seeds from basal fill 136193 produced a date of 1620–1320 (WK9375 cal BC 2 sigma). The seeds, however, may have derived from the earlier waterhole, 103040, since the pottery from 136193 clearly belonged to the Post-Deverel Rimbury ceramic tradition. Every and Mepham (CD Section 1) describe the vessels from this waterhole complex:

One carinated bowl formed part of a deliberate deposit at the base of a waterhole (136194; Fig. 3.37, no. 4) together with two carinated drinking vessels (Barrett's Class V; Fig. 3.37, nos 2–3). The latter have no known direct parallels in Thames Valley assemblages, although the profile of the form echoes

exactly that of the accompanying bowl form—both forms have convex neck profiles and omphalos bases, and these three vessels were almost certainly made at the same time as a 'matching set'. The two drinking vessels both have simple linear decoration around the neck and carination. All three of the vessels within this deposit had been partially burnt, with localised 'blistering' and refiring of exterior surfaces in each case, and the bowl has what appears to be a large post-firing perforation in the base (perhaps a deliberate 'killing' of the vessel?). While nearly all the fineware bowls have the short necks typical of the late Bronze Age, there is at least one example (from deposit 136188) of a long-necked form, which potentially has a slightly later (early Iron Age) date; this example is decorated with incised motif (Fig. 3.37, no. 5).

The deposition of a complete coarseware bipartite jar at the base of waterhole (103038; Fig. 3.37, no. 1) and the careful placing of a 'matching set' of carinated bowl and two carinated cups, all finewares, at the base of waterhole (see above) is clearly an act of deliberate deposition. In these instances, pots can be seen as similar to the to the 'sealing deposits' comprising wooden and other artefacts in other waterholes of the middle Bronze Age; the latter do not include whole vessels although occasional sherds are included, perhaps incidentally. All three fineware vessels, prior to their final deposition, had been subjected to high temperatures to produce slight localised burning, such as might result from being placed close to a bonfire, and the bowl had apparently been deliberately pierced through the base. The coarseware jar appears to show evidence of use prior to deposition, in the form of an external burnt residue over the rim and upper part of the vessel.

There may in fact be a further link between these vessels. Woodward (1998–9) has highlighted the deposition of communal 'feasting sets' from the Neolithic onwards. For the late Bronze Age (1150–750 BC), she defines these 'sets' as consisting of a single large, often thin-walled, vessel, one or more medium-sized jars, and one or more drinking vessels. If the two intercutting waterhole deposits are combined, the four vessels could conceivably be seen as one such 'set'.

(Every and Mepham, CD Section 1)

This pattern of deposition of complete pots has been observed elsewhere, most recently at Swalecliffe, Kent, where a complete vessel ('pot 3', resembling the bi-partite carinated jar from waterhole 103038) was placed at the base of a waterhole in a dense complex of other such features (Masefield *et al.* 2003, fig. 28, plate 11). Radiocarbon and dendrochronology date this deposit to the 'turn [ie early] of the eighth century BC' (Masefield *et al.* 2004, 338) and we can postulate a similar date for the deposition of the Perry Oaks vessel.

Hill (1989) has explored the representation of symbolic systems through the placing of deposits in pits. We would simply suggest that, sometime in the 8th century BC, the social gatherings and interactions which were necessary to hold communities together were as important as ever, and that these activities involved the deposition of artefacts at the base of waterholes 103040 /136194.

Right
Figure 3.36: Waterhole complex 103040, 103038, 136194

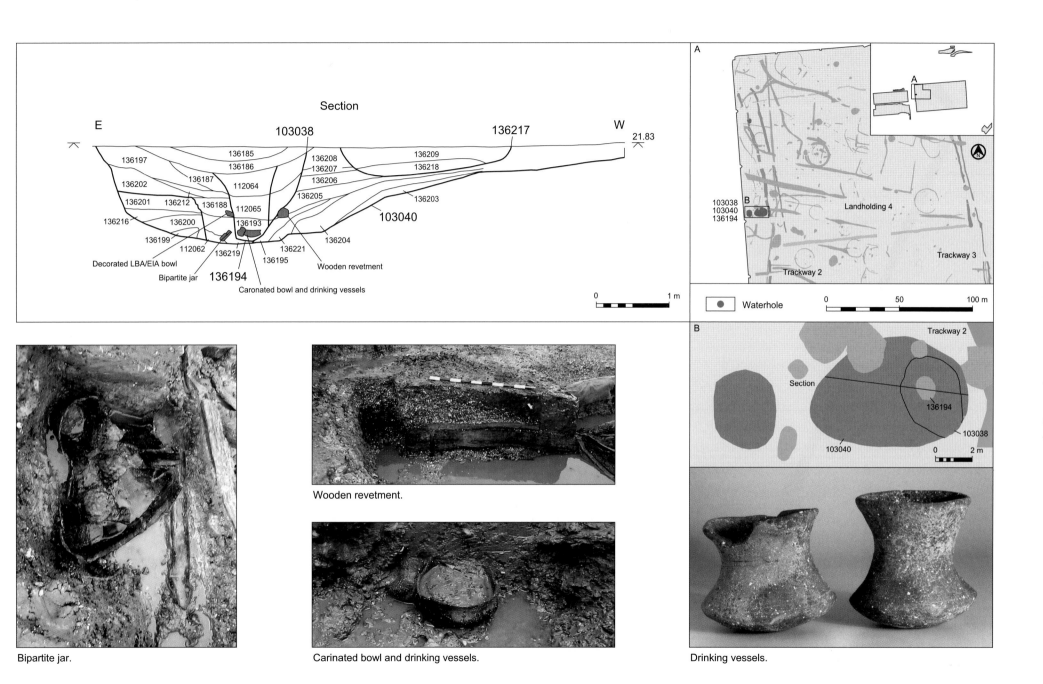

Section

E

103038   136217   W
21.83

136197   136185
136186
136202   136187   112064   136208   136209
136201   136212   136188   136207   136218
136216   136200   112065   136206   136203
136199   136193   136205
112062   136219   136194   136221   136204
136195

Decorated LBA/EIA bowl

Bipartite jar

Caronated bowl and drinking vessels

Wooden revetment

0   1 m

A

103038
103040
136194

B

Landholding 4

Trackway 3

Trackway 2

Waterhole

0   50   100 m

B

Trackway 2

Section

136194

103040   103038

0   2 m

Bipartite jar.

Wooden revetment.

Carinated bowl and drinking vessels.

Drinking vessels.

149

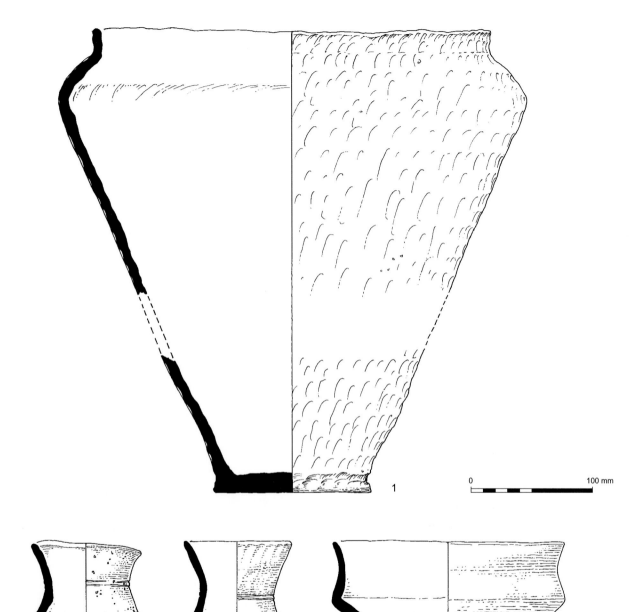

Continuity of tradition

A comparison of the waterholes and associated artefacts indicates a strong element of continuity between the periods 1700–1150 BC and 1150–750 BC, but also changes, which reflected how people shaped their society and community. The waterholes and associated artefacts of the middle Bronze Age period appeared to refer back to the Neolithic in their spatial arrangement (around the HE1 monument), act of deposition in pits and symbolism of the objects themselves. These elements were, however, affected by new constraints—the requirement to obtain water in a landscape where access to streams and rivers was now restricted by ditches, banks and hedges. Within this new landscape, the landholding kingroups still had to work and live side-by-side, and will have come together as a community to share labour, resources and participate in social events such as births, marriages and deaths. We have argued that the construction and use of waterholes in Landholding 3 and the burnt

Figure 3.37: Late Bronze Age pottery assemblage and decorated late Bronze Age/early Iron Age bowl from Waterhole complex 103040, 103038, 136194

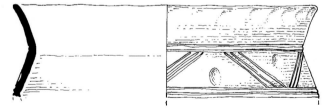

mound complex in Landholding 5 were shaped by practices that reflected these concerns. Moving forward to the period 1150–750 BC, we see a strong sense of continuity with the reuse of waterholes or the excavation of new examples adjacent to the originals. However, the water-holes of this later period derived their meaning from the more immediate past, the period 1700–1150 BC, not the ancient past of the 4th and 3rd millennia BC. The echoes and traditions of that ancient community which persisted into the latter half of the 2nd millennium BC had been swept aside in the making of the new world of the agricultural and pastoral landscape. In its place we see in the complete pottery vessels the agency of new mechanisms involving feasting and drinking that modulated the age-old dynamic tension between individuals, the kin-groups and the community.

Life and death during the 2nd and early 1st millennium BC at Perry Oaks

We have now explored how and perhaps why the landscape was divided sometime around 1700 BC into a series of landholdings, and how a system of fields, trackways, settlements and waterholes followed. We have suggested that the broader community may have become more loosely bound than previously, but we have shown how mechanisms resulting in the deposition of unusual artefacts and burnt flint in waterholes may have served to maintain the intra-community bonds.

In this section we will start by discussing the elements of life in the 2nd millennium BC that are surprisingly under-represented in our excavations, namely the use and deposition of metalwork and the disposal of the dead. We will then move on to discuss how the landholdings may have sustained the kin-groups through arable and pastoral agriculture. We will briefly discuss changes in settlement distribution in the early 1st millennium BC, and how this may represent the strengthening of the community as the individual kin-groups coalesced.

Burials and Metal artefacts: where are they?

In a period where we have demonstrated a thriving rural agricultural landscape, the scarcity of cremations or inhumations at Perry Oaks, either in cemeteries or singly is striking. Similarly, the only metalwork of note was the side-looped spearhead and the spiral finger ring described above. No metalwork was recovered from any of the possible settlement sites we have identified. In order to understand this, we must firstly remember the effects of truncation on the archaeological deposits at Perry Oaks and then we should consider the Heathrow landscape in a wider geographical context.

The varying degrees of truncation caused by the construction of the sludge works would have removed most shallow features which were confined to topsoil or upper subsoil. During the recent T5 excavations, a small un-urned

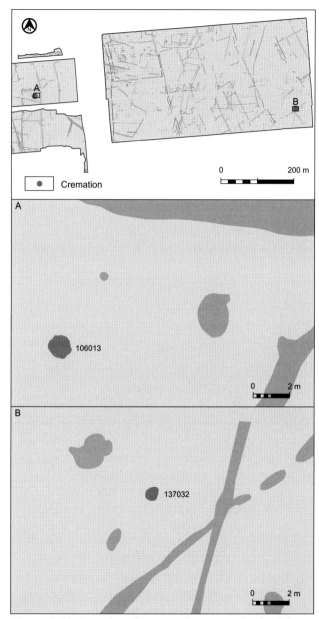

Figure 3.38: Location of Bronze Age cremation burials at Perry Oaks

cremation cemetery, probably dating to the 2nd millennium BC, was excavated on the edge of the Colne floodplain near the village of Longford (discussed in Volume 2). Truncation on the scale encountered at Perry Oaks would have removed all trace of these burials, while cremations contained within Deverel Rimbury urns and grouped into cemeteries such as that at Ashford Common (Barrett 1973) would also have been destroyed. Similarly, cremations inserted into the flanks of low mounds or barrows would have been removed, and so we must acknowledge that what remains at Perry Oaks is a very partial sample of what *could* have once existed.

Only two definite cremations were present at Perry Oaks: 106013 and 137032 (Fig. 3.38). Both contained an adult (probably female), and 137032 also contained fragments of copper alloy from probable grave goods and ten *Arrhenatherum elatius* (onion couch) tubers. The presence of edible tubers, such as *Arrhenatherum elatius*, in cremation deposits are particularly characteristic of Bronze Age cremations (eg Jones 1978, 108; Carruthers 1992, 63; Moffett 1999, 245), although their purpose in these assemblages is unclear. Unfortunately, a sample of this material produced a radiocarbon date of 3030–2870 (WK11473 cal BC 2 sigma). However, in view of the presence of copper alloy, and the known occurrence of these tubers in 2nd millennium BC cremations, we conclude that this date is probably from a contaminated sample. Cremation pit 106013 contained fragments of Deverel Rimbury pottery but Post-Deverel Rimbury pottery predominated, suggesting a date after 1150 BC.

The location of pit 137032 in Landholding 6 is relatively isolated, but pit 106013 was located between Settlements 2 and 4, south-west of the Neolithic HE1 monument. It could thus be seen to fit the model proposed by Barrett for the Thames Valley 'buffer zone', where, 'The correlation is between the inheritance of land and those rights of inheritance which find further expression through the burial of ancestors in close proximity to the settlement' (Barrett 1980, 84).

The marked absence of metalwork is particularly striking in view of the well-known concentrations of finds from the River Thames, and several terrestrial hoards in West London. There have been numerous attempts to reconcile the apparent dichotomy between rich metalwork evidence suggesting social differentiation, versus the settlement evidence that suggests little such differentiation (eg Bradley 1984). This paradox is particularly evident at Perry Oaks, and apart from the two bronze artefacts already described above; one cannot help but feel that almost all bronze artefacts were carefully removed and either recycled, or recast and reused, but ultimately deposited with particular care in certain contexts. For example, both wooden axe hafts were buried without their associated bronze axe heads. The context of deposition of the spearhead and spiral finger ring may also have been symbolic. The spearhead, an artefact with male associations, was placed in a field boundary, whilst the thumb ring, an artefact with possible female associations, was deposited in a waterhole. These symbols could suggest the different roles the genders played in matters of land inheritance and claim, provision

of water as a fundamental of life and the social mechanisms used to bind the community together.

How people lived: arable and pastoral agriculture at Perry Oaks 1700–750 BC

We have described above a complex landscape of fields, trackways, settlements and waterholes, which evolved from 1700 to 750 BC. We will turn now to how people may have used this landscape to produce the food they needed to exist.

Firstly it is worth reiterating that the landscape and agricultural regime of the latter half of the 2nd millennium represented a complete trans-formation from that of the 3rd millennium BC. It has been argued that once the concept of tenure and inheritance of formal blocks of land had been formalised by the first land boundaries, the trajec-tory of landscape development and agricultural transformation was altered. People had no choice but to shape their own, narrower world defined by the land boundaries so that they obtained the best return from their resources and labours. This is reflected in the different sizes and orientations of the fields and paddocks within each landholding.

Similar conclusions were reached for the Newark Road sub-site at Fengate, Cambridgeshire (Pryor 1980). However, in the light of his practical experience as a sheepfarmer, Pryor reviewed the situation that led to the creation of the 'planned' later prehistoric landscapes, and came to differ-ent conclusions (Pryor 1996, 316). Fundamental to the pattern of stock management proposed by

Pryor was the suggestion that livestock were grazed in the rich pastures of Flag Fen during the dryer summer months, but were moved and spent the late autumn, winter and early spring on the well-drained, higher ground of Fengate where they were kept and managed using the ditched fields and trackways. These trackways were spaced 50–100 m apart and ran down to the wetland edge (ibid., 314). Within this complex of droveways, Pryor suggested the existence of 'community stockyards' where major gatherings of people and animals occurred at the beginning / end of the dryland phase of grazing. The Newark Road complex was interpreted this way, and would have served to manage the confinement, sorting, inspection and exchange of hundreds if not thousands of animals, predominantly sheep.

In tandem with the 'community' stockyards, Pryor suggested 'farm' stockyards, serving single farms, and cited the Storey's Bar Road sub-site at Fengate as an example (ibid., 317–8). Pryor's model proposed very large flock sizes, running into thousands, which required increasingly elaborate stock control mechanisms. This redressed what he saw as a bias towards arable agriculture in the archaeological literature. He suggested that the long droveways, for instance, passed through paddocks 'not arable fields' and were to keep animals apart from other animals and overgrazed pasture rather than from crops.

The strength of Pryor's analysis is that it is based on large excavated areas and his own personal experience of raising and managing sheep,

and as such it deserves close comparison with the Perry Oaks landscape.

Firstly we can see many similarities between Fengate and Perry Oaks: the long trackways, instances of stock management features, sub-divided fields and waterholes. There is a clear example of a gateway in Trackway 1, for example, which was probably used for stock management (Fig. 3.39). Many of the trackways varied in width at different points along their length to allow sheep to be singled out and inspected. Many of the fields had entrances at their corners to take advantage of the funnelling effect of two hedgerows. Trackway 2, at almost 7 m wide, may have served as a 'main drove' for moving animals longer distances across the landscape. Even Settlement 1 could be interpreted as one of Pryor's 'community stockyards', with the buildings being sheds for animals. However, the flanking trackways narrowed to the south of the settlement, in contrast to the Newark Road stockyard where they widened as they moved away from the enclosure.

It is indisputable that much of the Perry Oaks landscape developed during the 2nd millennium BC to facilitate animal husbandry. However, there are differences between the Fengate model and Perry Oaks, some subtle, some more sharply drawn. Firstly, we maintain that the main trackways represented major landholdings, and the differences in field layout cannot be explained purely in functional terms. Secondly, the fundamental basis of the Fengate model is the movement of animals from the wetter summer

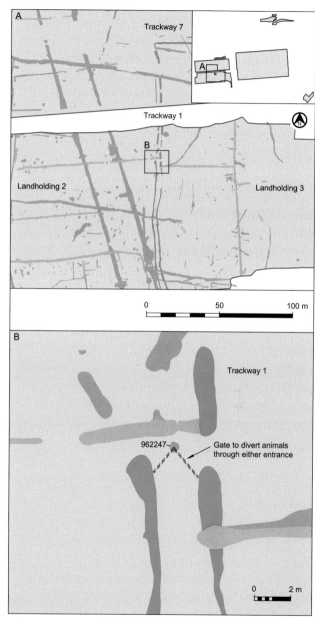

Figure 3.39: Gateway in Trackway 1, used for stock management

pastures to higher, dryer pastures during winter, hence the orientation of droveways to this effect. At Perry Oaks, all the major droveways were orientated parallel to the River Colne, roughly north-south. They could have been aligned to provide access to a loop in the Colne, 1.1 km to the north-west, but this seems unlikely. If access to and from the Colne Floodplain and the higher, dryer terrace was of crucial importance, then the major landholdings and certainly the trackways would have been aligned east-west. That way, all landholdings would have had access to the river, and could have moved and herded their animals easily between the two areas.

Palaeoenvironmental evidence from middle Bronze Age waterholes

The palaeoenvironmental evidence from Perry Oaks features dated to the middle Bronze Age shows quite clearly that the landscape maintained a mixed agricultural regime of cereal crops and animal husbandry, while insect remains clearly stress the importance of stock raising and animal husbandry, as detailed by Robinson:

All the Bronze Age insect assemblages gave strong evidence for grassland. The chafer and elaterid beetles of Species Group 11, such as Phyllopertha horticola and Athous haemorrhoidalis, comprised around 5% of the terrestrial Coleoptera. Another member of this group, Agrypnus murinus, which is characteristic of well-drained soils, was well-represented in Sample 856 from Feature 178108 and Sample 857 from Feature 178122, the intercutting pits. Many of the Carabidae (ground beetles) commonly occur in grassland including Pterostichus cupreus, Calathus fuscipes and some species of Amara. A warm sunny aspect to the site, with sheltered areas of permanent grass which was relatively short, was suggested by the occurrence of Brachinus crepitans (bombardier beetle) in several of the samples. Another beetle of warm dry habitat is the tenebrionid Opatrum sabulosum, which was represented by six individuals in Sample 857. It occurs in sandy areas where there are breaks in the vegetation cover and now has a distribution in Britain which is principally coastal, although it is known from parts of Berkshire and Surrey (Brendell 1975, 10). The lygaeid bug Aphanus rolandri, also found in this sample, only occurs in sheltered sunny habitats. Further evidence of broken sandy grassland was given by Calathus cf. ambiguus but there was no other evidence of the heathland vegetation with which this beetle is often associated, although heathland subsequently developed in the region.

Grass-feeding insects included cicadellid bugs from the genus Aphrodes. The phytophagous beetles gave some indication of the grassland vegetation. They included Ceuthorhynchidius troglodytes which feeds on Plantago lanceolata (ribwort plantain), Mecinus pyraster which feeds on P. media (hoary plantain) as well as P. lanceolata, Hydrothassa glabra which feeds on Ranunculus spp. (buttercups) and Galeruca tanaceti which is mostly associated with Achillea millefolium (yarrow). A more general association with Compositae is shown by Olibrus sp. Weevils from the genera Apion and Sitona which feed on clovers and vetches (Species Group 3) ranged from 2.3 to 3.7% of the terrestrial Coleoptera. Such values are not high enough to suggest hay meadow but are characteristic of grassland that has not been so heavily grazed as to prevent the flowering of clovers. Two of the more host-specific members of this group that were identified, Sitona hispidulus and S. lepidus mostly feed on Trifolium spp. (clovers) although they can also occur on Medicago spp. (medicks) (Morris 1997, 51, 57).

Evidence that the grassland was grazed by domestic animals was given by the scarabaeoid dung beetles of Species Group 2. These beetles feed on the droppings of larger herbivores on pasture. They ranged from 9.3% of the terrestrial Coleoptera in Sample 229 from Feature 135071 to 19.2% of the terrestrial Coleoptera in Sample 856 from Feature 178108. The lower value is what might be expected from a largely pastoral landscape but the higher value suggested that domestic animals were concentrated in the vicinity of the middle Bronze Age pit. It is possible that the enclosure in which this pit was situated was used for management of stock which grazed over a much wider area.

The most numerous of the scarabaeoid dung beetles were species of Aphodius: A. cf. sphacelatus in Samples 229 and 277, A. granarius in Samples 856 and 857. However, species of Onthophagus were also well-represented in samples 229 and 277, comprising 33.3% individuals in these two samples. Two species of Onthophagus in Samples 229 and 277, O. nutans and O. taurus, are now extinct in Britain. Individuals of Aphodius greatly outnumber Onthophagus in present-day dung faunas in Britain. The proportion of Onthophagus, however, rises further south in Europe. It is possible that mean summer temperatures were somewhat warmer when some of the middle Bronze Age deposits accumulated (see below).

The insects from the Bronze Age samples also included members of several other families of Coleoptera which commonly occur in the droppings of domestic animals. They included the hydrophilids Sphaeridium bipustulatum and Megasternum obscurum, the histerid Hister quadrimaculatus and the staphylinids Anotylus sculpturatus gp. and Philonthus spp. Some of these species are members of Species Group 7 and also occur in other categories of foul organic material including dung heaps and middens.

Coleoptera are very good at demonstrating the importance, species composition and use of grassland within the vicinity of a waterlogged deposit, but are less effective at indicating the presence of arable (Robinson 1983). This is because cereal crops in Britain do not commonly suffer from beetle pests. Sample 277 from Context 141024 did, however, contain a single example of Aphthona cf. euphorbiae, a beetle that as well as occurring on species of Euphorbia (spurges) also feeds on Linum usitatissimum (flax). Otherwise, possible evidence of arable was given by the carabid (ground) beetles of Species Groups 6a and 6b which are favoured by areas of bare or weedy disturbed ground. The two members of Species Group 6a, Agonum dorsale and Harpalus rufipes, beetles of general disturbed ground or arable, ranged from 0 to 3.5% of the terrestrial Coleoptera. The species of Amara such as A. apricaria and A. bifrons that belong to Species Group 6b, beetles of sandy or dry disturbed ground and arable, ranged from 0 to 0.7% of the terrestrial Coleoptera. Their abundance was certainly sufficient to show the occurrence of their habitat in the vicinity of the waterholes. However, it is much harder to establish whether they were from cultivated ground or disturbed, weedy and

bare ground as occurs around settlements. In the case of Sample 229 from Feature 135071, there was no evidence from the insects for the proximity of settlement whereas Sample 856 from Feature 178108 and Sample 857 from Feature 178122 contained synanthropic beetles and it is very likely that there would have been areas of bare and weedy ground between buildings (see below).

The phytophagous beetles included some that are dependent on potential arable weeds. For example Pseudostyphlus pillumus feeds on Tripleurospermum, Anthemis and Matricaria spp. (mayweeds) and many of the Ceuthorhynchinae feed on Cruciferae that are arable weeds. However, many of the phytophagous beetles feed on herbaceous plants that occur in several habitats. Chaetocnema concinna, which feeds on Polygonaceae, was present in all the Bronze Age samples but it is uncertain whether it was feeding on Rumex spp. (dock) at the base of the hedges, in waste ground, in grassland or growing in cultivated ground. It could also have been feeding on other plants such as Polygonum aviculare (knotgrass) growing on disturbed ground.

(Robinson, CD Section 12)

The pollen and waterlogged plant remains indicate direct and indirect evidence of cereal growing as well as animal husbandry. The best direct evidence for cereal growing was provided by the dump of crop processing waste in waterhole 135071 (see Fig 3.29 above).

Waterhole 135071

Six samples were examined for waterlogged plant macrofossils, four of which produced a wide range of well preserved remains. Sample 1141 (context 135040), taken from below the log ladder, was the lowest of the samples stratigraphically, but sample 1140 (context 135034), a thin layer higher up the profile, produced by far the greatest concentration of plant remains. 1140 also produced the largest amounts of emmer (Triticum dicoccum) and spelt (T. spelta) glume bases and spikelets, including some that were radiocarbon dated to 1260–910 BC (WK9374 cal BC 2 sigma). The presence of compacted layers of straw and chaff, interleaved with numerous wild parsnip (Pastinaca sativa) and common mallow (Malva sylvestris) fruits and stems in both samples from this thin layer (samples 1140 and 1135) suggest that crop processing waste mixed with ruderal weeds had been deposited in the waterhole. Crop processing waste was recovered from all four of the lower, better preserved samples, accounting for 2 to 10% of the identifiable remains. A few barley (Hordeum vulgare) rachis fragments provided evidence for the cultivation of barley, in addition to emmer and spelt. The absence of synanthropic insects from the deposit of crop processing waste, context 155028 (Robinson, CD Section 12), demonstrated that the straw had not been used for thatching, flooring or bedding before being deposited in the waterhole.

A few flax (Linum usitatissimum) capsule fragments were recovered from two of the samples. Waterlogged features often produce evidence of flax processing waste, since leaving the plants to rot in water (retting) is one of the stages in processing flax for its fibre. Because only a few capsule fragments and no seeds were present in otherwise very well-preserved samples there is no clear evidence for retting having taken place in this particular waterhole. Retting is a smelly process that would have fouled the water if it was being used for human or livestock consumption, and caused eutrophication. It is likely that flax processing waste had been fed to livestock and small amounts had been introduced into the feature in animal dung.

(Carruthers, CD Section 9)

The common mallow and wild parsnip found in waterhole 135071 are tall perennials (parsnip is a biennial) that grow primarily on dryer soils. Mallow shows a preference for calcareous soils, whilst parsnip is often found on nutrient-enriched soils. Being perennials, they would not have been growing as arable weeds, but may have survived around field margins. Alternatively, they may have become mixed with the straw in the early stages of threshing. Both plants are readily grazed by animals, but a threshing area is likely to have been situated on dryer ground which was fenced off from livestock. The plants would have been fruiting some time between July to September, which would correspond with harvesting arable crops. A beetle which feeds on mallow, Podagrica fuscicornis, was recovered from the same context as the seeds (Robinson, CD Section 12).

All the pollen samples from middle Bronze Age waterholes 178108, 124100, 156031 and 135071 provided evidence for cereal production and grazed grassland. We can take waterholes 178108

and 124100 as good examples, since they are spatially well separated (see Fig. 3.8 above). The following is derived from Wiltshire (CD Section 11):

Waterhole 171808 (Fig. 3.40)
If Feature 178108 is taken as an example, elements of mixed farming and landscape management can be seen. From the base of the waterhole, Zones 178108/1&2 relate to the earliest phase of the feature.

Zone 1 *shows relatively low levels of grass pollen, ruderal weeds, and pasture herbs, and this might indicate a fairly high grazing pressure in the environs of the feature. But cereals were well represented and these indicate the importance of arable farming in this area of*

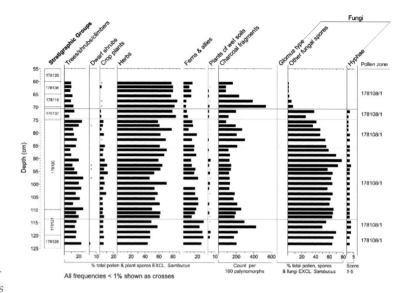

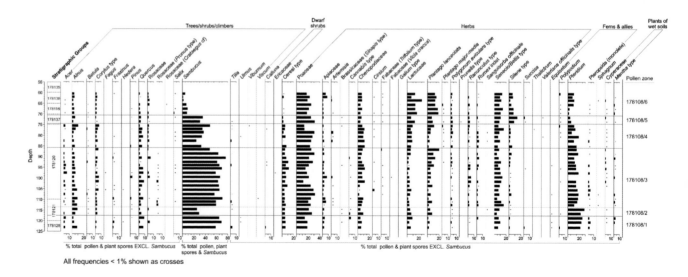

Figure 3.40: Pollen samples from waterhole 178108

the site. The soils around the waterhole were obviously wet, but the absence of obligate water plants might suggest that the feature was so intensively used that floating plants could not colonise. The ferns and many of the herbs recorded in the diagram could have been growing at the base of the adjacent hedge. The observed assemblage is often seen along boundaries of field systems today although, of course, they could also have been growing in grassland or on open, disturbed soils associated with ploughed fields.

Zone 2 shows some intensive activity in the vicinity of the feature. The local hedge was affected (particularly elder) and the changes might have been related to local burning. It is possible that hedge cuttings were burned very close to the feature. There was certainly no impact on local cereal growing but the rise in grasses and other herbs might indicate that animals could have been kept away from the area for a period.

Zone 3 coincides approximately with the re-cutting of the waterhole 178108 by Feature 178122. This was presumably an attempt to rejuvenate the original silted-up waterhole. Throughout this zone, the very local landscape seems to have been stable, and there were only small variations in the herb pollen spectra throughout. The hedgerow recovered and, indeed, more woody taxa were recorded. Bracken declined while some ruderal weeds and pasture plants increased. This implies that there was a greater availability of disturbed and broken soils. The wetness around the feature also increased.

In **Zone 4**, there appears to have been another management event and the hedge was adversely affected. Cereal growing also seems to have declined

slightly and there seems to have been trampling, grazing, or cutting of local herbaceous vegetation. However, there was better representation of smaller herbs such as plantains, buttercups, polypody fern, and cleavers. Common valerian and meadow rue (plants characteristic of meadow/pasture) were also recorded. The removal of taller grasses might have allowed better pollen dispersal of these plants. The effects in the herb flora might suggest that the impact on grasses (whether due to active management or grazing) occurred before the main grass flowering period in June; the later flowering plants are thus better represented.

In **Zone 5**, there seem to have been an even greater impact on the hedgerow and other trees and shrubs in the catchment. Values for cereal pollen and bracken also dropped while grasses and some other herbs were enhanced by events. It must be remembered that the timing of plant management can affect the palynological record very dramatically. The cutting of spring and summer flowering woody plants at any time will result in a diminishing of flowering in the following year or even longer. Cutting grasses and many herbs in late spring, and cutting bracken at any time between April and late July, will result in poor pollen and spore representation. The pollen spectra in this zone are probably reflecting the effects of small scale management although there is little doubt that cereal production had either moved away slightly, or had declined in areal extent in the immediate locality.

In **Zone 6**, the local elder bushes seem to have been severely cut and/or burned, but attention seems to have been directed mainly to this one shrub. Cereal production also declined near the feature. The increase

in pollen of herbaceous plants, particularly that of plantain, campion, dandelion-like plants and, eventually, bracken and hogweed/fool's parsley, suggest that the sward at the base of the hedge remained lush. It is possible that the herbs were actually growing in the ditch and out of reach of stock animals. There is little doubt that there were small-scale changes in the area but it is doubtful that there were meaningful alterations in the landscape further afield.

(Wiltshire, CD Section 11)

Waterhole 124100 (Fig. 3.41)

Zone 1 in the pollen diagram for this features shows that, as with the waterholes in Landholding 3 to the west of the site, this one was set in a cleared, agricultural landscape with both arable and pastoral farming being important in the immediate area. It was also close to diverse hedgerows. The vegetation dominating the open ground was also very similar to that recorded on the west of Perry Oaks for the same period.

Zone 2 shows changes in local management. Cereals appear to be grown or processed further away and flax was recorded. Flax is well known to produce tiny amounts of poorly dispersed pollen (values of less than 2% TLPS have been recorded within the crop fields) so a single pollen grain could, actually, represent a considerable area put to this crop. It is tempting to suggest that crops were being rotated, albeit at a small scale in an attempt to conserve soil fertility. At about 112 cm, Poaceae declined and continued to do so until the end of the zone. There was also a decline in some of the herbs that might have been abundant in the local grassland such as Fabaceae (clover family), Potentilla type (eg silver weed), and *Ranunculus* type (buttercups). It is possible that grazing intensity increased locally but it might also mean that the grassland was being managed for hay production. The lack of response of some of the herbs that were probably growing in the pasture community might simply reflect the relative flowering times at hay cutting. This interpretation is conjectural but quite feasible.

In **Zone 3**, the area around the waterhole seems to have been the focus of renewed agricultural pressure, and microscopic charcoal increased very greatly. There was little change in the larger woody taxa other than a slight but consistent lower representation of *Alnus*. However, *Acer* and *Viburnum* (guelder rose) were recorded and *Salix* increased while Rosaceae indet (probably bramble) declined. Nevertheless, the hedgerow remained diverse and was probably being managed carefully. Cereal pollen was more frequent along with ruderals which could have been growing at the field boundaries, on paths, or even in the crops themselves. Grasses recovered slightly but not to the levels of the earlier part of the previous zone. There was a marked decline in plantain and a reciprocal (quite large) rise in bracken.

The varying fates of these taxa must relate to relatively small-scale changes in local land use practices. It is feasible that brambles were being cleared from the hedgerow, freeing bracken from competition. It is also possible that more intense grazing allowed the unpalatable bracken to flourish. Stock animals often seek out the longer and more succulent herbage along field boundaries and hedgerows but grazing is selective. It is, of course, possible that a different stock animal was being grazed in the pasture, possibly sheep rather than

cattle. They have a very different effect on the sward from cattle by virtue of close nibbling rather than tongue pulling. Generally, they cannot cope with long vegetation and, today, are usually pastured when the grassland sward has been reduced in height (Bacon 1990). They can cope with a very short sward, and even crop stubble after harvest, whereas cattle need fairly lush, long grass (Owen 1980). Sheep will nibble young bramble and flowering heads of rosette plants (personal observation), but will usually avoid bracken; and they are not as effective as cattle at trampling down this invasive pastoral weed. Sheep are also less dependent upon waterholes and get much of their water from vegetation. It is feasible that drier conditions and repeated drying out of the waterhole favoured sheep over cattle in this particular field system.

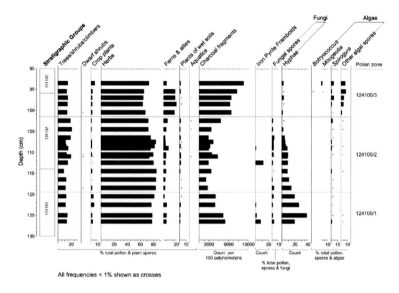

All frequencies < 1% shown as crosses

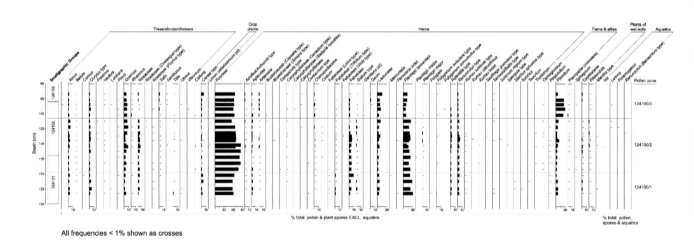

All frequencies < 1% shown as crosses

Figure 3.41: Pollen samples from waterhole 124100

158

Stocking densities and duration of grazing in any one area is known to affect the species composition of pasture very markedly. However, certainly in calcareous grassland, high species richness is maintained when sheep are kept at one animal/ha/yr on swards of low productivity, but at seven sheep/ha/yr where there is high productivity (Bacon 1990). The species richness in herbs in Zone 124100/3 certainly changed, and taxa such as Fabaceae (eg bird's foot trefoil, hop trefoil, clover), Galium type (eg bedstraws), Plantago lanceolata, and Potentilla type declined. It is possible that sheep grazing was responsible for this effect. Some of the shrub taxa growing locally certainly indicate that the soil was moderately calcareous (at least in patches) and, considering the rich assemblage of plants growing in the sward, it is possible that the grassland was at least moderately productive. Although it is highly conjectural, perhaps a stocking density of about seven sheep/ha/yr was being maintained.

It is very difficult to define precisely the nature of the stimulus to vegetation change, but any of the above suggestions is possible. In any event, none of the shifts in the relative performance of the plant communities created dramatic transformation of the local landscape. The effects were probably caused by relatively small scale changes in husbandry and land management such as selective cutting of different plants in the hedges, attempts at removing troublesome 'weeds', crop rotation, rotation of the use of areas for arable and pastoral husbandry, and moving sheep and cattle around to cope with varying states of herbage in the pastures.

(Wiltshire, CD Section 11)

Palaeoenvironmental evidence from late Bronze Age waterholes

Our evidence for arable and pastoral agriculture from 1150 to 750 BC is much less extensive. However, although the pollen diagram from late Bronze Age waterhole 155144 shows subtle differences when compared to the landscape of the period 1700–1150 BC, farming remained a mix of cereal production and animal husbandry:

Waterhole 155144 (Fig. 3.42)

Zone 1: *Arboreal pollen was highest in the basal sample and values ranged between 20–25% TLPS. The best represented taxon was Alnus, and the Corylus and Quercus which characterised the landscape of earlier times were much diminished by the time these sediments had accumulated.*

Both had either been exploited so extensively that their flowering was massively depressed, or they had been largely removed from the site for some considerable distance. Pinus and Betula were still growing in the catchment and Salix was growing not too far away. Ulmus (elm) had been exploited to extinction but the relatively high levels of Tilia throughout the zone are

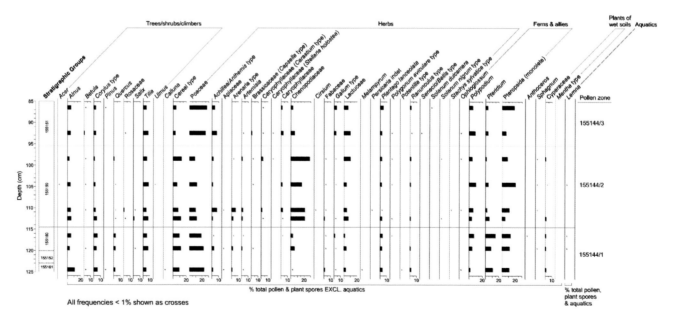

Figure 3.42: Pollen diagram from late Bronze Age waterhole 155144

159

quite surprising. In view of its poor pollen production and dispersal, its pollen percentages suggest that it must have been growing locally. However, it is also possible that faeces from stock animals fed on lime leaf fodder were finding their way into the feature. Ferns (undifferentiated) were growing locally and may have been species such as Dryopteris carthusiana (narrow buckler fern) that are, today, often found on the wet soils at the margins of ponds. Polypodium was also well represented and its spores may have been derived from ferns growing on field banks.

There is little doubt that the site was quite open and most trees were probably some distance away. The local area supported herb-rich grassland (probably pasture) and it is possible that the relatively abundant Pteridium (bracken) spores were derived from plants infesting drier areas of grazing; the presence of Calluna (heather) also suggests that heathland plants were starting to invade the acidic soils. Today, many of the herbs in the assemblage are certainly characteristic of lightly grazed pasture. These include Plantago lanceolata (ribwort plantain), Ranunculus type (buttercups), and Lactuceae (dandelion-like plants). However, the presence of ruderals such as Chenopodiaceae (goosefoot family), Artemisia (mugwort), Senecio/Bellis type (ragwort/daisy and others), and Polygonum aviculare (knotweed) indicate that there were open, broken, and possibly trampled soils around the site. Indeed, the high value for cereal type pollen suggests that ploughed arable fields were either very close to the feature or that the waterhole was situated close to the boundary between arable and pastoral land. It is interesting that a spore of Anthoceros (hornwort) was found since this is often an indicator of fallow ground.

Zone 2: *The most dramatic change in the record is due to the massive representation of Chenopodiaceae and enhanced representation of ruderals and weeds often associated with crop fields. These include Achillea/Anthemis type (eg yarrow/mayweeds), Arenaria type (sandwort), Artemisia (mugwort), Lactuceae (dandelion-like plants), Solanum nigrum type (black nightshade), and others. However, Poaceae declined quite markedly while cereal type pollen reached values similar to the earlier period in the life of the feature. These results suggest that this area of the site was being used more intensively. The lowered grass and eventual higher fern values might suggest higher grazing intensities since flowering heads of grasses would be removed by animals. By the same token, bracken might have been purposefully removed because of its toxic effect on stock animals while other ferns could have thrived because of their lack of palatability. The values for Tilia remained high and whether the pollen was derived from dung or from local trees must remain an enigma.*

The high levels of Chenopodiaceae and other ruderals might have been a response to the neglect of an area close to the feature. Weeds would be quick to capitalise on the open, fallow ground. On the other hand, the enhancement of weeds might simply be due to poor crop husbandry.

Zone 3: *Apart from Tilia, which continued to be represented as before, the local landscape was clear of trees other than those that were probably growing some distance away such as Alnus, Betula, and Corylus. Quercus seems either to have been removed altogether from the immediate area, or it was so intensively managed that it never flowered. There*

appears to have been some relaxation of land use in this zone and this continued for some time. The pollen spectra are reflected in the lower sediments of Sample 1181 above 1171. The area certainly seems to have become drier and no evidence of aquatics or plants of wet soils was found. The rise in Poaceae and the decline of many ruderal weeds also indicates that grazing was somewhat relaxed. Cereal pollen also declined but crops were still being grown in the area. Again, these conditions continued into the sediments above this zone.

This diagram would appear to indicate a very arable landscape in Zone 1, succeeded by more intensive grazing, and possible a period of fallow fields in Zone 2. The sequence culminates in a more relaxed grazing regime, but still with an arable component.

However it must be emphasised that these findings may reflect the activity in the handful of small fields surrounding waterhole 155144 and not the landscape at large.

(Wiltshire, CD Section 11)

Waterhole 180080 (Fig. 3.43)
Waterhole 180080 produced waterlogged plant macrofossil remains from its base:

The dominant group was weeds of disturbed / cultivated land, as usual (average = 49% of total remains). Nutrient-loving weeds such as fat hen, small nettle and common chickweed were fairly frequent, as were more specific arable weeds, such as parsley piert and scentless mayweed. Cereal grains and a few emmer/ spelt, spelt and barley chaff fragments were recovered from these samples, suggesting that domestic waste, fodder or dung had found its way into the well. No doubt many of the arable weed seeds had been introduced with these remains.

The second most important group was plants of wet grassland/marsh/banksides. This was mainly due to relatively high counts of blinks (Montia fontana ssp. minor) seeds. Meadowsweet (Filipendula ulmaria), wood-rush (Luzula sp.) and sweet-grass (Glyceria sp.) were also present in low frequencies, and drier grassland taxa were fairly well represented. This suggests that the surrounding vegetation consisted of grassland that was probably seasonally waterlogged and permanently damp in places.

This was the earliest sample to produce macroscopic evidence of heathland, with several heather (Calluna vulgaris) shoot tips and some cross-leaved heath (Erica tetralix) leaves. Pollen evidence for heathland vegetation was recorded in the earliest pollen zone in M/LBA pit F178108. Heather grows on sandy and peaty soils, but cross-leaved heath is typically found on wetter, boggy areas of heath. These remains could represent locally growing vegetation, in which case they indicate that the local soils had deteriorated following the clearance of scrub and/or woodlands. However, the presence of cereal waste also suggests that it could have been deposited in domestic waste, fodder or dung. The only woodland/scrub/hedgerow seed found in this feature was a single bramble seed, so some changes in the landscape appear to be taking place between the middle and late Bronze Ages.

(Carruthers, CD Section 9)

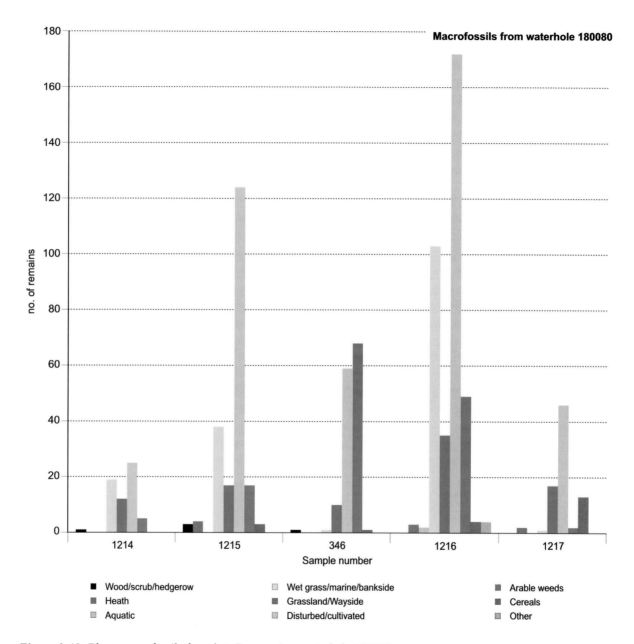

Figure 3.43: Plant macrofossils from late Bronze Age waterhole 180080

161

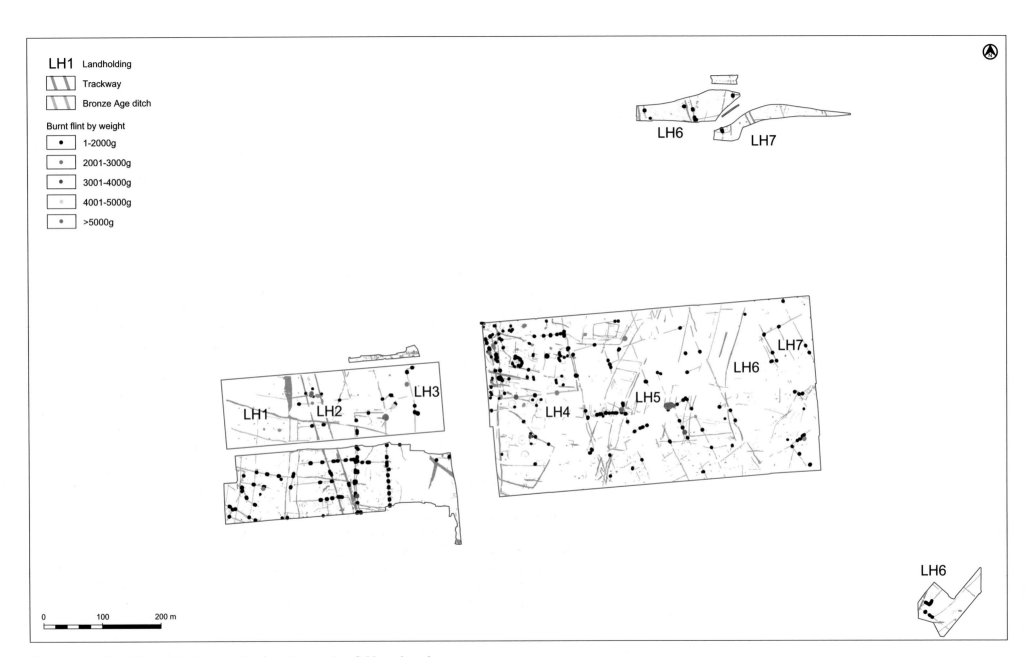

Figure 3.44: Burnt flint wt by intervention from Bronze Age fields and trackways

The presence of possible domestic waste, fodder and dung is especially interesting, since waterhole 180080 was located in the area which we believe to have been occupied by the larger, nucleated settlement form 1100 to 750 BC (see above).

Summary: farming practices in the middle to late Bronze Age

The assumption that the farming economy of the Thames Valley in the later 2nd and early 1st millennia BC was dominated by pastoralism has been fundamental to recent reviews of field systems in the region and West London (in particular Yates 2001, 67). However, the Langley Silt ('brickearth') capped Kempton Park, Taplow and Lynch Hill gravel terraces have long been known for their high agricultural productivity (eg Rackham and Sidell 2000, 17), so it should come as no surprise that the evidence from Perry Oaks demonstrates that arable agriculture formed an important part of a mixed agricultural regime. There is ample evidence from Southwark on the banks of the Thames downstream from Heathrow of ard cultivation in the 2nd millennium BC, probably associated with manuring of the soil (Drummond-Murray et al. 1994, 253–4). This cultivation occurred for a relatively short period around 1520–1220 BC (Sidell et. al. 2002, 36). It is likely that similar techniques were used at Perry Oaks, which would explain the small quantity and sherd weight of the pottery assemblage from the fields, together with the ubiquitous burnt flint (Fig. 3.44). The average sherd weight shown in Figure 3.45 demonstrates that similar depositional processes affected the ramped waterholes

and field boundaries of the landholdings. In other words, they formed part of the same agricultural complex, with artefacts (in this case pottery) being deposited in their fills following distribution in the fields through spreading midden material. The slightly higher average sherd weight from the trackway ditches reflects their dual roles as corridors of transport (for animals but also presumably of midden material) and field boundaries. We have already described how steep-sided waterholes performed a range of functions, and the high average sherd weight clearly reflects not only deliberate deposition of complete vessels in the late Bronze Age, but also significantly larger fragments of Deverel Rimbury pottery associated with settlements. These features can clearly be separated from the agricultural complex of ditches and ramped waterholes.

Most of our evidence for a mixed arable/pastoral economy comes from the period 1700–1150 BC, but at the moment there is nothing to suggest a radical change during the period 1150–750 BC. The development of double ditched trackways occured late in our sequence, but as we have shown it is difficult to know precisely when this happened. There was a slight increase in the number of ramped waterholes, between 1150 and 750 BC, but it is small. Taken together, these could demonstrate an increase in the importance of stock rearing, but the pollen evidence demonstrates the continued cultivation of cereals.

Mixed arable / pastoral agriculture, crop rotation and land management would explain the alteration of some steep-sided waterholes to ramped

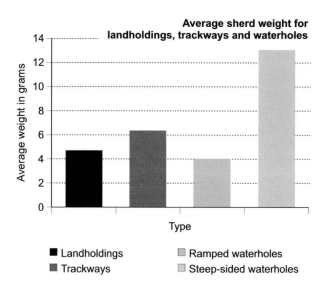

Figure 3.45: Average pottery sherd weight for landholdings, trackways and waterholes

access examples. It would also explain why the ramped access waterholes tended to be associated with more finely sub-divided fields, since these probably served as stock holding areas. In contrast, very few of the larger fields had any waterholes, and these could have been where arable crops were grown. If stock rearing was not the overriding economic concern then the Perry Oaks trackways could have developed along landholding boundaries to facilitate access across the landscape without disturbing neighbouring kin group's crops and pasture, as opposed to an overriding prerequisite to secure summer grazing on the floodplain of the Colne. As we have suggested earlier in this chapter, the original landholding boundaries formalised land tenure and control which had been facilitated through negotiation and ceremony in the 3rd millennium BC, and again these would have been driven by imperatives other than large scale sheep herding. For the trackways and boundaries to have been laid out with sheep management in mind, an economy already based on huge flocks would have to have already existed in the late 3rd millennium BC, and there is no evidence for this. Indeed, such thinking produces a 'chicken and egg' situation. For trackways to exist, large flocks of sheep must have been in existence, but without trackways and fields, how were these flocks managed? As Barrett has pointed out, It is [in] the social mode of production...... that explanations must be sought. The productive technology, and the ecosystem itself, can only represent a changing pattern of constraints acting upon the mode of production. They do not determine its actual path of development' (1980, 77).

Changes in settlement patterns in the early 1st millennium BC

We have shown how the mixed farming economy of the 2nd and early 1st millennium BC operated in conjunction with the development and adaptation of the landholdings in terms of hedges, trackways and waterholes. We have also shown how small possibly kin-based settlements may have existed in each landholding during the period 1700–1150 BC, and how ceremonies enacted around waterholes throughout our period served to tie the community together.

Unfortunately as discussed above, the evidence from the Perry Oaks excavations for where people lived during the period 1150–750 BC is less clear. It is possible that some of the earlier settlements such as Settlement 1 continued to be occupied, although it appears that the main focus of activity in this period lay within Landholding 3 (Settlement 4) and an adjacent zone (Twin Rivers) excavated during the later T5 excavations. Whether this represented a trend towards nucleation of settlement into fewer, larger locations, or whether it was an accumulation of debris and rubbish (by whatever mechanism and for whatever purpose) will be explored in Volume 2. For now, we will pursue the former theory, that during the period 1150–750, many of the settlements of the last half of the 2nd millennium BC were abandoned in favour of fewer, more nucleated settlements.

The plan in Figure 3.46 shows how this model might look. The trackway boundaries of the original kin-based land holdings would now simply be used for movement and stock management. In effect, the landholdings would coalesce and become one large pastoral / arable system, farmed by a community living in a single larger settlement. The usual causes for this change in society include deterioration in climatic conditions and soil quality which leads to increased 'pressure' on resources. 'Pressure' is a frequently encountered term in the archaeological literature, and is often used in a variety of contexts to explain change or impetus for development. Unfortunately, exactly what is meant by 'pressure' is rarely specified or

discussed in detail. If we take the insect evidence from Perry Oaks, Robinson (CD Section 12) makes a case for

'...possibly a brief episode towards the end of the middle Bronze Age when southern England had significantly warmer summers than at present.'

This was followed by a decline in temperature. Lambrick proposed a rise in the water table in the Upper Thames Valley from the late Bronze Age (Lambrick 1992, 217), and the recutting to a shallower depth of waterholes during this period at Perry Oaks suggests a similar occurrence in the Middle Thames. Our pollen, insect and waterlogged plant evidence show the presence of heathland at Perry Oaks from the latter half of the 2nd millennium BC. Such evidence for deteriorating climate and worsening soils could well explain the 'pressure' on land and productivity, which forced people to abandon individual landholdings and pool their resources.

But what of changes in the 'social mode of production'? If we are to avoid rounding up the usual archaeological suspects as causes of settlement pattern changes in the early 1st millennium BC, then we must look at our model of the dynamics between the kin-groups and the individuals. Yes, climate and soils must have had some effect on how people lived, but firstly, these changes were far from catastrophic, and secondly we would argue that the way people dealt with these conditions led to changes both in their own relationships and in the landscape.

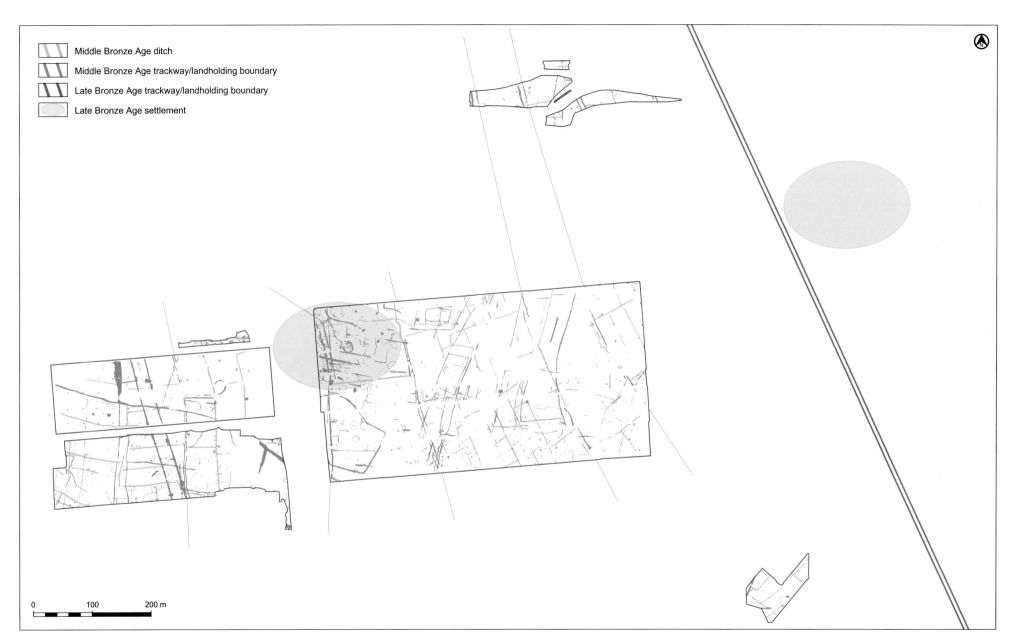

Legend:

- Middle Bronze Age ditch
- Middle Bronze Age trackway/landholding boundary
- Late Bronze Age trackway/landholding boundary
- Late Bronze Age settlement

0   100   200 m

Figure 3.46: Late Bronze Age - early Iron Age settlement and landholding

We have shown that the Perry Oaks landscape was very fertile and facilitated the successful development by the individual kin-groups of their landholdings through the 2nd millennium BC. The mixed economy of arable and pastoralism would have allowed greater flexibility in the way landholdings were used, and we can see this in crop and pasture rotation. The key here is to emphasis just how successful this way of life must have been, both economically and socially. However, we do not have the metalwork and burial evidence with which we can explore the kinship and exchange networks which some have taken to underpin 2nd and early 1st millennium BC society. For instance, Rowlands (1980, 46) stated that dominance and hierarchy depend on the relations of circulation and exchange rather than control of production, but that these cannot be separated, since the former depends on the latter. Therefore the success of the kin-groups through the latter half of the 2nd millennium BC in terms of production of crops and animals needed to be translated into increased prestige through gift exchange with other kin-groups outside the area. In order to make these exchanges and form these networks, kin-groups would have been too small, and instead the importance of the community would have again come to the fore. The external imperatives of exchange networks would have increased the need for the kin-groups to develop closer ties within their community.

Turning to the landscape, the successful development of the individual landholdings may paradoxically have required even more co-operation between the kin-groups. The increasing sub-division and 'enclosure' of the landscape led to more elaborate routeways, but must also have required increasing co-operation between the different landholdings. In other words, successful development would have reached a point where it could only continue by landholdings working in co-operation, rather than in isolation.

We believe that it is these social factors which, allied with agricultural success, led to the trend towards settlement nucleation in the early 1st millennium BC. However, as has been discussed many times before, such a dependence on complex networks of gift exchange made the community vulnerable to the changes of the 8th century BC, and it is to the early Iron Age that we now turn.

The early Iron Age landscape at Perry Oaks

Little evidence was recovered for early Iron Age activity during the Perry Oaks excavation, but results from the recent excavations at T5 have provided information that will enhance the narrative for landscape use in the Heathrow area during this period. Details of the recent findings will form part of Volume 2. Major elements of the Bronze Age agricultural landscape appear to have persisted well into the Iron Age, and the position of late Bronze Age and early Iron Age waterholes indicates that many field boundaries remained in use, mainly in the form of hedgerows, as the ditches had largely silted up by the early Iron Age. Some degree of expansion of land division eastwards occurred during this period, new waterholes were cut and earlier ones kept open, mostly in the eastern part of the site. Waterholes appeared to have retained their status as places of offering for generations of farmers during the late Bronze Age/early Iron Age whilst hedgerows were maintained and ancient trackways respected.

Precise dating of these developments in landscape use and settlement activity is not clear. Pottery belonging to the Post-Deverel Rimbury tradition was recovered from field ditches across the site, particularly in the central and eastern sector. Late Bronze Age and early Iron Age pottery fabrics are, however, generally indistinguishable in the region and the most undiagnostic body sherds can be dated only broadly to the late Bronze Age/early Iron Age. At the end of the Bronze Age the frequency of sandy fabrics escalated and distinctive decorative motifs emerged, and a few deposits and archaeological events can be assigned with some confidence to the early Iron Age. The recovery of distinctive early Iron Age pottery from waterholes and other features exposed in the recent T5 excavations indicates continuity of activity following the late Bronze Age at a higher level than the Perry Oaks evidence suggested (see Vol. 2).

The small dispersed settlements of the middle Bronze Age were abandoned during the late Bronze Age (see above) and there is no conclusive evidence for the re-emergence of nucleated settlement until the middle Iron Age, when a substantial settlement was established between

Figure 3.47: Pottery distribution showing the process of settlement nucleation from the middle Bronze Age to the middle and late Iron Age at Perry Oaks

field blocks in what may have been an area of common land (see Chapter 4). The process of settlement nucleation may, however, have begun as early as the late Bronze Age or early Iron Age, based on the concentrations of Post-Deverel Rimbury pottery found in the central part of the site (Fig. 3.47). The maps in Figure 3.47 demonstrate the process of settlement nucleation from the middle Bronze Age to the middle and late Iron Age, but also indicate that the use of the field system changed over time. Manuring of fields and the construction of middens seem to have been elements of the agricultural regime during the later part of the Bronze Age and the early Iron Age, and this may explain how pottery came to be scattered across the fields at this time.

The sparse and disparate strands of evidence for late Bronze Age/early Iron Age settlement suggest a slight concentration of features set amongst the pre-existing field systems, including waterholes and a small number of structural features. Evidence for early Iron Age occupation activity was also exposed during excavations in advance of the Northern Runway extensions in 1969 (Canham 1978). Nonetheless, the relatively limited evidence from the Perry Oaks excavations, along with past and recent fieldwork at Heathrow, is insufficient to allow us to fully characterise the scale and nature of early Iron Age activity or to determine the role of the settlement within a larger economic and social scheme of the Thames Valley at this point in the history of the landscape. Nor is it possible to clearly depict the early Iron Age settlement as an architectural expression of any wider unit of economic or political control in the region. Nonetheless, as agricultural activity continued, habitation persisted in some form at Perry Oaks until, at some point in the period preceding about 400 BC, the central part of the site was transformed by the establishment of a substantial nucleated settlement.

CHAPTER 4

The development of the agricultural landscape from the middle Iron Age to the end of the Romano-British farmstead (*c* 400 BC-5th century AD)

by Nicholas Cooke

CD-Rom queries
Middle Iron Age landscape
Distribution of middle Iron Age pottery
Middle Iron Age settlement
Middle Iron Age waterholes
Late Iron Age - early Roman landscape
Early and mid Roman landscape
Roman buildings
Late Roman landscape
Post-Roman use of the 'ladder' enclosure system

Introduction

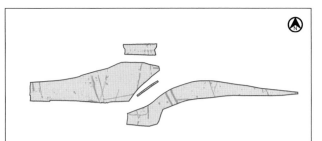

After the abandonment of the small, dispersed settlements occupied by the Bronze Age inhabitants, and following the early Iron Age, the Perry Oaks landscape came under new cultural and economic influences and political designs. These resulted in the emergence of a nucleated settlement of round-houses in the middle Iron Age, which remained the focal point for activity during the late Iron Age and Roman period. The daily and seasonal routine of the Perry Oaks inhabitants continued to be dictated by the requirements of a localised agricultural regime, and remnants of the ancient Bronze Age field systems continued to guide these practices.

Significant changes to these field systems were only made during the later Iron Age and early Roman period, when many of the landscape boundaries were realigned.

The Perry Oaks landscape of the later Roman period bears testimony to the gradual pressure of social, political and economic demands, perhaps produced by upheavals within the regional and imperial Roman administration during the 3rd century AD. The result, in archaeological terms, was the appearance of a system of enclosures and a major droveway that seemed to overwrite the previous land divisions and swallow up previously farmed tracts. The new arrangement focussed

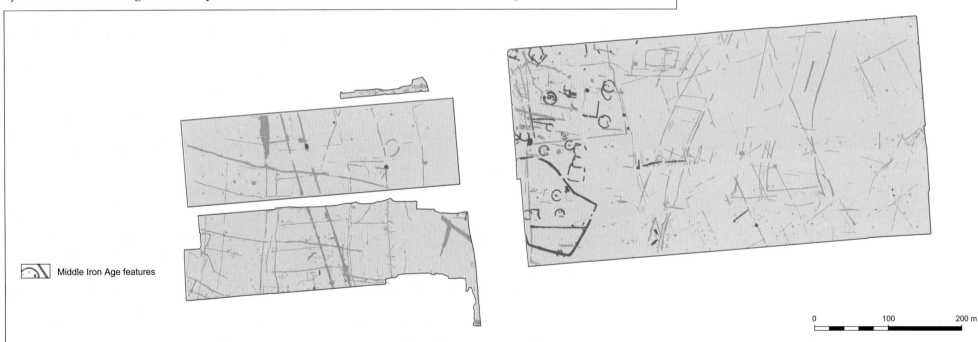

Middle Iron Age features

0   100   200 m

Figure 4.1: Extent of middle Iron Age occupation at Perry Oaks

outwards and away from the ancient local community. Although it had undoubtedly developed piecemeal, and probably had its origins in the Iron Age, the patterns resemble cumulative 'ladder enclosures'. Livestock and other commodities were moved across the Perry Oaks site along the central droveway of the ladder enclosures, penned overnight in the flanking enclosures, and driven away towards markets to the north and south. These markets were perhaps controlled by elite landlords of large Roman villas.

Some residue of this late Roman landscape can be traced in the medieval ridge and furrow and the alignment of a post-medieval trackway that survive at Perry Oaks. But the extent of the medieval field systems and the scale of the trackway imply that the site reverted to localised rural inhabitation and agricultural activity.

The middle Iron Age settlement (Fig. 4.1)

The agricultural landscape of Perry Oaks, established during the early and middle Bronze Age, remained relatively unchanged well into the Iron Age, although as we have seen, there is little evidence for activity during the early part of the Iron Age. The locations of late Bronze Age and early Iron Age waterholes (see Chapter 3) indicate that many of the field boundaries remained in place, and although no obvious effort had been made to maintain the ditches associated with the original hedgerows, there appears to have been no motivation to significantly alter the pattern of the Bronze Age field enclosures.

This continuity of land-use suggests that there was a recognised system of land control. If and when land changed hands, it did so without significant alteration to the general field system. This area of the Heathrow landscape may have been farmed in *broadly* the same way for over 1500 years, beginning in the early Bronze Age and continuing into the middle Iron Age.

Despite the apparent continuity of agricultural practice, the pattern of dispersed small settlements concentrated within the extensive field system appears to have been abandoned in favour of nucleated settlement. There is clear structural evidence for this settlement dating to the middle Iron Age (Fig. 4.1), but its development may have begun earlier, during the late Bronze Age or early Iron Age. The nucleated settlement was preserved in the form of penannular gullies representing at least eighteen roundhouses and ancillary post-built structures. One of the roundhouse gullies (no. 8; see Figs 4.6 and 4.10 below) had been recut at greater depth than the original, more properly a surrounding ditch. This particular structure or location may have been special in some way, perhaps incorporating a non-domestic function (see below). It is clear that the structures formed the main focus of settlement, which continued into the late Iron Age and Roman period.

The new settlement occupied a previously open area that may have been common land during the Bronze Age, and the inhabitants certainly farmed fields that were originally laid out during this earlier period. Relatively large numbers of Bronze Age pottery sherds were recovered from the

ditches belonging to the field systems either side of the settlement, along with small quantities of early and middle Iron Age pottery. The lack of middle Iron Age pottery from these features could suggest a change in farming practices during the Iron Age, whereby waste material from the settlement was no longer being used to fertilise the arable fields. However, a more likely explanation is that the original field ditches had fully silted by the middle Iron Age and only the hedges survived to define the field boundaries. In these conditions, Iron Age pottery from manuring material would remain on the ground surface, subject to weathering, scatter and ultimately loss in the truncated landscape.

Chronological indicators

The dating of Iron Age settlement sites generally relies upon associated ceramics, but much of the Iron Age pottery from Perry Oaks was not closely datable and artefacts associated with the settlement were scarce overall, in common with other Iron Age sites excavated in the region. No scientific dates are available for the origin of settlement or for the sequence of excavated structures. The absence of suitable organic or charred material from penannular gullies representing the middle Iron Age structures, and the likelihood of contamination by intrusive material, ruled out radiocarbon dating as a practical option.

The pottery

The change from small scattered occupation of the Bronze Age to a more nucleated settlement broadly corresponded with the adoption of sand-tempered pottery fabrics. The origin of the nucleated settlement and the adoption of a new pottery tradition may have been broadly contemporary, although the shift in preference to sandy-tempered wares was clearly a gradual process. Flint-tempered wares of this transitional period are classified as late Bronze Age/early Iron Age, whilst the sandy wares are dated to the early and middle Iron Ages. Analysis of the ceramic distribution demonstrates that sandy wares were

Feature Type	No. sherds	Weight (g)	Mean sherd Weight (g)
Ditch	407	2532	2532
Gully	106	550	550
Pit	1462	8273	8273
Posthole	126	655	655
Penannular gully (8)	350	3088	3088
Penannular gullies (other)	685	4610	4610
Tree-throw	26	109	109
Waterhole	30	219	219

Table 4.1: Quantification of pottery by feature type for the middle Iron Age

concentrated in the area of the middle Iron Age settlement, whilst the flint-tempered wares had a more widespread distribution.

Most of the Middle Iron Age pottery recovered from beyond the core settlement area came from waterholes and tree-throws (Fig. 4.2). Waterholes were commonly located close to the boundaries or corners of the extant Bronze Age fields, whilst the tree-throws captured material circulating in the topsoil and subsoil of the fields.

Quantification of pottery by feature type for the middle Iron Age is presented in Table 4.1. The majority of middle Iron Age sherds came from structural features associated with the settlement (Fig. 4.2), most from the pennanular gullies representing the sites of roundhouses, with smaller amounts from pits and ditches. Penannular gully 8 was most productive and its mean sherd weight highest, suggesting that the pots were deposited fairly rapidly following breakage. The more fragmentary pottery from tree-throws and other small features is likely to have derived from manuring of fields or dispersed middens. The mean sherd weight for the waterhole assemblages reflects to some degree deliberate deposits of large vessel fragments.

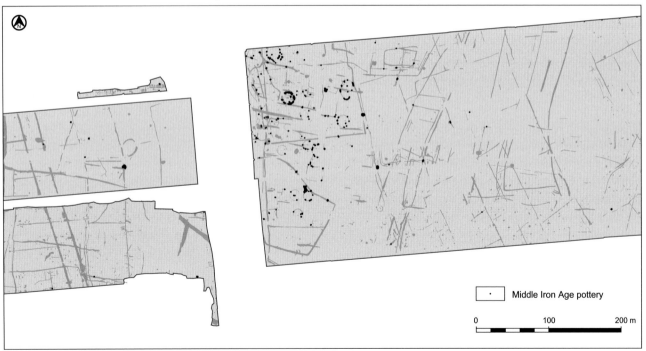

Middle Iron Age pottery

0   100   200 m

Figure 4.2: Distribution of middle Iron Age pottery

172

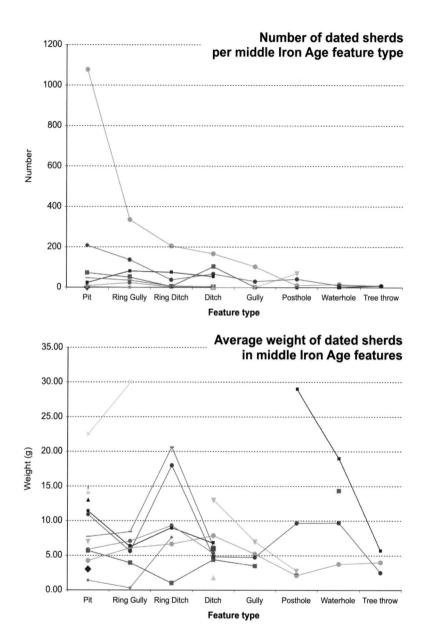

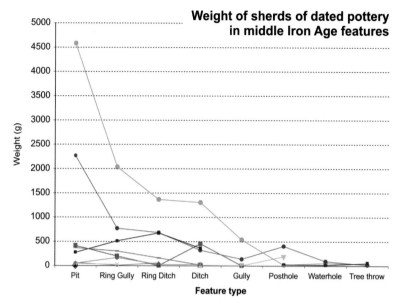

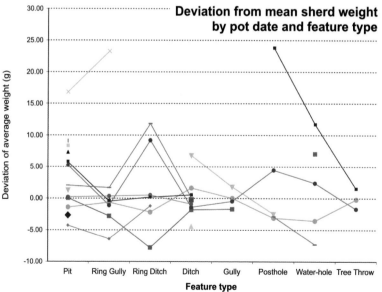

Figure 4.3: Distribution of pottery by middle Iron Age feature type

173

The pottery recovered from the fills of middle Iron Age features dated from several different periods, ranging from the early Neolithic through to the Roman period (Fig. 4.3). Most of this pottery was residual and the small quantities of late Iron Age and Roman pottery recovered from these features was intrusive in the upper fills, or came from later Iron Age or Roman deposits within the top of these features.

An anomaly in the pattern is demonstrated by the late Bronze Age/early Iron Age pottery, which occurred in greater numbers in ditch fills than in any other feature type. However, given the small size of the assemblage, this may not be significant. The graph displaying the total weights of the dated pottery lost by middle Iron Age feature type shows a similar pattern to that displayed by the sherd numbers (Fig. 4.3).

The two remaining graphs on Figure 4.3 show the average weights of sherds by feature type along with the deviation of these values from the mean for the feature type. These display a similar pattern. Many of the values can be discounted, as these are skewed by the small number of sherds. The only periods containing more than 100 sherds were the late Bronze Age/early Iron Age, the middle Iron Age and the late Iron Age.

The pattern that emerges is that the largest sherds tend to occur in pits and penannular gullies, and smaller sherds in other gullies and waterholes, although there is some difference between sherd groups of different dates. Interestingly, the pattern also supports the

suggestion that the late Bronze Age/early Iron Age sherds are residual, in that they generally fall below the mean weights for pits. Conversely, those for the late Iron Age are generally slightly above average, suggesting that these are more likely to date the layers in which they occur.

The second set of graphs (Fig. 4.4) presents the distribution of dated material in different fill types of middle Iron Age features. The main context types recorded are primary, secondary and tertiary fills, with small numbers of deposits recorded as deliberate placements of material and miscellaneous unclassified 'other fills'.

The first graph in Figure 4.4 shows a number of sherds of different date following similar patterns within the main fill groups. Most of the pottery was recovered from secondary fills with smaller quantities in primary and tertiary fills.

When the average weights were examined, some interesting patterns emerged. The middle Iron Age pottery produced the expected profile, with the largest sherds recovered from the primary fills and the smallest from the tertiary fills, with the caveat that quantities of pottery from the latter were low overall. The late Bronze Age/early Iron Age pottery showed a different pattern, with small sherds recovered from both the primary and secondary fills.

The general pattern of pottery loss and deposition suggests that secondary fills contained the most pottery and the largest sherds by average weight (taking into account sample size). This pattern

could be predicted on the basis that these fills formed as a result of activity associated with the use of the relevant features, and as such, are relatively high energy deposits. The material they contained was incorporated more rapidly than the material recovered from the tertiary fills, which accumulated slowly, and incorporated higher levels of badly abraded material.

Other finds categories

Turning to the other finds categories from the middle Iron Age features, it is clear that there is some variation between artefacts recovered from the different feature types (see graph in Fig. 4.4). The most notable pattern is that displayed by the animal bone and the burnt flint, which appear to have an inverse relationship to each other within particular features, especially in the case of pits, penannular gullies and ditches.

Burnt flint was more common in penannular gullies and ditches than animal bone whilst animal bone was more common in the roundhouse gully 8 and in pits. Although the graph in Fig. 4.4 is based on finds by count in these features, the total weights produce a similar picture (see Fig. 4.5). Animal bone and burnt flint rarely occur at the same levels of distribution, and this may reflect two key factors—the general paucity and poor condition of animal bone from the site overall, and the range of activities that produced burnt flint.

There is also a clear difference between the material recovered from pits and from penannular gully 8.

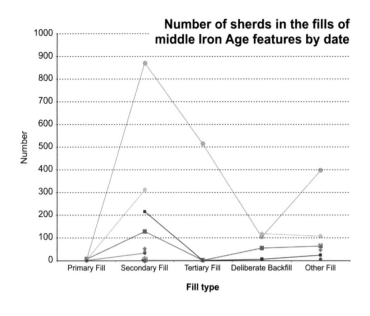

Number of sherds in the fills of middle Iron Age features by date

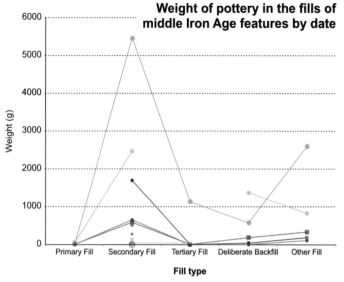

Weight of pottery in the fills of middle Iron Age features by date

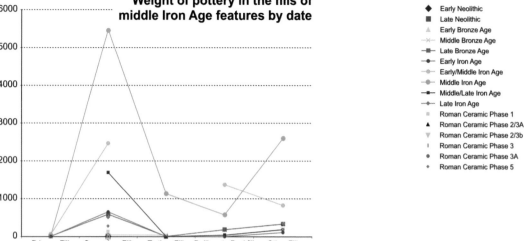

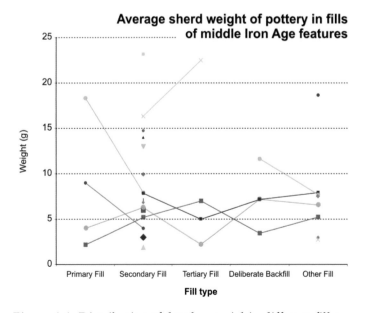

Average sherd weight of pottery in fills of middle Iron Age features

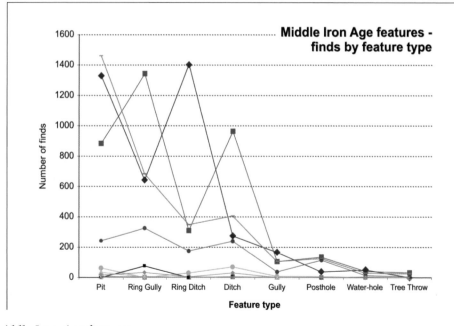

Middle Iron Age features - finds by feature type

Figure 4.4: Distribution of dated material in different fill types of middle Iron Age features

Plotting the weight of animal bone from pits against that of burnt flint indicated that the pits did not form a coherent group. Rather, there were a small number of pits with high levels of animal bone that influenced the overall ratios. The feature types which did show a high level of correlation were the ditches and penannular gullies. The finds groups recovered from sections through the penannular gullies showed remarkable similarities, with none containing more than 200 g of animal bone, and most containing far more burnt flint than animal bone. The ditch groups produced a similar result. Penannular gully 8, on the other hand, contained far more animal bone on average than burnt flint. This may well reflect different depositional practices at these locations. A plot presenting the overall distribution of burnt flint by weight (Fig. 4.5) shows that the material was relatively widespread, and not concentrated on any particular feature type or area. It does show peaks in some of the penannular gullies, as well as a concentration in the northern arc of penannular gully 8.

A plot of the animal bone by weight (Fig. 4.5) also shows a clear concentration in the in the northern arc of gully 8 and in two of the pits. The relatively low proportions of animal bone recovered from the penannular gullies is also clear.

This preliminary examination of the finds assemblage from the different feature types associated with the newly created middle Iron Age settlement has raised several points for further discussion. However, prior to focussing on the settlement itself, it is perhaps worth looking at its raison d'être. The

location of the settlement points to continuity both of the field system and also potentially the basics of agricultural exploitation. This suggests that the inhabitants of the settlement farmed the surrounding land intensively, with the shift in settlement location perhaps reflecting a need to free up land previously containing settlements for agricultural exploitation, and indicating a possible change in working practices.

The settlement

The middle Iron Age settlement was established in what had apparently been an open, possibly common, block of land in the Bronze Age landscape of Perry Oaks, which was intersected by two west-east aligned Bronze Age ditches (Fig. 4.6).

The location of the settlement within the wider landscape is intriguing. Its position on the edge of the Taplow terrace ensured that it was ideally placed to exploit the possibilities afforded by the different landscape zones surrounding it. The wetter lower terrace to the west would have been suited to specific forms of activity such as animal grazing, whilst the nearby River Colne would have been an important resource. The location is paralleled at a similar settlement at Mayfield Farm, which also lies on the edge of the Taplow terrace, to the south of Heathrow (Merriman 1990). It may be significant, however, that the major alignments of the structures of the Perry Oaks settlement faced eastwards. Whilst this is due in part to the most common alignment of the roundhouse doorways, it is also reflected in the location of the entrance to a

large irregular ditched enclosure (see below), and the fact that the major structures were built on the eastern edge of the settlement. It may have been that the main focus of agricultural activity lay to the east, in the extensive field systems of the upper terrace.

The penannular gullies/roundhouses (Fig. 4.6)

The settlement contained at least 18 roundhouse sites, represented by penannular gullies which were either eaves drip gullies or enclosures around buildings. Few structural features in the form of postholes or wall slots survive. Most of the gullies had south-east facing entrances, but one (penannular gully 8) faced north-west.

The south-easterly orientation of roundhouse entrances is well known, with a sheltered doorway through which the sun will shine having practical and cosmological implications (Fitzpatrick 1997; Oswald 1997). Three of the Perry Oaks roundhouse gullies may also have had smaller north-westerly entrances in addition to their south-east entrances, including penannular gully 3, the northernmost of the structures excavated. If it were the case that these gullies had dual entrances—and the depth of the gullies suggests that these are genuine gaps rather than the product of truncation—then it may represent a re-enforcing of the cosmological references within the structure itself, with the smaller north-west facing entrance aligned on the direction of sunset at the midsummer solstice. The possibility that similar causeways existed in some of the other gullies cannot be excluded, as

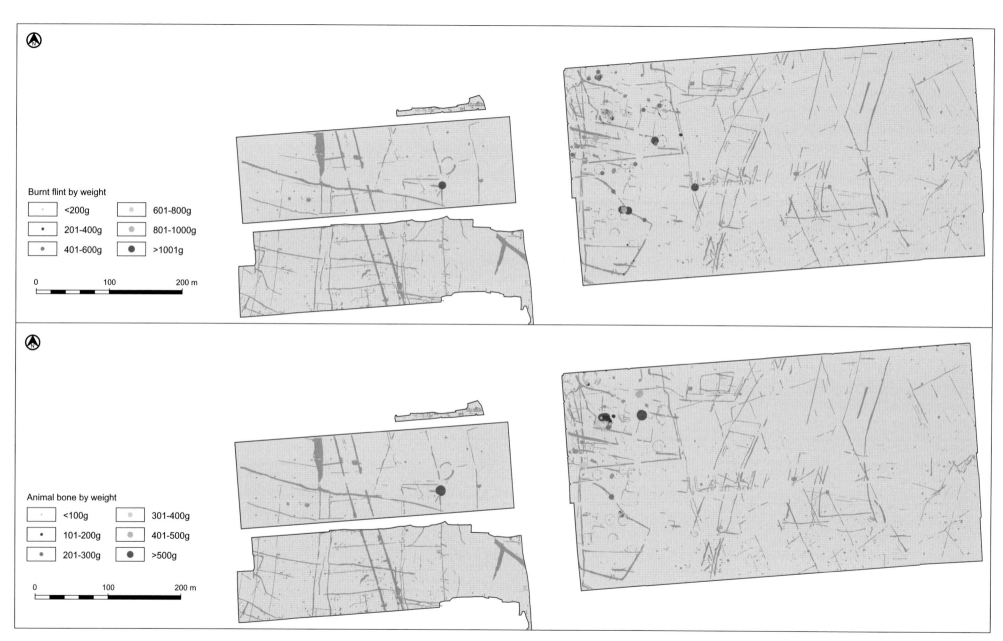

Figure 4.5: Burnt flint and animal bone in middle Iron Age features

these were either only partially preserved or not fully exposed in the excavated area.

The gullies representing the 18 roundhouses can be divided into three distinct groups on the basis of internal diameter. Penannular gully 8, which was originally *c* 13 m diameter, but larger (*c* 15 m dia.) and much deeper when recut (see Fig. 4.10 below), has been included twice, creating a total of 19. Table 4.2 shows the variation in diameter of penannular gullies at Perry Oaks.

The three major groups are as follows:

- Group (a) Two gullies of 9 m diameter.

- Group (b) Eleven gullies ranging from 11 to 14 m diameter.

- Group (c) Six gullies with diameters greater than 14 m (*nb some diameters are calculated based on surviving short lengths of gully and may be inaccurate*).

Diameter (m)	No. of penannular roundhouse gullies
9-10	2
10-11	0
11-12	5
12-13	4
13-14	2
14-15	1
15-16	3
16-17	1
19	1

Table 4.2: Diameter of roundhouses at Perry Oaks

Figure 4.6: Plan of the middle Iron Age settlement core, with roundhouses highlighted

The six largest gullies, Group (c), were all sited along the eastern edge of the settlement. The intermediate sized gullies, Group (b), were more widely dispersed, whilst the two smallest gullies, Group (a), lay within the centre of the settlement area (Fig. 4.6). There is some significance apparent in the distribution, which has been further defined by examining the quantities of domestic material in the gully fills (Fig. 4.7). Penannular gully 8 is a special case, due to the substantial size of the recut and the generally greater quantity of finds recovered from its fill.

The first graph in Figure 4.7 shows a correlation between the diameters of the penannular gullies and the number of sherds of pottery in each. This assumes that pottery loss is one of the main indicators of domestic activity. The smaller gullies of Group (a) contained very little pottery, whilst the Group (b) gullies produced 0–49 sherds. The largest gullies, Group (c), generally produced the most pottery, although one, Gully 1, was aceramic. This feature, however, survived only as short stretches and its classification by size was somewhat tenuous. Gullies 3 and 8, both of which may have incorporated a non-domestic function, produced the largest numbers of sherds.

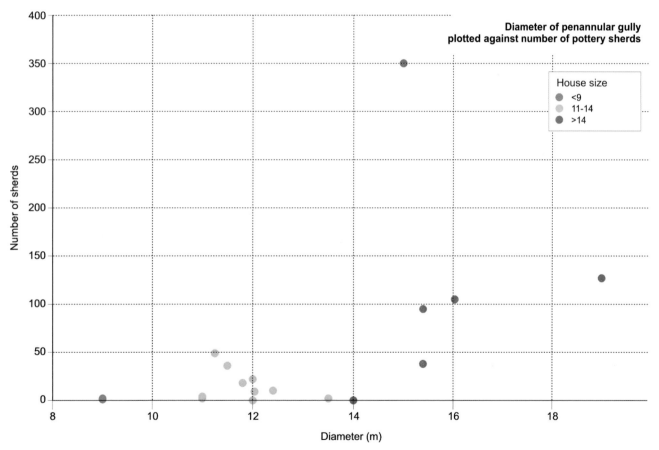

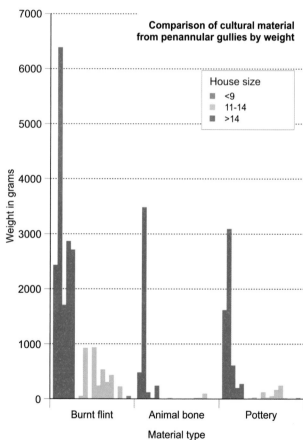

Figure 4.7: Correlation between the diameters of the penannular gullies and the quantities of finds within them

The use of pottery sherds as a sole indicator of domestic activity is unreliable, and therefore the second graph on Figure 4.7 considers three components of the finds assemblage from the gullies—the total weight of pottery, the total weight of animal bone and the total weight of burnt flint.

The results indicate greater quantities of material from the larger penannular gullies, with especially large amounts from gullies surrounding structures 3 and 8. These features may have been foci for deliberate deposition, with the large numbers of animal bones from the partially silted ditch of penannular gully 8 being of particular significance. There was also a marked difference between the

average sherd size of pottery recovered from these two roundhouse gullies and the other four Group (c) gullies, as demonstrated in Table 4.3. Also included in this table are the figures for the weight of fired clay, burnt stone and ceramic building material (CBM) from each feature, which are, again, more common in the larger gullies. On the basis of this, it seems reasonable to suggest that most of the Group (c) structures were more likely to have been used for domestic purposes (although structures 3 and 8 may have been exceptions; see below) than the smaller Group (a) structures, whilst the Group (b) structures may have had a secondary domestic role.

Group (a) gullies

The two smallest gullies, 4 and 9 of Group (a), were situated close to one another (Figs 4.6 and 4.8). Gully 9, the more easterly of the two, enclosed a group of posts possibly representing a four-post structure. Four postholes of similar size lay c 2 m apart, forming a rough square, while a fifth, smaller, posthole lay outside the square and may have been unrelated or may indicate the position of a ladder or steps. This structure was centred within the gully, aligned on the south-east facing entrance (the other gaps are the result of truncation). The traditional interpretation of similar four-post structures is that they were

Penannular gully#	Group	Internal diameter (max)	Pottery No.	Pottery weight (g)	Pottery average weight (g)	Animal bone weight (g)	Burnt flint weight (g)	CBM weight (g)	Fired clay weight (g)	Burnt stone weight (g)
4	a	9	2	17	8.5	0	49	0	2	0
9	a	9	1	4	4	0	0	0	0	0
6	b	11	2	3	1.5	94	222	0	51	0
13	b	11	4	13	3.25	18	0	0	69	0
11	b	11.25	49	241	4.92	17	433	0	15	0
14	b	11.5	36	164	4.56	2	300	0	4	0
7	b	11.8	18	50	2.78	0	533	0	148	0
2	b	12	9	23	2.56	2	239	0	1	0
5	b	12	22	123	5.59	4	934	0	178	0
18	b	12	0	0	0	2	0	0	0	0
10	b	12.4	10	24	2.4	17	924	0	41	0
17	b	13.5	2	10	5	0	51	0	4	0
1	c	14	0	0	0	0	0	0	0	0
15	c	15.4	95	269	2.83	237	2707	108	261	41
16	c	15.4	38	195	5.13	13	2863	6	232	0
12	c	16	105	607	5.78	116	1705	22	348	60
8	c	15	350	3088	8.82	3482	6386	0	1802	66
3	c	19	127	1613	12.7	479	2429	0	702	0

Table 4.3: Quantities of material from roundhouse gullies

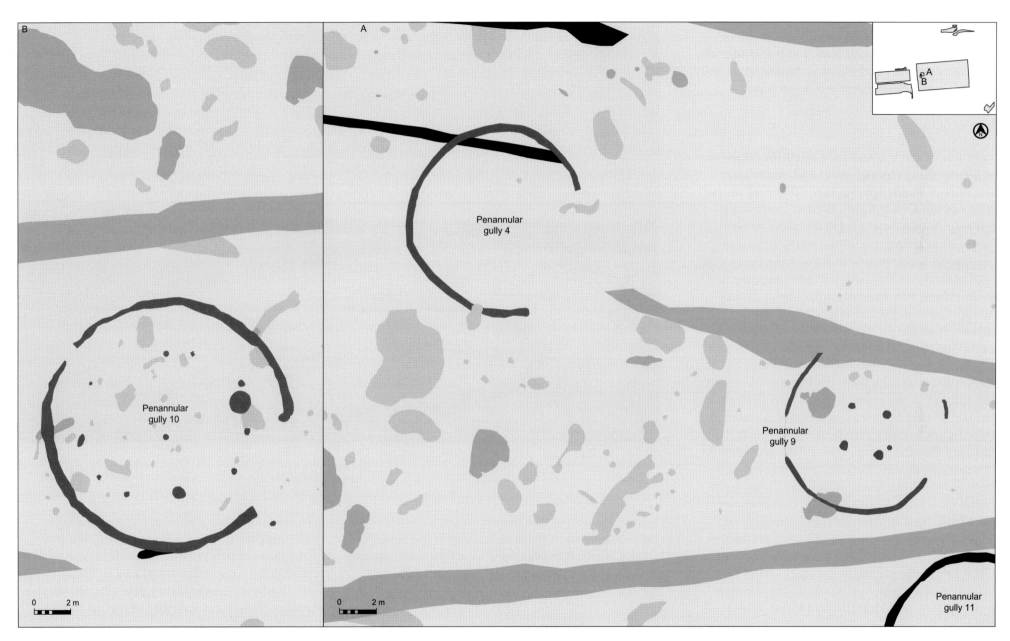

Figure 4.8: Group (a) gullies 4 and 9 and Group (b) gully 10

raised granaries designed to store grain above the ground surface, away from damp and animals. Alternatively, the postholes may represent the only surviving structural features of a roundhouse.

Group (b) gullies

Very few of the intermediate sized roundhouses of Group (b) preserved structural evidence in the form of postholes (Fig. 4.6). This may be the result of modern truncation, or of construction techniques that employed stake walls or post pads rather than ground-fast posts. Whilst truncation is certainly a feature of the Perry Oaks site, some postholes have survived in truncated areas. These may have originally been deeper features as many occur at or close to the entrances of the gullies, probably representing porch supports. However, a similar dearth of postholes was noted in the excavations at Caesar's Camp (Grimes and Close-Brooks 1993), interpreted as the result of plough truncation and the use of slight plank or stake built walls in the roundhouses. Close-Brooks (ibid.) felt that it was unlikely that the penannular gullies represented the remains of wall trenches, and this has also been judged to be the case at Perry Oaks. Some of the structural elements of the roundhouses may have been constructed of clay or cob, of which little or no trace would have survived.

Only one of the gullies in Group (b) showed evidence of a possible post circle. Penannular gully 10 (Fig. 4.8; Plate 4.1) appeared to enclose a partial ring of postholes, although these varied in depth and form, and many were very shallow.

Plate 4.1: Penannular gully 10 looking south-east

It is worth noting that this structure lay within the central area of the eastern beds of the sewage works, which had been used as a haul road, and was, therefore, subject to far less truncation than the rest of the site.

The diameter of the circle of posts was *c* 8 to 9 m, leaving a gap of *c* 2 m between it and the gully.

It is likely that this post ring marked the main roof supports, but was not necessarily the line of the main structural wall of the building. A pair of postholes some 2.2 m apart and equidistant from the south-east entrance probably marks the position of the main doorway of the roundhouse.

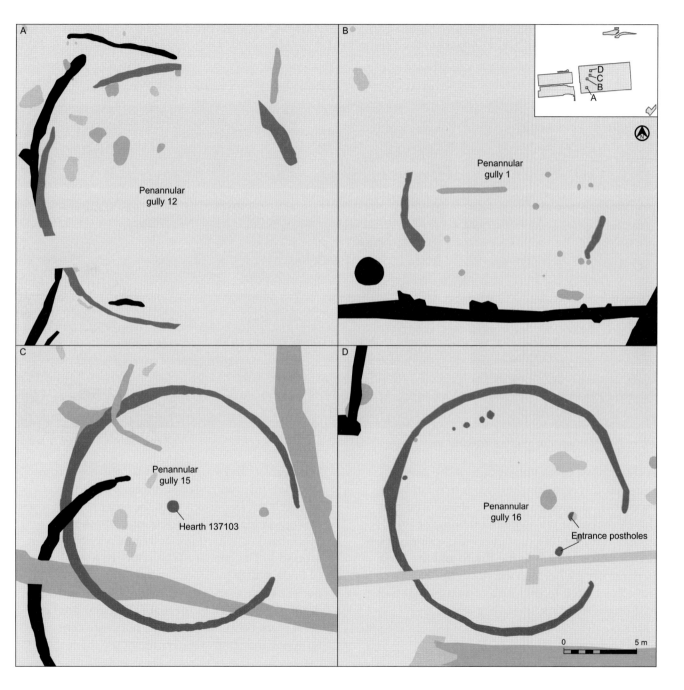

Group (c) gullies

The best preserved postholes associated with the larger penannular gullies of Group (c) also lay within the entrance area (Fig. 4.9). The clearest example is gully 16, which had a pair of posts 2.5 m apart and set back *c* 3 to 3.5 m from the gully termini, perhaps part of an entrance structure. As only these postholes survived later truncation, it supports the view that porch postholes were dug deeper than other structural components. Both gully 1 and gully 15 also had surviving postholes which may represent entrance posts, but the door area of gully 12 lay below the concrete walls of the sewage beds. In considering the likelihood that the structures enclosed within the larger gullies were entirely post-built, it is notable that a sunken hearth (137103) located at the centre of gully 15 survived truncation. This might suggest that the superstructure of this roundhouse at least was not constructed with ground-fast posts.

Two of the roundhouse gullies in Group (c) (3 and 8) appear to have been functionally divergent, and will now be discussed separately.

Figure 4.9: Penannular gullies of Group (c)

Penannular gully 8

Penannular gully 8 was represented by two phases, the original shallow gully (113117) recut as ditch 113114 (Fig. 4.10; Plate 4.2). The original gully enclosed an area *c* 13 m in diameter and the later ditch enclosed an area of *c* 15 m, allowing space for a structure 10–12 m or more in diameter. The profile of the recut ditch varied from V-shaped to a flat bottomed U-shaped and the depth was also variable (see sections, Fig. 4.10). An apparent terminus observed in one of the deep sections on the western side of the ditch indicated that it was dug in segments, which could suggest the demonstration of a division in labour, reinforcing the anomalous character of this structure and location within the settlement. The sequence of fills was similar throughout the ditch, suggesting that the segments filled contemporaneously.

The entrance to one or both phases of the roundhouse was probably represented by a number of postholes, some unexcavated, clustered within the north-west facing gap in the gully/ditch. Two wide, shallow features, 147136 and 125123, were almost certainly the truncated bases of large postholes designed to hold porch or door posts. They produced no datable finds but their position and size are comparable to large roundhouses excavated elsewhere such as Pimperne (Harding *et al.* 1993) and Longbridge Deverill (Hawkes 1994). Various internal features, some interpreted as tree-throws, produced middle Iron Age pottery and may represent internal divisions or be the result of activity within the structure. Most produced no pottery or other dating evidence.

Plate 4.2: Penannular gully 8 looking west

Although we cannot be certain of the precise role that this structure served, it may, in both its early and later guises, have influenced the development of the settlement. None of the gullies representing contemporary roundhouses lay closer than 15 m to the ditch, and the large penannular gully (3) to the north appears to have been sited to enclose a structure that had a strong visual link towards gully 8.

The number and variety of finds recovered from the ditch fills contrasted sufficiently with the assemblages associated with the other roundhouses to suggest that these distributions represent specialised activity if not within the structure then around it. The primary fills contained a small group of finds, which included animal bone, flint and pottery (four sherds dated to the middle Iron Age). A small amount of burnt flint (177g) and fired clay (131g) was concentrated in the north-western terminal and south-western arc of the ditch.

184

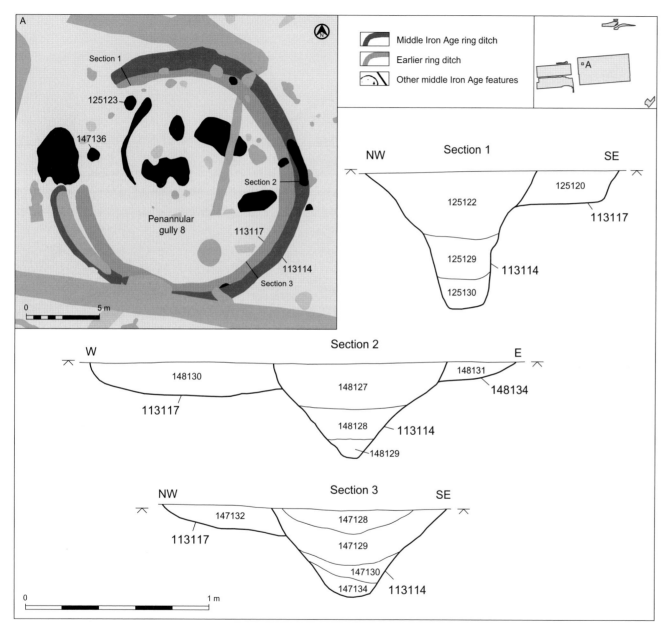

Figure 4.10: Penannular gully 8

The sequence of lower secondary fills comprised a series of shallow lenses and localised deposits. These related to the first period of prolonged use of the structure, and occurred along much of the length of the ditch, but were absent within the western arc and the south-western terminus. Pottery was recovered from only three sections containing these fills, with largest group of sherds (43) coming from the north-west terminal. The small quantities of animal bone, burnt flint, worked flint and fired clay in these fills showed no significant concentrations. These lower secondary deposits were sealed by a relatively thick fill (113107), which contained the majority of the finds recovered from the ditch. The pottery was of predominantly middle Iron Age date, although early and late Iron Age and Roman pottery was also present in small quantities. The latter may be intrusive, but may point to limited accumulation in the ditch during these periods (in some stretches of the ditch, context 113107 represents the final deposit). The pottery was distributed more or less evenly within this fill, except in the north-western terminus. Thirty-three sherds weighing over 1.4 kg, many belonging to a single vessel, came from this terminus deposit. The pottery was associated with a deposit of degraded organic matter (deposit 146141) and may represent a special deposit. The organic material was too highly degraded to identify.

The distribution of the animal bone from penannular gully 8 showed no significant pattern.

185

The animal bone report states:

There was no evidence of deliberate burial, articulation, or of the association of animals bones with other artefacts. There is nothing therefore in the character of the animal bones... that would suggest a ritual aspect to their deposition....

(Bates, CD Section 14)

This roundhouse was one of the few features at Perry Oaks in which animal bone and burnt flint occurred in relatively large quantities, both concentrated in the northern arc of the ditch. In some parts of the ditch, this deposit was sealed by further fills which also produced pottery, animal bone, fired clay and burnt flint, but in relatively small amounts. Where concentrations of these finds did occur (notably of pottery and animal bone), they tended to cluster in the south-eastern or north-western sectors.

Penannular gully 3 and associated rectilinear enclosure/structure 108018

Penannular gully 3 survived as a roughly circular feature, over 18 m in diameter at its widest (Fig. 4.11; Plate 4.3). If it were a domestic roundhouse gully, it could have accommodated a structure of 15 m or more in diameter, on the scale of the Pimperne (Harding *et al.* 1993), Little Woodbury (Bersu 1940) and Flint Farm roundhouses (Payne *et al.* 2005), and would represent the largest middle Iron Age structure on the site. As such, it would have been a significant building within the settlement.

Plate 4.3: Penannular gully 3 looking south-east from the north-west corner of WPR98 Bed C

The gully appears to have had two entrances, one opening out to the south-east and a wider gap facing south-south-east. The latter may have been designed to oppose the north-west facing entrance to penannular gully 8, although the two lay some 50 m apart. No associated postholes were identified within the enclosed area, although surviving postholes in the vicinity indicate that the lack of such features may not be entirely due to truncation. The absence of structural features could suggest that this enclosure was not designed to accommodate a building, but was rather an animal enclosure or

served some other function. The scale and position of gully 3 might imply a non-domestic function.

When penannular gully 3 fell into disuse, the location was occupied by a rectilinear feature (108018) represented by a shallow gully that defined a building or enclosure measuring *c* 14 m by 13 m. The gully as exposed in excavation was discontinuous, although it was clear that the northern corner suffered recent localised truncation. The rectilinear feature lay within the entrance gaps of the earlier penannular gully, the north-eastern and south-western sides coinciding

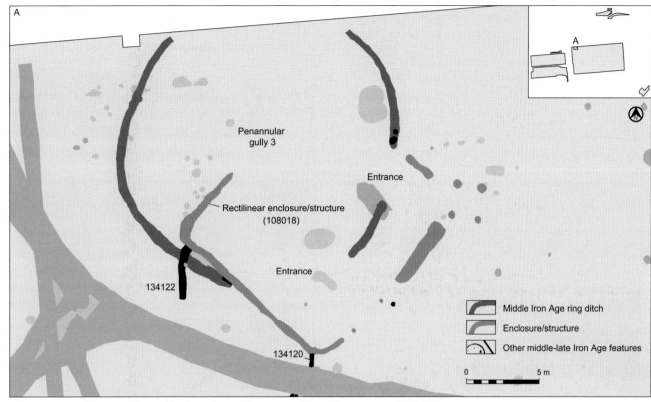

Figure 4.11: Penannular gully 3 and rectilinear enclosure/structure 108018

Airport (Grimes and Close-Brooks 1993), Little Waltham (Drury 1978), Danebury (Cunliffe 1995), and Stansted (Havis and Brooks 2004). Such structures have often been interpreted as shrines, although in most cases the evidence is far from conclusive and overall the evidence for specialised religious structures in Iron Age Britain remains slight (Smith 2001, 67). The Perry Oaks rectangular structure shares some common features with a number of the structures mentioned above, including its wall trench construction and the easterly or south-easterly orientation of the entrance. It may have been a direct replacement for penannular gully 3 and possibly served a similar function. It is tempting to suggest that the location was somehow special and the structures or enclosures represented a focus of spiritual life within the Iron Age community, possibly linked to penannular enclosure 8. The evidence is, as ever, slight.

Settlement development

It is unlikely that all the roundhouses were contemporary; gully 18 is among the latest on site, and possibly wholly late Iron Age in date (see below). Neither the dating nor the stratigraphic evidence is sufficiently clear to allow us to refine the sequence, and in the absence of a detailed chronology for the settlement, it is difficult to trace its development. It is also unclear whether the settlement extended further to the north and north-west. If the analysis of function based on the finds assemblages is correct, and penannular gullies 3 and 8 are accepted as anomalous, then the larger, probably domestic, roundhouses

with the terminals of the entrances. The north-eastern side had been recut on at least one occasion. The gully appears to have had two entrances, one opening out at the east corner, the other facing south-east. The latter entrance was marked by two postholes and their position suggests that the gully probably marked the line of the wall, possibly a sill beam. Alternatively, they may have represented the gate posts to an enclosure. The eastern entrance opened onto a four-post structure, conceivably a porch, although it was possibly unrelated. Pottery from three of the

postholes indicated a date of middle to late Iron Age, but the gully itself produced only prehistoric sherds of indeterminate date. Two short lengths of very shallow north-south gully (134122 and 134120) were traced up to the southern and western corners of the rectangular enclosure/structure and may have represented part of an adjoining enclosure, most of the which has been truncated.

Similar rectangular structures are known from the Iron Age across southern Britain, notably from Caesar's Camp at the eastern end of Heathrow

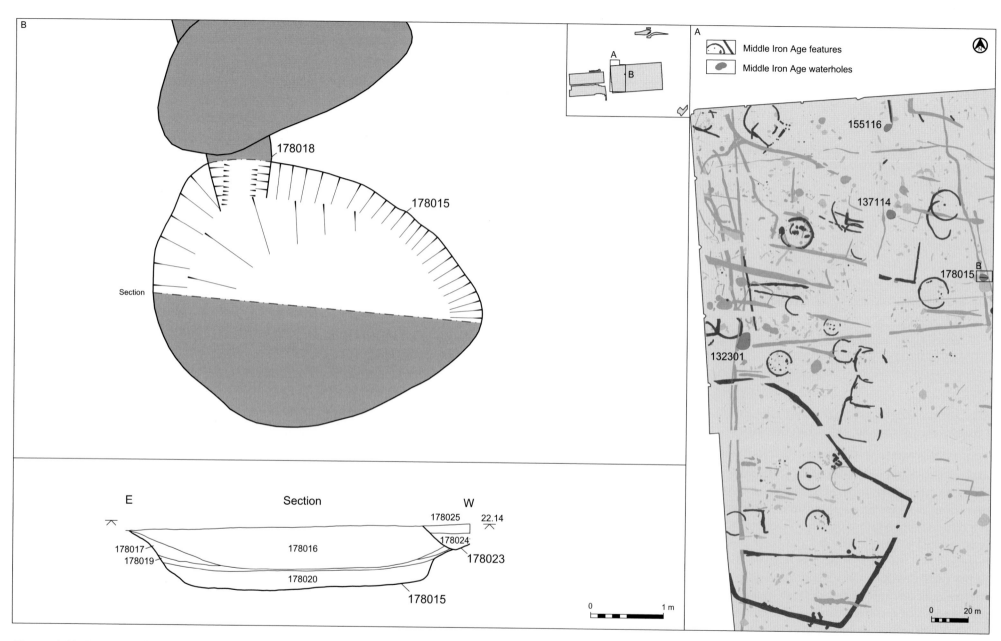

Figure 4.12: Location of middle Iron Age waterholes with detail of waterhole 178015

occupied the eastern fringe of the settlement
and the smaller roundhouses lay to the west.
A number of the larger roundhouses appear
to have had associated enclosures (see Fig. 4.6
above), which may have served as animal
stockades or enclosed ancillary buildings.

Waterholes

Water for the settlement was provided by several
waterholes—two located on the eastern edge of
the settlement (155116, 178015) and two within
the settlement itself (132301 and 137114) (Fig. 4.12;
Plate 4.4). The latter were substantial features
and were open for considerable periods of time.
The lower fills of waterhole 137114 were securely
dated by pottery to the middle Iron Age, and
contained fills characteristic of water-lain silts
that form within standing water. A reasonable
quantity of late Iron Age pottery from the
middle fills of this waterhole suggests
continued use into this later period (see below).

Waterhole 178015, lying between the settlement
and agricultural fields to the east, was a catchment
for organic material from both the farming of the
fields and crop-processing within the settlement
(Fig. 4.12; see discussion below). The waterhole
was dug in an area known to be have a high water
table and no great depth was required before
water filled its base. The lowest fill, 178020, was
water-lain and showed evidence of gleying. This
deposit was sealed by a thin layer of iron stained
silt with patchy inclusions of grey clay. This in
turn was overlain by 178017, derived from the

Plate 4.4: Excavation of Iron Age Waterhole 155116

erosion of the pit top and sides, and representing
a rapid accumulation of material. The upper fill,
178016, formed slowly, showing evidence of
gleying and leaching of minerals, again suggesting
that it formed in a watery environment.

Although the absence of gravels in the lower fills
suggests that there was little initial erosion of the
sides of the pit, there was no clear evidence of a
revetment constructed to maintain the purity of

the water. The waterhole may therefore have
been used by animals. The fill sequence was
relatively well dated as contexts 178017 and
178019 contained small assemblages of middle
Iron Age pottery, and the upper fill, 178016,
contained a single late Iron Age sherd,
suggesting the feature survived as a shallow
hollow in the late Iron Age. The environmental
material from this waterhole is discussed below.

The southern enclosure

After the settlement had been in existence for some time, a number of the roundhouses in the southernmost area were enclosed by a substantial bank and ditch (Fig. 4.13). This irregular enclosure appears to have cut the eastern end of a shallow east-west linear gully (121075), although the main part of the gully may have continued in use, dividing the enclosed area into different zones such as domestic settlement and animal corrals. Analysis of the finds recovered from the fills of the enclosure ditch (see Figs 4.2 and 4.5 above) show marked differences in distribution. Most of the artefacts were recovered from the stretches north of the dividing gully, and particularly from the north-eastern part of the ditch. This probably reflects a higher level of domestic activity in the area. The only finds from the southern part of the ditch were a few pieces of struck or burnt flint.

The ditch and bank would have formed an impressive barrier. The ditch varied in profile, but was steep sided and over 1 m deep in places. The evidence of fill profile suggests that the enclosure had an internal bank, perhaps topped with a palisade, fence or a hedge (see reconstruction in Fig. 4.19 below). A south-east facing entrance was exposed in the excavated area, but the unexcavated western side of the enclosure may have also have had an entrance.

Although unlikely to have been defensive, the enclosure seemed designed to accommodate at least four roundhouses, while excluding others. The north-eastern stretch of the ditch changes alignment, respecting the ancillary subrectangular enclosures of roundhouse 12 to the north and enclosing an area devoid of roundhouses. It also cut one of a small complex of Iron Age pits dug in this area (see discussion on pits below).

It is possible that no more than three or four roundhouses were extant at any particular time during the middle Iron Age, and that the enclosed buildings represented a single phase of enclosed settlement. Activity within the enclosure continued into the late Iron Age and the only securely dated late Iron Age roundhouse (18) was constructed within its confines and over the area of the putative bank (see below). Regardless of its significance in terms of the settlement pattern, the construction of the enclosure represents a major investment of labour.

Pollen samples taken from the terminus of the ditch provided some evidence for the nature of the surrounding landscape (see below for full discussion). The landscape was predominantly:

…herb-rich grassland. Bracken was relatively abundant and may have been encroaching on the pasture. The presence of reedmace indicates that the water table was high within the ditch, although it may not have been waterlogged. The relatively high frequency of ferns might also represent plants growing in the moist and protected microenvironment offered by the ditch. No cereal pollen was found and there was no evidence that the feature represented a boundary between arable fields and other areas. The only woody taxa recorded were alder, pine, oak and hazel, with the latter being the most abundant.

(Wiltshire, CD Section 11)

This evidence suggests that pasture was an important element of the agricultural system to the east of and within the settlement, whilst the woody taxa identified suggest the presence of a hedge associated with the ditch. This pattern of enclosure of a later settlement is paralleled at Caesar's Camp, Heathrow (Grimes and Close-Brooks 1993).

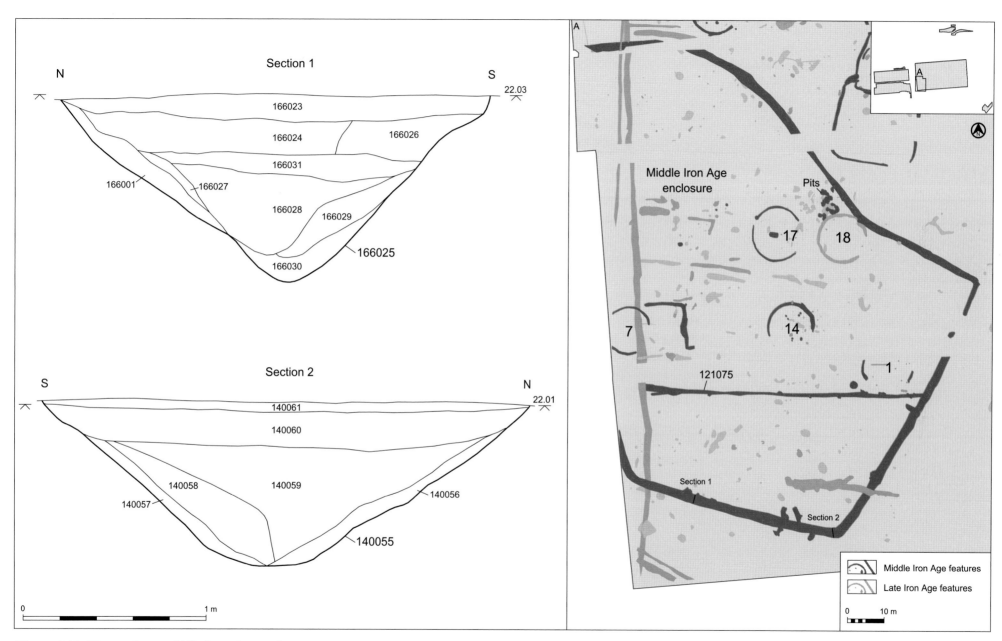

Section 1

N   S
                                                                  22.03

166023

166024   166026

166031

166001   166027

166028   166029

166030   166025

Section 2

S   N
                                                                  22.01

140061

140060

140058   140059

140057   140056

140055

0   1 m

A

Middle Iron Age
enclosure   Pits

17   18

7   14

121075   1

Section 1

Section 2

Middle Iron Age features

Late Iron Age features

0   10 m

Figure 4.13: The southern middle Iron Age enclosure

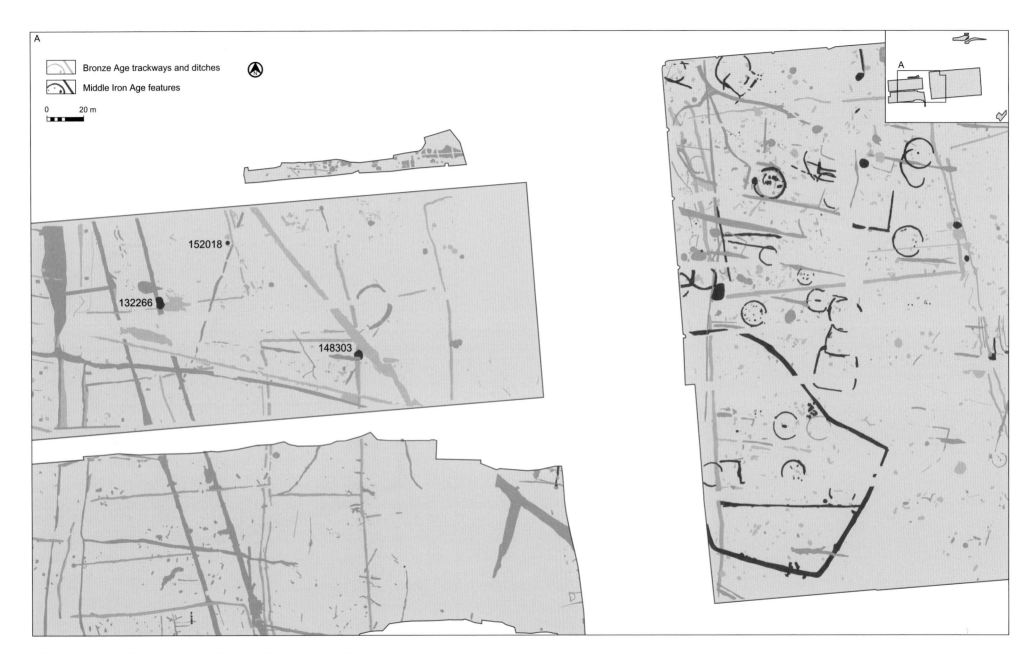

Figure 4.14: Middle Iron Age activity in the western field system

Middle Iron Age activity in the western field system

Three pits or waterholes located in the western fields on the lower gravel terrace were dug with the intention of providing a source of water, presumably for the watering of both cattle and crops (Fig. 4.14).

The westernmost waterhole, 132266, was situated in the corner of a middle-late Bronze Age field and cut the fills of the eastern Stanwell Cursus ditch. The waterhole was poorly dated, with the main fills producing pottery sherds that could only be broadly dated to the early-middle Iron Age, and the lowest excavated fill contained two small late Bronze Age sherds.

A second waterhole, 152018, was also apparently sited with reference to middle and late Bronze Age field boundaries. It was also poorly dated, with only two small sherds of middle Iron Age pottery recovered from one of the upper fills. A third waterhole (148303), also located at the edge of an earlier field, was well dated (Fig. 4.15). Waterhole 148303 was some 1.77 m deep, with the earliest fill, 148309, representing the rapid collapse of the sides shortly after it was dug. This gravel-rich deposit contained only a few fragments of animal bone. Two subsequent fills, 148310 and 148308, represented slow silting episodes in a watery environment, and both contained wooden twigs and middle Iron Age pottery. Other finds included animal bone, burnt flint and fired clay, including possible fragments of a loomweight or oven brick. These deposits

Context number	Number of objects	Specific date	Material type
148298	7	Bronze Age	Flint
148298	2	Late Neolithic/Bronze Age	Flint
148298	1	Mesolithic	Flint
148298	2	Middle Bronze Age	Pottery
148298	1	Neolithic	Flint
148299	1	Late Bronze Age	Pottery
148300	2	Late Bronze Age	Pottery
148306	1	Bronze Age	Flint
148306	4	Early Bronze Age	Pottery
148304	2	Late Bronze Age	Pottery
148305	1	Late Bronze Age	Pottery
148308	2	Early Iron Age	Pottery
148308	1	Neolithic	Flint

Table 4.4: Dated residual material from contexts of waterhole 148303

were sealed by a sequence of well-dated, gravel-rich secondary fills and tertiary fills.

Considerable quantities of finds were recovered from the fills of the waterhole, the variety of which suggests a range of intense activity in the vicinity. Some 348 sherds of pottery weighing over 2 kg were recovered—a significant amount for the site—along with over 1 kg of fired clay, 1.3 kg of animal bone, over 1.5 kg of slag and 5 kg of burnt flint. Several struck flints and flint debitage were residual.

A sequential analysis of this material produced some interesting results. The primary fill and the water-lain fills contained mixed assemblages of finds, with significant quantities of pottery and animal bone and only small amounts of burnt flint

and fired clay. In contrast, the assemblages from the gravel-rich secondary fills were dominated by burnt flint, fired clay and slag. The finds indicate industrial activity in the area of the pit, the debris from which was dumped into the feature.

Almost all of the slag from the feature was recovered from contexts 148305, 148304 and 148306, along with over 850 g of the fired clay and over half of the burnt flint (2.8 kg) (Fig. 4.15). The amount of pottery and animal bone recovered from these deposits was proportionally lower. Amongst the fired clay were fragments of two loomweights (or oven bricks), and a partially vitrified fragment of a tuyere. The slag was identified as waste from iron smithing with some possible smelting waste. Of the 3 kg of slag recovered from all middle Iron Age features, over half of this total came from waterhole 148303. The tertiary fills of the waterhole also produced large quantities of burnt flint and fired clay, and a single piece of slag, debris perhaps derived from middens associated with this industrial activity.

The entire waterhole sequence appears to date to the middle Iron Age, as there was no evidence of later material in the secondary and tertiary fills. There was a relatively large quantity of early residual material, predominantly burnt flint and pottery, ranging in date from the Mesolithic and Neolithic through to the late Bronze Age. This is unsurprising given the proximity of the feature to the middle and late Bronze Age field boundary and the Neolithic monument. It is the distribution of the finds within the fill sequence that is particularly interesting (see graph in Fig. 4.15). Small amounts of residual material were present in most fills, including one of the water-lain fills (148308, shown in red), the secondary fills (in blue) and the tertiary fills (indicated in yellow). It is notable that more residual material was recovered from the tertiary fills than the lower deposits. When analysed further, another pattern emerges (Table 4.4).

The sequence of water-lain (148308) and gravel-rich secondary fills (148300, 148304–6) all contained some residual material, most of which was late Bronze Age or early Iron Age in date. The material in the upper fills was more varied, and included Neolithic and undiagnostic Bronze Age flints. The increased quantity of this material suggests that it was derived from different and more wide ranging sources. The artefacts in these upper fills may represent material deposited by a re-introduction of ploughing. If this were the case, it highlights a shift from pasture to increased cereal cultivation (see discussion below).

The pattern of activity in the western field system during the middle Iron Age is difficult to define on the basis of the limited evidence available. It does appear, however, that waterholes and pits continued to be dug close to existing boundaries, whilst the absence of newly created boundary ditches implies a degree of continuity of the pre-existing field systems. We have no firm evidence for the nature of the farming undertaken in this area, but the circumstantial evidence from waterhole 148303 suggests that there may have been a change from pasture to crop growing in the later part of the middle Iron Age. This waterhole deposit also shows that iron working, and possibly other aspects of pyrotechnology, were taking place to the west and outside the main area of the settlement.

Middle Iron Age activity in the eastern field system

Waterholes and pits were also dug within the field system to the east of the middle Iron Age settlement. Two were cut along the line of the defunct Bronze Age trackway which formed the eastern limit of the settlement (Fig. 4.16). One, 178015, has been discussed above. A second waterhole, 156100, dug some 18 m to the south, contained no datable material apart from a single middle Iron Age sherd. Other waterholes and pits in the area may have been contemporary, but were not investigated as part of the excavations.

A group of four intercutting pits, 161099, 161103 161093 and 161089, lay further to the south along the line of the disused trackway. The precise stratigraphic relationships of the earlier pits were not recorded, but all are likely to be of similar date and none was very deep. The most closely dated was pit 161093, which was dug to a depth of 0.8 m and contained two fills, neither providing evidence of standing water. Both fills produced small numbers of middle Iron Age sherds. The function of the three earliest pits is difficult to ascertain.

All were cut by a later pit, 161089, which was excavated to a depth of 0.55 m. It contained two fills, both of which produced large quantities of pottery. The lower fill, 161091, represented a gradual erosion of the sides and top of the feature. It contained 66 sherds of middle Iron Age pottery, along with a deliberate dump of 154 sherds (161088), all dated to the middle Iron Age or the middle/late Iron Age. The upper fill of the pit (161090) was also likely to have accumulated slowly, and contained 304 sherds of similar date. Neither fill contained significant quantities of other find types—a small amount of animal bone was recovered from 161090 and a very small quantity of slag, fired clay and burnt flint came from 161091. The pit has few contemporary parallels in terms of the quantity of pottery, and the absence of other components of a 'domestic' assemblage points to a specific pattern of deposition (see discussion below).

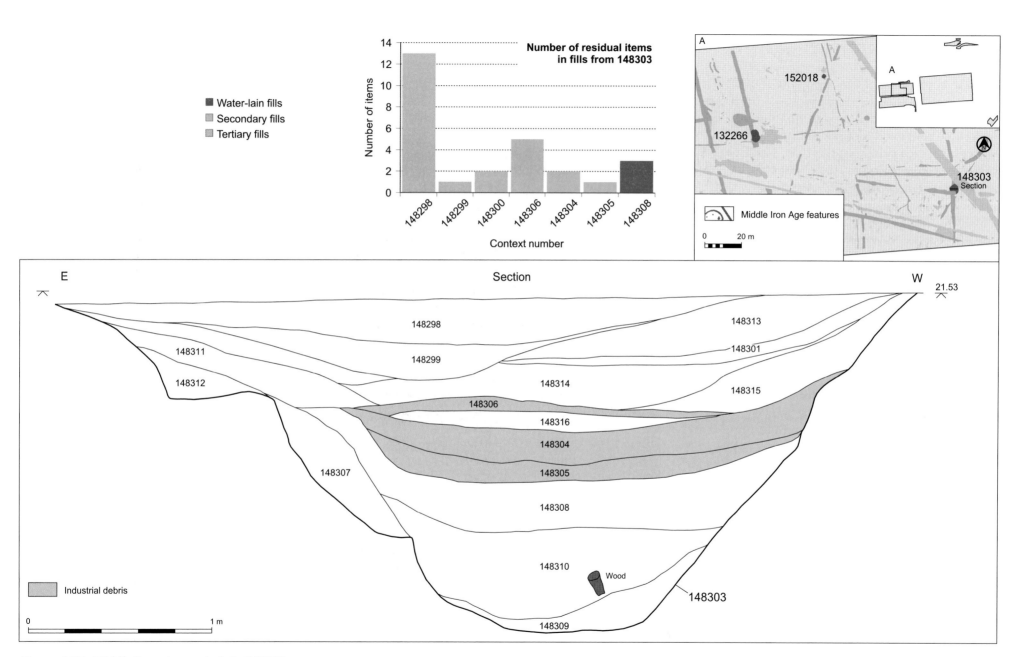

Number of residual items in fills from 148303

Water-lain fills
Secondary fills
Tertiary fills

Industrial debris

Middle Iron Age features

Figure 4.15: Middle Iron Age waterhole 148303

Another waterhole, 105027, lay *c* 180 m to the south-east of this pit group. It was roughly circular in plan, and 0.8 m deep. The southern edge formed a shallow slope, probably an access ramp, whilst the northern edge was steeper. The waterhole contained a classic silting sequence, with gravel-rich primary fills (105028 and 130195) sealed by two successive layers which formed in standing water (layers 105029 and 105031). The upper fill of the feature (105032) formed over a long period. A date for the feature, which cut one of the silted ditches of the middle/late Bronze Age field system, was provided by a few sherds of early/middle Iron Age pottery recovered from the lower part of the fill sequence. The only other material recovered was a small residual assemblage of struck flint and small quantities of fired clay.

A steep sided pit, 163005, excavated close to the eastern end of the site also dated to this period, but its function was unclear. The primary fill, which contained no finds apart from a single sherd of early Iron Age pottery, was sealed by a charcoal rich dump of domestic material. This contained a small quantity of animal bone, burnt and worked flint, along with 19 sherds of pottery. The uppermost fill represented a gradual silting episode.

Other middle Iron Age features in the area east of the settlement included a small number of tree-throws and a single posthole. All of the tree-throws were dated by a few abraded sherds of middle Iron Age pottery. This material may represent domestic waste from the settlement

Plate 4.5: Surveying the middle Iron Age features in the eastern field system

used to fertilise the fields. If this were the case, it would correspond with the pollen evidence, which suggests a mostly open landscape with few trees during this period.

Further evidence for middle Iron Age activity within these fields consisted of a number of approximately east-west aligned ditches

(128296, 163060, 160184 and 160092) that seem to subdivide Bronze Age land divisions. All may have recut earlier ditches and none were particularly well dated, containing very small quantities of middle Iron Age pottery. This points to continued activity in the eastern fields, although it is unclear whether the entire system remained in use (see discussion on farming below).

Figure 4.16: Middle Iron Age activity in the eastern field system

Pit digging, middens and propitiation in the middle Iron Age

A group of 32 shallow, inter-cutting pits lying within the boundary of the later middle Iron Age enclosure should be noted (Figs 4.16–7). The pits had been infilled by the time the enclosure was built. One was cut by the digging of the middle Iron Age enclosure ditch, all must have lain in the area occupied by the enclosure bank, and one pit was also cut by the late Iron Age penannular gully of house 18 (Fig. 4.17).

The concentration of shallow and intercutting pits is unusual. One of the stratigraphically earliest pits contained a quantity of Bronze Age sherds. Iron Age pottery and residual Bronze Age sherds were recovered from the remainder of the pit fills along with animal bone, burnt flint and stone, fired clay and worked flint (some of which was residual). Pit 141202 produced a complete miniature vessel dating to the middle Iron Age (Fig. 4.17, no. 1).

The repeated activity, and the mixed and residual nature of the fills might imply that these pits were associated with a range of well established activities in the immediate vicinity that generated a reasonable amount of debris, perhaps resulting in the creation of a midden. It is noticeable that the pits lie at the point where the middle Iron Age enclosure ditch diverts from its line to curve around a large area devoid of any surviving evidence for buildings. This might indicate that enclosure was designed to incorporate an area of earlier activities, of which the pits are our only surviving trace.

Figure 4.17: Distribution of pottery within the middle Iron Age pit group within the settlement

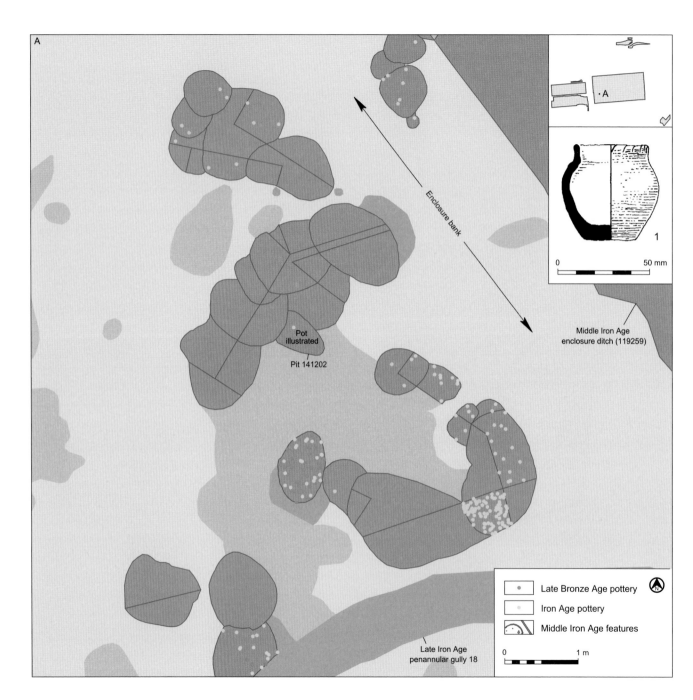

Farming in the middle Iron Age at Perry Oaks

The inhabitants of the middle Iron Age settlement continued to cultivate the earlier landscape. It is possible that the nucleated settlement represented an agglomeration of earlier farmsteads, although whether its location within earlier common land indicated increased pressure on resources is unclear. If this were the case it would imply social or even political change.

Whatever the significance of the reorganisation of the settlement, it is clear that agriculture remained the primary focus of activity. Construction within the confines of pre-existing landscape boundaries indicates continued use of the earlier fields for agriculture. There is little evidence for any significant reworking of field boundaries, and the land divisions were defined by banks and mature hedges, the ditches having long been infilled.

Three main sources are available to us in analysing the nature of the agriculture of this period—pollen, charcoal from the fills of the features, and animal bones. Although the preservation of animal bone was generally very poor, there was a reasonable assemblage of material from the settlement, largely recovered from the fills of the recut ditch of penannular gully 8. However, the animal bone assemblage from gully 8 is probably the result of selective activity and cannot be treated as a reflection of species proportion in the general animal population at the time.

The proportions of animal bones identifiable to species was very low, and the poor preservation of animal bone in general made it impossible to estimate the relative proportions of species in the assemblage (Bates, CD Section 14). Cattle and sheep bones were both present, and likely to have formed the main elements of the animal stock of the settlement. Small numbers of pig bones were also recovered along with a few red deer bones. Bates' specialist report on the assemblage states that:

The predominance of cattle over sheep/goat may simply be the result of low-lying areas, such as the Perry Oaks environment, being more suited to cattle husbandry. Similar proportions of species are found on other Iron Age sites on the gravel terraces of the lower Thames Valley (Grant 1984, 103–105).

(Bates , CD Section 14)

The low occurrence of pig on Iron Age sites is not unusual, but pig is almost certainly under-represented at Perry Oaks, often being described in the archive records as poorly preserved, presumably due to low bone density in comparison to other animals of similar size. Horse bones and a few dog bones were also recovered from the middle Iron Age site.

The best evidence for land management in the middle Iron Age was recovered from one of the waterholes excavated at the eastern edge of the settlement (178015; see Fig. 4.12 above). Analysis of pollen samples taken through the fills of this waterhole have given us good evidence for the surrounding landscape. The pollen diagram for this feature is summarised in Figure 4.18, and described below:

The lowest deposit is characterised by very high levels of microscopic charcoal and an exceedingly open landscape. The feature itself was wet although there is no palynological evidence for standing water in this zone. Sedges, water mint, and meadow sweet were growing very close, probably at the wet edges of the pit. Fungal spores were also high in this zone and that might indicate that the pit dried out from time to time so that deposits became aerated enough to allow fungi to grow on organic debris falling into the feature. The area around the feature seems to have been very open, with woody taxa accounting for only about 5% of TLPS. Alder, pine, hazel, and oak were recorded but they were probably some distance away as single trees, or else all the trees and shrubs in the catchment were severely coppiced or pollarded.

(Wiltshire, CD Section 11)

These results suggest that grazing pressure was particularly high when this waterhole was open, and that the abundant weeds identified from the pollen were avoided by grazing animals, or may have been growing on the edges of arable fields, on grassy banks between fields, or on open broken ground. Cereal pollen also points to arable cultivation in the area.

Higher up the sequence (Zone 2 of pollen column in Fig. 4.18) there is evidence for a drop in the intensity of grazing, in the form of a slight increase in woody taxa with some scrub/hedge plants also present. Whilst grasses increased, there was a slight decline in some weeds. The levels of microscopic charcoal were also lower, supporting the suggestion that there was a shift in activity, including a lowering of grazing pressure on the land surrounding the waterhole. Small amounts of cereal pollen were found, pointing to continuation of arable farming in the vicinity.

In pollen Zone 3, there was further evidence for an even greater decline in grazing and management of woodland plants. Both grasses and woody taxa were more common, whilst the decline of ruderals (weeds) noted in Zone 2 continued. Again, the presence of cereal pollen pointed to continued arable cultivation. The presence of *typha* (reed-mace) also indicated that the feature or its margins were very wet. This accorded with the recorded stratigraphy, which showed evidence of formation in a watery environment (see above).

The upper Zone (4) of the pollen diagram suggested a continuation of open landscape, with only a slight increase in tree and shrub growth, a significant increase in the representation of grass pollens, a smaller increase in cereal pollen, and a decline in ruderals. These point to continued decline in grazing in the area, although it is possible that the evidence was distorted by hay-making or some similar practice:

If the cut were made after grass flowering but before the main flowering season of the grassland weeds, it is not difficult to see how this activity could affect the palynological record. Grass must be viewed as a crop (Lockhart and Wiseman 1983) and there is no reason why these Iron Age peoples should not have been making hay for overwintering animals or for some other domestic purpose.

(Wiltshire, CD Section 11)

The general picture that emerges is one of a fairly open landscape, where the:

...middle Iron Age settlement was set in a very clear landscape with very few trees and shrubs. If they were present, then they must have been pollarded and/or coppiced very regularly so that woody taxa were not able to flower. Cereal growing /processing was being carried out at the site but marked changes in the pollen spectra *show that either grazing pressure was lower than before or that the timing of hay making influenced the sward. There was no convincing evidence for hedges in this part of the site in the middle Iron Age and boundaries might have consisted of earth/grassy banks. These banks would have provided havens for many of the herbaceous plants found in the sample.*

(Wiltshire, CD Section 11)

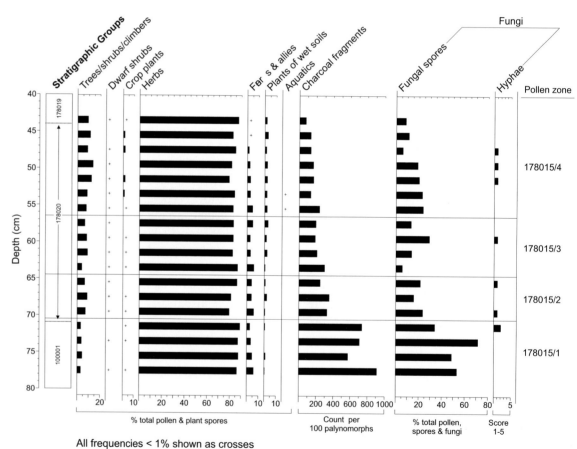

Figure 4.18: Pollen diagram for waterhole 178015

Summary

The evidence for middle Iron Age agriculture is sparse. Developing out of the major landscape divisions of the Bronze Age, the construction of the new settlement seems to have been allied to changes in the way the land was farmed, with inevitable consequences for the layout of the landscape. The continued digging of waterholes within the bounds of the western field system suggests the survival of some, if not all, of the field boundaries in this area, with animal grazing probably being the primary agricultural activity. There was also some evidence for iron smelting and smithing in this locality.

The evidence for the eastern field system is more ambiguous. Although a number of pits or waterholes were dug, some of these may have served the settlement rather than the fields. Only one, 105027, lay on the edge of an earlier field, with the remainder being dug across the line of a derelict Bronze Age trackway, which for much of its length marked the eastern limit of the middle Iron Age settlement. Equally ambiguous was the only pollen evidence, obtained from one of the waterholes (178015), which appears to show that the landscape was extremely open, and that grazing pressure on grasses appeared to decline through the life of the waterhole, whilst the levels of cereals grown remained relatively constant. Despite the fact that the waterhole was acting as a catchment for material derived both from the settlement and from the field system, it does hint at an open landscape in which grazing in this area at least was less intensive.

Figure 4.19: Artist's reconstruction of the middle Iron Age settlement at Perry Oaks, looking west through the entrance in the southern enclosure

The likelihood is that this small settlement was one of a large number of similar settlements which were bound politically and may have owed a degree of allegiance to an elite group or individual. It is unclear how this political structure worked. If dues were paid, this could have been by agricultural surplus or labour service and military obligation.

201

Transforming the landscape—
late Iron Age-early Roman settlement
and re-organisation

Large-scale and quite fundamental changes took place in the late Iron Age, although they may also be the most archaeologically ephemeral (Figs 4.20–1). The system of small co-axial fields which had characterised the landscape for almost two thousand years seem to have been largely replaced or cleared and a field system aligned roughly north-east to south-west was constructed in its place (Fig. 4.20; see below). We will first look briefly at the ceramic data for this period and then examine the evidence for a settlement focus, before commenting in more detail upon the newly created field system.

Ceramic evidence

The earliest ceramic material from this phase comprised 'Belgic' type wares, which have a date range beginning in the 1st century BC, indicating that the significant landscape developments may well have taken place some time before the Roman conquest (see below). However more precise dating that would enable the transition from the middle Iron Age settlement to be better understood is not possible, as Every and Mepham state:

Ceramic developments within the late Iron Age can be seen within the wider context of the late Iron Age ceramic sequence for southern England. The introduction of wheelthrown 'Belgic' wares in necked and shouldered jar forms, and their handmade imitations, is generally

Figure 4.20: Late Iron Age - early Roman landscape at Perry Oaks

dated no earlier than the second quarter of the 1st century BC. It is likely that there was some period of overlap between these wares and the preceding middle Iron Age traditions, although the isolation of well stratified early groups containing both types has not proved possible at Perry Oaks.

(Every and Mepham, CD Section 1)

The pottery assemblages from this late Iron Age-early Roman phase include some 'Romanised' forms and fabrics, but these only became numerous during the 2nd century AD. Prior to this point the inhabitants continued to use pottery developed from the well-fired, wheel thrown ceramic tradition of the late Iron Age. In many cases it is generally difficult to determine whether this material is pre- or post-conquest in date, creating a corresponding difficulty in phasing certain elements of the site.

This particular issue is highlighted in the Roman pottery report:

Although there is a substantial amount of these [late Iron Age/early Roman 'Belgic' type] wares there is very little 'Romanised' material that could be dated earlier than the early-mid 2nd century AD. Contexts that contained this early material with Roman wares such as Verulamium and some unsourced sandy wares defined the early Romano-British period. Early forms within these groups are restricted to bead-rim and high-shouldered/necked jars, with the single example of a 'Surrey' or 'Atrebatic' bowl. Early flagons and mortarium types are completely absent and there are virtually

no amphorae. Not until the end of the first quarter of the 2nd century AD does Roman material really start to occur in quantity.

(Brown, CD Section 2)

The pottery of the period 100 BC–AD 120 was largely composed of a narrow range of coarsewares. Only four sherds of a total of 506 dated to this phase were finewares, including three small samian ware fragments. Small quantities of pottery in Romanised forms and fabrics could be confidently dated to the post-conquest period, including shell-tempered wares, Alice Holt sandy wares and samian ware. In contrast, the pottery assemblage post-dating AD 120 was dominated by these 'Romanised' wares although the proportion of finewares was relatively low.

Settlement focus

Despite the paucity of evidence for late Iron Age-early Roman domestic structures (see below), it is likely that main focus of occupation remained in the area of the middle Iron Age settlement (Fig. 4.21). The northern area of the earlier settlement was cut through by two boundary ditches (147253 and 108027) which had been dug partly with reference to the two largest middle Iron Age structures (gullies 3 and 8). One of these, represented by penannular gully 8, was still clearly in use as a segment of the gully was recut in this period. This work may have been contemporary with the cutting of a large pit (148342) through the southern ditch of the penannular gully.

Another pit (147153) was dug within the gully interior, its fill including a deposit of burnt material including cremated animal bone.

The southern edge of gully 8 was skirted by the late Iron Age-early Roman boundary ditch 147253, which appeared to continue (after a possible gap) westwards as ditch 113131 and then curved back to the north-west as ditch 108028 (Fig. 4.21). A small irregular shallow penannular gully (126155) was dug against the north lip of this boundary (113131). Further modifications were to come when gully 8 was incorporated into the corner junction of the reworking of this boundary complex (by ditch 147237) in the middle Roman period (see below).

A second ditch (108027) curved around the southern edge of the rectangular enclosure/structure 108018, which overlay middle Iron Age gully 3. It is quite possible that feature 108018 could actually date to the late Iron Age, but the chronological evidence remains uncertain. In any case the implication is that both middle Iron Age gullies 3 and 8 continued to have an impact on the landscape in the later Iron Age and Roman periods.

The one recognisable late Iron Age-early Roman domestic structure is represented by penannular gully 18, located *c* 120 m to the south of the northern activity area (Fig. 4.20). This must have cut into the denuded internal bank of the irregular middle Iron Age enclosure, the upper ditch-fills of which were continuing to accumulate in this period.

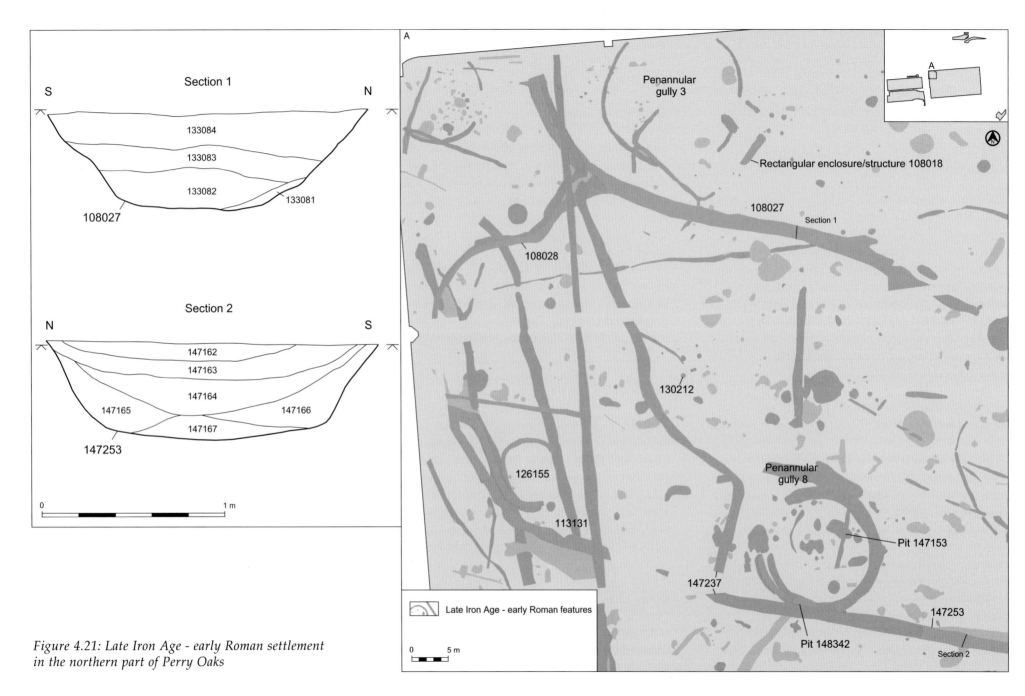

Section 1

S   N

133084

133083

133082

133081

108027

Section 2

N   S

147162

147163

147164

147165   147166

147167

147253

0   1 m

A

Penannular gully 3

Rectangular enclosure/structure 108018

108027

Section 1

108028

130212

126155

Penannular gully 8

113131

Pit 147153

147237

147253

Pit 148342

Section 2

Figure 4.21: Late Iron Age - early Roman settlement in the northern part of Perry Oaks

Late Iron Age - early Roman features

0   5 m

Feature type	Number of objects	Weight (g)	Average weight (g)
Cremation	7	35	5
Ditch	937	5088	5.43
Gully	39	250	6.41
Pit	350	4803	13.72
Posthole	2	13	6.5
Penannular gully	101	775	7.67

Table 4.5: Quantities of pottery recovered from late Iron Age features

The difficulty of identifying late Iron Age structures is a more general problem in southern British settlement studies, one which presumably indicates a change in the nature of domestic architecture rather than necessarily implying a decline in settlement activity. Consequently some of the undated postholes within the earlier settlement area may be late Iron Age-early Roman in date.

The quantities of late Iron Age-early Roman pottery recovered from these features are presented in Table 4.5. Most sherds were recovered from the earlier settlement area, and those with the highest average weight came from pits and waterholes (notably 130212, 137114 and 167119, the only such features to produce more than 20 sherds) and penannular gully 8. The limited but relatively large sherd fragments from the middle Iron Age pennanular gullies (3, 10, 11 and 15) and later Iron Age-early Roman ditches (eg 108027 and 108028) may reflect the proximity of these features to the core of the settlement area.

The fills of the northern ditch (108027) produced a diverse assemblage of finds, including pottery, fragments of fired clay and animal bone. Amongst the bone assemblage was a complete cattle mandible, which was found in the ditch fill immediately to the south of the entrance of rectilinear enclosure/structure 108018. The quantity of finds from this ditch suggests that there was fairly intensive activity in the area.

The southern ditch segments (113131, 147253), which slighted the southern curve of gully 8, also produced large quantities of occupation material, including animal bone, pottery, burnt flint and fired clay, particularly from 147235 in the south-eastern section (Fig. 4.21).

Other features in the probable area of occupation that were definitely associated with this phase of occupation included a group of three intercutting pits or waterholes (180106–8) lying in the zone between the southern roundhouse (18) and the northern activity area (Fig. 4.20). The most

southerly of these, pit 180106 was relatively shallow at 0.85 m deep and none of the fills indicated the presence of standing water. The pit had, however, been heavily truncated by a later pit, and its original dimensions and fill sequence were unclear. Two large sherds of late Iron Age pottery were recovered from the surviving fill.

The second pit in this group, 180107 contained a clear sequence of water-lain primary and secondary fills. No datable material was recovered from this feature, or from 180108, which was dug to replace it. The latter was not cut sufficiently deep to have served as a waterhole and may not have been open for very long. There is some evidence that pit 180107 was deliberately backfilled.

Eastern field system

The evidence for the nature and extent of the late Iron Age-early Roman field system is slight—only a few shallow ditches survive on this alignment (Fig. 4.20 and 4.22). Nevertheless, it still marks an important shift in landscape organisation in this area, being a complete realignment of the previous fieldwork system that had been used for almost 2000 years. The realignment was largely confined to the higher gravel terrace to the east of the probable settlement focus, in an area that would eventually be divided by a late Roman 'ladder' enclosure system (see below). There was no evidence for any change to the Bronze Age field system established on the lower gravel terrace to the west (Fig. 4.22), and it is possible that all or some elements of this system remained in use throughout later prehistory and into the Roman period. In fact continuing excavation at Heathrow has established that enclosure ditches relating to the Bronze Age field system in the area were re-cut in the medieval and post-medieval periods, suggesting that these fields survived relatively unchanged until fairly recent times (see Volume 2 for a wider discussion).

It was impossible to identify a coherent single system of fields within the pattern of the eastern boundaries, although some groupings of ditches were identified, including those (eg 137125, 155062, 155047) cut by middle Roman enclosure E1 (see Figs 4.20 and 4.24 below). In general there was insufficient stratigraphic and dating evidence to establish their chronological sequence in detail, although it is clear that they post-dated the field system created during the Bronze Age, and some were cut by a Romano-British 'ladder' enclosure system (see below).

Datable material was recovered from the fills of several of these boundary features, some clearly residual and others intrusive. The residual material included Neolithic and Bronze Age worked flint, along with late Bronze Age and early and middle Iron Age pottery. The most significant assemblage recovered, however, comprised late Iron Age and Roman pottery and ceramic building material. A collection of 14 sherds of Roman pottery from ditch 129067 probably dates to sometime after AD 150, and may reflect the latest phase of cleaning or re-cutting of this boundary, which cut through the silts of a large deep waterhole, 151132 (see below).

The overall stratigraphic and ceramic evidence suggests that the field system was being constantly modified from its inception in the late Iron Age right through into the early and middle Roman period, perhaps only falling into disuse with the establishment of the 'ladder' enclosure system in the later Roman period (see below).

Two waterholes were located within the eastern field system, and were broadly contemporary with it (Fig. 4.20). Waterhole 119380 to the north was 0.85 m deep, and contained a complex sequence of fills, some of them deposited in standing water. The dating of this waterhole is problematic as the only fills that produced pottery were relatively high in the sequence, and contained both late Iron Age and early Roman sherds. That this feature was completely backfilled, possibly deliberately, before being cut by the mid Roman enclosure (E1), suggests that it was originally cut during the late Iron Age-early Roman period.

A large deep waterhole, 151132, lay to the south of 119380 and was cut by ditch 129067 of the eastern field system (Fig. 4.20; see above). The precise date of the waterhole could not be determined, but it contained a few early Roman sherds along with larger numbers of undatable Roman pottery. The feature was probably dug in the early Roman period to provide water for agricultural activities, and had silted up by the time the final recut of the ditch was undertaken. A few late 3rd or 4th century Oxfordshire wares recovered from the upper fills of the waterhole are likely to be intrusive.

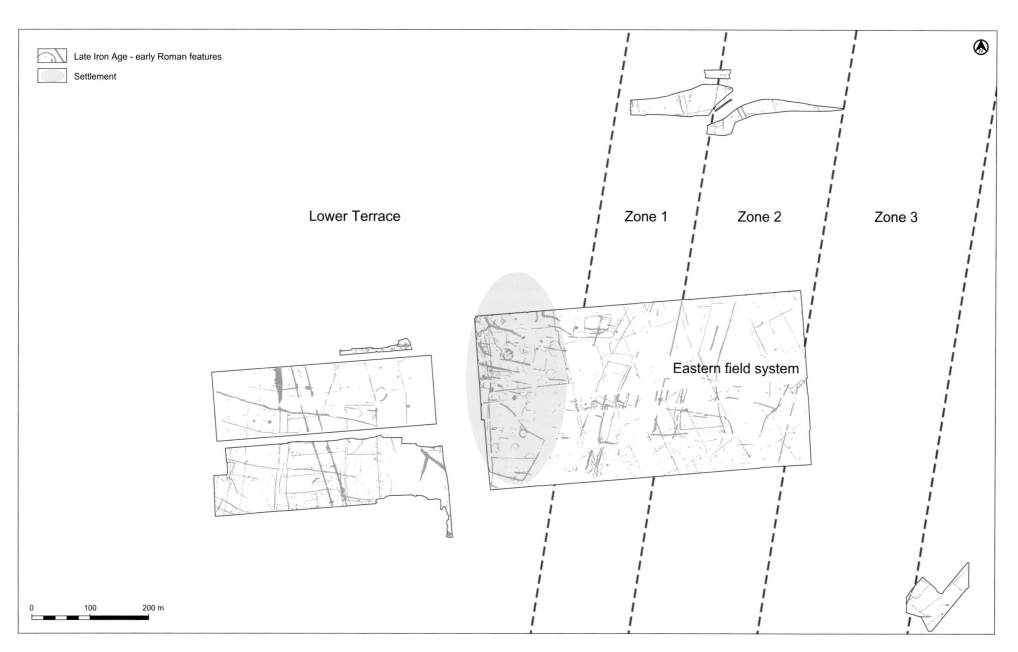

Figure 4.22: Late Iron Age - early Roman landscape showing different zones of activity

Key:
- Late Iron Age - early Roman features
- Settlement

Lower Terrace

Zone 1   Zone 2   Zone 3

Eastern field system

0   100   200 m

Form and function of the eastern field system (Fig. 4.22)

The precise form and function of the early Roman field system is impossible to determine, largely because of the effects of the heavy truncation. On the basis of the surviving evidence, a few details were identified. The re-alignment of the landscape appears to have been confined to the upper gravel terrace to the east of the Iron Age and Roman settlement. It seems likely that the landscape was divided into zones, much as previous Bronze Age field systems had been, although these do not appear to have been equally spaced land divisions. Three zones have been tentatively identified (Fig. 4.22), each defined by what appears to have been a substantial boundary ditch. Zones 1 (bounded to the west by the settlement) and 2 were the most obvious, whilst Zone 3 is somewhat more conjectural as most of it lay outside of the area of excavation.

As was the case with the Bronze Age field system, the large landscape zones appeared to be subdivided in different ways. The surviving internal subdivisions of the central Zone (2) were irregular and lacked coherence. This may indicate that boundaries in the area changed rapidly, or that the land was subdivided into a number of small landholdings, perhaps belonging to particular individuals or kin-groups. We cannot be certain that all of the subdivisions belonged to this field system, or even to a single phase of activity. It may be that the landscape was at this stage divided into large fields, or that internal boundaries were only hedged or demarcated

by shallow drainage gullies that did not survive subsequent truncation. This suggestion is supported by the evidence from Zone 1, where a slightly more coherent pattern of subdivision was apparent. The best evidence for a regular system of enclosures lay in the central strip across the site. During the operation of the site as a sewage treatment plant, this central spine was used as an access road for vehicles, and subsequently did not suffer the same level of truncation as the beds to the north and south. These ditches and gullies lay on the same alignment as each other and may represent the remains of a series of fields or enclosures. If these belong to a single phase of activity, they are likely to have been a series of enclosures of different sizes, with trackways providing access between them.

Settlement activity in the mid Roman period

The settlement activity of the 2nd-early 3rd centuries AD appears to have been a continuation of the late Iron Age-early Roman occupation in the area and on the evidence of quantities of artefacts recovered, occupation was probably on a similar scale (Fig. 4.23). Boundaries were re-worked and maintained, and there is no clear evidence for changes in the way the landscape was organised. The focus of settlement activity remained broadly similar and the most of the eastern field system that was first laid out during the late Iron Age (see above) appeared to continue in use.

Organisation of the settlement

The core of the mid Roman settlement corresponded to the middle Iron Age and late Iron Age-early Roman settlement nuclei, indicating continuity of occupation at some level throughout this long period. The area around penannular gully 8 persisted as a major focus, with the ditches immediately to the south and west being recut (147237). However, it is unlikely that gully 8 itself remain in use, as a shallow north-south gully (126099) was dug across the feature, through the fills of the silted ditch. There is little evidence to suggest that roundhouse 18 continued in use beyond the start of the 2nd century AD, although there is evidence for rectangular buildings (B1–4) dating to the Roman period lying further north (Fig. 4.23).

At some point in the mid Roman period, two enclosures (E1 and E2) were constructed on the western side of the eastern field system (Fig. 4.23). The ditches of the northernmost enclosure (E1) were heavily re-worked and cleaned over a relatively short period of time, from the mid 2nd to late 2nd/3rd century AD (Phases 2–3 on Fig. 4.24). The earliest rectangular enclosure clearly cut the line of partially silted late Iron Age-early Roman field boundaries such as ditch 155062 and gully 137125 (Phase 1 on Fig. 4.24). This enclosure was sub-divided by north-south ditch 110042, and its northern boundary (156047) was later re-dug along a slightly different alignment. At some point after its initial establishment, the enclosure was expanded to the west (137136, 134058) and a droveway was created along its

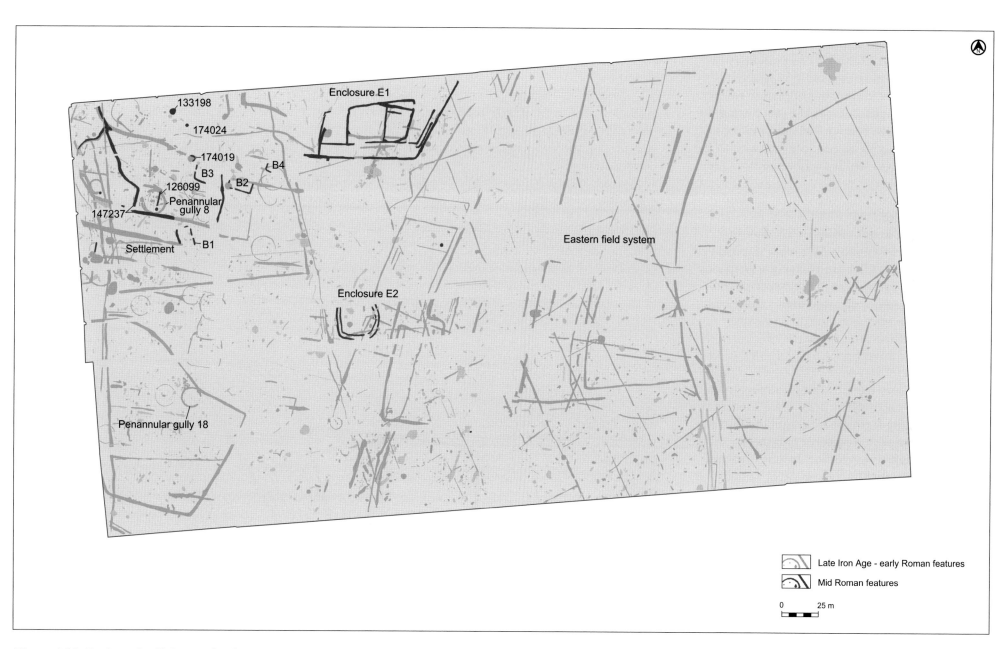

Figure 4.23: Early and mid Roman landscape

southern and eastern margins (110078, 134058, 137129, 119352 and 134046). The chronology of this droveway is uncertain and it may actually have been designed to link this enclosure complex with the 'ladder' enclosures to the east during the 3rd century AD (see below). The morphology of the enclosure complex and its integration with the droveways suggests that it may been a stockade.

There were concentrations of pottery and to a lesser extent fired clay and CBM in the area of enclosure E1. Insufficient ceramic building material was recovered to suggest that it originated from a building in the vicinity, but the fired clay is more likely to represent the presence of cob built or wattle and daub structures. It may be that part of this area was occupied by non-domestic structures, such as barns or agricultural outbuildings.

Another enclosure complex (E2) was constructed c 100 m further south (Fig. 4.23). Two concentric ditches were dug forming an irregular subrectangular enclosure with a possible entrance to the south. The ditches were quite shallow and may have been separated by a bank. Most of the enclosure lay within the central band of the site which was subject to a lesser degree of truncation (see above), while the northern side, which lay outside, did not survive. Stratigraphically the enclosure post-dated ditches of the late Iron Age-early Roman field system and was cut by ditches of the late Roman 'ladder' enclosure. Furthermore its north-south alignment deviated from both the early and late Roman field alignments. This is important because if this were an agricultural

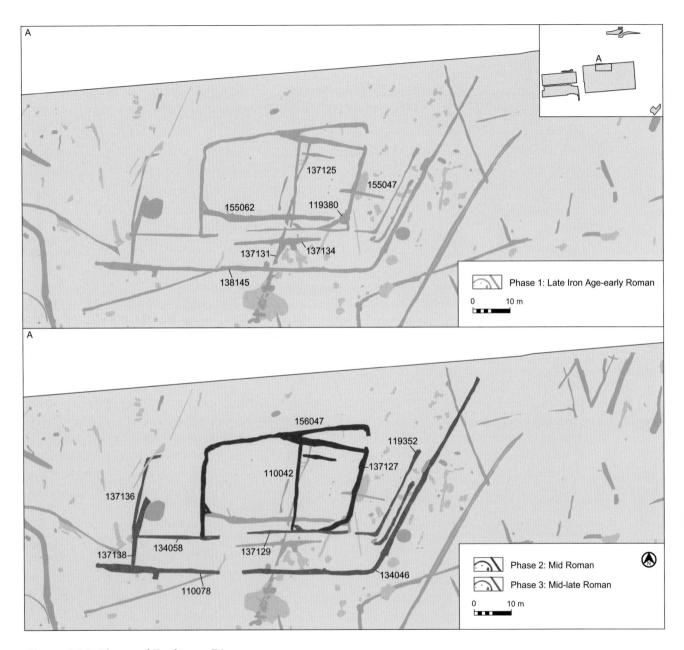

Figure 4.24: Phases of Enclosure E1

210

enclosure, we may expect it to be integrated within the field system, not set apart from it. Therefore it is possible that this enclosure was not part of a wider agricultural landscape, but purposely set aside from it.

A small assemblage of Roman pottery recovered from a number of ditches associated with both of these enclosures (E1 and E2) provided the only dating evidence. The assemblage included reduced wares, the most common fabrics, along with whitewares and oxidised wares. The absence of samian wares and the small numbers of whiteware and 'Belgic' pottery sherds within the associated ceramic assemblages suggests that the enclosures were probably constructed during the second half of the 2nd century AD, and were silting up during the late 2nd or 3rd centuries. They were probably, therefore, short lived features, in use for no more than three or four generations before being replaced by enclosures and boundaries which made up the larger 'ladder' enclosure system of the 3rd–4th century AD (see below).

Roman buildings and activity areas

Five probable buildings (B1–5) could be dated to the Roman period, all of which lay close to the site of penannular gully 8, thus demonstrating some continuity with the earlier settlement focus (Figure 4.25). Four could not be closely dated (B1–4), but could well span the middle to late Roman phase and so are described here. A fifth (B5) was certainly late Roman and is described separately below.

One building (B1) was represented by a series of segmented gullies defining a roughly rectangular area *c* 17 x 8 m. The gullies may be interpreted as foundation trenches for a building, which have been badly truncated. Numerous finds were recovered from the building trenches, including a small assemblage of undiagnostic Roman pottery. A single sherd belonging to Roman ceramic phase 1 (100 BC–AD 100) provides scant evidence for an early date for this structure, but it may be residual. However the possibility that this building belongs to a different phase than the other buildings (see below) is suggested by the fact that it lay upon a different alignment, echoing that of the earlier agricultural landscape.

Other finds from the trenches of Building 1 suggest that it had an industrial function. A relatively large quantity of burnt flint and fired clay was found, along with small quantities of burnt stone, slag and ceramic building material. The fired clay assemblage included burnt daub. Some of the building gully fills also produced charred plant remains.

The charcoal from soil samples in three trenches (126121, 148155, 126129) of Building B1 was found to derive from a very restricted range of taxa, dominated by oak *(Quercus)*. These were compared with a typical assemblage from a Roman ditch (160102) (Figure 4.25), and the difference in proportions led the charcoal specialist to suggest that, 'a greater degree of care was taken when selecting the fuelwood for a specific purpose than in the general field system assemblages.' (Challinor, CD Section 10).

Charred plant material from the foundation trenches of Building B1 produced an assemblage rich in weed and chaff (147253 and 113079) and grain (148155 and 126121) (Fig. 4.26). As Challinor concludes:

It is reasonable to assume that the samples are the result of crop processing activities which were being carried out in the close vicinity of the structure. The grain-dominated assemblages are likely to have resulted from accidental over-burning during crop processing while the chaff-rich assemblages would be the by-product of the process.

(Challinor, CD Section 10)

The building was clearly situated within an area of crop processing, presumably surrounded by threshing floors, and itself may have functioned as an agricultural barn.

A second possible Roman building (B2) (Figs 4.25–6) was represented by a rectangular arrangement of gullies, which—as with B1—probably represent foundation trenches for a wooden building. The building measured *c* 15 m by at least 7 m, and the northern section appears to have been truncated.

The dating of this building relied on the stratigraphic relationship between the foundation trench and the fills of a middle Iron Age waterhole (137114). This waterhole continued in use into the late Iron Age and its upper fills (137106, 137107, 137108 and 137109) were dated to the early Roman period on the basis of late Iron

211

Age/early Roman pottery. The feature was completely backfilled prior to the construction of the building, probably during the mid to late Roman period. Only a few pieces of burnt flint were recovered from the building gullies, with nothing to indicate its function.

A number of shallow gullies in the vicinity of B2—and on the same alignment—probably represent the structural remains of at least two other rectangular buildings (B3 and B4; Fig. 4.25). Although none produced many finds, sherds dated broadly to the Roman period were recovered from some of the foundation gullies.

Circumstantial evidence from the specialist analysis of the insect remains supported the interpretation of structures in this area, at least in the late Roman period. Samples from a 4th century waterhole (174069; the latest in a sequence—see discussion below) lying just to the west of gully 163097 included several species characteristic of settlements, indicating the proximity of timber buildings in particular:

Beetles which infest structural timber comprised 4.3% of the terrestrial Coleoptera. They were all Anobium punctatum (woodworm). In the almost complete absence of other woodland insects, they provide very strong evidence for the presence of timber structures.

(Robinson, CD Section 12)

A significant proportion of the Coleoptera assemblage also comprised *Ptinus fur*, which inhabits buildings amongst stable debris, old hay, granary waste and food scraps. Other insects recovered that favour the environment of buildings included:

…examples of Mycetaea hirta, a fungal feeder which occurs in damp places inside buildings, sometimes feeding on the dry rot fungus and Typhaea stercorea, another fungal feeder which occurs in old haystack bottoms as well as in such indoor habitats as stable bedding.

(Robinson, CD Section 12)

Some species, whilst not necessarily diagnostic of settlement habitats, also suggested the presence of buildings. These included fungal feeders such as *Lathridius minutus* gp. and *Xylodromus concinnus*. Robinson was able to conclude on the basis of the waterhole assemblage that it was:

…clear that the pit was either next to a building or that organic refuse from inside a building had been dumped in it. It is possible that the building was domestic or agricultural. However, it is unlikely to have been used for the long-term storage of fully cleaned cereals because even the minor grain pests were absent.

(Robinson, CD Section 12)

Furthermore, the presence and proportions of other insects within the assemblage indicated that the deposit also contained small quantities of domestic organic refuse, but that there was unlikely to be much in the way of animal dung or naturally accumulated decaying material.

If the possible building(s) to the east of the waterhole were the source of these insects, they may have been either domestic dwellings or agricultural buildings. If this were the case, the structure(s) would have had to have been occupied during the lifetime of the waterhole in the 4th century AD (see below).

Other insects found in high concentrations in the waterhole sample were honey bees (*Apis mellifera*), evidence of bee-keeping within the settlement:

There were the remains of at least 16 workers in a 3-litre sample. Honey bees need a source of water to dilute their honey when they are feeding on it during the winter. Once a colony has found a source of water, its location is communicated amongst the workers and they will all tend to use it. Inevitably, some fall in and drown. The waterhole appears to have been used as such a water source. It is unlikely that the occupants of the settlement would have tolerated a bee colony other than a managed hive.

(Robinson, CD Section 12)

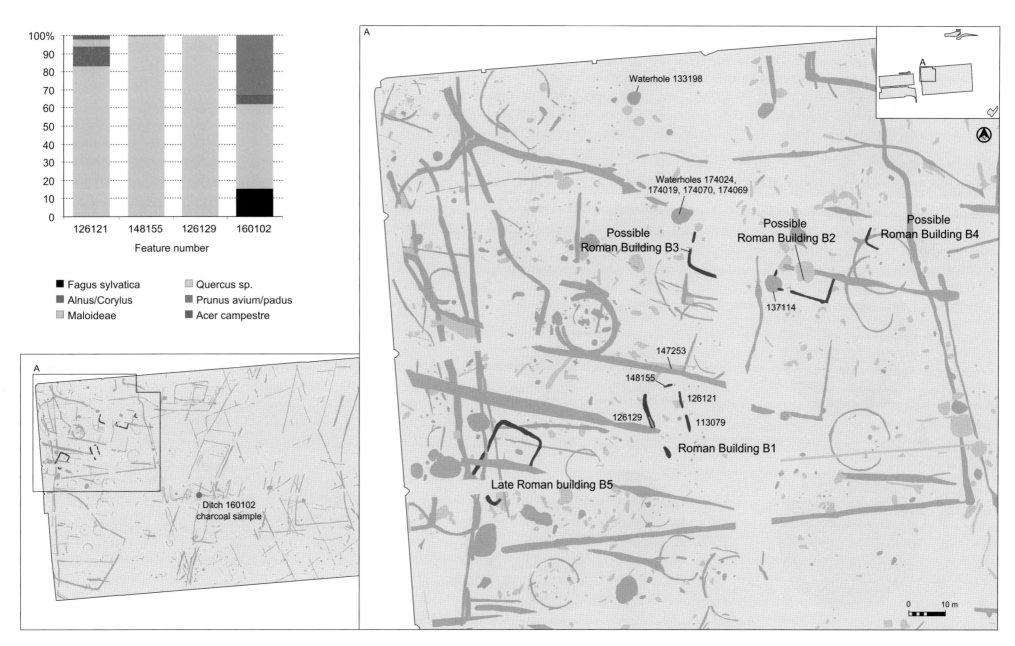

Figure 4.25: Mid to late Roman buildings and graph showing distribution of charcoal remains

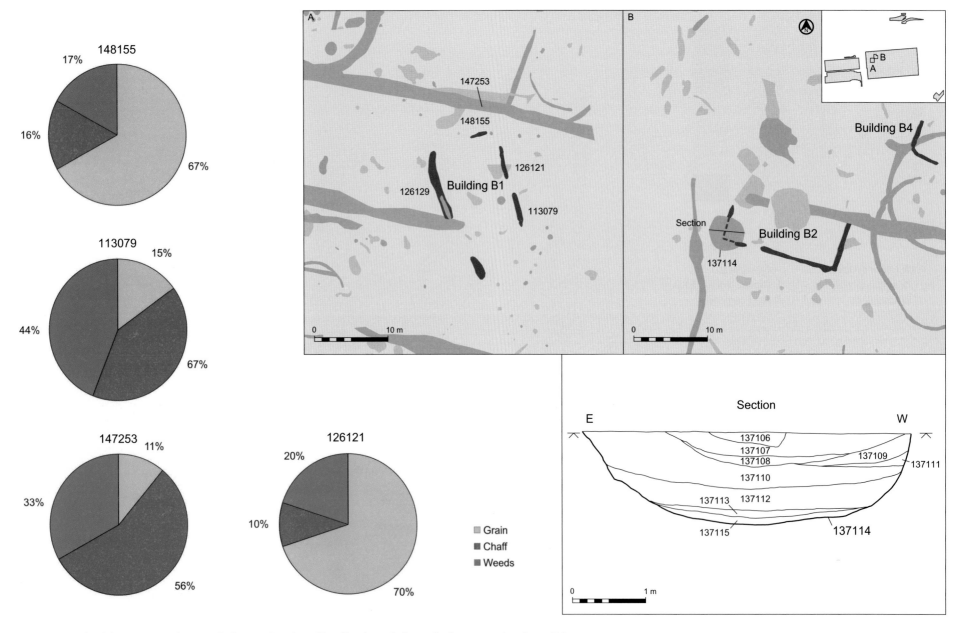

Figure 4.26: Roman buildings B1 and B2 and charts showing distribution of charred plant remains from B1

214

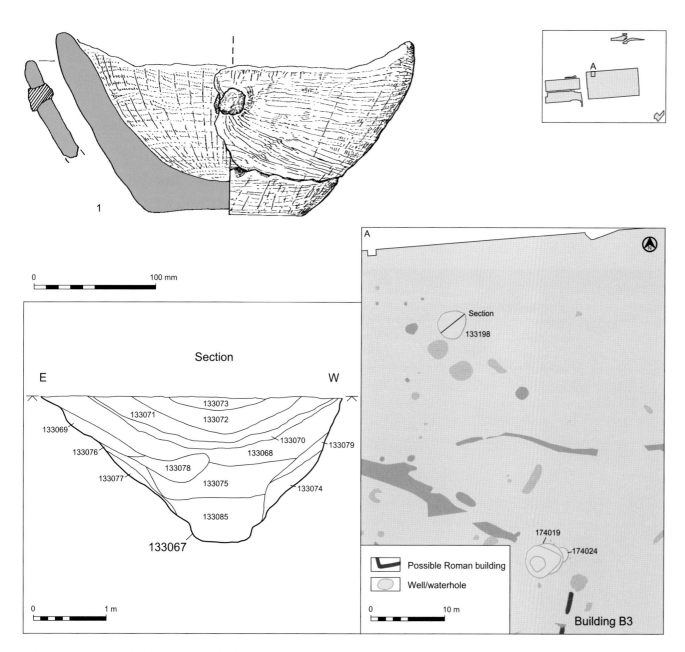

Figure 4.27: Waterhole 133198 with illustration of wooden bowl

Water for the settlement – Roman waterholes and wells

A number of waterholes were dug around the Roman settlement focus and probably met the needs of the Roman community at Perry Oaks for nearly four hundred years. Those relating to the mid Roman phase of settlement are described here.

Waterhole 133198 (1st–2nd century AD)

A substantial Roman waterhole lay *c* 35 m to the NNW of the possible Roman building group (B2–4) described above (Fig. 4.27). It was dated by pottery and coin evidence to the early-mid Roman period (1st–2nd century AD) and was probably the earliest of the waterholes to relate to these buildings.

Plate 4.6: Plan view of collapsed wooden/wattle lining within Romano-British well 133198

215

Plate 4.7: Close up of wattle inside Romano-British well 133198

A wattle structure had been placed in the bottom of the cut immediately after its digging and may have been pre-fabricated, with gravel backfilled around it (Plates 4.6-7). The pattern of the gravels and evidence from the full length wooden stakes suggest that the revetment was only ever about 1.2 m high, which would have meant descending part-way into the feature before lowering a container down to scoop up water. The slightly more shallow and stepped eastern edge is the likely place for such an entrance into the waterhole. Many finds were retrieved from the various fills, including withy rope, a wooden bowl (Fig. 4.27, no. 1) and a leather shoe. One tightly packed group of finds from context 133078, comprising tweezers, pottery, an iron bar and animal bone, may have been a deliberate deposit after the waterhole had gone out of use.

Well/waterhole sequence 174024 and 174019

A sequence of wells/waterholes were constructed near to possible building B3 within the main settlement area (Fig. 4.28; Plate 4.8). The sequence had a lifespan of close to 400 years, throughout the Roman period. Those (174024 and 174019) relating to the mid Roman (*c* 2nd–mid 3rd century AD) period are described here, whilst the later Roman (*c* late 3rd–4th century AD) period waterholes are looked at below.

Well 174024 (1st century AD – first half of the 2nd century AD)

The earliest cut in the sequence was a deep pit, probably a well (174024), cut over 1.5 m into the gravel (Fig. 4.28). The steep sides suggest that the feature originally had a wattle lining, which would have prevented erosion of the gravel sides. Some initial erosion did occur, however, resulting in the fills 174028 and 174029 at the base of the feature. This is likely to have occurred rapidly, and four relatively unabraded sherds of pottery were recovered from the upper of the two fills, 174028, two being late Iron Age and two Roman.

Plate 4.8: Excavation of Romano-British waterhole sequence 174024, 174019, 174070 and 174069

The remaining fills formed more slowly, with a higher silt content than the lower fills. The lowest of these, 174027, representing the main period of use, was a dark silt with few inclusions, formed in a watery environment. It produced a more varied finds assemblage than any other deposit within the feature, including small quantities of animal bone, burnt flint and fired clay. The pottery from this fill was mostly undiagnostic Roman sherds.

Subsequently, the lining of the well was removed and the feature silted naturally. The high levels of gravel present in deposit 174026 represent collapse from the exposed sides. Following the collapse, the well continued to silt slowly, and although it still contained standing water (both of the subsequent fills, 174025 and 174042, were waterlain) it is not clear whether it continued in use as a well. Only fill 174025 produced finds, a small group of fired clay, burnt flint and pottery, including white ware from the Verulamium region and a South Gaulish samian sherd. There was no material dating later than *c* AD 160.

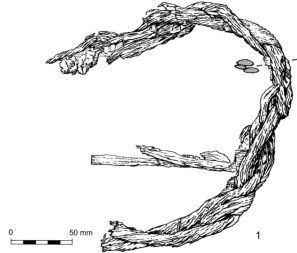

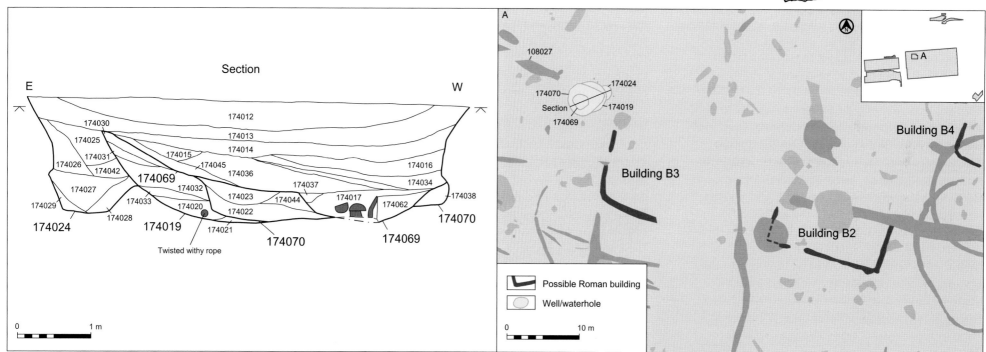

Figure 4.28: Well/waterhole sequence (174024, 174019, 174070, 174069) within the Roman settlement with illustration of twisted willow rope from 174019

Waterhole 174019 (mid–late 2nd century AD –
2nd half of 3rd century AD)

After the well had largely silted up, it was cut by
a second, larger, waterhole (174019) slightly to its
west (Fig. 4.28). This waterhole was itself largely
truncated by the construction of a later well
(174070; see below), but nonetheless it was
possible to establish its shape, function and date.
Although only the eastern edge of the feature survived, the evidence suggests that it was unlikely
to have been constructed in the same way as
the earlier waterhole; there was no evidence
for a wooden or wattle liner and the profile was
shallower and bowl-shaped. The lowest surviving
fill, 174021, was very gravelly, probably the product of rapid erosion of the pit walls. Seven sherds
of pottery from this deposit included a sherd of
samian ware, broadly dated to before AD 240,
and a number of residual prehistoric sherds.

This fill was sealed by a waterlain silt, 174020,
which produced pottery, animal bone, fired clay,
waterlogged wood and some non-local stone.
The pottery was mainly undiagnostic oxidised
and reduced sherds, but some samian fragments
dated to between AD 120 and 240, and a single
sherd dated to between AD 160 and 300. The
poorly preserved animal bone assemblage included cattle and horse. Small quantities of wood
included twigs which had been blown into the
waterhole, woodworking chips and a small
skein of twisted willow 'rope' comprising
three plaited willow strands (Fig. 4.28, no. 1).

The remaining fills comprised alternating layers
of silt and dumps of gravel. The silts, 174030 and
174032, indicated the continued presence of
standing water. The gravel rich deposits, 174031
and 174033, did not represent collapse as they lay
on the eastern edge of the pit, which cut through
the fills of the earlier waterhole and not natural
gravel. The dearth of artefacts from the fill was
notable.

Extent and nature of the settlement

The putative structures and the waterholes
described above may represent the full extent of
mid Roman activity on the site, although given
the level of truncation this seems unlikely. The
number of wells and waterholes corresponded to
that of the middle and late Iron Age periods, and
their location across the area of settlement points
to a more widespread settlement area than was
evident from the preserved remains.

Work to the north during the recent T5 excavations undertaken by Framework Archaeology,
established that Roman activity continued to the
north of the excavated area (see Volume 2), and
on the evidence to date, it seems unlikely that
these remains represent structures of any
higher level of sophistication or status than
the Perry Oaks group.

A surprising paucity of Roman coins and other
metalwork was recovered from the settlement.
Even a small settlement which continued in use
throughout the Roman period might be expected
to produce a reasonable number of coins. Despite
the use of a metal detector, only a single coin, a

2nd century AD As of one of the Antonine
Empresses (likely to be Faustina Junior (146–175)
or Crispina (177–before 192)), was found. The
absence of coins suggests that coin use on the site
was very low, and probably also indicates that—
despite the presence of small quantities of
finewares and ceramic building material—
activity on the site was fairly 'low status'.

Settlement development within the later Roman period

At some point in the 3rd century AD the pattern of
field boundaries to the east of the main settlement
as altered by construction of a 'ladder' enclosure
system (Fig. 4.29; see below). This system was
focussed outwards and away from the ancient
local community, thus representing a significant
break with the past, possibly influenced by external
socio-economic and political factors (see discussion below). Nevertheless an element of continuity
remained, with the settlement focus remaining
in the same place as it had been since the middle
Iron Age, and the enclosure boundaries remaining
on approximately the same alignment as the
late Iron Age-Roman field system.

Settlement focus

Most if not all of the Roman buildings described
above (B1–4) could have persisted in use into the
late Roman period, although only one building
within the settlement (B5), lying to the west of B1,
could be closely dated to this time (Figs 4.29–30).

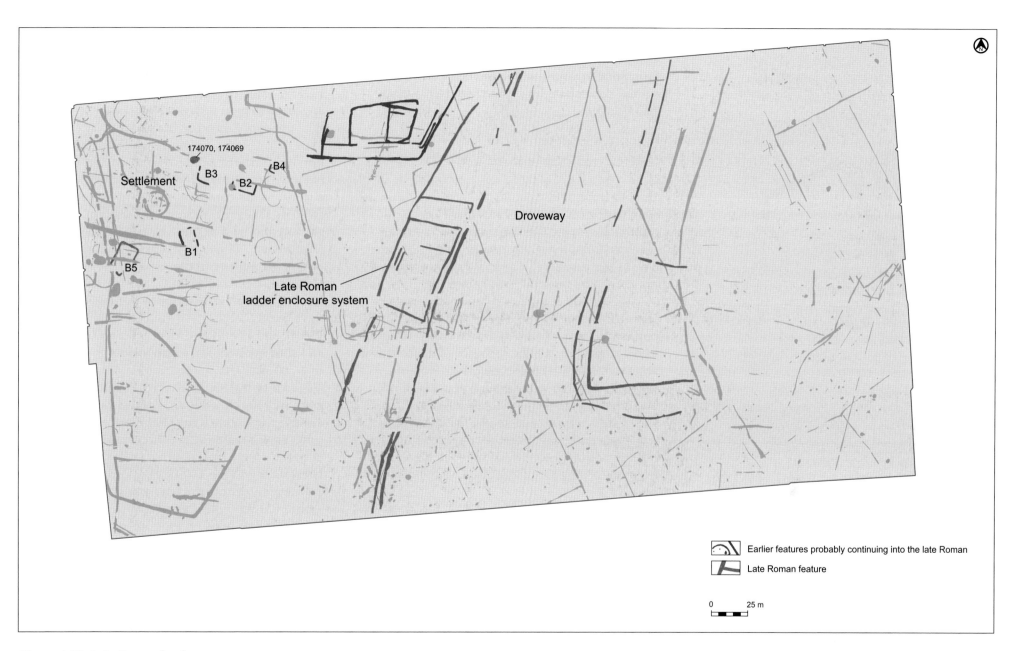

Figure 4.29: Late Roman landscape

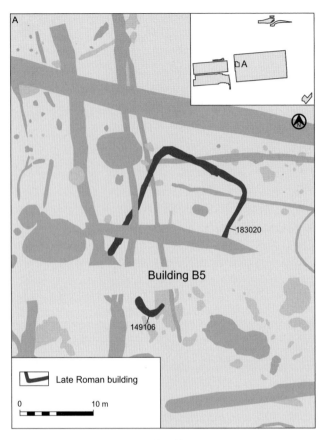

Figure 4.30: Late Roman building B5

As was the case with the other proposed buildings described above, the only surviving feature was a shallow foundation trench with short sections of narrow beam slots. A break along its south-eastern side could have been an entrance, although it may have just been truncated at this point. The gully had a shallow 'U'-shaped profile, and enclosed a roughly rectangular area measuring *c* 18 m by 11 m. The finds from the gradually accumulated gully

fill included 36 sherds of pottery, some dating to the latest Roman ceramic phase (AD 240 to 410). Small quantities of fired clay, burnt flint, animal bone and a fragment of roof tile were also recovered.

Waterhole 174070. (?3rd or early 4th century AD)

The sequence of intercutting waterholes within the main settlement area described above (see Fig. 4.28) continued into the late Roman period, thus suggesting continuity of occupation. The third waterhole in this sequence, 174070, was the most poorly preserved and most difficult to interpret (Figs 4.28 and 4.31). Little of its plan could be discerned, although it clearly cut the fill of 2nd to early 3rd century AD waterhole 174019 (see above). Despite heavy truncation, a basic sequence of deposits was observed. The sides of the waterhole were steep, suggesting that they had been revetted in timber. The three lowest gravel-rich fills (174022, 174044 and 174023; see Fig. 4.28 above) may have been deliberate dumps intended to support a timber revetment similar to that identified in the final waterhole (174069) of the sequence (see below).

Most of the artefacts recovered from this waterhole came from the lower fill, 174022. They included Roman pottery and fragments of fired clay. A second residual late Iron Age pottery sherd came from fill 174023, along with pieces of burnt flint. A fragment of shale was recovered from fill 174068. The stratigraphic evidence suggests that the feature is likely to date to the 3rd or 4th century AD.

Waterhole 174069 (?4th century AD)

The final phase of the waterhole sequence, 174069, dated to the 4th century AD and appeared to be roughly contemporary with the final phase of Roman settlement activity (Fig. 4.31, Plate 4.9). This feature may have resembled its heavily truncated predecessor. A wooden revetment was constructed in the centre of the deepest part of the cut comprising several timber planks (174055, 174056, 174057 and 157058) roughly stacked and held in place by two driven stakes (174059 and 174060) to the front, and by a stack of re-used timbers to the rear (174050, 174051, 174052, 174053 and 174054). Most of the timbers were oak (*Quercus sp.*), but two of the stakes were hazel (*Corylus sp.*). Timbers 174050, 174051 and 174054 had clearly been reused and showed evidence of lap joints.

One half of the pit divided by this timber revetment was backfilled with a gravel rich deposit, 174067, to provide a firm flat platform for the collection of water. Forty-three residual sherds of pottery were incorporated in this deposit, the latest dating to the 2nd or early 3rd centuries AD. For much of its life the well was periodically scoured to keep the water clean; artefacts came from silts that built up after its final cleaning in the western part of the feature.

Most of the pottery from this silt was residual or undiagnostic, but a virtually complete Alice Holt flagon had been deposited immediately in front of the wooden revetment (see Fig. 4.31). The rim was missing but a finger impressed rilled flange

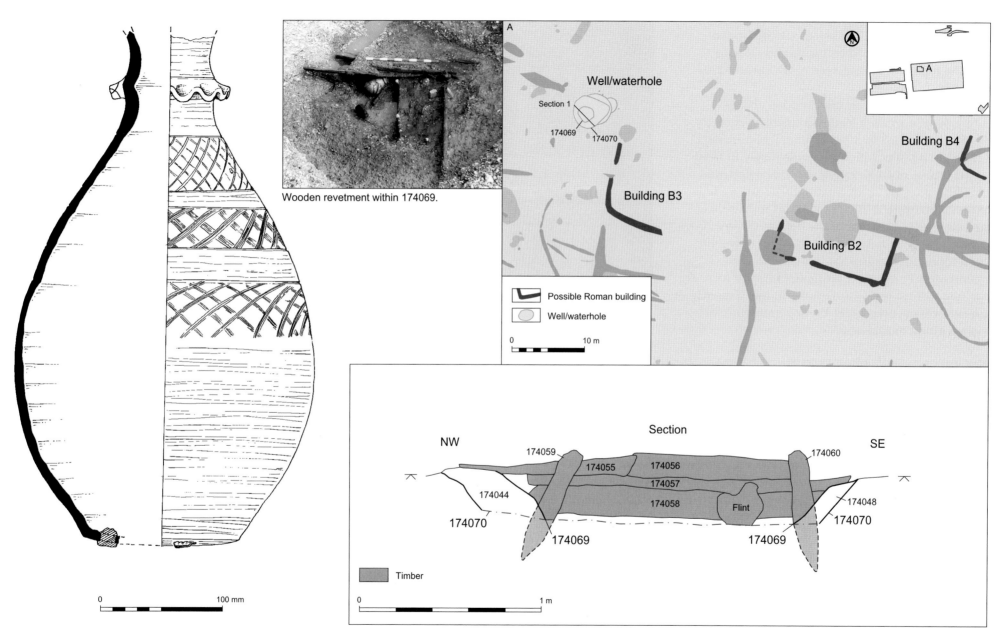

Figure 4.31: Late Roman well/waterhole 174069 with illustration of Alice Holt flagon

on its neck survived. The vessel was decorated with alternating burnished bands and latticing, and the type dates to between *c* AD 330 and 420.

Other finds included several wooden objects, a fragment of worked leather (possibly a shoe fragment), a small number of animal bones and a large flint nodule, which lay immediately in front of the timber revetment (Fig. 4.32). The flint was roughly spherical, with a naturally occurring hole through one side. Although it seems to have been used to wedge the front of the timber revetment, it may originally have served as a counterweight for a lifting mechanism associated with the waterholes. Three small postholes adjacent to the two earliest wells/waterholes in this sequence (see above) may represent the superstructure of such a lifting mechanism.

Other finds included two quernstone fragments, and wooden finds, including a withy tie made of twisted willow (Fig. 4.32, no.1), a 'crook crop' and an object tentatively identified as a 'reliquary' (Allen, CD Section 6; Fig. 4.32, no. 2). The withy tie was similar to others found in waterholes dating from the middle Bronze Age to the late Roman period. It was made up of four strands plaited to form a half loop. The object described as a 'crook crop' was a curved length of ash with a truncated fork at one end which may represent nothing more than part of a wattle structure (Allen, CD Section 6). The 'reliquary' was a box made from a halved block of oak, rectangular in cross section, with the edges hewn to a blunt apex. One face had seven blind sockets cut into it, in a regular pattern but of varying depths and dimensions. There is evidence

Plate 4.9: Excavation of the wooden revetment in the base of late Roman waterhole 174069

for insect damage prior to its loss. The closest recognised parallels are post-Roman reliquaries (Allen, in archive), the sockets used to hold relics or other religious items, although this identification is advanced in the absence of more obvious interpretations.

Other finds from the lower fills (174036, 174015, 174034, 174016; see Fig. 2.28 above) produced small amounts of animal bone (including cattle and red deer), fired clay and Roman pottery, along with small quantities of non-local stone, an iron nail and a copper alloy fitting.

Once the waterhole had silted up, there appear to have been no further attempts to replace or preserve the water source at this location,

suggesting that this marked the end of the settlement sequence here.

The final levelling was a deliberate dump composed mainly of gravel, 174014, which produced a small assemblage of largely residual material, including pottery, animal bone, ceramic building material and burnt and worked stone. The filling of the hollow, 174012 and 174013, contained relatively large assemblages of material, representing the remains of five or six hundred years of activity at the same location incorporated in topsoil and sub-soil deposits before being dragged by the plough into the top of the waterhole. The date of final deposition is unclear, but it may have been as late as the 11th or 12th century, when a small farmstead was established to the south-west (see below).

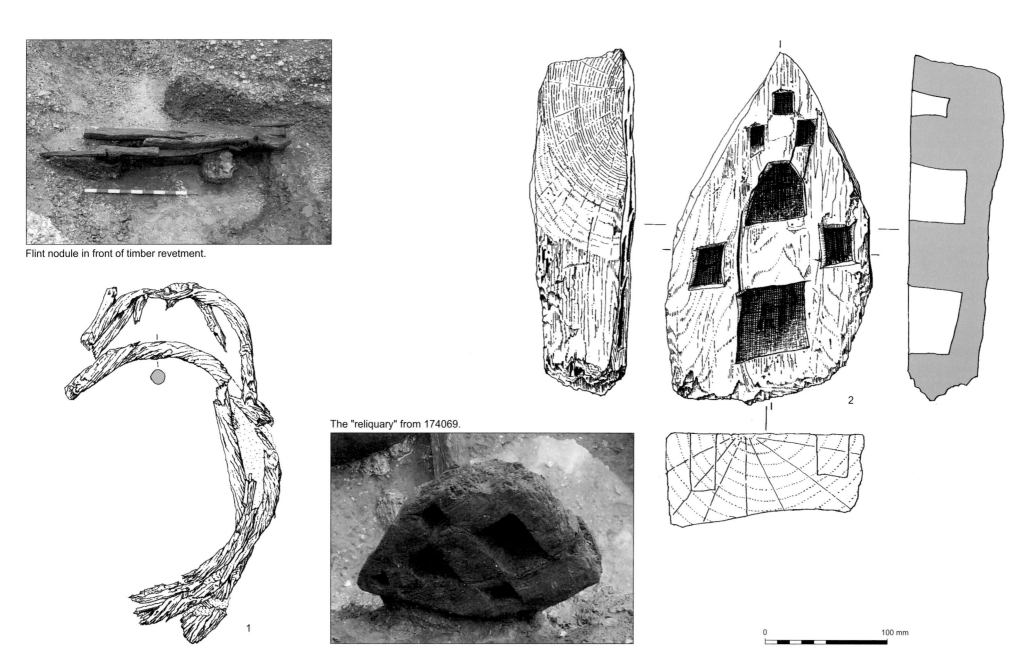

Flint nodule in front of timber revetment.

The "reliquary" from 174069.

1

2

0   100 mm

Figure 4.32: Other finds from Well 174069. No. 1. twisted willow withy tie; No. 2. 'reliquary'

The Roman 'ladder' enclosure system

The later Roman period saw the building of an enclosure system to the east of the settlement area (Figs 4.29 and 4.33). The resulting 'ladder' arrangement was visible in cropmark surveys and took the form of a linear series of linked enclosures extending in a piecemeal process on either side of a wide central droveway.

The main purpose of these enclosures and ditches appears to have been to facilitate movement of animals by the construction of a large central corridor, the main axis of which lay on a roughly NNE-SSW alignment, and an east-west corridor allowing access further to the east (Fig. 4.33). The environmental evidence provided no information as to the function of the enclosures flanking the droveway, the fills being generally sterile secondary and tertiary deposits derived from the surrounding topsoils and brickearth.

The scale of this system is impressive. The central corridor provided a droveway some 90 m wide in places, designed to accommodate high levels of traffic, even if only seasonally. The most likely purpose would have been the need to move large numbers of stock animals, perhaps cattle, through this part of the landscape, either to markets for sale or slaughter, or the seasonal movement of animals between summer pasture and over-wintering. The latter might indicate the existence of large managed estates within the Heathrow area during the late Roman period. Similar 'ladder' enclosures, interpreted as droveways, have been excavated to the north-east, on archaeo-

Figure 4.33: Late Roman 'ladder' enclosure system

logical excavations at Imperial College Sports Ground (Crockett 2002; Wessex Archaeology 2004) and Wall Garden Farm (Thompson *et al.* 1998).

The 'ladder' enclosures at Imperial College Sports Ground (Fig. 4.34) developed from an earlier enclosure system, which had its origins in the Iron Age. It also continued the line of one of the Roman roads out of London, and the axis of the Perry Oaks 'ladder' enclosures meets this line at roughly right angles to the north-east. Meanwhile to the south-west, the Perry Oaks droveway may have continued on to the Roman town of Staines. The implication is that the Perry Oaks and Imperial College Sports Ground 'ladder' enclosures formed part of a network of droveways that served a wider region during the late Roman period.

The extent to which the reorganisation of the greater Roman landscape in late Antiquity affected the Perry Oaks settlement is unclear, although clearly a significant area of farming land was lost to the droveways and enclosures. Elements of earlier enclosure systems (E1) were incorporated into the 'ladder' systems, presumably prolonging their use into this later period (Fig. 4.29). The central droveway was flanked by narrow trackways, which might have provided access into the enclosures for human traffic. The relatively narrow scale of these paths suggests that any hedges and banks must have lain on the outer sides of the ditches (see Fig. 4.33).

The 'ladder' enclosure system was the latest in a series of changes to the landscape during the Roman period, cutting the eastern field system ditches, which had developed from the late Ion

Age to middle Roman period. However the 'ladder' enclosure system itself it is not well dated. The pottery from the ditch fills ranges in date from late Bronze Age to late Roman, with a high level of residuality (see below). None of the ceramic building material can be closely dated. The earliest ditch fills had been scoured out by successive episodes of cleaning, which may possibly account for why none of the material recovered from the enclosure ditches showed any significant distribution pattern.

Pottery from the 'ladder' enclosure ditches

Very small quantities of pottery were recovered from the enclosure ditches, especially considering their huge scale. Most pottery was of Roman date but included residual Bronze Age and Iron Age sherds. A small number of sherds could be dated with some precision, assigned to Roman ceramic phase 3 (AD 120–240), and Roman ceramic phase 4 (AD 240–410) (Brown, CD Section 2). An examination of the fabric types of the different Roman pottery assemblages within these two different 'phases' (3 and 4) indicates minor differences between them. Although various types of pottery were found in both assemblages, the ditches abandoned earlier also contained sherds of mortaria, whitewares, and shell tempered pottery, with some residual Gallo-Belgic finewares. In contrast, the only pottery recovered from the later ditches was a few sherds of white-slipped fabrics. The different fabric types may hint at a slightly different assemblage accumulating within these ditches, possibly indicating a change in pottery use over the lifetime of the 'ladder' enclosure.

Chronology of the 'ladder' enclosure system

The dating of the enclosure system relied on stratigraphic relationships with earlier features, and limited information provided by pottery from the ditch fills. Subsequently, the dating of the 'ladder' enclosure can only be expressed in general terms.

Given the datable pottery and the clear stratigraphic relationships with the earlier field systems, we can suggest that the enclosure system originated during the 3rd century AD, and remained a focus of activity well into the 4th and even 5th centuries. After the original ditches had silted up, only one or two cases of recutting were observed, but there were other examples where the recutting took a slightly different alignment, suggesting that traces of the initial ditch were no longer visible.

Clearly the need to facilitate movement across the Perry Oaks landscape was such that by the 3rd century AD it was considered worth sacrificing several hectares of agricultural land to meet this need. This may have seriously disrupted the local farming regime. If the land was farmed by the inhabitants of the adjacent small settlement, it is likely that a higher authority may have imposed the reshaping of the land, and we might conclude that we are witnessing the management of one or more large estates. Once constructed, the enclosure ditches were maintained, and associated hedges and banks were probably also maintained and exploited.

Whilst we cannot accurately determine the life span of the 'ladder' enclosure system, it remained a major feature of the post-Roman landscape (see below).

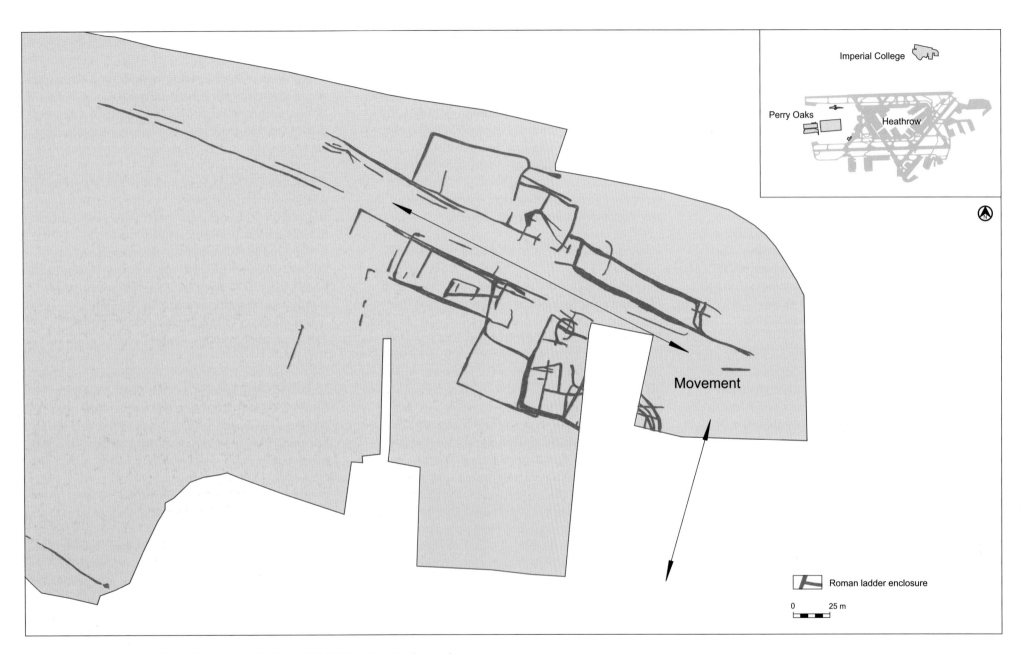

Imperial College

Perry Oaks   Heathrow

Movement

Roman ladder enclosure

0   25 m

Figure 4.34: Roman ladder enclosures at the Imperial College Sports Ground

Summary of 'ladder' enclosures

The evidence suggests that an increasing requirement to move stock and other commodities on a large scale through the Perry Oaks landscape was such that the construction of a substantial droveway was undertaken during the 3rd century AD, at the cost of a significant area of farmed land. The ditches and associated hedges were maintained for a period, after which the former were allowed to silt up. We cannot be certain of the late history of the droveway. The scale of the later post-medieval trackway (see below) suggests that by this period the necessity for large scale movement had abated and once the droveway had gone out of use, much of the land it had occupied reverted to farmland, although without a wholesale change in the existing boundaries. This transition may have occurred during the very late Roman or early post-Roman period, at a time when the centralised system of power that had stamped itself so firmly on the landscape in the form of the 'ladder' enclosures was waning.

It was within this period of change and confusion that a fragment of lead tank came to be buried within a waterhole (135087) to the west of the main settlement.

The final act – deposition of a lead tank

At some point, late in the 4th or early in the 5th century AD, some of the inhabitants of the small collection of half-timbered buildings that occupied the edge of the upper gravel terrace overlooking the floodplain of the River Colne deposited the remains of a badly damaged lead tank in a small waterhole (135087) to the west of the settlement (Figs 4.35–6; Plates 4.10-12). The following is derived from David Petts' report (CD Section 7).

The remains of this circular lead tank comprised a circular base which had been soldered to the curved side. The side was divided into a series of panels by a horizontal strand of cable pattern, and within each panel was a floating saltire or *crux decussata* ('St Andrew's Cross') drawn with similar cable strand. The tank had clearly been broken up prior to burial, with an axe used to cut the base into at least two pieces, and the sides being bent and twisted until they tore. It was one of these pieces which was buried at Perry Oaks, with its side folded over to meet the base, perhaps to make it more easy to transport.

Plate 4.10 Withy ropes and straps (135088 and 135089) within late Roman waterhole 135087

Plate 4.11: Excavation of the lead tank from late Roman waterhole 135087

The object belongs to a group of around twenty late Roman Christian lead tanks, found only in Britain (Guy 1981; Watts 1988). Predominantly found in the East Midlands and East Anglia this tank is towards the southern edge of their distribution; its nearest neighbour was one found at Caversham, near Reading (Frere 1989).

Other than the *crux decussata*, this object bears no other possible indications of a Christian function. Other members of this group are decorated with *chi-rho* symbols (first two letters of Christ in Greek), *orans* figures (a standing figure with both arms raised in prayer) (Flawborough; Elliot and Malone 1999) and even the probable depiction of a baptism (Walesby; Petch 1961). Their precise function is, however, uncertain. Thomas has argued that they were used for the rite of baptism by affusion (the pouring of the baptismal water over the head of an unclothed candidate) (Thomas 1981, 221–5). Watts has however suggested that they may instead be related to the rite of *pedilavium*, a ritual washing of the feet (Watts 1991, 171). Their final placement in pits and watery contexts is common, and there may well be a ritual element to their disposal in such a manner, reflecting a wider late Romano-British tradition of depositing lead and pewter objects in such contexts (Petts 2004). Its presence at the site is certainly an indicator of a small Christian community in the surrounding area, and adds to the relatively sparse evidence for Christianity in the London region.

We cannot be certain exactly when the tank was dismantled and buried, or even why this was done. Its burial may relate to one of the occasional reversions to paganism during the late 4th century, such as the reign of Julian (AD 361–3) or perhaps to one of the periodic persecutions of Christians within the Empire. Equally, it may relate to activity after the Emperor Honorius had told the inhabitants of Britain to look to their own defences in AD 410 because the Empire could no longer protect them from growing menaces to its shores.

Plate 4.12: Excavation of the lead tank from late Roman waterhole 135087

It remains uncertain if the pit was dug specifically for deposition of the tank, as it was deeper than was necessary to dispose of it. The feature may instead have been an earlier waterhole, although minimal silting suggests that it had not been open for too long prior to the tank's deposition.

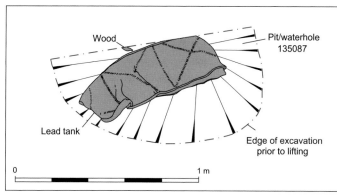

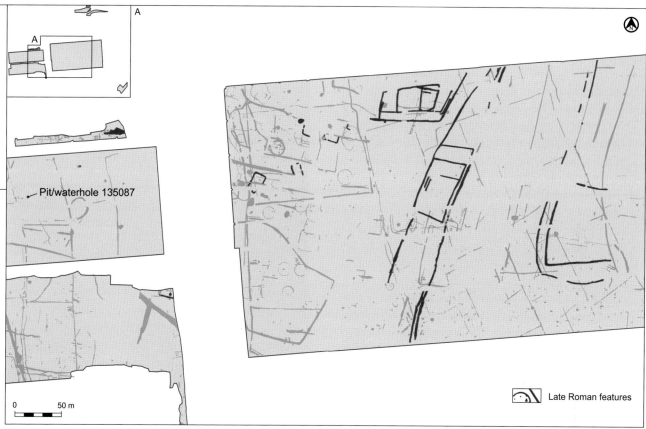

Figure 4.35: The late Roman lead tank

The location of the burial spot, adjacent to a shallow hollow, perhaps a dew pond, formed in the hollow of an earlier feature, may have been a significant place in the landscape. The font was placed on the base of the pit, and the ropes of twisted hazle that had served as carrying straps, were deposited with it.

Whatever the reason for the burial of this hacked-up object, its carefully constructed final resting place can be viewed as a metaphor for the end of Roman activity on the site. This object, imbued with the attributes and significance of a foreign religion within a waning imperial system, was buried in a fashion reminiscent of pre-imperial deposition practices. With the burial, the inhabitants of the gravel terrace may have drawn a line underneath their association with a failing continental Empire and faced their uncertain future unencumbered by the trappings of the past. Even if the alternative interpretation is more credible, and that the burial of the tank was an act of reverence, a holy relic placed in a safe location, the very fact that this artefact was never recovered highlights the shifting nature of the

political, social and religious situation in the area. The lead tank, perhaps uniquely amongst the artefacts recovered from the site, symbolises the impact of the Roman Empire on Britain. The Empire had, within a relatively short time, changed the physical appearance of the landscape, the material culture of the inhabitants, and perhaps most importantly and intangibly the hopes, desires, expectations and understandings of everyday people. The old political systems,

social networks and even the old gods had been replaced, modified or absorbed within a greater and infinitely more powerful whole. The gradual realisation that the power which had controlled and influenced daily life in so many ways and which had been equally an irritant and a source of security was now in decline must have engendered a terrible uncertainty. Years of economic decline and political uncertainty caused by eternal power struggles amongst the ruling elite must have acted as some preparation for the blow that was to come, but the dawning realisation that the Empire could no longer defend the inhabitants of Perry Oaks, and that the barbarians were at the gates, must have been a terrible one indeed. In this context, the dismemberment and burial of the remains of the Christian tank is a poignant symbol of the ultimate demise of the Roman Empire in Britain.

The horses grazing in the middle distance watched curiously as a small knot of people made their way out of the settlement and down the slope to the small well in the middle of the field. Three men walked slowly in the middle of the group, treading uncertainly on the damp ground. Each walked awkwardly, stooping slightly to counter the weight they each carried, slung between them on crude carrying straps fashioned from twisted hazel. After a while, the going became easier, and their progress quickened. Shortly they reached the edge of the well, and the sweating men lowered their load to the ground.

They stood in a rough circle around the well as one of the men made a short speech. Then, slowly, and with a sense of ceremony, two of the men rose and lifted their precious burden. It was heavy and awkward, and the size of the well made manhandling it into position difficult. After a few efforts, and the occasional curse, they positioned it over the southern half of the pit, a move which necessitated them leaning awkwardly over the wooden revetting which lined the well. The man who had spoken gave a solemn nod, and the two men lowered the object as far as they could into the glassy water of the well before releasing it and allowing it to sink into the depths. They stood silently for a while,

Figure 4.36: *Artist's impression of the ceremony leading to the deposition of the lead tank into pit/waterhole*

watching the ripples fade and the cloudy water clear. It could still be seen on the base of the well, its torn and scarred edges glittering silver in the depths. By chance, it had come to rest with the decoration facing upwards, and the raised cordons could just be made out standing proud of the surface of the lead. This done, the men cast the twisted wooden straps into the water, where they sank to the base of the pit. It was done.

Gradually, one by one, they turned and walked away, leaving the horses to return to their grass.

Post-Roman landscape

Medieval activity on site was apparently confined to an area west of the late Roman 'ladder' enclosure system, and seemed to respect the position and orientation of this earlier landscape feature (Fig. 4.37). A concentration of early medieval activity lay on the southern edge of the excavations, and recent excavations at T5 have exposed remains of a small early medieval farmstead to the south-west of the Perry Oaks site (see Vol. 2).

The apparent continuation of the 'ladder' enclosure system in the post-Roman landscape must point to the survival of the hedges of the main boundaries and possibly even of continued use of the trackway. The westernmost boundary of the 'ladder' enclosure appeared to form the eastern boundary to an area of land on which a 'ridge and furrow' system formed,

with channels cutting into the underlying gravels and brickearth in places. The distance between the shallow furrows was generally between 14 m and 17 m. These earthworks could not be closely dated, but two sets of ridge and furrow cut across the remains of late Roman buildings. This agricultural system was therefore probably associated with the medieval farmstead identified to the south-west of the Perry Oaks site.

The post-medieval trackway and field boundary excavated to the east of the site shared a similar alignment with the 'ladder' enclosure system, supporting the case for continuity (Fig. 4.37). The trackway is visible on John Rocque's map of the area, the earliest known depiction of this part of the agricultural landscape, and could have had its origins in the medieval period.

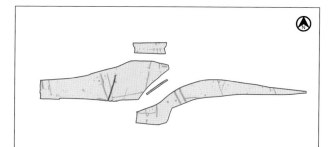

Figure 4.37: Post-Roman use of the 'ladder' enclosure system

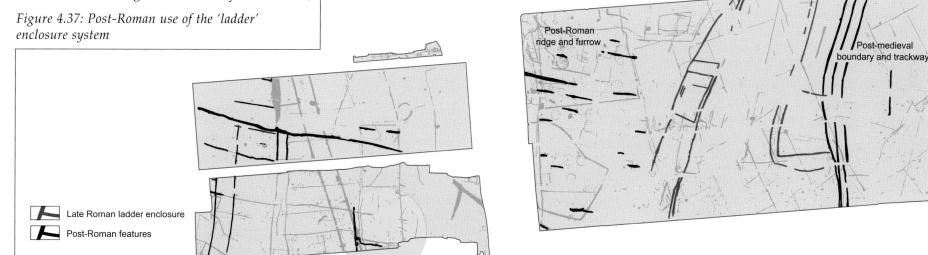

Late Roman ladder enclosure

Post-Roman features

Post-Roman ridge and furrow

Post-medieval boundary and trackway

Focus of early medieval activity

0   100   200 m

CHAPTER 5
Epilogue and prologue

by John Lewis

This chapter is intended as both an epilogue to this volume and a prologue to Volume 2, which will include the results of the excavations undertaken at Terminal 5 from 2002 to 2007.

Epilogue to Volume 1

This volume has looked at the historical processes and the choices that people have made during the period from the late Mesolithic, *c* 6500 BC, to the end of the Romano-British period at the start of the 5th century AD.

Chapters 2 and 3 took as their underlying theme the major concern of access to land and resources, and how this affected the relationships between individuals, family groups and the broader community. We have tried to show how at various points in history (for instance between 3600 and 3300 BC) people adopted new solutions to conditions which required a rebalancing of the tensions between components of society to achieve a new equilibrium (for instance the construction of the C1 Stanwell Cursus). Often these new solutions appear to us to have created a landscape which was radically different to that which went before (eg the monumental landscape of the late 4th millennium BC), but which in many ways was a logical result of the traditions and tensions which were the products of history. We have shown how sometimes people looked to the past as a mechanism which would maintain bonds between family groups at times when such groups had greater importance than the overarching community. Perhaps the best example here is

the deposition during the middle of the 2nd millennium BC of wooden and stone artefacts that refer to the past in waterholes ringing the Neolithic HE1 enclosure.

Sometimes, the choices and solutions people adapted to particular circumstances had unforeseen but profound consequences. For instance we have argued that it is unlikely that anyone could have foreseen that the first land divisions of the early 2nd millennium BC would produce that patchwork pattern of fields, lanes and settlements which has characterised the southern English countryside ever since.

It is clear that even when major changes such as land division are adopted to achieve a new social equilibrium, social relationships exert forces that lead to imbalances in the equilibrium and thus require new adjustments. At Perry Oaks this process can be seen in the change from dispersed to nucleated settlement at the end of the 2nd millennium BC, with an increase in the use of communal feasting to hold the community together. The most visible manifestation of a large community living in a nucleated settlement is the Iron Age settlement of the mid- 1st millennium BC. Here we see people living in a single settlement which developed adjacent to its predecessor in the late Bronze Age, and was accommodated within a landscape of fields and boundaries that were already 1000 years old. Of course, over time, people modify those ancient boundaries, sometimes replacing them with new alignments as old tenures and methods of agricultural working were replaced by new forms of tenure

and practice. Within the Iron Age settlement we can detect from the different size of the houses and their finds assemblages differences in use and perhaps status of their inhabitants.

Whilst the Roman occupation of Britain in the 1st century AD resulted in the adoption by the Perry Oaks inhabitants of different forms of architecture and artefacts, the fundamentals of the small agricultural settlement seem to have continued. However the settlement was now tied into the economic, legal and political construct of the Roman Empire, and the effect of these much wider forces can be seen in the construction of the droveway and associated enclosures which overwrote the ancient fields of prehistory, and were concerned with linking agricultural production with towns which in turn were linked by the road network. Of course, the Romano-British world was in constant flux, and the lead font is a perfect illustration of this. The mere existence of this object is testament to the profound effect on spiritual and political life that Christianity had on the Roman Empire. Its destruction and burial in a pit in the late 4th or early 5th century AD is a strong metaphor for the end of the Roman world in Britain.

The historical themes we have explored in this volume have been deliberately broad: we have not focused in the published text on detail, much of which is available on the accompanying CD-Rom. Primarily, this is because we were conscious that although the area excavated at Perry Oaks was large, many key components remained unexcavated.

For instance:

- the north-eastern terminus of the Neolithic C2 Cursus was undetected

- we had excavated a comparatively small length of the C1 Stanwell Cursus

- our understanding of the 3rd and the early 2nd millennia BC was extremely thin

- we did not have a complete middle or late Bronze Age settlement

- the field system was obviously far more extensive and complex than the small area captured by the Perry Oaks excavations

- the middle Iron Age and Romano-British settlement clearly extended into unexcavated (and destroyed) areas

- very little Saxon or medieval evidence for human use of the landscape was recorded at Perry Oaks

Whilst this volume was being written, excavations in advance of the construction of Terminal 5 were being undertaken, which covered a much larger area on and around the Perry Oaks sludge beds. Some of the data recovered in these excavations has been alluded to in this volume, but it will be integrated fully with the current data set and published in Volume 2.

Prologue to Volume 2

The second volume will use the additional data to re-evaluate some of the interpretations expressed here, as well as explore different historical themes and different periods of human inhabitation. Further excavation of the C1 Stanwell and C2 Cursus, together with that of a third cursus shows that their constructional histories are more complicated than first thought.

A handful of new circular monuments, pit groups and finds will be used to consider in more detail the period of the late 4th and 3rd millennia BC, when people lived in a world shaped by these monuments and their associated ceremonies.

A scattering of artefacts and features dated to the late 3rd and early 2nd millennia BC will provide a little more detail on the period just prior to the construction of the first major land boundaries.

A greatly expanded map of the 2nd millennium BC field system will allow us to more fully understand how society developed the concept of land tenure, and how agricultural production and processing was undertaken. It will also allow us to reconsider the validity of the model of family versus community presented in this volume.

The excavation of a complete settlement and the identification of a few new 2nd millennium BC settlements provide the opportunity to look in some detail at how family groups organised

their domestic space and architecture. This theme will be continued into the Iron Age and Romano-British settlements that are now more fully excavated.

The post Romano-British landscape can now be considered, with the Saxon origins of the present village of Longford being revealed. On the main Terminal 5 site, excavation of a small rural medieval settlement will allow us to consider this aspect of the site's history.

Volume 2 will be fully integrated with the Perry Oaks data and inevitably there will be differences between the data sets presented in Volumes 1 and 2. Volume 2 will take a similar form to Volume 1, and the entire digital archive will be deposited with the Archaeology Data Service (ADS) in York. A Web-based version of the dataset, hosted by ADS, will be made available. The web interface to this data will be similar to that provided by the Freeviewer software on the CD-Rom which accompanies this volume, with similar levels of functionality.

It its intended that the finds and the physical archive will be deposited with the Museum of London.

Bibliography

Allen, T, Barclay, A, and Lamdin-Whymark, H, 2004 Opening the wood, making the land: the study of a Neolithic landscape in the Dorney area of the Middle Thames Valley, in J Cotton and D Field (eds), *Towards a New Stone Age: aspects of the Neolithic in south-east England*, CBA Res. Rep. **137**, 82–98

Ambers, J, 2003 The Radiocarbon Dating, in S Preston (ed.), *Prehistoric, Roman and Saxon Sites in Eastern Berkshire*. TVAS Monograph **2**, Reading

Andrews, G, and Barrett, J, 1998 Heathrow Archaeological Research Design, BAA Unpubl. document

Andrews, G, Barrett, J, and Lewis, J, 1998 Perry Oaks rescue excavations: post-excavation assessment report, BAA/TWUL/MoLAS

Andrews, P, 1996 Prospect Park and Hurst Park: the Settlements and the Landscape, in P Andrews and A Crockett, *Three excavations along the Thames and its Tributaries, 1994*, Wessex Archaeol Rep **10**, Salisbury, 108–11

Atkinson, R J, 1961 Neolithic Engineering, *Antiquity* **35**:140, 292–9

BAA /905, 1996 Heathrow Terminal 5 Report of Archaeological Evaluations at the western end of Heathrow Airport and Perry Oaks Sludge Works, Unpublished Rep, MoLAS 1996

Bacon, J C, 1990 The use of livestock in calcareous grassland management, in S H Hillier, D W H Walton and D A Wells (eds), *Calcareous grasslands: Ecology and management*, Huntindon, 121–127

Barclay, A, and Bayliss, A, 1999 Cursus monuments and the radiocarbon problem, in A Barclay and J Harding (eds), 11–29

Barclay, A, and Harding, J (eds), 1999 *Pathways and Ceremonies: the Cursus Monuments of Neolithic Britain and Ireland*, Neolithic Studies Group Seminar Papers **4**, Oxford

Barclay, G J, and Maxwell, G S, 1998 *The Cleaven Dyke and Littleour: monuments in the Neolithic of Tayside*, Soc. Antiquaries of Scotland **13**, Edinburgh

Barfield, L M, and Hodder, M, 1987 Burnt Mounds as saunas and the prehistory of bathing, *Antiquity* **61**, 370–9

Barrett, J C, 1973 Four Bronze Age cremation cemeteries from Middlesex, *Trans. London & Middlesex Archaeol. Soc.* **24**, 111–34

Barrett, J C, 1980 The evolution of Later Bronze Age settlement, in J C Barrett and R Bradley (eds), *Settlement and Society in the British Later Bronze Age*, BAR British Series **83**, 77–100

Barrett, J C, 1985 Hoards and related metalwork, in D V Clarke, T G Cowie and A Foxon, *Symbols of Power at the Time of Stonehenge*, HMSO, Edinburgh

Barrett, J C, Bradley, R, and Green, M, 1991 *Landscape, Monuments and Society. The prehistory of Cranborne Chase*, Cambridge

Bates, S, and Wiltshire, P, 2000 *Excavation of a Burnt Mound at Feltwell Anchor, Norfolk*, 1992, Norfolk Archaeol. Vol. **XLIII** Part III, 389–414

Branch, N P, and Green, C P, 2004 The environmental history of Surrey, in J Cotton, G Crocker and A Graham (eds), *Aspects of Archaeology and History in Surrey*, Surrey Archaeol. Soc., Guildford, 1–18

Bell, M, Fowler, P J, and Hillson, S W, 1996 *The Experimental Earthwork Project* 1960–1992, CBA Res. Rep. **100**, London

Bersu, G, 1940 Excavations at Little Woodbury, Wiltshire, part I. *Proc. Prehist. Soc.* **6**, 30–111

Bird, D G, Crocker, G, and McCracken, J S, 1990 Archaeology in Surrey 1988–1989, *Surrey Archaeol. Col.* **80**, 201–27

Black, E W, 1986 Romano-British Burial Customs and religious Beliefs in South East England, *Archaeol. J.* **14**, 201–239

Bradley, R, 1984 *The social foundations of prehistoric Britain*, London

Bradley, R, 1998 *The Passage of Arms: Archaeological Analysis of Prehistoric Hoards and Votive Deposits*, Oxford

Bradley, R, and Gordon, K, 1988 Human skulls from the River Thames, their dating and significance. *Antiquity* **62**, 503–9

Brossler, A, 2001 Reading Business Park: the results of phases 1 and 2, in J Brück (ed.), *Bronze Age Landscapes Tradition and Transformation*, Oxford, 129–138

Brown, A G, and Keough, M, 1992 Palaeochannels, palaeoland-surfaces and three-dimensional reconstruction of environment floodplain change, in P A Carling and G E Petts (eds), *Lowland floodplain rivers; geomorphological perspectives*, Chichester, 185–202

Brown, K, in prep. The mid–late Iron Age and Roman pottery from Eton Rowing Lake, Oxford Archaeology

Brown, N, and Cotton, J, 2000 The Bronze Age, in *The archaeology of Greater London*, MoLAS Monograph. London, 81–94

Buckley, V, 1990 *Burnt offerings: international contributions to burnt mound archaeology*, Dublin

Burgess, C, 1986 "Urns of no small variety": Collared Urns Reviewed, *Proc. Prehist. Soc.* **52**, 339–51

Burleigh, R, and Clutton-Brock, J, 1977 A radiocarbon date for Bos primigenius from Charterhouse Warren Farm, Mendip, Proc. *Univ. Bristol Spelaeol. Soc.* **14** (3), 255–7

Canham, R, 1978 Excavations at Heathrow Airport, 1969, *Trans. London Middlesex Archaeol. Soc.* **29**, 1–44

Carruthers, W J, 1992 The plant remains, in C A Butterworth and S J Lobb, *Excavations in the Burghfield Area, Berkshire; developments in the Bronze Age and Saxon landscapes*, Wessex Archaeology Report, **1**, Salisbury, 63–65

Case, H, 1993 Beakers: deconstruction and afterwards, *Proc. Prehist. Soc.* **59**, 241–68

Clarke, D V, Cowie, T G, and Foxon, A, 1985 *Symbols of Power at the Time of Stonehenge*, HMSO, Edinburgh

Cleal, R, 1992 Significant form: ceramic styles in the earlier Neolithic of southern England, in N Sharples & A Sheridan (eds.), *Vessels for the Ancestors*, Edinburgh, 286–304

Cleal, R, 2004 The dating and diversity of the earliest ceramics of Wessex and south west England, in

R Cleal and J Pollard, *Monuments and material culture papers in honour of an Avebury Archaeologist: Isobel Smith*, Salisbury

Coles, J M, 1976 Forest farmers: Some archaeological, historical and experimental evidence, in S J De Laet (ed.), *Acculturation and Continuity in Atlantic Europe*, IV Atlantic Colloquium, Brugge, 59–66

Cotton, J, 1990 Finds from the Cursus Ditches, in N O'Connell, Excavations during 1979–1985 of a multi-period site at Stanwell, *Surrey Archaeol. Coll.* Vol 80, 28–29

Cotton, J, 2004 Surrey's early past: a survey of recent work, in J Cotton, G Crocker and A Graham (eds), *Aspects of archaeology in Surrey: towards a research framework for the county*, Surrey Archaeol. Soc., Guildford

Cotton, J, Elseden, N, Pipe, A, and Rayner, L, in Press Taming the Wild: A final Neolithic/Earlier Bronze Age Aurochs Deposit from West London

Cotton, J, Mills, J, and Clegg, G, 1986 *Archaeology of Middlesex*

Crockett, A, 2001 The archaeological landscape of Imperial College Sports Ground part 1, prehistoric, in *London Archaeologist* Vol. **9**, No. 11, Winter 2001, 295–99

Crockett, A, 2002 The archaeological landscape of Imperial College Sports Ground part 2, Roman to medieval, in *London Archaeologist* Vol. **9**, No. 12, Spring 2002, 341–5

Cunliffe, B, 1995 *Danebury, an Iron Age hillfort in Hampshire, Vol. 6: a hillfort community in perspective*, CBA Res. Rep. **102**

Drummond-Murray, J, Saxby, D, and Watson, B, 1994 Recent Archaeological work in the Bermondsey district of Southwark, in *London Archaeologist* 7 (10), 251–7

Drury, P J, 1978 *Excavations at Little Waltham 1970 – 71*, CBA Res. Rep. No. **26**, Chelmsford Excavation Committee Report 1

Edwards, K J, 1993 Models of mid-Holocene forest farming for north-west Europe, in F M Chambers (ed.), *Climate Change and Human Impact on the Landscape*, London, 133–145

Ehrenburg, M R, 1977 *Bronze Age Spearheads from Berks, Bucks and Oxon*, British Archaeol. Rep. **34**, Oxford

Elliot, L, and Malone, S, 1999 Archaeology in Nottinghamshire, 1998: Flawborough, *Trans. Thoroton Soc.* **103**, 88–9

Ellis, C J, forthcoming, Excavations at Battlesbury Bowl, Warminster, Wiltshire, 1998

English Heritage, 1991 *Management of Archaeological Projects* (2nd ed.), English Heritage

Evans, C, Pollard J, Knight, M, 1999 Life in woods: tree throws, "settlement" and forest cognition, *Oxford J. Archaeol.*, **18**, 241–54

Fairweather, L, and Sliwa, J A, 1970 *AJ Metric Handbook*, Architects Journal, London

Field, D, and Cotton, J, 1987 Neolithic Surrey: a survey of the evidence, in J Bird and D G Bird (eds), *The Archaeology of Surrey to 1540*, Surrey Archaeol. Soc., 71–96

Fitzpatrick, A, 1997 Everyday life in Iron Age Wessex, in A Gwilt and C Haselgrove (eds), *Reconstructing Iron Age Societies*, Oxbow Monograph **71**, Oxford, 73–86

Ford, S, 1986 A newly discovered causewayed enclosure at Eton Wick, near Windsor, Berkshire, *Proc. Prehist. Soc.* **52**, 319–20

Framework Archaeology, 1999a Perry Oaks Sludge Works: Archaeological Fieldwork Phase 2 Project Design, Unpubl. client Rep.

Framework Archaeology, 1999b Perry Oaks Sludge Works: Archaeological Fieldwork Phase 2 Project Design Update Note 1, Unpubl. client Rep.

Framework Archaeology, 2000 Perry Oaks Sludge Works, Western Perimeter Road, Heathrow, London Borough of Hillingdon, Project Design Update Note 2, Unpubl. client Rep.

Framework Archaeology, 2002 Heathrow Terminal 5: General Project Design for Archaeological Mitigation, Unpubl. client Rep.

Framework Archaeology, 2003 Excavations at Mayfield Farm, East Bedfont, London Borough of Hounslow by Framework Archaeology, *Trans. London and Middlesex Archaeol. Soc.* **54**, 9–21

Frere, S S, 1989 Roman Britain in 1989: sites explored, *Britannia* **20**, 258–326

Garwood, P, 1999 Grooved Ware in Southern Britain: chronology and interpretation, in R Cleal and A MacSween (eds), *Grooved Ware in Britain and Ireland*, Oxford, 145–76

Gibbard, P L, 1985 *Pleistocene history of the Middle Thames Valley*, Cambridge

Gibson, A, 2002 *Prehistoric Pottery in Britain & Ireland*, Stroud

Gibson, A, and Kinnes, I, 1997 On the urns of a dilemma: radiocarbon and the Peterborough problem, *Oxford J. Archaeol.* **16** (1), 65–72

Göransson, H, 1982 Man and the forests of nemoral broad-leaved trees during the Stone Age, *Striae* **24**, 143–152

Grant, A, 1984 Animal Husbandry in the Thames Valley, in B Cunliffe and D Miles (eds), *Aspects of the Iron Age in Central Southern Britain*, CBA, London, 102–119

Green, H S, 1978 Late Bronze Age wooden hafts from Llyn Fawr and Penwyllt, *Bulletin of the Board of Celtic Studies* **28**, 136–141

Green, H S, 1980 *The Flint Arrowheads of the British Isles: a detailed study of material from England and Wales with comparanda from Scotland and Ireland*, British Archaeol. Rep. **75**, Oxford

Grimes, W F, 1961 Settlements at Draughton, Colsterworth and Heathrow, in S S Frere (ed.), *Problems of the Iron Age in Southern Britain*, London, 21–8

Grimes, W F, and Close-Brooks, J, 1993 The excavation of Caesar's Camp, Heathrow, Harmondsworth, Middlesex, 1944, in *Proc. Prehist. Soc.* Vol **59**, 303–60

Guy, C J, 1981 Roman Circular Lead Tanks in Britain, *Britannia* **12**, 271–6

Harding, D W, Blake, I M, and Reynolds, P J, 1993 *An Iron Age Settlement in Dorset - Excavation and Reconstruction*, Monograph Series No. **1**, Department of Archaeology, University of Edinburgh

Harding, J, 1999 Pathways to new realms: cursus monuments and symbolic territories, in A Barclay and J Harding (eds), *Pathways and Ceremonies. The cursus monuments of Britain and Ireland*, Neolithic studies Group Seminar Papers **4**, Oxford

Havis, R, and Brooks, H, 2004 *Excavations at Stansted Airport, 1986–91, vol. 1, Prehistoric and Romano-British*, E Anglian Archaeol. Rep. **107**

Hawkes, S C, 1994 Longbridge Deverill Cow Down, Wiltshire, House 3: A Major Round House of the Early Iron Age, *Oxford Journ. Archaeol.* **13** (1), 49–69

Hedges, J, 1975 Excavations of two Orcadian burnt mounds at Liddle and Beaquoy, *Proc. of the Soc. of*

Antiquaries of Scotland **106**, 38–98

Herne, A, 1988 A time and a place for the Grimston Bowl, in J C Barrett and I A Kinnes (eds), *The Archaeology of Context in the Neolithic and Bronze Age: Recent Trends,* Sheffield, 9–29

Hill, J D, 1989 Re-thinking the Iron Age, *Scottish Archaeological Review* **6**, 16–24

James, H, 1986 Excavations of Burnt Mounds at Carne, Nr Fishguard, 1979 and 1981, *Bulletin of the Board of Celtic Studies* **33**, 245–65

Jones, M, 1978 The plant remains, in M Parrington, *The excavation of an Iron Age settlement, Bronze Age ring-ditches and Roman features at Ashville Trading Estate, Abingdon, Oxfordshire, 1974–76,* Oxfordshire Archaeological Unit Report **1**, London, 93–110

Jones, P, 1995 An Interim report on the excavations of an Upper Palaeolithic site in Staines, Surrey, Unpublished report of Surrey County Archaeological Unit

Kinnes, I, Gibson, A, Ambers, J, Leese, M, and Boast, R, 1991 Radiocarbon dating and British beakers, *Scottish Archaeological Review* **8**, 35–68

Lacaille, A D, 1963 Mesolithic Industries beside Colne Waters in Iver and Denham, Buckinghamshire, *Records of Bucks* **17** (3), 143–181

Laidlaw, M, and Mepham, L, 1996 The Pottery, in P Andrews and A Crockett, *Three Excavations Along the Thames and its Tributaries, 1994,* Wessex Archaeological Report No. **10**, Salisbury

Lambrick, G, 1992 Alluvial archaeology of the Holocene in the Upper Thames Basin 1971–1991: a review, in S P Needham and M G Macklin (eds), *Alluvial Archaeology,* Oxbow Monograph **27**, Oxford, 209–226

Lawson, A J, 2000 *Potterne 1982–5: Animal Husbandry in Later Prehistoric Wiltshire,* Wessex Archaeology Report **17**, Salisbury

Lewis, J S C, 1991 Excavation of a Late Glacial and Early Flandrian site at Three Ways Wharf, Uxbridge: Interim report., in R N E Barton, A J Roberts and D A Rowe (eds), *Late Glacial Settlement in north-west Europe,* CBA Res. Rep. **77**

Lewis, J S C, 2000 The Neolithic, in MoLAS, *The Archaeology of Greater London: an assessment of archaeological evidence for human presence in the area now covered by Greater London,* Museum of London Archaeology Service, MoLAS monograph, London, 63–80

Lewis, J S C, in prep. Three Ways Wharf, Uxbridge: A Late Glacial and early Holocene hunter-gatherer site in the Colne Valley. MoLAS Monograph Series

Lewis, J S C, and Welsh, K, 2004 Perry Oaks - Neolithic inhabitation of a west London landscape, in J Cotton and D Field (eds), *Towards a new stone age: aspects of the Neolithic in south-east England,* CBA Res. Rep. **137**, York, 105–109

Lewis, J S C, Wiltshire, P E J, and Macphail, R, 1992 A Late Devensian/early Flandrian site at Three Ways Wharf, Uxbridge: environmental implications, in S P Needham, and M G Macklin (eds), *Alluvial Archaeology,* Oxbow Monograph **27**, Oxford, 235–46

Lockhart, J A R, and Wiseman, A J L, 1983, *Introduction to crop husbandry,* Oxford

Lovell, J, and Mepham, L, 2003 Excavations at East Park Farm, Charvil, **Berkshire: evidence** for prehistoric and Romano-British activity on the Thames floodplain, *Berkshire Archaeol. J.* **76**

(1998–2003), 17–36

Masefield, R, Branch, N, Couldrey, P, Goodburn, D, and Tyres, I, 2003 A Later Bronze Age Well Complex at Swalecliffe, Kent, *Antiquaries Journal* **83**, 47–121

Masefield, R, Baylis, A, and McCormac, G, 2004 New Scientific Dating of the Later Bronze Age Wells at Swalecliffe, Kent, *Antiquaries Journal* **84**, 334–9

McK. Clough, T H, 1970–73 A late Bronze Age socketed axe from Horsford, Norfolk, *Norfolk Archaeology* Vol. **35**, 491–493

McOmish, D, 1996 East Chisenbury: ritual and rubbish at the British Bronze Age-Iron Age transition, *Anitquity* **70**, 68–76

Mercer, R M, 2002 Review of Cadbury Castle Somerset, by J Barrett *et. al., Antiquaries Journal* **82**, 358–65

Merriman, N, 1990, *Prehistoric London,* London

Mitchell, A, 1974 *A Field Guide to the Trees of Britain and Northern Europe,* London

Moffett, L, 1999 The prehistoric use of plant resources, in A Barclay and C Halpin, *Excavations at Barrow Hills, Radley, Oxfordshire, volume 1: the Neolithic and Bronze Age monument complex,* Thames Valley Landscapes, **11**, Oxford Archaeological Unit, 243–247

MoLAS, 2000 *The archaeology of Greater London. An assessment of archaeological evidence for human presence in the area now covered by Greater London,* London

MoLAS, forthcoming The West London Gravels Project, MoLAS Monograph

Needham, S, 1996 Chronology and periodisation in the British Bronze Age, in K Randsborg (ed.), *Absolute chronology: archaeological Europe 2500–500 BC,* Acta. Archaeol. **67** (supp. 1), 121–40

Needham, S, and Spence, T, 1996 *Refuse and Disposal at Area 16 East, Runnymede.* Runnymede Bridge Research Excavations, Volume **2**, The British Museum Press, London

Needham, S, and Spence, T, 1997 Refuse and the formation of middens, *Antiquity* **71**, 77–90

Needham, S, and Trott, M R, 1987 Structure and Sequence in the Neolithic deposits at Runnymede, *Proc. Prehist. Soc* **53**, 479–98

O'Connell, M, 1990 Excavations during 1979–1985 of a multi-period site at Stanwell, with a contribution on Moor Lane, Harmondsworth, by Jonathan Cotton, *Surrey Archaeol. Col.* **80**, 1–62

O'Drisceoil, D A, 1988 Burnt Mounds: cooking or bathing? *Antiquity* **62**, 671–80

Oswald, A, 1997 A doorway on the past: practical and mystical concerns in the orientation of roundhouse doorways, in A Gwilt and C Haselgrove (eds), *Reconstructing Iron Age Societies,* Oxbow Monograph **71**, Oxford, 87–95

Owen, J, 1980 *Feeding Strategy,* Oxford

Parker Pearson, M, 1993 *Bronze Age Britain* English Heritage, London

Payne, A, Linford, N, Linford, P, and Martin, L, 2005 Flint Farm Iron Age settlement, in *Research News. Newsletter of the English Heritage Research Department.* No **2**. English Heritage (http://www.english-heritage.org.uk/upload/pdf/Research-News-N2.pdf)

Petch, D F, 1961 A Roman lead tank, Walesby, *Lincolnshire Archit. Archaeol. Soc.* Rep. **9**, 13–15

Preston, S (ed.), 2003 *Prehistoric, Roman and Saxon Sites in Eastern Berkshire,* TVAS Monograph **2**, Reading

Petts, D, 2004 Votive Hoards in Late Roman Britain: Pagan or Christian? in M Carver (ed.), *The Cross*

Goes North: Processes of Conversion in Northern Europe, AD 300–1300 , York

Pryor, F, 1980 Excavation at Fengate, Peterborough, England: the Third Report, Royal Ontario Museum archaeological Monograph **7** and Northants Archaeological Society Monograph **2**

Pryor, F, 1996 Sheep, stockyards and field systems: Bronze Age livestock populations in the Fenlands of eastern England, Antiquity **70**, 313–24

Rackham, J, and Sidell, J, 2000 London's Landscapes: the changing Environment, in The Archaeology of Greater London, MoLAS Monograph, London, 11–27

Rackham, O, 1986 The history of the countryside, London

Ray, K, 1990 Science and Anomaly: Burnt Mounds in British Prehistory, Scottish Archaeological Review **7**, 7–14

Raymond, F, 2003a The earlier prehistoric pottery, in S Ford, R Entwistle and K Taylor (eds), Excavations at Cippenham, Slough, Berkshire, 1995–7, Reading: Thames Valley Archaeological Services Ltd. Monograph **3**, 66–78

Raymond, F, 2003b The Neolithic pottery, in S Ford and J Pine, Neolithic ring ditches and Roman landscape features at Horton (1989–1996), in S Preston (ed.), 2003, 33–43

RCHME, 1995 Heathrow Mapping Project: Air Photographic Transcription and Analysis. Unpubl. report

RCHME, 1997 Mayfield Farm, Heathrow: Aerial Photographic Transcription and Analysis. Unpubl. report

Robertson-Mckay, R, 1987 The Neolithic causewayed enclosure at Staines, Surrey: Excavations 1961–63, Proc. Prehist. Soc. **53**, 23–128

Robinson, M A, 1983 Arable / pastoral ratios from insects? in M Jones (ed.), Integrating the subsistence economy, British Archaeol. Rep Int. Ser. **181**, Oxford, 19–55

Rowlands, M J, 1976 The Organisation of Middle Bronze Age Metalworking, Brit. Archaeol. Rep. **31**, Oxford

Rowlands, M J, 1980 Kinship, alliance and exchange in the European Bronze Age, in J C Barrett and R Bradley (eds), Settlement and Society in the British Later Bronze Age, BAR Brit Series, **83**, 15–55

Scaife, R, 2000 Palynology and palaeoenvironment, in S P Needham (ed.), The Passage of the Thames - Holocene Environment and Settlement at Runnymede, Runnymede Bridge Research Excavations, Vol **1**, London, 168–187

Sidell, J Cotton, J, Rayner, L, and Wheeler, L, 2002 The prehistory and topography of Southwark and Lambeth, MoLAS Monograph **14**, London

Smith, A T, 2001 The Differential Use of Constructed Sacred Space in Southern Britain from the Late Iron Age to the 4th Century AD, BAR British Series 318, Oxford

Startin, D W, 1982 The labour force involved in constructing the causewayed enclosure, in H J Case and A W R Whittle (eds), Settlement Patterns in the Oxford Region: Excavation at Abingdon Causewayed Enclosure and Other Sites, CBA, London, 49–50

Startin, D W, 1998 Estimating the labour required to build the Cleaven Dyke, in G J Barclay and G S Maxwell (eds), The Cleaven Dyke and Littleour: monuments in the Neolithic of Tayside. Soc of Antiq. of Scot. Monograph Series **13**, Edinburgh, 52

Tauber, H, 1965 Differential pollen dispersion and the interpretation of pollen diagrams, Geological Survey of Denmark **11**, Series No. 89

Taylor, M, 1992 Flag Fen: The Wood, Antiquity Vol. **66**, 476–498

Taylor, M, 1995 The worked wood, in A Mudd et.al., The excavation of a late Bronze Age/early Iron Age site at Eight Acre Field, Radley, Oxoniensia **60**, 21–66

Thomas, C, 1981, Christianity in Roman Britain to AD 500, London

Thompson, A, Westman, A, and Dyson, T (eds), 1998 Archaeology in Greater London 1965 – 1990: a guide to records of excavations by the Museum of London, The Archaeological Gazetteer Series Vol. **2**, London

Tilley, C, 1994 A phenomenology of landscape: places, paths and monuments, Oxford

Tinsley, H M, (with Grigson, C), 1981 The Bronze Age, in I G Simmons and M Tooley (eds), The Environment in British Prehistory, London, 210–49

Townend, C B, 1947 West Middlesex Main Drainage- Ten Years Operation, Journal of the Institution of Civil Engineers, Paper **5599**, 351–414

Wainwright, G J, and Longworth, I H, 1971 Durrington Walls: Excavations 1966–1968, Rep. Res. Comm. Soc. Antiquaries of London **29**, London

Watson, D M, 1937 West Middlesex Main Drainage, Journal of the Institution of Civil Engineers, Vol. **5**, 1936–1937, Paper 5120, 463–568

Watts, D J, 1988 Circular lead tanks and their significance for Romano-British Christianity, Antiq. J. **68**, 210–22

Watts, D, 1991 Christianity and Pagans in Roman Britain, London

Wessex Archaeology, 2004 Imperial College Sports Ground, Sipson Lane, Harlington, London Borough of Hillingdon: Post-Excavation Assessment Report, unpublished client report no. 42282/4

Wiltshire, P E J, 2003 Palynological analysis associated with human remains in woodland. Unpublished report for Surrey Constabulary

Whittle, A, 1977 The Earlier Neolithic of Southern England, British Archaeological Report **35**, Oxford

Woodward, A, 1998-1999 When did pots become domestic? Special pots and everyday pots in British prehistory', Medieval Ceramics **22-23**, 3-10

Yalden, D, 1999 The History of British Mammals, London

Yates, D, 2001 Bronze Age agricultural intensification in the Thames Valley and Estuary, in J Brück (ed.), Bronze Age Landscapes Tradition and Transformation, Oxford, 65–82

Young, R, and Humphrey, J, 1999 Flint use in England after the Bronze Age: time for a re-evaluation? Proc. Prehist. Soc. **65**, 231–42

Index

NOTE: References in *bold italics* denote illustrations; those in **bold figures**, feature numbers.

and horseshoe enclosure HE1 77
modified to accommodate settlement 118, 122,
  123-4, 132
monuments superseded by 30, 87, *88*, 92, 116, 122
pits as boundary markers 91-2, 106, *106*, 107-8
and Stanwell Cursus (C1) 48, *48*, 98, *99*, 101, 108,
  (C2) *70*, 71, *99*, 101, 106, *106*
social context 25, 30, 87-92, 105, 234
and stock management 152-5
and topography 6, 108, *109*
trackways develop along 105-8, 112, 122
within landholdings 25, 108, *109*, 114, 131
early Iron Age eastward expansion 166
middle Iron Age *192*, 193-4, *195*, 196, *196-7*, 199,
  200, 201
late Iron Age/early Roman realignment 170, 202,
  203, 206, *207*, 208
late Roman realignment x, 14, 25, 170-71, 234
continuity 206, 218, 234
  Bronze-Iron Age 166, 170, *170*, 171, 194, 199,
    206, *207*
  to post-medieval x, 25, 171, 206, 227, 231, *231*
1980s excavations 11
see also enclosures; field systems; hedgerows;
  Landholdings; trackways
land tenure, ceremonial basis of 30, 89, 91-2, 152
  superseded by enclosure 30, 87, *88*, 92, 116, 122
landholdings, Bronze Age *94*, 104-12
  chronology of development 108, 110-12, *110-11*, *113*
  distribution of finds *110*, *162*, 163, *163*
  land divisions within 25, 108, *109*, 114, 131
  settlements located within 114, *115*, 116
  BY NUMBER
  1 – *94*, 108, *110*
    see also settlement (2)
  2 – *94*, 108, *110*, 138
    stratigraphy 98, *99*, 101, 106, *106*
  3 – *94*, 108
    cremation *151*, 152
    environmental material *103*, 126, *127*, 128
    pottery 110, *110*
    radiocarbon dates *96*, 97, *98*
    stratigraphy 98, *99*, 101, 106, *106*
    trackways 106, *106*, 126

waterholes *103*, 138, *139*, 140-41, *140-41*, 142,
  144-5, 150-51
  see also settlement (4)
4 – *94*, 95, 106-7, *106*, 107, 108, *110*
  waterholes 148, *149-50*
  see also settlement (5)
5 – *94*, 108, *110*
  burnt mound complex 145-7, *147*, 150-51
  internal divisions 131, 138
  radiocarbon dates *96*, 97, 102
  waterholes *96*, 97, *103*, 137, 138, *138*, 145-7, *145-7*
  see also settlement (6); spearhead
6 – *94*, 108, 110, *110*, *151*, 152
  see also settlement (1)
7 – *94*, 107, *107*, 108, *110*
Landscape Generic stage of excavation 20-21
Landscape Specific stage of excavation 21-2
land-use, modern 10-11, 12
Langley Silt Complex 5, *5*, 13
lead tank, late Roman Christian viii, 227-30, *227-30*
leadership groups *see* elites
leather objects, Roman
  shoe 216
  worked fragment 222
lifting mechanism, possible late Roman 222
lime pollen 62, 63, 104, 159-60
Little Waltham, Essex 187
Little Woodbury, Wilts 186
location of site *2-4*, 5
Londinium 14
Longbridge Deverill, Wilts 184
Longford (excavation) 23
Longford River *5*, 11
Longford village 151-2, 235
loom weights and fragments 114, 129, 193

Manor Farm, Horton, Berks 34, 86
manuring 163, *167*, 168, 171, 172
marginality, spaces of 16
marshland plants 61, 62, 161, 199, 200
Mayfield Farm, Heathrow *12*, 13, 176
Meadlake Place, Egham, Surrey 61
medieval period 14, 25, 231, 235
  land divisions x, 25, 171, 231, *231*

memory
  superseded by monuments 24, 58
  see also continuity (of place)
Mendip, Somerset; Charterhouse Warren Farm 137
Mesolithic period 13, 24, 28, 29, 39-42
  chronology 30, 31, 41-2
  continuity from Neolithic 24, 41, 42, 43-4, 45, 47,
    58, 59, 77, 80
  see also under flint, burnt; flint, worked; pits
metalwork
  Bronze Age viii
    scarcity 89, 151, 152, 166
  see also copper alloy objects; iron objects, Roman
metalworking 193-4, 201, 211
metaphysical world, mediation with 53
microburins 76, 82
midden deposits
  Mesolithic 58, 59, 86
  Neolithic 86
  Bronze Age 129, 131, 133, 163
  middle Iron Age 172, *197*, 198, *198*
mitigation, archaeological 2, 22-3
Mogden sewerage purification works 10
MoLAS *see* Museum of London Archaeological Service
monuments
  Neolithic 29-30, 45-81, 234
    and clearance 30, 38, 54, 61, 65-7
    continuing use in Bronze Age 86, 87, 150
    memory superseded by 24, 58
    settlement adjacent to 112, 114, 116, 126
    see also circular monuments; cursus monuments;
      horseshoe enclosures; Stanwell Cursus
  early Bronze Age 90-91
    see also barrows
moss, Neolithic *Sphagnum* 43, 61, 62
Museum of London Archaeological Service (MoLAS) 235
  earlier excavations 11, 14, 22, 23
  see also POK96

nail, late Roman iron 222
Neolithic period x, 13, 24, 28-38, 45-81
  chronology 29, 30-38, 39-42
  late Neolithic/early Bronze Age 36-7, 82-92, 95-104
  see also individual aspects throughout index

144-5, 148, *149-50*, 228, 234
Watson, John D 10
wattle structures 210
  see also revetments
weeds and ruderals
  Neolithic/early Bronze Age 62, 63, 85
  Bronze Age 155, 156, 157, 159, 160-61
  middle Iron Age 199, 200
  Roman 211
wells 114
  Bronze Age *127*, 128

with copper alloy ring *100*, 101, *101*, 152
Roman 216-17, *216-17*
  see also waterholes
Wessex Archaeology ix, 2, 11
West Middlesex Main Drainage Scheme 10
wet areas, plants of 61, 62, 161, 199, 200
wicker revetments 135, 145, *145-6*
willow ropes and ties *217*, 218, 222, *223*
withy rope and tie 216, 222, *223*
wood *see* charcoal; timber structures; wooden objects,
  waterlogged

wooden objects, waterlogged viii, 135, *139*, *141*, 222
  see also bowl; crook crop; hafts; 'reliquary';
  revetments
WPR98 excavation *4*, 5, 6, *7*, *8*, 23
  see also gullies, pennanular (**3**)
WXC96 excavation 23
WXE96 excavation 23

Yeoveny Lodge causewayed enclosure, Staines 11, 13,
  38, 52, 85, 86